Foundations *of* Early Childhood

Principles and Practice

Foundations *of* Early Childhood

Principles and Practice

Edited by

Penny Mukherji and **Louise Dryden**

SAGE | AdvantEDGE Teacher Resources

Los Angeles | London | New Delhi
Singapore | Washington DC | Melbourne

Originally published in 2014 by

SAGE

Los Angeles | London | New Delhi
Singapore | Washington DC | Melbourne

SAGE Publications Ltd
1 Oliver's Yard
55 City Road
London EC1Y 1SP

This SAGE AdvantEDGE edition published in 2017 by

SAGE | AdvantEDGE Teacher Resources

SAGE Publications India Pvt Ltd
B-1/I-1, Mohan Cooperative Industrial Area
Mathura Road
New Delhi 110 044

Published by Vivek Mehra for SAGE Publications India Pvt Ltd and printed at Saurabh Printers Pvt Ltd, Greater Noida.

ISBN: 978-93-860-6256-7 (PB)

Contents

Acknowledgements

We wish to give heartfelt thanks to our partners, Ashu and Windy, without whose support and encouragement this project would have been extremely difficult. We also wish to acknowledge the huge contribution made by the hundreds of students we have worked with over the years who have generously shared their experiences with us.

We have been privileged to work with an amazing team of authors who have contributed their knowledge and specialist expertise to bring this project to fruition. We thank them for all the time and effort which went into producing their individual chapters.

Finally, we wish to recognise the huge contribution made by the team at SAGE, in particular Jude Bowen and Amy Jarrold, and the external readers who provided such helpful feedback during the writing process.

Publisher's Acknowledgements

The publishers would like to extend their warmest thanks to the following individuals for their invaluable feedback.

Jo Albin-Clark, Senior Lecturer in Early Years Education, Edge Hill University

Jane Beniston, Senior Lecturer, Early Childhood Education and Care, Newman University

Joy Chalke, Principle Lecturer, School of Education and Continuing Studies (SECS), University of Portsmouth

Rose Envy, Senior Lecturer (Education), School of Social Sciences and Law, Teesside University

Jessica Johnson, Senior Lecturer in early years education, Kingston University

Janet Kay, Principal Lecturer in Childhood Studies, Sheffield Hallam University

Susan Lewis, Associate Leader of Education Studies and Multiprofessional Practice, Manchester Metropolitan University

Jackie Musgrave, Senior Lecturer in the Centre for Early Childhood, University of Worcester

Ruby Oates, Assistant Subject Head, Early Childhood & Education Studies, School of Education & Social Science, University of Derby

About the Editors and Contributors

About the Editors

Penny Mukherji is an established author who has been involved in the education and training of early childhood practitioners for over twenty-five years. After setting up a Foundation Degree in Early Childhood in an inner city Further Education college, Penny transferred to London Metropolitan University as a Senior Lecturer on the Early Childhood Studies Degree programme. Penny has a health background, and her areas of interest include the health and well-being of young children and care and education of children under 3. Penny has recently retired from full-time teaching to concentrate on her writing.

Louise Dryden is an experienced early years educator. After working with children directly for many years she moved into the adult education field, lecturing on early years practitioner courses and teacher training programmes. She has lectured in both Further and Higher Education establishments and was the academic liaison tutor for a foundation degree in early childhood studies. Currently Louise is working as a free-lance educator, and is a visiting lecturer at Middlesex University teaching on several undergraduate programmes, including the new practitioner pathway leading to Early Years Teacher Status.

About the Contributors

Hilary Fabian has taught in primary schools and the university sector (Manchester Metropolitan University, University of Edinburgh, Glyndŵr University, and Edge Hill University). Her MSc dissertation in Education Management explored staff induction; her PhD thesis, books and journal publications reflect her research into transitions, particularly children starting school, children transferring between schools and the way in which the process for children and adults is managed. Currently she is mainly retired, but continues to write about transitions.

Ros Garrick is a Principal Lecturer in Early Years at Sheffield Hallam University. Following professional experience as an early years teacher and Teacher Adviser, she currently teaches and supervises early years practitioners on a range of undergraduate and postgraduate courses. Ros undertook doctoral research into young children's mathematical development while teaching in an inner-city nursery class. She recently co-directed a study of young children's experiences of the Early Years Foundation Stage for the DfE.

Jonathan Glazzard has taught across EYFS, KS1 and KS2. Since 2005 he has worked as a Senior Lecturer in Primary Education at the University of Huddersfield. He currently leads the Primary QTS provision at the University and is responsible for leading the MA in Early Childhood Studies.

Justine Howard is an Associate Professor in the College of Human and Health Science, Swansea University and is the Programme Manager for their MA in Developmental and Therapeutic Play and MA in Childhood Studies. She is a Chartered Psychologist specialising in child development and is trained in therapeutic play. She worked in a variety of early years settings before developing her academic career. She is well published and regularly speaks on play and child development at a national and international level. Her most recent book is *The Essence of Play* (Routledge).

Tricia Johnson is an assessor for Early Years Professional Status and member of the Sector Endorsed Foundation Degrees in Early Years Network. She has a breadth of experience in Early Years having been a Senior Lecturer and Department Head in FE and HE and Childcare Management at the Norland College with children from birth to 9 years. This included multi-agency work and involvement with guidance for the National Standards for Regulation of Childcare (2003).

Gianna Knowles is a Lecturer in Educational Studies at London South Bank University, having previously worked at the University of Chichester and the University of Jönköping in Sweden. She has over 12 years of experience of teaching in primary schools in England, in London and the Midlands. She has worked in Local Authority Advisory services and as an Ofsted Inspector.

Claire Majella Richards is a Senior Lecturer within the Institute of Education at the University of Worcester. She has extensive experience of multi-agency partnership working, having been employed within the voluntary and statutory sectors. Her roles have varied in the fields of mental health, substance misuse and domestic abuse. As a qualified barrister she remains a committed advocate of the rights of children and young people, and is engaged with the activities of the Local Safeguarding Children Board and is a member of the British Association for the Study and Prevention of Child Abuse and Neglect (BASPCAN).

Julia Manning-Morton has worked as a practitioner, manager, inspector and advisor across a range of early childhood settings. She has an MA in Early Childhood Education with Care, and was Principal Lecturer for Early Childhood at London Metropolitan University for 13 years; she is now an independent consultant for 'Key Times Professional Development'. Julia's research and writing is focused on the needs of children from birth to 3 years old and on the personal, social and emotional well-being of children and practitioners.

Edwina Mitchell worked in a variety of early years settings before moving into training childcare students at Levels 2 and 3. As a very mature student she gained her degree in Early Childhood Studies at London Metropolitan University (where she now lectures) and followed this with a Masters in Early Years Education at the Institute of Education. She is also on the UK committee of the World Preschool Organisation (OMEP).

Vicky Mummery is a Senior Lecturer at London Metropolitan University. Before going to the university Vicky taught in Further Education for four years, teaching students from entry level through to Foundation Degree. Vicky qualified as a Level 3 early years practitioner in 1997, and has since completed her BA (Hons) in Early Childhood and MA in Education. She has held various roles, from practitioner to manager, across a range of settings for children from birth to 5.

Linda Pound has worked in three universities and was an LEA inspector responsible for the early years for almost ten years. In addition she has been head of a nursery school and deputy head of a primary school. In her current role as an education consultant, she provides training for early years practitioners around the UK and beyond. Linda writes extensively for a range of audiences on a range of topics related to early childhood care and education.

Judy Stevenson, OBE has worked in London as a Nursery Teacher, Nursery School Headteacher, Ofsted Inspector and Head of an Early Years Centre, joining London Metropolitan University in 2007 as Programme Manager for both the National Professional Qualification in Early Years Leadership (NPQICL) and Early Years Professional Status. Having worked as a Principal Lecturer for Early Childhood at the university, she is currently the Distance Learning Coordinator for the Early Childhood degree. Judy has a particular interest in leadership and management alongside the development of reflective practice.

Rita White was previously Course Leader for the BEd Early Years Teaching course at London Metropolitan University. As a qualified teacher she taught in infant and primary schools and coordinated provision for ICT, SEND and the Early Years before leaving as a Deputy Head. Since moving into Higher Education Rita has worked as a teacher educator in three universities on Foundation Degrees, undergraduate and PGCE courses convening modules related to Inclusion and Diversity, ICT, Education and the Early Years. In addition she coordinated funded courses for refugee teachers.

Carolyne Willow started her career as a child protection social worker in the 1980s and has since held a variety of children's rights roles. She ran the Children's Rights Alliance for England between 2000 and 2012, where she prioritised making an impact on law and policy and upholding the rights of children to be heard and taken seriously. Carolyne has researched and written widely, and has consistently advocated the rights of babies and young children.

Introduction

What happens in children's earliest years will affect them throughout their lives.

All those involved in supporting children and their families in these early years, have a huge responsibility because, for any individual child, the window of opportunity is brief. We are still learning about influences that affect children's life chances; however, research findings indicate that children are more likely to achieve their full potential if:

- They experience positive relationships within their family and have a home environment which encourages their learning and development
- They attend high quality early childhood provision
- The childcare practitioners are well qualified
- Settings have staff who are qualified to Foundation Degree level and above. (DfE, 2012a)

This book is primarily designed for those of you who are studying for degrees or foundation degrees in early childhood subjects. However, students on courses leading to Qualified Teacher Status in the early or primary years, those on programmes leading to Early Years Professional Status and students studying for qualifications in health and social work, will also find this book essential reading.

Foundations of Early Childhood is designed to give students a good introduction to the main topics covered by Early Childhood Studies Foundation degrees, and levels 4 and 5 of traditional early childhood studies degrees. The text contains information that directly relates to the *Statutory Framework for the Early Years Foundation Stage* (DfE, 2012b) which is the early years curriculum for England, however, those of you working in different countries will find that the general principles explained within this book will still be applicable. It is not possible to cover all the information that you will need for your studies and, inevitably, some topics that you may have expected to be included have not been covered. For example there is no chapter related specifically to children from birth to 3. The *Statutory Framework for the Early Years Foundation Stage* (DfE, 2012b) does not make this distinction and in this textbook you will find the chapters cover all ages. Likewise there is no chapter specifically written about children with disabilities and special educational needs; you will find that this information is included throughout the chapters.

The book is divided into five distinct parts:

- **Part 1: Introduction to Studying Early Childhood.** This part of the book is designed to support you in your studies as you begin your course, helping you to develop the key skills and attributes needed to work with very young children.
- **Part 2: How Children Develop.** This section of the book looks at some of the ways in which children learn and develop. It includes a chapter which specifically looks at the role of play in children's learning.
- **Part 3: Influencing Factors.** In this section you will find chapters that describe historical and legislative influences on early childhood practice. Factors that influence children's health are described together with social influences that can lead to inequality in outcomes for children.
- **Part 4: Approaches and Practice.** In this part of the book we look at some of the main principles that underpin childhood practice in the UK and in other countries. The importance of safeguarding children and of working closely with parents is explored. This part concludes with a look at the role managers and leaders in settings play in delivering the curriculum and upholding the principles of early childhood practice.
- **Part 5: Implementing the Curriculum.** It is in this section that the threads are drawn together and we look at how theory underpins the practical implementation of the Early Years Foundation Stage (DfE, 2012b). There is a chapter on each of the three 'prime areas of learning', with an extended chapter on the 'specific areas'. Finally, we look at the transitions children encounter, both when entering early provision for the first time and the transition between the Foundation Stage and year one of compulsory schooling.

Although we have divided the text into specific parts and chapters, in reality this is a somewhat artificial divide and you will find that some topics are discussed in several different chapters. For example you will find that the fundamental importance that parents play in promoting children's health and development is looked at in the chapters on child development, children's health, social inequalities, working with parents, and personal, social and emotional development. We recognise that it is unlikely that you will read each chapter in sequence so, where relevant, you will find directions within chapters to indicate where the topic is discussed in other areas of the book.

The team of writers who have contributed to *Foundations of Early Childhood* are all highly experienced professionals in their fields and many are also experienced lecturers on early childhood courses. We (the editors) have been involved in the education and training of early childhood practitioners in Further Education, University and in early childhood settings. We have participated in running the Foundation

Degree in Early Childhood for many years and have a profound understanding of the needs of Foundation Degree students both during the programme and their transition to Honours degree study. With this in mind we have designed each chapter to include features that aim to help students get the most from the book.

The text is written in accessible language. That is to say, that although we have used an academic style of writing, we have endeavoured to use straightforward language. We know that many students (especially those who are experienced practitioners but have been out of education for many years) find reading and understanding academic writing a challenge. To become a skilful reader of academic texts takes practice and, like any other skill, takes time and application to perfect; this book will support you while your skills develop. If you do not understand terms used within the text, look to see if they are included in the glossary at the end of the book, where the contributors have compiled a list of definitions explaining many of the more technical terms. The following describes a list of features, contained within each chapter, that have been included to support your learning and to help you apply what you have learned to practice.

- *Foundations of Early Childhood* is designed to cover the material for levels 4 and 5 of early childhood studies degree programmes. It is our experience that students who have completed levels 4 and 5 find that there is a huge leap with regard to expectations when they transfer to level 6 (the final Honours year). To prepare students for this challenge we have included extension activities. At level 6 you will be expected to rely less on textbooks and more on journal articles. Often students are anxious about finding and using articles, so to prepare you we have included journal tasks within the text. If you find it difficult accessing journal articles your university's library or learning resource centre should be able to help.
- Within the text you will find suggestions for reflection. These are designed to help you consolidate your learning by reflecting upon your own understanding and practice. Many of you studying for early childhood degrees will be experienced practitioners and throughout the book you will be encouraged to draw upon your own experience. If you are new to the field you will be encouraged to relate what you have learned to your practice placement if you have one.
- It is impossible to cover all the information you need within the text, so sometimes the 'reflection' feature will direct you to resources for you to investigate on your own. To help you, internet locations have been included within the text; these were all current at the time of writing, but inevitably some links will be broken by the time you read the text. An internet search using the document name will usually locate what you are looking for.
- Each chapter includes at least one case study. This feature is designed to help you understand theoretical concepts by placing them within a practical context.
- At the end of each chapter you will find a list of recommended further reading which is designed to help you access material that will extend your knowledge of the topic being discussed within the chapter.

- Each chapter finishes with a reference section which contains details of all the texts used within the chapter. We have used the Harvard system of referencing which is explained in Chapter 1. Your own institution will have specific guidelines on referencing that you should follow.

We hope that you enjoy *Foundations of Early Childhood* and that you will be motivated to look more deeply into the topics covered in each chapter. The theory and research findings which you will find in this book will help you to become a reflective practitioner who can meet the needs of the children and families in your care.

References

Department for Education (DfE) (2012a) *Early Years Evidence Pack*. London: DfE.

Department for Education (DfE) (2012b) *Statutory Framework for the Early Years Foundation Stage*. London: DfE. http://media.education.gov.uk/assets/files/pdf/e/eyfs%20statutory%20framework%20march%202012.pdf (accessed 20 April 2013).

Companion Website

Visit the following website to access a wide variety of additional and very useful online resources that accompany this textbook:

www.sagepub.co.uk/mukherji

- A flashcard glossary to test you on the key terms from the study of early childhood.
- Online versions of all the tables from Chapter 1 to help you improve your study skills.
- 'Cheat sheets' of key theorists and early years legislation to help with revision.
- All the journal articles from the end of chapter tasks in one easy place for you to read and develop your skills.

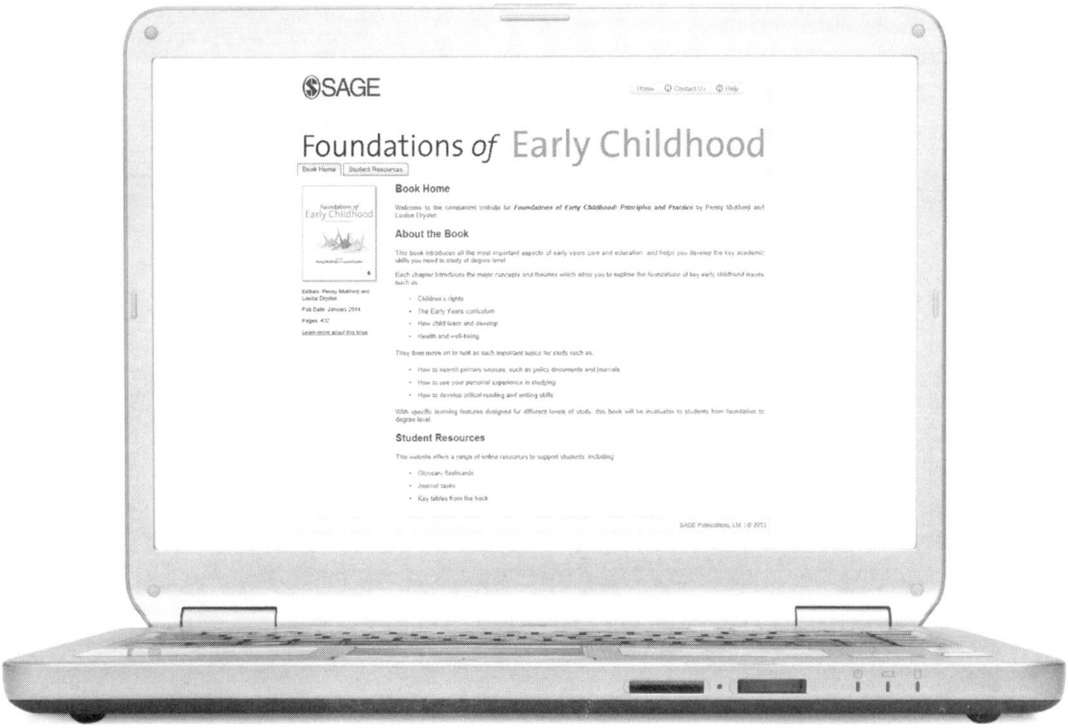

Part 1

AN INTRODUCTION TO STUDYING EARLY CHILDHOOD

Part one of *Foundations of Early Childhood* is designed to support you as you start your early childhood degree. We strongly advise that you read these chapters thoroughly, even if you have recently undergone a course of study or are an experienced early childhood practitioner.

Beginning a new course is always challenging. Students vary in the amount of recent study they have undergone and the amount of practical experience they have in working with very young children. If you are lucky you will find yourself studying in a group with a wide range of complementary skills so that students confident in academic studies can support those who have been out of education for a while, whilst experienced practitioners can support those with no knowledge of working with very young children. You may be studying on your own, and will seek support from the online community or colleagues at work. Whatever your situation most of you will be new to studying at degree level, and in Chapter 1 Louise Dryden gives you a comprehensive introduction to starting your studies. Louise's chapter draws upon very many years' experience of supporting students at the start of a new course, and she emphasises that success depends on hard work and good organisational skills. In our experience it is not always the very brightest students with high grades in previous exams who are the most successful; it is often those who did less well in school or college, but who work hard and have a passion for Early Childhood, who succeed. Success also depends upon how well you are supported both at home and in your workplace. Before you start, everyone involved should be aware of how *your* course may impact *their* lives. There is nothing worse than starting a course and finding out later that your workplace cannot give you the time off to attend class or that family members are unwilling to look after young children when you need to work at home. Success also depends upon how well you interact with the institution where you are studying and in Chapter 1 you will find information to help you access support during your course.

Lahman (2008) considers children to be competent yet vulnerable, and in Chapter 2 Carolyne Willow points out that early childhood practitioners play a critical role in upholding children's rights. She explains that children are not always respected as people and that their rights can so easily be overlooked. As students of early childhood you are required to know and understand the general principles of the Convention on the Rights of the Child (UNICEF 1989) and Chapter 2 supports you as you seek to implement these principles within early childhood settings.

In your degree course you will learn about different theories regarding how children learn and develop and you will be introduced to relevant research findings that can be used to help you implement quality provision for children and families. In Chapter 3 Judy Stevenson explains that an academic understanding on its own is insufficient to promote quality practice and she explains how *reflective practice* can be used to make positive changes within settings. Reflective practice involves learning through and from experience; it involves challenging assumptions about your everyday practice and becoming self-aware.

The final chapter within Part 1 is about observation and assessment. The ability to observe children and make an assessment of their strengths, abilities and interests is the foundation upon which early childhood practice is based. It is fitting that this chapter concludes Part 1 as it draws on material from the preceding chapters. Jonathan Glazzard explains how observation and assessment have to be conducted within an ethical framework that upholds children's rights and encourages children to be partners in the assessment process. The ability to analyse observational material using research findings, theory and your own experience is integral to the assessment process and contributes to reflective practice. Finally, the information from Chapter 1 will support you in the skills you need to produce written observations in the style that is required by your setting or university.

References

Lahman, M. (2008) 'Always othered: Ethical research with children', *Journal of Early Childhood Research*, 6(3): 281–300.

United Nations Convention on the Rights of the Child (1989) http://www.unicef.org.uk/UNICEFs-Work/Our-mission/UN-Convention/ (accessed 29 April 2013).

1

Studying for a Degree

Louise Dryden

This chapter will:

- Help you to prepare for your new programme of study
- Encourage you to organise your time effectively
- Build your confidence, helping you to become familiar with expectations at this level of study
- Explain the skills and strategies that will enable you to study successfully
- Help you to prepare for different types of assessment.

This is the first chapter of the book and is placed here to help you prepare for your study experience. Some of you will feel confident as you embark on this new course at degree level, whilst others may feel a little anxious, especially if it is some time since you last did any academic work. I shall begin by reassuring you that the most important attributes for successful study are organisational skills and hard work; the more carefully you prepare for your studies, the more successful you will be.

In this chapter I will ask you to assess your existing skills, and then help you to consider a range of strategies which could assist you in producing work of a quality you can be proud of. Once you have organised yourself and your resources, then you will be ready to explore the subjects themselves. You will need methods for taking notes, in lectures or whilst reading; strategies for collecting and organising material from a variety of sources, for essays, presentations and portfolios; and the confidence to present your knowledge and ideas in a clear, analytical manner. I hope that what follows will help you on your journey towards success.

Reflection

Before you start

Your previous academic history

Take a few minutes to recall your previous learning experiences. Using the chart below, consider your school and college careers – what were the high points; what did you find more challenging? Then consider the factors which contributed to the achievements and disappointments.

Use this chart to set yourself some initial study goals – examine the list of contributing factors and (a) determine the strategies you think it would be helpful to use, and (b) remind yourself of those factors to avoid.

Table 1.1 Your academic history

	Successes	**Challenges**	**Contributing factors**
Primary school			
GCSEs			
A levels/Level 3 National Diploma			
Further study			
Recent staff/professional development			

Finding time to study

Many Foundation Degree students are childcare practitioners working full-time whilst studying, and many have substantial family commitments. Alternatively, you may be younger, working part-time to support yourself through your studies. Whatever your personal circumstances, you need to organise your time efficiently and effectively. You should consider your lifestyle and current commitments, and plan a realistic study timetable (Table 1.2).

Draw a chart and begin by putting in your domestic commitments. Then add your work schedule and periods required for College/University attendance. Next include times you normally spend on leisure pursuits with family and friends, adding times for exercise and hobbies.

Looking at this chart, realistically locate the spaces available for private study. Highlight times which you can put aside for organising lecture notes, and allocate several hours for academic reading/research each week. Whilst working on assignments, you may need to sacrifice some of your social activities, which will mean adjusting your timetable during busy periods.

Table 1.2 Proposed study-timetable

Time	Early morning	9.00–13.00	13.00–17.00	Late afternoon	Evening
Monday					
Tuesday					
Wednesday					
Thursday					
Friday					
Saturday					
Sunday					

You will also need to plan your time efficiently across the whole academic year. Using a diary or a year-planner, note down all the important dates in your personal and work calendars, put in the University term dates and indicate where assessments are due. It is useful to work backwards from assignment deadlines to block in extra study time.

Negotiating with family, friends and workplace colleagues

Most of your acquaintances will be genuinely delighted that you are returning to study, however, you need to be sensitive to the ways in which your decision affects those closest to you. It is important to negotiate with your family and work colleagues, as their support and understanding will be crucial to your success. Early years settings function as learning communities, and hopefully your fellow workers will support your studies and engage in your interests. However, recognise that study is empowering and members of your family or colleagues might feel worried about the changes taking place; in some instances they may become envious. Ensure that major decisions are made with these key people's consent and cooperation.

CASE STUDY

Maria, a working mother, was studying for her Foundation Degree. She was excited about returning to study, and also hoped to be a positive role-model for her own children. Maria was conscientious, ensuring she attended all the lectures

(Continued)

(Continued)

and maintaining careful study habits. However, as the first semester progressed she found it increasingly hard to juggle her family and work commitments with the home study requirements of the programme. To her surprise, her family and friends were not as supportive as she had hoped, and Maria began to panic as the time approached to prepare her first set of academic assignments.

Sensibly, Maria made an appointment with her personal tutor to discuss these concerns. She explained that it was hard to create time for study at weekends because her family wanted her attention. Her partner and children felt she was neglecting them whenever she did work associated with her assignments. Maria's tutor was able to reassure her that this was a common problem for students with family responsibilities, and that together they could look for possible solutions. The tutor explained that it can be quite threatening for partners when the student appears to be changing, with a new set of aspirations. The partner can fear that they will be neglected, or even believe that their status within the family unit is threatened. To counter this, the tutor suggested that Maria sought her family's cooperation when planning her study schedule. Maria agreed that her family were feeling left out, and she decided it would be beneficial to re-negotiate their family time together.

- How do you think Maria should approach this with her family?
- What suggestions could she make that could resolve these issues and ensure that her family do not feel left out?
- If you are studying in a group, share your experiences and how you have overcome this type of challenge.

The right environment

Another practical aspect of private study is finding a suitable place to work. At home, you need somewhere to store your course materials safely, and a table to work at. You should take advantage of your institution's learning resource centre. Library facilities provide an environment conducive to uninterrupted study – helpful if you live in a busy household, where it is hard to find a quiet space, without fear of interruption.

Getting to know your institution

Degree programmes are run under the auspices of a university, but some of you on Foundation Degree programmes could be attending lectures in a further education college.

Universities and colleges have large campuses which may feel impersonal, but information about your programme will be available online. Academic institutions have websites which provide you with access to important information on enrolment, fees, degree and assessment regulations, student services and access to library resources. Make yourself familiar with these before you start the programme.

Your course should have a Virtual Learning Environment (VLE), a web platform, giving you information relating to your specific programme of study. VLE systems vary, but usually include a message board, provide detailed course information, and the facility to blog (converse) with fellow students and tutors. You may be required to submit coursework via this system.

Degree programmes have a handbook, a document (in paper form or online) which provides important information, including curriculum content, and guidelines pertaining to assessment regulations and degree requirements. Read this carefully and refer to it frequently. Module handbooks, written by the lecturers who deliver individual subjects, will explain the module content, giving details of expected learning outcomes, assessment requirements, reading lists and synopses of each lecture.

The difference between FE and HE

Higher education students are required to take responsibility for their own learning. For example, lectures will be just one source of your academic knowledge; you are expected to read and research widely, using the lectures and handbooks as a guide to further independent study. Degree-level study requires you to not only acquire knowledge, but also to demonstrate that you have understood and analysed it. In childcare settings, being educated to degree-level indicates that you are able to take responsibility and articulate your ideas clearly to colleagues, parents and outside agencies. Studying will help you to develop the skills required to consider theory and practice, look objectively at evidence and make reasoned decisions in the workplace; academic discussion, presentation skills and essay writing all contribute to the development of these attributes.

Let us turn to the opportunities afforded by your lecturers, fellow students and work colleagues. The other students on your programme will be important to you, sharing the highs and lows of the study process. Get to know all your fellow students, but seek out the company of those you feel most comfortable with; tea breaks provide excellent opportunities for forging friendships, as well as discussing the content of recent lectures. Find individuals you can work with to become your study buddies; you may agree to share books, meet periodically to study together, and can support one another when the going gets tough.

Student support

Be assured that help is available from your institution while you are studying. You may be assigned a personal tutor who can support and guide you through the general aspects of your degree, and colleges and universities provide support services to assist students with general issues. These departments are staffed by people with specialist knowledge in areas such as student finance, ICT, academic writing support and personal counselling. It would be your responsibility to approach these agencies for help.

Reflection

Being a strategic student

Look at the list below and rate how important you think these resources will be to your study success:

Handbooks

Lectures

Lecturers & tutorials

Fellow students & study buddies

Reading lists

Resource centre

Subject-specific librarian

Web-based resources

Your choices will reflect your learning style preferences. As an adult learner you need to be continually monitoring your progress, recognising the aspects of study or curriculum you find most challenging, and seeking help when you are struggling.

Starting to study

Getting the most out of lectures/teaching sessions

Having read the course materials (handbooks, etc.) identify exactly what the individual modules cover. Before the lectures begin, think about what you already know on the subject, and highlight aspects you think may prove challenging. You should prepare before each lecture by reading the synopsis to find out what the session will cover, look through the indicative reading list, and see whether you recognise any authors/theorists. Some lecturers require you to do preparatory reading – if you do not complete this you will find it harder to participate in the learning experience.

Note taking

Reflection

There are several techniques for taking notes in lectures. To evaluate your current techniques it would be helpful to analyse notes you have taken recently at a lecture or perhaps during a staff development event. Rereading your notes now, how useful are they? Did they capture enough information or jog your memory?

Have you used any of the following techniques?

Table 1.3 Note-taking techniques

Have you:	Yes/No?	If yes, has it helped you to organise the material more effectively?
Tried to write down everything the presenter said?		
Annotated a handout that you were given by the presenter? (Doodles don't count!)		
Used your own shorthand for words you use frequently?		
Used headings?		
Underlined important information?		
Used highlighter pens to make particular information stand out, or link related items?		
Used columns or margins to separate information into categories?		
Drawn a mind-map?		

Most of the techniques in Table 1.3 can be very helpful, *except the first one.* It is not possible to concentrate on a lecture and write everything down. This is the least productive method, though it may appear to be an insurance policy; whilst concentrating on capturing every word, you are not participating in the lecture, nor are you making sense of the material.

You need to find your preferred style of note taking. Here are ideas which you may wish to consider as you experiment with a variety of techniques:

1. Prepare a list of the things you want to find out during the lecture. If any of these questions remain unanswered, ask the presenter at the end of the session.
2. Capture the essential facts in the quickest possible way. Devise your own form of shorthand to increase your speed e.g. using abbreviations and symbols: i.e. ch > 6mths = sit unaided [this means a child over six months can sit unaided].

3. Organise your notes as you write them: using headings, columns, or underlining and using capitals for important words. Using colours to highlight different aspects or topics can also help. For example you could use red to highlight theories, yellow for legislation, etc.
4. Cornell notes (http://coe.jmu.edu/learningtoolbox/cornellnotes.html) enable you to organise your notes in columns with the left-hand column giving the heading/focus and the right-hand the information.
5. Diagrammatic methods are visually effective (e.g. mind-maps: Buzan and Buzan, 2000; pattern notes: Burns and Sinfield, 2012).

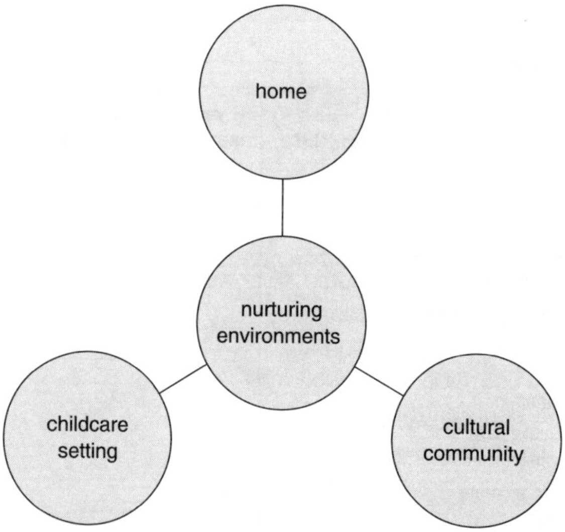

Figure 1.1 Pattern Notes. Using headings on the spokes, add information as the lecture proceeds; you can also indicate connections between ideas using arrows and colour coding

6. Reviewing your notes soon after the lecture enables you to add details that were missed. If you were actively involved in the discussions, you should be able to fill in these gaps quite easily, even 24 hours later.
7. Many tutors provide notes electronically, possibly their PowerPoint slides. If these notes are available prior to the session, print them off. This means that you can concentrate more effectively on the content of the lecture, and just annotate (make notes on) the handout.

8. Some students take notes using a laptop; whilst these will be more legible, you must be proficient at touch typing so you are not distracted from the lecture.

As discussed earlier, information from lectures is only one source of knowledge. Whichever note-taking method you employ, to get the most out of lectures you need to be attentive and participative. Like an athlete you will build up your powers of concentration and find ways to ensure that you are actively engaged.

Field notes

A practice-based programme such as a childhood studies degree will require you to make field notes and observations in practical situations. You need to capture details of events quickly and efficiently so you have sufficient information to write reports and case studies. Preparing charts in advance, and devising a variety of shorthand abbreviations will help you to make effective field notes.

Participating in lectures

Taught sessions are usually structured so that direct information giving is followed by opportunities for group work, enabling students to discuss and analyse material to gain a better insight into the topic. To participate fully in the tasks and discussions, sit with students with whom you work well, establishing a stable group where you feel confident to make a contribution.

Working in groups

Collaborating in these groups is excellent preparation for writing discursive essays. Discussions you have with colleagues will mimic the balanced arguments you need to provide in your written work. Members of groups will have varied experiences and knowledge to bring to discussions, and may offer different ideas and hold alternative opinions. The more lively the debate, the more you will benefit from working together. The group needs to ensure that no one dominates, and that shyer individuals are encouraged to contribute their ideas. If there is an imbalance, some students may feel that they are sharing their ideas and getting little in return; this may discourage them from participating fully on subsequent occasions. Being part of a stimulating group will enhance your studies; once established the group may wish to meet between lectures. In my experience, students who do this get better grades because they are engaged in a vibrant learning community.

Journal Task

Cavanagh, M. (2011) 'Student's experiences of active engagement through cooperative learning activities in lectures', *Active Learning in Higher Education*, 12(1): 23–33.

Levels 4 & 5

Read the article and:

1. Consider what constitutes 'active learning' and the concept of 'lectorials' described by Cavanagh.
2. How does this researcher suggest these techniques help students to engage in university lectures?

Level 6

Consider the way in which the author presents his research:

1. Make notes on the structure of the article and how Cavanagh takes the reader through the different stages of the research process.
2. How does he provide an overview of the issues, including the views of other academics, and analyse the data gathered from the students?

To download this task as well as other useful online resources please visit:
www.sagepub.co.uk/mukherji

Distance learning

Some of you may be about to embark on your studies as a distance learner. This method of study can fit in better with your work commitments and personal life, and is a good alternative when attending lectures is difficult. Studying this way requires motivation and determination; you need to be very disciplined, setting aside adequate periods of time to read the course materials which replace lectures. You should not rely exclusively on the course materials; you will need to access further reading by visiting a library or using the internet.

A benefit of working as a distance learning student is that you will be assigned a personal tutor. This provides you with the opportunity to communicate regularly with a tutor on an individual basis, an advantage not generally available to those on taught courses. Some distance learning programmes encourage students to meet other students; becoming a member of a self study group would enable you to participate in the type of discussion and lively debate mentioned previously.

Academic reading

Studying at degree level will require you to reassess the way you approach texts. When you read for academic purposes you need to concentrate in a systematic way, searching for specific information. Remember that you should *always* carry pen and paper (or a laptop) to make notes.

Reflection

You will rarely read a book from cover to cover; this may seem surprising, but let us take this textbook as an example. Suppose you are studying a module on the development of children's language would you:

Look down the **contents page**, searching for relevant chapter headings?
Look up key words (such as speech, language acquisition) in the **index**?
Read the chapter **introduction/aims**, which provide a summary of the material covered?
Scan the **headings** for relevant words/themes?
Skim across **paragraphs** to gauge the general content?

All the textual features (in **bold** above), help you to find the information you seek, and are commonly found in paper texts, and are also apparent in the structure of internet articles. Strategies such as **skimming** (to get the gist of a passage) and **scanning** (searching for particular words/ names) will help you to quickly assess whether the text suits your purposes. Once you have found something of interest, you need to slow down the pace in order to digest the passage carefully.

To engage in 'deep' reading, you should prepare in advance. Organise your search by pre-determining the focus of the reading session, considering carefully what specific information you wish to gather, and making a list of questions that need answering. Always make a note of the title and author before you start note-taking – this way you can return to the text.

Books

You may wish to own particular textbooks suggested by your tutors, but you will need to read more widely. Become familiar with your institution's library systems and understand how the books are classified (sorted and labelled). Libraries cannot buy sufficient copies for every student studying in a particular discipline, however, once you have a classification number from the electronic catalogue, search the shelves to find alternative books on the subject by different authors.

Academic journals

The most current information on any subject is to be found in academic journals. The articles are written by experts in their field and are often based on recently conducted research. The articles are 'peer reviewed', this means that other academics have checked the content so you can be sure of the quality of the information.

Articles begin with an **abstract**, this paragraph provides a summary of the content, and allows you to assess whether it contains material you are seeking. Reference lists at the end of articles provide a rich source of further reading material on the subject. Generally, daily papers and weekly magazines do not provide a balanced view; avoid using them as references in academic writing unless you are exploring public opinion or trends.

Most journals are now published electronically and you should be able to access them through your institution's library system. Colleges and universities pay annual subscriptions for these journals, and your tutors will have selected titles they think most relevant to your programme.

The internet

The internet provides limitless information from around the globe, which can be bewildering. You need to distinguish between sources that have academic legitimacy, and those that are written by students in Detroit – *never* use Wikipedia as an academic reference.

To begin your search, use a search engine (such as Google Scholar) or a library catalogue, selecting **key words**. Remain focused on one search at a time; it is easy to get side-tracked. If you discover something useful for a different essay, jot down a reminder so you can return to the pages at a later date.

Once you have found what you are searching for, settle down to some uninterrupted 'deep reading', making notes as you go. Take time to read slowly and carefully, pausing to think about what you have read; sometimes you need to reread a passage to ensure that you have fully understood the content. During your studies you will constantly encounter new ideas and concepts, many will challenge your ideas. Take time to reflect on your current understanding, and explore alternative views with an open mind. This strategy will help you to develop two really important study skills: **analysing** (exploring different ideas and opinions) and **synthesising** (using these ideas for your own purposes).

As you read, carefully extract the details most useful for your purpose; pre-prepared questions will help you to quickly identify relevant information. Whilst reading, frequently check whether you have maintained your focus, and at the end of the session take a few moments to summarise what you have learnt in a series of bullet points; this will help consolidate your understanding.

Preparing for assessments

Academic referencing

Work you produce for module assessments needs to demonstrate both your knowledge and your understanding of the topic. To show that you have explored the subject in depth, you must make reference to the views, theories and research of other writers, *and* discuss what you have read.

As mentioned earlier, you should note the title and the author of any text you read. You will need additional information if you mention the ideas in an essay or presentation. The chart below sets out what information you are going to need.

For a book:

Table 1.4 Information required for referencing a text

Title
Author/editor
Date of publication
Chapter title and author if it is an edited text where different contributors have written chapters, as is the case in this textbook
Place of publication
Publishing house (not printers)
Page numbers when quoting the author's words directly

For a journal article:

Table 1.5 Information required for referencing a journal article

Title of Journal
URL if using electronic copy
Publishing house
Date of publication
Article title and author(s)
Pages the article covers
Specific page, if making a direct quote

From the internet: this is more complicated since not all material on the internet provides such detailed information. *Cite Them Right* (Pears and Shields, 2010) is an excellent publication which I would suggest you refer to. However, as a guide you should find out your institution's specific requirements.

Table 1.6 Information required for referencing an internet source

URL
Date you accessed it from the internet
Publisher/author/organisation who has written the material
Title of article, if available (such as piece from online newspaper, or government website)
Date published, if available

References: citations and reference lists

There are two ways in which you will include reference information in your academic work. The first is during the assignment itself when you refer to the text, known as a **citation**. This proves that the ideas you present come from reliable sources. The second is at the end of the essay or presentation, where you provide details of every text you have used. This can be called a **reference list** (showing texts you have referred to), or a **bibliography** (a list which includes your preparatory reading). At undergraduate level you will mostly be required to provide a reference list, however you may need to compile a bibliography for an extended essay or a research project at Level 6.

Reference lists include all the detailed information you have collected about the text, and must be arranged in alphabetical order using the authors' surnames, and should be listed as follows (please note the punctuation used in the list, this is important):

Surname, initials. (date) Title. Place of publication: Name of publishers.

Citations

To refer to a text in your essay, you will use a form of shorthand. You are only required to give (cite) the surname of the author: Wyse (2012), or organisation: CWDC (2011), plus the date of publication. If there are two authors: Mukherji & Albon (2011), you name them both, but if more than two, you name the first author, for example Bruce et al. (2010).

Take a moment when you are next reading to examine how the author cites (refers to) other texts. This will be a good model for your own work. There are a number of websites which help you to organise your references such as Neil's Toolkit (http://www.neilstoolbox.com/articles/harvard-reference-generator.htm), and online journals provide the details ready to paste into your reference list. Most British universities use the Harvard Referencing system (see Middlesex University: http://libguides.mdx.ac.uk/content.php?pid=220238&sid=1828721), but you may be allowed to use footnotes.

Quotations

You must be extremely careful when making notes. If you copy out the *actual words* used by the author, then note the page number, to include in the citation. Put quotation marks around the quoted words, so you can identify which sentences are *direct quotes*, and which are ideas you have summarised.

Sometimes the author has phrased something so well that you decide to use their exact words, but keep quotations brief. Remember that a quote only demonstrates your ability to extract information, whereas summarising an author's ideas in your own words will indicate that you have considered the meaning and understood the material you are discussing.

Citing secondary sources

Sometimes you will mention ideas an author has referenced in their work – this is known as a secondary source. Since you have not directly read this yourself, you must indicate where you found it. This is done by referring to the secondary source, but adding the primary source in brackets. For example if you have found information about Piaget's stage theories from Bruce's book you would show the reference as follows:

Piaget's theory suggested .... (cited in Bruce et al., 2010)

Academic writing

Academic writing can cause students anxiety, but as with other aspects of study, the ability to organise yourself will be crucial. It can be helpful to practise expressing yourself in writing by, for example, keeping a diary or a study journal (such as Bassot, 2012).

Preparing for different types of assignment

Modules are likely to be assessed through a series of formative and summative assessments, and course documentation will clarify what these are, and when they will be required. Summative assessments provide grades towards your degree, while formative pieces may be designed to develop your understanding without contributing to your grades.

Your initial strategy should be to read the title/task extremely carefully; read it several times and highlight the key words. What are you being asked to do? The following table provides an explanation of terms:

Table 1.7 Assessment requirements

Report	A descriptive, factual piece of writing about a particular event
Observation	A detailed account of an event
Portfolio	A collection of material gathered for a specific purpose
Reflective writing	A personal response to an event or experience
Case study	A detailed description and analysis of a particular subject
Balanced argument	Providing evidence of opposing theories and opinions on a subject
Analysis	An in-depth exploration of facts and opinions
Evaluation/a critical appraisal	A considered opinion, drawing on ideas from sources possibly on opposing sides of an argument
Synthesis	Bringing together ideas to use in a new way

Reflection

Consider the differences between these terms which are frequently used in assignment questions:

Table 1.8 Terms commonly used in essay questions

		Differences?
Describe	Analyse	
Summarise	Discuss	
Outline	Explain	
Compare	Contrast	

Planning essays

Once you are confident about the task (rephrase the question to check your understanding) make a plan using either linear notes or a diagram. Highlight the topics you need to include and write what you already know under each heading. Next, consider who the main theorists are, and which texts and authors will help to reference your work; reread the module learning outcomes, and refer back to your lecture notes for clues. A good plan will enable you to be systematic and time-efficient, provide a clear focus when you begin to research, and highlight gaps in your knowledge.

Be sure to search for different opinions and theories from a variety of sources to build a balanced argument. Placing opposing views under a heading on your plan will ensure that you discuss them together in your essay, avoiding repetition. Once you have researched the topic thoroughly, you can start structuring your essay. Meticulous planning will facilitate a speedy write-up, as all the information will be at your finger-tips.

Points to remember when structuring your essay are:

- Start with an introduction explaining how you intend addressing the question.
- Organise your essay in a logical order, for example in chronological/historical order. Paragraphs should discuss one point; the first sentence should introduce the point, followed by further sentences which discuss the idea.
- Avoid returning to a different aspect of the same topic later in the essay.
- Check that the essay flows well; ensure that ideas lead into one another in a logical manner. Using words or phrases which signpost when you are comparing ideas (However ......), or changing the subject (Next ......) will help cohesion.
- The concluding paragraph should provide a neat ending; it signals to the reader that you have reached the end of your discussion. You may highlight particularly interesting ideas, explaining how you hope to pursue them further. Reports or case studies often require you to make recommendations.

Drafting and editing

It is a common misconception that competent writers produce perfect essays in one sitting. When you write an email or text you probably check it before you press send to ensure it makes sense. The best essays are drafted, redrafted and edited several times, which is why you should give yourself sufficient time to perfect an essay; leaving assessments to the last minute will result in less polished work.

Once you have a good draft leave it aside for a day or two, so you can return to it with fresh eyes. Check again to ensure that you have answered the question and provided sufficient supporting evidence. Read through to see how it flows – you may decide to move paragraphs or sections around, and cut parts that are irrelevant or repetitive.

Once you are happy with the work carefully edit it, checking that you have expressed yourself clearly, detecting grammar and spelling mistakes. Ask someone to help you to proofread your work – they need have no knowledge of the subject; in fact if they do not, they can tell you whether you have explained yourself adequately.

You may need to reduce the essay to keep within the required word limit (usually you are allowed 10% over or under). When reducing an essay take care not to lose essential information. It is tempting to cut whole paragraphs, a quick solution, but it can mean losing vital information or affect the critical balance of an essay. If you are just a few words over the limit, you can rephrase sentences, or take out unnecessary descriptive words (adverbs/adjectives). Finally, do remember to revisit your reference list to remove any texts that you have taken out of the essay.

Plagiarism

Another important aspect of editing is ensuring that you have referenced your work meticulously. Remember that **plagiarism** is a very serious offence and can lead to your work being disqualified. Ensure that all supporting evidence is correctly cited in the main body of the essay, and that references are listed in alphabetical order in the list at the end of the essay. Check that you have put page numbers with every direct quote, and that publication dates are correct.

Anonymity

Check through your essay and the appendices to ensure that individual and institutional identities have been disguised, or in the case of documentary evidence, permission letters and policy documents, that names are blanked out. Photographs should be used sparingly and never show children's faces.

Other features

Abbreviations

Always put the full name of an organisation or document the first time you mention it, giving the acronym in brackets [for example: United Kingdom Language Association (UKLA)], thereafter in the essay you can use the abbreviated form.

Appendices

Appendices allow you to provide additional information, and are useful because they are not included in the word count. However, appendices provide supporting material and *must* be referred to in the essay. Appendices are numbered after you have completely finished writing, as they must be listed in the order they occur in the essay. Refer to them as follows: (see Observation 2, Appendix 6).

Presentations

You will probably be required to do oral presentations during your course. A presentation allows you to share your knowledge and understanding of a particular topic with an audience, and, whilst they need careful planning, they are an opportunity to express your ideas verbally rather than in writing. Where presentations are for assessment purposes, two tutors will watch and agree marks, and you may be required to provide a handout outlining your talk with a list of references.

Presentations require the same thorough research as an essay. You may be asked to present a case study or explain other practical information you have gathered, but you still need to support your discussion with evidence from your reading including pertinent theory. Having gathered the material, plan your talk using a linear or diagrammatic method, focusing on approximately five main points. Take each heading in turn and decide how best to explain the information to your audience. Check that the ideas are in an order which ensures the talk will flow smoothly.

A presentation, like an essay, should start with an introduction explaining how you are going to proceed. If you are using PowerPoint, the first slide can provide a visual guide indicating the order in which you plan to explore the topic.

During the main body of the presentation, use PowerPoint slides as prompts; avoid putting all the information on the slides and then just reading them aloud. Prepare notes or prompt cards to remind yourself of the key points you want to make, and endeavour to present in a relaxed manner, maintaining some eye contact with your audience. Consider the style of delivery your tutors use, and model yourself on the most engaging.

Your talk should end with a strong conclusion which sums up your ideas, possibly providing recommendations or ideas for further research, and indicating to your audience that the presentation is finished.

You will be given a time limit which should be treated as seriously as a written word limit. It always takes much longer than you think to talk through a series of points, so practise your timing using a stop-watch. You may need to adjust your material if you cannot fit everything in; remember that for assessment purposes, you will be penalised for running over time, possibly stopped in mid-flow, so it is important that you practise aloud before the event.

You may also be required to be part of a group presentation. This should be an enriching experience, with students bringing different knowledge and expertise to the joint process. However, occasionally certain members of a group prove to be less committed, failing to participate fully. It is up to the group to self-regulate, ensuring that each member takes responsibility for specific tasks. Agree appropriate deadlines and ensure that there is time to meet to run-through (and time) the presentation. In extreme circumstances, where one individual has been uncooperative, you may need to bring this to the attention of the assessing tutors.

Facing challenges and overcoming difficulties

Studying is full of unexpected challenges and most students encounter periods of uncertainty, when they question their ability to complete a particular task or even the degree itself. When you are feeling overwhelmed, take some time out and return to it later from a fresh perspective. It also helps to find someone to talk things over with.

Using tutorials effectively and listening to advice

The ability to listen to advice, and act on feedback, is crucial to successful study; failure to do so will result in your continuing to make the same mistakes.

Tutorials will be available with your module tutors, and these provide an excellent way of gauging your development. Take advantage of every opportunity to meet with your lecturers; prepare some questions in advance and when appropriate, take an essay plan with you to discuss. Always make notes during tutorials as you are unlikely to remember the details afterwards, and listen carefully to the tutor's remarks on your ideas and your written style.

It is hard when you have put great effort into a piece of work, to hear that it is flawed. However, if you take advice in the spirit in which it is given, viewing it as an opportunity to improve your performance, you will make better progress. You may share your ideas and draft essays with your study buddies; make sure that you all behave as 'critical friends', providing constructive support for one another in a kind manner. Always begin by pointing out the positive aspects and then make suggestions for improvement.

Tutors provide feedback on your written assignments; regrettably students often focus on the grade they receive and ignore the comments. You should read and digest these comments carefully when your work is returned; however high your mark, there will be suggestions for further development. If you fail a piece of work, you should read the feedback, decide what you need to do to improve the essay, and then arrange to meet your tutor to discuss your plans for the re-sit assessment.

Getting help, student support services

If you find yourself struggling with your studies, and in particular find it hard to express yourself in writing, there should be support available in your institution. If you have a known disability, such as dyslexia, inform your tutors *before you begin* the course so that appropriate help is available from the start. You may receive individual support from a specialist tutor, be able to keep library books longer, and be allowed extra time to submit your written work when needed.

The transition from HE level 4 to levels 5 and 6

Your academic skills will be developing as you progress through your degree. In the same way that you need to assess your study skills at the beginning of the course, you also need to recognise that the bar is raised at each further level of study. As you enter the second year (level 5) there are expectations of much wider reading, including greater access to academic journals. You will be expected to demonstrate deeper engagement with the texts you read, and show that you are developing analytical skills.

At Honours level (6) you will need to show advanced study skills, with emphasis on independent study and the ability to fully analyse and synthesise new material. You will need to demonstrate advanced research skills, and the capacity to use the material to defend your views based on a deep understanding and analysis of the subject. At Honours level you will be required to carry out a piece of research, collecting your own data on a subject of your choosing. This independent piece of work requires you to utilise all the skills that you have gained along the way, and is the culmination of your development towards being a graduate.

Table 1.9 Academic writing at undergraduate levels

	Demonstrate:
Level 4	your ability to gain an understanding of new knowledge and concepts; much of your work at the beginning will be descriptive.
Level 5	your ability to show a more confident attitude towards your reading, be able to analyse and apply new ideas appropriately.
Level 6	your ability to evaluate opposing opinions on a subject, and use these to support/justify your own views in a rational, systematic manner.

Summary

In this chapter we have looked at how to prepare for study at degree level. I do hope that this will have helped you to examine your attitude towards study, clarified some questions you may have had about expectations at degree-level learning, and provided you with practical information regarding academic writing skills. This would be a good moment to return to the notes you made in response to the first reflective point and consider whether you feel better prepared for the work that lies ahead.

Further reading

Levels 4 & 5

Bassot, B. (2012) *The Reflective Diary 2012–13*. Leicester: Troubador Publishing. This is an excellent academic-year diary, which includes informative pages on developing and recording reflective practice.

Burns, T. and Sinfield, S. (2012) *Essential Study Skills: The Complete Guide to Success at University* (3rd edition). London: Sage. Chapter 11: 'How to make the best notes' will help you to review in greater detail the different note-taking methods available, and make an informed choice.

Northedge, A. (2005) *The Good Study Guide*. Milton Keynes: Open University Press. Chapter 10: 'Writing the way "they" want' helps you to recognise what your tutors will be looking for when they read your assignments.

Norton, L. and Pit, E. (2009) *Writing Essays @ University: A Guide for Students by Students*. London: CETL Write Now. Chapter 7: 'Developing argument' explains how to write a discursive essay

Sambell, K., Gibson, M. and Miller, S. (2010) *Studying Childhood & Early Childhood: A Guide for Students* (2nd edition). London: Sage. Chapter 3: 'Producing a good assignment' has general tips for successful writing.

Wyse, D. (2012) *The Good Writing Guide for Education Students* (3rd edition). London: Sage. Chapter 2: 'Searching for reading materials' explores how to gather material for your essays.

Level 6

Judge, B., Jones, P. and McCreery, E. (2009) *Critical Thinking Skills for Education Students (Study Skills in Education)*. Exeter: Learning Matters. This text will help you to consider how you present and critically analyse your ideas, an essential skill at Level 6.

Mukherji, P. and Albon, D. (2011) *Research Methods in Early Childhood: An Introductory Guide*. London: Sage. An excellent, clear text which will support your final research project.

Wyse, D. (2012) *The Good Writing Guide for Education Students* (3rd edition). London: Sage. Chapter 6: 'Structuring your writing' will help when you are writing up your final project/dissertation.

Online resources

Open University website: http://www.open.ac.uk/skillsforstudy/
Sage online study resources: http://www.uk.sagepub.com/studyskills.sp
Sinfield, S. How to make better notes: http://www.youtube.com/watch?v=M1IHsPt_Nmg

To download all of the tables in this chapter as well as other useful online resources please visit: **www.sagepub.co.uk/mukherji**

References

Bassot, B. (2012) *The Reflective Diary 2012–13*. Leicester: Troubador Publishing.

Bruce, T., Meggitt, C. and Grenier, J. (2010) *Child Care & Education* (5th edition). London: Hodder Education.

Burns, T. and Sinfield, S. (2012) *Essential Study Skills: The Complete Guide to Success at University* (3rd edition). London: Sage.

Buzan, T. and Buzan, B. (2000) *The Mind Map Book* (Millennium edition). London: BBC Publications.

Cavanagh, M. (2011) 'Student's experiences of active engagement through cooperative learning activities in lectures', *Active Learning in Higher Education*, 12(1): 23–33.

Cornell notes: http://coe.jmu.edu/learningtoolbox/cornellnotes.html

Middlesex university: http://libguides.mdx.ac.uk/content.php?pid=220238&sid=1828721

Mukherji, P. and Albon, D. (2011) *Research Methods in Early Childhood: An Introductory Guide.* London: Sage.

Neil's Toolbox: http://www.neilstoolbox.com/articles/harvard-reference-generator.htm

Northedge, A. (2005) *The Good Study Guide.* Milton Keynes: Open University Press.

Norton, L. and Pit, E. (2009) *Writing Essays @ University: A Guide for Students by Students.* London: CETL Write Now. www.writenow.ac.uk/assessmentplus

Palgrave study guides: http://www.palgrave.com/skills4study/index.asp

Pears, R. and Shields, G. (2010) *Cite Them Right* (8th edition). Basingstoke, Hampshire: Palgrave Macmillan. http://www.palgrave.com/products/title.aspx?PID=410850

Sambell, K., Gibson, M. and Miller, S. (2010) *Studying Childhood & Early Childhood: A Guide for Students* (2nd edition). London: Sage.

Wyse, D. (2012) *The Good Writing Guide for Education Students* (3rd edition). London: Sage.

2

Upholding Children's Rights in Early Years Settings

Carolyne Willow

This chapter will:

- Establish the importance of early childhood and the critical role played by early years practitioners in upholding children's rights
- Show that young children are not always respected as people, within the law and in their everyday interactions with adults
- Introduce the general principles of the Convention on the Rights of the Child and explore how they can be implemented in early years settings
- Outline the main themes in the children's rights literature and their implications for early years settings.

This chapter introduces you to children's rights ideas and practice, beginning with a discussion of the importance of early childhood then moving on to recognising young children as individual people with their own thoughts, wishes and feelings. You are asked to consider how you communicate respect to young children and to analyse different early years scenarios from a children's rights perspective.

Five themes are discussed in more detail, with case studies, in order to develop your understanding of what it means to uphold the rights of young children. These themes cover the capacity of young children to make choices and influence their surroundings; the ways in which adults can nurture or suppress children's capacities;

the interrelationship between what is in a child's best interests and their wishes, feelings and views; how children's rights relate to all aspects of child well-being and development; and the responsibility of us all to uphold the rights of young children.

The chapter ends with a reminder of the extraordinary opportunities that early years practitioners have, to show young children they are valued; to offer them respectful relationships where they are heard and taken seriously; and to provide pleasurable experiences. Upholding young children's rights should be at the centre of every early years setting, and I hope this chapter will inspire you to strengthen your efforts to make this happen.

The Importance of early childhood

That early childhood is a critical period of human growth and development is now firmly established in public policy (Allen, 2011; Feinstein, 2003; Field, 2010; Tickell, 2011). The quality of care, relationships, stimulation and opportunities offered to babies and young children is fundamental to their present happiness and well-being, and will also affect their adulthood. The Childcare Act 2006 has given prominence to the state's role in supporting early childhood: since April 2008, English local authorities have been required to promote the well-being of young children in their area and reduce inequalities between them.

Babies and young children require special attention from policy makers, partly due to their innate vulnerability and dependency on adults, but also because the economic and social conditions of early childhood can be extremely challenging. Statistics show that the homicide rate in England and Wales is highest in the first year of life (Smith et al., 2012: 44). Forty-five per cent of UK families living in severe poverty includes a child aged 4 or under (Magadi and Middleton, 2007: 19). Over one-third of children of imprisoned mothers are aged under 5 (Howard League for Penal Reform, 2011) and 144,000 babies in the UK live with a parent who has a mental health problem (Cuthbert et al., 2011: 5). In the year ending 31 March 2012, 40,990 children under the age of 10 years were looked after by local authorities, accounting for 40 per cent of children in care (Department for Education, 2012a).

The international monitoring body for children's rights, the United Nations Committee on the Rights of the Child, has issued guidance on young children's rights. This urges governments to adopt a 'positive agenda for rights in early childhood' (UNCRC, 2006: 2) and explains:

> Work with young children should be socially valued and properly paid, in order to attract a highly qualified workforce, men as well as women. It is essential that they have sound, up-to-date theoretical and practical understanding about children's rights and development; that they adopt appropriate child-centred care practices, curricula and pedagogies; and that they have access to specialist professional resources and support ... (2006: 11)

Children are people

The UN Committee's guidance explains that international law now 'requires that children, including the very youngest children, be respected as persons in their own right' (2006: 2–3).

The idea that children are people may seem obvious. But if you think carefully about their everyday lives, and the attitudes and behaviour within wider society, it becomes clear that children are commonly treated as *human becomings* (Lee, 2001; Qvortrup et al., 1994) rather than human beings. The law on assault is probably the greatest signifier that children are not accorded the same human worth and dignity as adults. Parents and others acting *in loco parentis* can use a legal ('reasonable punishment') defence if they are charged with the common assault of a baby or child. This defence is not available to those who are prohibited in law from inflicting corporal punishment, such as early years practitioners and teachers. There is no statutory definition of reasonable punishment: the court must look at the facts of each case. The defence dates back to 1860 when a schoolmaster in Eastbourne beat to death a teenage boy. The judge in that case advised the jury (who found the schoolmaster guilty of manslaughter) that: '... a parent or schoolmaster ... may for the purpose of correcting what is evil in the child inflict moderate and reasonable corporal punishment' (*R v Hopley*). Husbands were similarly permitted to chastise their wives until 1891, when the Court of Appeal ruled that this was now obsolete. But the situation remains that babies and children are the only people in the UK not to be fully protected under the law. A study for the Department of Health found that 52 per cent of 1-year-olds were hit/smacked weekly or more often by their parents (Nobes and Smith, 1997: 276–7). The NSPCC found that 39 per cent of primary-school-aged children had been physically punished/smacked by a primary carer in the past year (Radford et al., 2011: 89). The legal situation in the UK and elsewhere led the Deputy Secretary-General of the Council of Europe to declare: 'children are not mini-persons with mini-rights, mini-feelings and mini-human dignity' (de Boer-Buquicchio, 2005).

Laws mirror social attitudes, and at the same time influence thinking and behaviour. This is why the campaign for equal protection from assault for children is so intertwined with seeking greater respect for them as people. Sweden was the first country in the world to give children the same protection as adults from assault, in 1979. A government publication two decades later reflected on the country's growing respect for the child's mental and physical integrity, and Sweden's rejection of violence in child-rearing:

> At the beginning of the 20th century it was still implicitly assumed that the child should obey its parents and authorities without murmur. Children were ascribed no independent standing and as a rule were not allowed to voice their opinions ... Gradually society has changed ... The concept of the child as an individual with rights of its own has become more prominent. This calls for a form of child education based on interaction, care and mutual respect. (Hindberg, 2001: 11–12)

Early years practitioners have countless opportunities to provide care and respect to children. Your role in encouraging positive behaviour among children is vital and uncontested, whether this be administering warnings against snatching, stealing, pushing or interrupting, or reminders to be kind, patient and considerate. But how many of the courtesies enjoyed by adults are available to young children?

How do you talk to children?

Playgroup leader Judy Miller in her book about young children taking responsibility and making decisions gives this advice: 'Tape yourself talking with children and compare this with how you talk with adults. Is there a difference in your tone of voice? Are there things you say to children that you wouldn't say to adults' (2003: 31). Miller is not saying that children are miniature adults, nor is she advocating that people of different ages should be treated exactly the same. She is questioning how much respect (or disrespect) we communicate to children as a matter of routine.

Reflection

Recall the last time you had a conversation with a child. Consider the purpose and nature of the conversation and whether there was anything else you could have said or done to communicate respect to the child.

Young children are very often aware of the lack of respect given to them. The child that told me some years ago that '[Adults] don't treat us like humans. They treat us like babies who can't talk' (Willow, 1999: 32) was pointing to children's inferior social standing and depicting a pecking order with babies at the bottom. Another child eloquently described children's low status to Ofsted's Children's Rights Director: '[Adults] think we're there to become adults – you're only a child because you can't be born as an adult' (cited in Morgan, 2004: 16).

The idea that childhood's value rests in its production of adults is embedded in our society's culture and education system. The 'What do you want to be when you grow up?' question, so frequently asked of children, epitomises the belief that childhood is simply a passing stage to a full and valued adult life. The way in which play, the mainstay of early childhood, is viewed by some as a mere pastime that can be interrupted or ended without warning shows little regard for what children find fulfilling. The National Children's Bureau's first Director, Mia Kellmer Pringle, wrote almost 30 years ago:

> The phrase 'he is only playing' is still too often heard, implying that play is only slightly superior to doing nothing at all. In fact, it is an intensely absorbing experience and even more important to the child than work is to the adult. (1975: 43)

Communicating respect

Most of us have answered a question for a young child when they were capable of responding themselves. Sometimes questions are not even asked. The demands of working in a group setting can mean that enquiring of children's basic needs is replaced by assumption: Hamid has eaten oranges before so there's no reason he shouldn't eat one today (what if Hamid doesn't want an orange right now); Megan looks hot so she should take off her cardigan (wouldn't it be polite to ask Megan if she is feeling uncomfortable); it's time for morning nap, Anka must sleep (but Anka has only just found all the pieces to her toy).

How many of us have lifted a young child without informing them of our intentions or seeking their permission to do so? Or dismissed a child when they were telling us something important? Miller (2003) cautions us to 'resist the temptation to find the teaching point in every exchange', giving this example:

> Child: My mum's car broke down on the way to nursery!
>
> Adult: Did it? And what colour is your mum's car? (2003: 32)

In this scenario, the adult is interrupting the child's flow and expression. They are also denying themselves the enjoyment of listening to an interesting anecdote told by an enthusiastic child. Leaving aside the educational benefits of conversation, probing and testing children in this way is not treating them with respect. This kind of interchange would appear very odd were it between two adults.

Treating children courteously tells them they are valued and worthy of respect. Crucially, it also reminds us we are interacting with fellow human beings who have dignity and feelings just like us. Indeed, we encourage very young children, babies included, to say thank you and take turns long before they can properly understand the social meaning of such actions. Writing about the rights of babies, Priscilla Alderson explains: ' … rights partly become real in being respected, just as babies learn to speak through being spoken to for months as if they can already speak' (Alderson et al., 2006: 47).

Children's rights agreed worldwide

The rights of children were first codified internationally in the 1920s and then the Declaration of the Rights of the Child was passed by the United Nations in 1959.

Twenty years later, the Polish Government recommended that a dedicated children's rights treaty be drafted. Its proposal was accepted and, after a 10-year drafting period, the UN adopted the Convention on the Rights of the Child (UNCRC) in November 1989. Two years later the UK ratified the Convention, which was a legal undertaking that the treaty would be upheld in all settings and for all children.

The UNCRC has 54 sections, called articles. These prescribe the rights of children, set out the obligations of governments and explain the membership and working practices of the UN Committee on the Rights of the Child. When it was formed in 1991, the UN Committee on the Rights of the Child selected four articles – 2, 3, 6 and 12 – as general principles. These are key to the implementation of all the other rights in the Convention.

Article 2 is every child's entitlement to enjoy his or her rights without any form of discrimination. This includes protection from discrimination relating to his or her parents' actions or status. Implementing children's right to non-discrimination in early years settings entails treating every child with respect and fairness, and ensuring individual needs are understood and met. Positive action will sometimes be necessary to ensure children can enjoy their rights on an equal basis with other children. The case study below shows the harm that can be caused by breaching a child's right to privacy, which in this situation arose from a mother being arrested for shoplifting.

CASE STUDY

The right not to be discriminated against

Four-year-old Chantelle arrives at nursery with her grandmother who tells the nursery manager that Chantelle's mother was arrested for shoplifting and detained at the police station for several hours over the weekend. Later that day, Chantelle and three other children overhear staff talking about Chantelle's mum being arrested. One member of staff says Chantelle's mum is likely to be sent to prison as she has been in trouble with the police before.

On the bus journey home, Chantelle asks her grandmother if she can live with her when her mum goes to prison. The grandmother is furious when she hears what has happened and makes a formal complaint. She threatens to remove Chantelle from the nursery. Staff say the children were playing together and they hadn't realised any of them were listening to their conversation.

- What kind of information should be shared in early years settings?
- How can this be done in a manner consistent with children's right to privacy?

Article 3 of the UNCRC requires that the child's best interests be a primary consideration in all actions concerning the child. In certain circumstances, the Convention gives absolute priority to the child's best interests, for example in adoption and other legal processes where the separation of the child from his or her family environment is being considered (articles 21 and 9 respectively). The best interests of children are not defined in the treaty itself: they have to be constructed from analysing 'the sum total of the norms in the Convention' (Hammarberg, 2008). Where the best interests of an individual child in a particular situation is under consideration – for example, when decisions are being made about the child's home, relationships and education following parental separation – it will be necessary to scrutinise those parts of the Convention which are most pertinent. The case study below illustrates the challenges of seeking to act in the best interests of a child when other children are affected too.

CASE STUDY

Acting in the child's best interests

Two-year-old Sonny has been with the same childminder since he was nine weeks old. Both his parents work full-time. He is with his childminder three days a week and grandparents two days.

Sonny is thriving and enjoys being with his childminder. His parents are expecting another child and would like both their children to be looked after by the same childminder. Looking after Sonny's sibling would breach the childminder's conditions of registration. Sonny's parents are therefore considering moving Sonny to another childminder who can look after both their children.

- What factors would you take into consideration when determining the best interests of the two children?
- Would you ask Sonny his views?

Article 6 requires all those states that have ratified the UNCRC to ensure every child's right to survival and maximum development. This encompasses all aspects of the child's development. In educational settings it is also useful to refer to article 29, which sets out the aims of education, starting with the development of the child's personality, talents and mental and physical abilities to their fullest potential. The case study below considers the role of early years practitioners in championing the rights of young children.

CASE STUDY

The child's right to develop fully

Mohammed is 5 years old and is a very quiet, placid child. He seems to be a bit of a daydreamer and doesn't have any friends at his after-school club which he attends with his 7-year-old brother.

Mohammed's older brother often speaks and makes decisions for him when they attend after-school club together. After-school workers have noticed Mohammed takes books to his brother to read aloud to him. One of the workers mentions this to his father and he says he is also concerned about Mohammed's development but does not know what to do. Mohammed's class teacher believes he is easily distracted but his parents think he may be having difficulties in learning.

- How can early years practitioners assist families in accessing support for children whose additional needs have not been recognised by other service providers?

Article 12 is the right of every child who can form a view to freely express this view. Due weight should be given to the child's views in accordance with his or her age and maturity. Every child has the right to be heard in any court or administrative proceeding concerning the child, and views can be communicated directly or through a representative.

The right to be heard and taken seriously is critical to respecting the child as an individual person with feelings, thoughts and wishes. The UN Committee on the Rights of the Child stresses there is no minimum age for the enjoyment of this right. The case study below describes a young child suggesting an improvement to the way her children's centre is organised. The child is concerned about minimising disruption to her own play, but may be highlighting a general problem. She is showing insight and problem-solving skills that could be used to good effect by the children's centre.

CASE STUDY

The child's right to be heard and taken seriously

Three-year-old Sophie attends a children's centre once a week with her mother. She loves going to the children's centre and particularly enjoys building things with K'Nex® and Lego®, which she doesn't have at home.

(Continued)

(Continued)

Sophie gets frustrated when other children take pieces from her construction or knock into it when they are running around. She asks one of the workers if she can take a box of Lego® into the baby changing room as only babies go in there and they don't run around. The worker says it is a nice idea but floors in toilets are not hygienic so all playing must be done in the main play area. Sophie decides to play with something else.

- Could staff in the children's centre have responded more positively to Sophie's ideas?
- How might Sophie be enabled to give advice on other aspects of the organisation of the children's centre?

Children's rights: Themes and implications for practice

There are five main themes within the UNCRC, and children's rights literature generally, and these have implications for how early years practitioners interact with children and deliver their services:

- Children of all ages have human agency – the capacity to make choices, shape their own lives and influence others.
- Human capacity evolves over time. In seeking to protect children's rights, we must always consider the individual child's evolving capacities.
- The best interests of children are shaped by an understanding of the child's wishes, feelings and views.
- Children's rights are interrelated and interdependent and concern all aspects of child well-being and development.
- Whilst governments are responsible, under international law, for ensuring the UNCRC is implemented, we must all uphold children's rights.

Recognising and supporting young children's agency

Human agency is the abiding need and capacity of human beings to make choices and influence our surroundings. Young children's agency is increasingly recognised, within the UK and internationally (Bernard van Leer Foundation, 2006; David et al., 2003). Alderson has conducted research with others on the different ways newborn babies in neonatal units contribute to their care and treatment (Alderson et al., 2006). This work provides compelling evidence that *very young* human beings interact with their carers and environments, make sense of, and respond to, their surroundings, and constantly communicate their needs and desires. The UN Committee notes that very young children:

> make choices and communicate their feelings, ideas and wishes in numerous ways, long before they are able to communicate through the conventions of spoken or written language. (2006: 7)

Listening to babies and young children, and actively seeking to understand their wishes and feelings, is fundamental to respecting them as people. The former Director of the municipal early childhood centres in the Reggio Emilia city in northern Italy, Carlina Rinaldi, says that active listening legitimises the person being listened to. In noting that 'children cannot bear to be anonymous' (2005: 20), Rinaldi reminds us that properly listening, and tuning in, to children ensures they are known. There are many actions that early years practitioners can take to promote the agency of babies and young children, as the example below demonstrates.

Young children making choices about sleep and rest

Babies at Riverside Children's Centre in North Tyneside each have their own padded wicker basket that they can access independently when they want to sleep, rest or play. Staff at the children's centre decided some years ago that placing babies in and out of cots unnecessarily restricted their movement and choices (Gordon-Smith, 2008: 20).

Reflection

In what ways do the physical surroundings of your setting encourage the agency of babies and young children? What choices can babies and young children make?

Evolving capacities central to protecting children's rights

The concept of evolving capacities challenges theories about child development that purport that all babies and children follow rigid, predictable stages of development.

Probably the most famous of all developmental psychologists, Jean Piaget, conducted experiments that concluded children below the age of 7 are unable to comprehend the other person's point of view. Later experiments showed this to be false but Piaget's theory was already well established across the Western world. Its central claim is that young children are unable to empathise, to think about other people's feelings and needs. The idea that they are lacking this basic ability – and there is nothing they can do about this except grow up – is damaging to young children. For once they are seen to be lacking such a fundamental characteristic, it is easier to deny other human qualities. From this perspective, the purpose of childhood is to acquire adult attributes, skills and capabilities. And that takes us back to the child who told the Children's Rights Director that children only exist because it's impossible to be born an adult!

No doubt aware of the risks of adopting a fixed 'age and stage' approach, the authors of the Early Years Foundation Stage (EYFS) non-statutory guidance material include this reminder on every single page:

> Children develop at their own rates, and in their own ways. The development statements and their order should not be taken as necessary steps for individual children. They should not be used as checklists. The age/stage bands overlap because these are not fixed age boundaries but suggest a typical range of development. (Early Education, 2012)

Read alongside the EYFS principles, which are set out in the Government's statutory framework (Department for Education, 2012b), this guidance makes it clear that early years practitioners are expected to get to know and relate to each child as a unique person.

An acceptance of children's evolving capacities means that we recognise the capabilities and potential of *every* child. We understand the ways in which we help (or hinder) the development of capacities; and see that children's relationships, opportunities and environments affect what they are capable (and incapable) of. In 1971, 80 per cent of 7- and 8-year-olds walked to school without an adult. Twenty years later this figure had reduced to less than 10 per cent of children (Hillman et al., 1990). The researchers found that parents were accompanying or chauffeuring their children to and from school because of their own fears associated with traffic and abduction. The following case study reports on a children's centre that engages young children in staff selection, making sure they have a role that is both meaningful and enjoyable.

CASE STUDY

Young children involved in staff recruitment

Young children attending First Steps Twerton Children's Centre in Bath and North East Somerset are involved in staff recruitment by assessing candidates' ability to read them stories. Children assess individual performances by using smiley and sad faces and this information helps the recruitment panel make its decisions. This is one of two local children's centres to be awarded the Gold Standard in the Children and Young People's Charter Scheme run by The Children's Society (The Bath Chronicle 3 Feb 2011).

Reflection

What does an early years setting gain from involving young children in staff recruitment? What positive messages would you communicate to candidates by involving young children in their selection process?

Children's best interests shaped by their wishes, feelings and views

As discussed above, two of the UNCRC's general principles relate to the child's best interests (article 3) and the child's right to be heard and taken seriously (article 12). The UN Committee on the Rights of the Child states 'there can be no correct application of article 3 if the components of article 12 are not respected' (2009: 15) which means that children's views must always be taken into account when considering what is best for them. A report I wrote for the Council of Europe put it this way:

> The right to be heard and children's best interests are often seen as being in competition, when in reality they are mutually dependent. Try asking yourself which you would be prepared to relinquish – the right to live in conditions conducive to your well-being or the right to be heard and respected. It's an impossible and meaningless choice – the right to express oneself to others is part of being a fully functioning human being. (Willow, 2008: 130)

The importance of listening and responding to children's views is reflected in many UK laws. For example, nursery schools are required by the Education Act 1996 to have regard to Government guidance on pupil participation in decision making. When a court is deciding what is best for a child it must have regard to the child's wishes and feelings, as must social workers, before making any decision about children's care and treatment. These duties apply to all children, irrespective of their age. Local councils must have regard to the expressed views of young children when carrying out their duties under the Childcare Act 2006. Directors of Children's Services are now required by statutory guidance to have regard to the general principles of the UNCRC and to ensure that children are involved in the development and delivery of services (Department for Education, 2012c: 3). The Mosaic Approach, summarised below, has been adopted by many early years settings as a means of delivering better services to children.

Learning through dialogue what children need and want

Alison Clark and Peter Moss developed The Mosaic Approach (2011) as a way of eliciting the views and experiences of young children in early years settings. This multi-method approach aims to create a 'living picture' of the child in the early years setting (it can be used in other contexts too) and starts with observation then uses an assortment of techniques to obtain additional information, including:

- Interviewing the child
- Giving children cameras to take photographs of important things
- Accompanying children on tours of their early years setting (the child is the leader and guide)
- The researcher and the child make a map based on the child's photographs and tour: these give a focus to dialogue and conversation about the setting
- Role-play using play figures
- Dialogue with children, practitioners and parents.

Reflection

Consider how your setting elicits the views and experiences of children using your service? Has anything changed in your setting as a result of listening to children?

Children's rights concern all aspects of children's well-being and development

There are parts of the UNCRC which relate especially to early childhood: the right to a name, nationality and to know and be cared for by both parents whenever possible (article 7); parents having the child's best interests as their basic concern and being entitled to assistance in their parenting role (article 18); the child's right to protection from all forms of violence (article 19); the right to play and recreational activities (article 32); and government's duties to ensure the reduction of child deaths, to encourage breastfeeding and to provide health guidance to parents (article 24).

There are numerous other rights that young children share with older children, including: civil rights, such as freedom of expression (article 14), freedom of association (article 15) and the right to privacy (article 16); the right to an adequate standard of living (article 26); the right to education which helps them develop fully as people and the duty on education providers to ensure discipline is carried out in a way which respects the child's human dignity (articles 28 and 29); the right to special care and assistance if they are separated from their family environment (article 20); the right of disabled children to lead full and decent lives and enjoy active participation in their communities (article 23); and children's entitlement to have information about their rights (article 42: the Government is also under a duty to inform parents and professionals about the UNCRC). The Children's Rights Alliance for England has produced an activity book for young children that explains all 54 articles of the UNCRC in an accessible way (Willow, 2006).

Many early years settings promote a rights-respecting ethos, and some are working towards UNICEF UK's Rights Respecting Early Years Award. But all early years settings have a crucial role to play in promoting and protecting children's rights. Indeed, as well as being prohibited from using corporal punishment themselves, early years providers must now, so far as is reasonably practicable, ensure other people caring for, or in regular contact with, children, do not use corporal punishment. This new duty came into force in September 2012 and should lead to greater promotion of non-violent parenting, though it falls far short of giving children the same legal protection from assault as adults.

Young children talk about smacking

When the UK Government last consulted the public about the law on smacking, two children's charities consulted 75 young children, aged 4 to 7 years, about physical punishment (Willow and Hyder, 1999).

A storybook was created with an appealing character called Splodge who was introduced to the children as not knowing much about this world. Questions to the children included 'what is a smack' and 'how does it feel to be smacked'. Children described smacking as a hit or very hard hit and told Splodge:

> 'It feels like someone banged you with a hammer' 5 year-old girl
>
> 'Sometimes may feel that inside like their tummy hurts' 5 year-old boy
>
> 'You're hurt and it makes you cry [and] drips come out of your eyes' 5 year-old girl
>
> 'It hurts and it's painful inside – it's like breaking your bones' 7 year-old girl
>
> (Willow and Hyder, 1999: 46–51)

Similar research has since been carried out in Wales, Scotland, Northern Ireland and New Zealand; and the perspectives of 2- to 4-year-olds have been elicited through focus groups in early years settings in England (Milne, 2009).

Reflection

How can early years practitioners ensure methods of discipline are consistent with children's human dignity? What action could early years practitioners take to implement their new duty to seek to stop parents and carers from using corporal punishment?

We are all responsible for promoting and protecting children's rights

It is now 20 years since the UK ratified the UNCRC, so the idea of children being rights holders should be well established across all children's services. The Human Rights Act (HRA), which places legal duties on many professionals working with children, has also been in force for over a decade.

The HRA was passed by Parliament in 1998 and makes it illegal for public authorities to act in a way that is incompatible with a right in the European Convention on Human Rights (ECHR). There are 16 rights in the ECHR, including the right to respect for private and family life; the right to protection from inhuman and degrading treatment or punishment; and the right to manifest your religion.

Publicly funded nursery schools and children's centres are public authorities, so staff working in those settings must follow the HRA. HRA duties may also apply to childminders and early years practitioners working in private nurseries, as the Act's definition of a public authority includes 'any person certain of whose functions are functions of a public nature'. Victims of rights violations can take public authorities to court and claim compensation. People of all ages are protected by the HRA, including babies and young children.

Some of the rights in the UNCRC resemble the rights protected by the HRA, such as the right to privacy, the right to education and the right to effective participation in official proceedings. But the UNCRC has not been made part of UK law so our courts cannot enforce its rights. Nevertheless, cases involving children that do go to court *can* refer to the UNCRC obligations. For example, article 3 of the UNCRC (the child's best interests) was given prominence in a High Court case in 2012 about imprisoned mothers being allowed temporary home leave to spend time with their children, even though this was a HRA case (*R (MP & P) v Secretary of State for Justice*). In a different HRA case, considered by the Supreme Court in 2010, it was stated that a child's best interests must always be a primary consideration when the authorities are deciding whether to deport a parent, consistent with the UNCRC (*ZH (Tanzania) v Secretary of State for the Home Department*).

Some years earlier, the UNCRC featured prominently in a HRA case brought to the House of Lords (since replaced by the Supreme Court) about the lawfulness of a ban on corporal punishment in schools. A group of Christian parents argued that their human right to manifest their religion was being breached by the ban. They believe that Christian parents have a duty to use physical punishment and teachers should be able to lawfully assault children if parents request this. The parents' claim was strongly rejected, with the leading judge, Baroness Hale of Richmond, stating:

> A child has the same right as anyone else not to be assaulted … Above all, the state is entitled to give children the protection they are given by an international instrument to which the United Kingdom is a party, the United Nations Convention on the Rights of the Child. (*R (Williamson and ors) v Secretary of State for Education and Employment* [2005] UKHL 15, [80])

The UN has established a new complaints mechanism that children can use when their UNCRC rights are violated and they have exhausted all remedies in their own country. The UK has yet to sign up to this procedure, though the coalition Government has indicated it will consider early ratification (Human Rights Council, 2012). Acceptance of this mechanism would significantly strengthen the protection given to children's rights in the UK. But laws, policies and complaints procedures do not on their own change the lives of babies and young children. It is the people that love, nurture and care for children that make rights real. And it is here that early years practitioners play an incredibly important role.

Showing respect, listening to young children's views, being sensitive to their feelings, getting to know them as individuals, offering a range of enjoyable and fulfilling experiences, always having their best interests at heart and being an advocate when necessary – this is what upholding the rights of young children is in practice. When the Children's Rights Director for England asked children to define what well-being means to them, one child replied: 'being able to know that there will be more nice things to come' (Morgan, 2010: 28). Unlike many other professionals, early years practitioners can deliver on this each and every day.

Journal Task

Woodhead, M. (2005) 'Early childhood development: A question of rights', *International Journal of Early Childhood*, 37(3): 79–98. http://oro.open.ac.uk/35894/2/64CC5394.pdf

This article signposts two broadly different approaches to child development – one that sees all babies and children following a set of natural and predictable stages towards maturation, whereby an unformed and incomplete human being grows into a capable, autonomous adult; and the other that sees child development as being variable across communities and cultures and which places great value on the child's dignity and capacities. The second approach recognises children as rights holders and critiques the notion of adulthood being an end-stage of supreme independence and competence.

Levels 4 & 5

Consider how these two ways of understanding child development might affect the way in which early years practitioners approach their work and relationships with young children.

Level 6

Reflecting on this article, and using material you have researched yourself, what key points would you include in a strategy for promoting and protecting children's rights in your setting?

To download this task as well as other useful online resources please visit:
www.sagepub.co.uk/mukherji

Summary

This chapter discussed the importance of early childhood and the vital role of early years practitioners. We explored the status of babies and young children and the need for respectful relationships and laws. The development of the UNCRC was discussed and we looked in-depth at articles 2, 3, 6 and 12 (the general principles). Although the Convention is not part of UK law, early years practitioners should be implementing it and are also bound by the HRA. We examined the main themes in the children's rights literature – including children's agency, evolving capacities and the relationship between children's views and their best interests – and looked at case studies showing children's rights being upheld in a variety of early years settings.

Further reading

Levels 4 & 5

Leach, P. (2012) 'Babies are people', *Nursery World*, 7 February. This short article powerfully advocates the rights of babies.

Miller, J. (2003) *Never Too Young: How Young Children Can Take Responsibility and Make Decisions* (2nd edition). London: Save the Children. This text explores the implementation of children's rights in early years settings through discussion and numerous practical examples and tried-and-tested methods.

Level 6

Alderson, P. (2000) *Young Children's Rights: Exploring Beliefs, Principles and Practice*. London: Jessica Kingsley Publishers Ltd. This accessible and thought-provoking book explores attitudes towards young children and shows how adults in different settings can implement children's rights.

Convention on the Rights of the Child. The United Nations' treaty setting out the rights of children and the responsibilities of governments and others. This is a particularly important document for early years managers and policy makers.

References

Alderson, P., Hawthorne, J. and Killen, M. (2006). 'The participation rights of premature babies', in Freeman, M. (ed.) *Children's Health and Children's Rights*. The Netherlands: Martinus Nijhoff Publishers.

Allen, G. (2011) *Early Intervention: The Next Steps. An Independent Report to Her Majesty's Government*. London: Cabinet Office.

Bernard van Leer Foundation (2006) *A Guide to General Comment 7: Implementing Child Rights in Early Childhood*. The Hague: Bernard van Leer Foundation.

Clark, A. and Moss, P. (2011) *Listening to Young Children: The Mosaic Approach*. (2nd edition). London: NCB.

Cuthbert, C., Rayns, G. and Stanley, K. (2011) *All Babies Count: Prevention and Protection for Vulnerable Babies*. London: NSPCC.

David, T., Goouch, K., Powell, S. and Abbott, L. (2003) *Birth to Three Matters: A Review of the Literature*. Nottingham: Department for Education and Skills.

de Boer-Buquicchio, M. (2005) 'Raising children without violence', Conference Speech, Berlin, 21 October.

Department for Education (2012a) *Children Looked After by Local Authorities in England (including adoption and care leavers) – Year Ending 31 March 2012*. Table B1. London: Department for Education.

Department for Education (2012b) *Framework for the Early Years Foundation Stage*. London: Department for Education.

Department for Education (2012c) *Statutory Guidance on the Roles and Responsibilities of the Director of Children's Services and the Lead Member for Children's Services*. London: Department for Education.

Early Education (2012) *Development Matters in the Early Years Foundation Stage (EYFS)*. London: Early Education.

Feinstein, L. (2003) 'Inequality in the early cognitive development of British children in the 1970 cohort', *Economica*, 70(277): 73–97.

Field, F. (2010) *The Foundation Years: Preventing Poor Children Becoming Poor Adults. The Report of the Independent Review on Poverty and Life Chances*. London: Cabinet Office.

Gordon-Smith, P. (2008) 'All about … children's rights', *Nursery World*, 3 July.

Hammarberg, T. (2008) 'The principle of the best interests of the child – what it means and what it demands from adults', Lecture, Warsaw, 30 May.

Hillman, M., Adams, J. and Whitelegg, J. (1990) *One False Move … A Study of Children's Independent Mobility*. London: PSI.

Hindberg, B. (2001) *Ending Corporal Punishment. Swedish Experience of Efforts To Prevent All Forms of Violence Against Children – and the Results*. Stockholm: Ministry of Health and Social Affairs and Ministry for Foreign Affairs, Sweden.

Howard League for Penal Reform (2011) 'The voice of child', Submission to the UN Committee on the Rights of the Child's: Day of General Discussion.

Human Rights Council (2012) *Report of the Working Group on the Universal Periodic Review. United Kingdom of Great Britain and Northern Ireland*: 'Addendum: Views on conclusions and/or recommendations, voluntary commitments and replies presented by the State under review'. New York: UN General Assembly.

Lee, N. (2001) *Childhood and Society: Growing Up in an Age of Uncertainty*. Buckingham: Open University Press.

Magadi, M. and Middleton, S. (2007) *Severe Child Poverty in the UK*. London: Save the Children.

Miller, J. (2003) *Never Too Young: How Young Children Can Take Responsibility and Make Decisions* (2nd edition). London: Save the Children.

Milne, E. (2009) *I Don't Get Sad, Only When My Mum Smacks Me: Young Children Give Advice About Family Discipline*. London: Children are Unbeatable Alliance.

Morgan, R. (2004) *Children's Views from Care and Residential Education on Proposals in the Green Paper: Every Child Matters*. London: National Care Standards Commission.

Morgan, R. (2010) *Children on Rights and Responsibilities. A Report of Children's Views by the Children's Rights Director for England*. London: Ofsted.

Nobes, G. and Smith, M. (1997) 'Physical punishment of children in two-parent families', *Clinical Child Psychology and Psychiatry*, 2(2): 271–81.

Qvortrup, J., Bardy, M., Sgritta, G. and Wintersberger, H. (1994) *Childhood Matters: Social Theory, Practice and Politics*. Aldershot: Avebury.

Radford, L., Corral, S., Bradley, C., Fisher, H., Bassett, C., Howat, N. and Collishaw, S. (2011) *Child Abuse and Neglect in the UK Today*. London: NSPCC.

Rinaldi, C. (2005) 'Documentation and assessment: what is the relationship?', in Clark, A., Kjørholt, A.T. and Moss, P. (eds), *Beyond Listening: Children's Perspectives on Early Childhood Services*. Bristol: The Policy Press.

Smith, K., Osborne, S., Lau, I. and Britton, A. (eds), (2012) *Homicides, Firearm Offences and Intimate Violence 2010/11: Supplementary Volume 2 to Crime in England and Wales 2010/11*. London: Home Office.

The Bath Chronicle (2011) 'Centre wins gold award for giving children a say'. Available online at: http://www.bathchronicle.co.uk/centre-wins-gold-award-going-children-say/story-11319918-detail/story.html (accessed 30th oct 2013)

Tickell, C. (2011) *The Early Years: Foundations for Life, Health and Learning. An Independent Report on the Early Years Foundation Stage to Her Majesty's Government*. London: Department for Education.

UN Committee on the Rights of the Child (UNCRC) (2006) *General Comment No. 7. Implementing Child Rights in Early Childhood*. Geneva: United Nations.

UN Committee on the Rights of the Child (UNCRC) (2009) *General Comment No. 12. The Right of the Child to be Heard*. Geneva: United Nations.

Willow, C. (1999) *It's Not Fair: Young People's Reflections on Children's Rights*. London: The Children's Society.

Willow, C. (2006) *Convention on the Rights of the Child Activity Book*. London: Children's Rights Alliance for England.

Willow, C. (2008) *Promoting the Participation by Children in Decisions Affecting Them: Report for Social, Health and Family Affairs Committee*. Strasbourg: Council of Europe.

Willow, C. and Hyder, T. (1999) *It Hurts You Inside. Young Children Talk About Smacking*. London: NCB.

Legal judgements

R v Hopley [1860] 2 F&F 202.

R (MP & P) v Secretary of State for Justice [2012] EWHC 214.

ZH (Tanzania) v Secretary of State for the Home Department [2010] EWHC 2397.

R (Williamson & ors) v Secretary of State for Education and Employment [2005] UKHL 15.

3

Becoming a Reflective Practitioner and Practitioner Research

Judy Stevenson

This chapter will:

- Consider the nature of reflective practice
- Examine why reflective practice is important in early childhood
- Explore the process and ways of developing personal practice
- Look at the skills and role of the reflective practitioner
- Highlight how practitioner research may inform reflection.

Reflective practice and being a reflective practitioner are highlighted as essential skills for those working in early childhood settings, to the extent where they are at risk of becoming meaningless. However, they are the key to improving your own practice, the practice in childcare settings, and thereby the outcomes for the young children in your care. The focus on early childhood and the qualifications of the workforce are still high on the government agenda, with both the Nutbrown Review, *Foundations For Quality* (Nutbrown, 2012) and the policy paper *More Great Childcare* (DfE, 2013) raising important issues for the profession. Change has become a way of life for all those involved. It is important that we hold on to the values and principles our profession believes in, and define our own professionalism through high quality practice. Gardner (2006) is very clear that no one can be considered a professional until they have developed reflective practice. This chapter aims to define the meaning of the terms 'reflective practice' and being a 'reflective practitioner' and examine how you can ensure that reflection is a vital and vibrant part of your daily routine. It will look at the skills you need to develop and the key role of practitioner research as part of the process.

Why reflective practice is important in early childhood

The term reflective practice is in common usage within early childhood, indeed, the Statutory Framework for the Early Years Foundation Stage (DfES, 2012) calls on practitioners to reflect on several areas of their practice, such as the different ways that children learn. However, there is no clear authoritative guidance on exactly what this means, how to go about it or the benefits to either the individual or the setting. The term 'reflective practice' is open to many interpretations, as Bolton (2005: 1) states, reflective practice has become 'a catch-all name for a wide range of activities from deep life, work and organisation changing critique to rote box-ticking practices seeking to make professionals accountable to and controllable by increasingly bureaucratic and market-led organisations'.

In the early childhood context reflective practice is possibly best defined as the process you use to improve and maintain the quality of your own practice and that of your setting. It involves asking yourself rigorous and critical questions about your daily work, but these may be summarised by three simple questions: 'Am I doing a good job?', 'Am I doing the best for the children in my setting?' and 'How can I do things better?'

Reflective practice is the process by which we continually seek and achieve changes in our personal and professional work to improve the outcomes for the children. Using the idea of a reflection, you may find it useful to think about how you use a mirror. There are times when you have a quick glance to make sure that your appearance is acceptable, and there are times when you look in more detail, focusing on one particular aspect of how you look. Reflective practice is very much the same; the quick glance around a room or the quick thought about something you are doing alongside the more detailed, thoughtful evaluation of your provision and your practice.

However, reflective practice is also about taking responsibility for yourself as a professional working with children, their families and the other adults in your setting. Every day we are called upon to make countless decisions; some of these are small and seemingly of little consequence, whilst others are larger and may have a long-lasting effect. A reflective practitioner thinks back on these decisions with a critical and analytical eye, hoping to improve the process for the next time a situation arises.

Reflection

Think about your last day in your setting. Make a list of the decisions you had to make, maybe about provision or routines, or particular incidents with the children. What process did you go through to make those decisions? Would you change your decisions now? Why might this be?

So far, I have focused on the idea of you looking at your own practice, but another equally important aspect of being a reflective practitioner is the feedback we receive from others, which may be full of praise or which, on occasion, may be more constructive, or even negative. Feedback is not necessarily part of a formal supervision, appraisal or performance management process, although it may well be. It also exists in the throw away comments from your colleagues and managers – something they particularly liked or something they observed that caused them concern. A good leader is somebody who knows you well and will intuitively know when to encourage or to intervene. Such comments often linger in our minds, and can have a great impact on our personal reflections.

The Early Years Foundation Stage Statutory Framework (DfES, 2012: 17) calls on providers to establish supervision for staff who have contact with children and families. It states that: 'Effective supervision provides support, coaching and training for the practitioner and promotes the interests of children. Supervision should foster a culture of mutual support, teamwork and continuous improvement which encourages the confidential discussion of sensitive issues'. Although supervision will be new for many providers, it has always been there as a key to supporting practitioners and raising the quality of provision. It is clear that there is now an expectation that through supervision, staff will 'receive coaching to improve their personal effectiveness' [ibid]. This element of feedback will now become part of a reflective cycle to which everyone will have access.

Reflection

Think about the last time someone gave you feedback on something you had done. Was it positive and encouraging, or more negative with points for you to improve on? Which type sticks most in your memory? Why might this be?

Remember that in the end, reflective practice is about the way you work, how you think about it, how you could improve your practice and how this could improve outcomes for the children and families in your care.

The reflective process

To reflect on your own practice in a way that will make a difference requires specific skills and attitudes. You need to be able to review and analyse every aspect of your practice, but you also need to do so honestly and to be open to making changes in the way you do things. This requires time. If reflective practice is viewed as learning through and from experience, it involves challenging assumptions about your everyday practice and being self-aware.

Dewey (1933) was one of the forerunners in identifying reflection as a particular way of thinking. He argued that reflective thinking moves people away from their everyday routines and actions towards a more purposeful and constructive way of solving problems. He stated that we need to start by looking at our experiences and then develop ideas as to how we could do things differently. This concept was developed further by Schön in his book *The Reflective Practitioner* (1983) where he identified two main ways for professionals to learn from experience. These can be summarised as the ideas of: reflection in action – the ability of professionals to think more deeply about what they are doing while they are doing it; and reflection on action – where you think about things after the event. Many people have challenged Schön's ideas and Moon (1999) asserts that reflection-in-action is unachievable. This view is supported by Ekebergh (2007), who also argues that it is impossible to reflect in the moment and that reflection can only be achieved retrospectively.

Kolb (1984) developed a theory of experiential learning that also provides a useful model for a reflective practice cycle, which, as already stated, relies heavily on learning from our experiences. This is called the Kolb Cycle, the Learning Cycle or the Experiential Learning Cycle. It is made up of four different stages of learning from experience, which must be followed in sequence for learning to take place. The Learning Cycle suggests that it is not sufficient to have an experience in order to learn. It is necessary to reflect on the experience and come up with new ideas to apply to the same or similar situations if they arise again. The four stages are summarised as: Concrete Experience (doing or having an experience); Reflective Observation (reviewing or reflecting on the experience); Abstract Conceptualisation (concluding and learning from the experience); and Active Experimentation (planning and trying out what you have learned).

Cable et al. (2007) suggest a structured four-stage Reflective Practice Cycle to support practitioners in reflecting on their practice: thinking about practice – the visible layer which is our daily practice; exploring practice – which is the vocabulary, theories, knowledge and values that underpin our work; reflecting on practice – which is the hidden layer that needs exploring; and documenting evidence – when the first three stages come together in a coherent form.

It is also important to think about another term which is in common usage, reflexivity. This is very much both part of and a follow-on from reflective thinking. It is the process by which we use our reflective learning to impact on our practice, going deeper than problem solving. Reflexive practitioners do not only question their actions, they look at a deeper level and question the assumptions, values and beliefs that underpin their whole approach to children and families. It also involves thinking about the way others perceive us and changing deeply held attitudes and behaviours. Reflexivity is therefore a potentially more complex process (Moon, 1999).

So far, I have implied that reflective practice is quite a solitary experience, and while this may be the case, it is also important to stress that it might also be a process you undertake consciously with your colleagues. As early years practitioners we all work as members of a team, and need to take the time to evaluate not only the daily experiences that we have provided for the children, but also the longer-term impacts of our provision, our routines and our attitudes to children and families. Observations on children are generally made individually, but again, other adults working in the room will have seen different things and may have a different perspective to share. This critical dialogue becomes more than discussion if it is approached with an open mind. There are also questions about how, when and where reflection should take place. We live busy lives and it requires self-discipline if it is to be meaningful. It can also be quite painful to stand back from something that has happened and to try to take an analytical approach. In the next section, we will look at some of the ways of embedding reflection into our daily practice.

Reflection

In this section you have read much about the theories that underpin the reflective process. Take some time to think about how much you reflect on your practice. Is this a quick thought at the end of the day or do you make a conscious effort to reflect on your practice? Is this something you do by yourself or with others?

Ways of developing as a reflective practitioner

Whilst most people have the natural skill to be thoughtful and to reflect, some will find it easier than others. However, like most things, if we play with it and practice it, the process becomes easier. There are many ways to develop your reflective skills, and you may find that some suit you better than others. It is worth trying each of them, and deciding which approach suits you best. Turner (cited in Bolton, 2005: xviii) encourages us to 'fly', to 'see how it can be done if you just let go', and this is very much what I encourage you to try. Any concrete form of recording your reflections can be helpful simply because it slows the brain down, begins to remove the emotional aspects and allows critical thought to commence. Remember, the methods are personal to you and need not be shared with anyone – so there is no need to worry about 'getting it right'.

Reflective drawing

Everyone has their own way of drawing. Some like cartoons and story boards where you begin with an event and create a series of pictures which tell the story of an event or an incident. Others prefer a more abstract approach and rely on symbols such as arrows, dots and lines or clouds and sunshine. You could approach your drawing in the form of a mind map with the incident you are reflecting on in the centre and lines of new thoughts spreading out. For it to become part of the reflective cycle, remember to also draw the future, what you want to be different next time around.

Writing a letter or an email

Have you ever lain in bed at night and composed the letter you will never send about something or someone that has upset you? This skill can be utilised as a powerful reflective instrument. Write exactly what you are thinking or feeling and then most importantly, why you are feeling like that. Move on, and in the final paragraph, write about what and how you want to change. If you are doing this as an email, remember never to fill in the 'to' address line – you do not want to accidentally send your deepest thoughts to someone.

Free-flow writing

For many people, this can be the hardest approach, putting pen to paper and simply writing down what you are thinking about, detailing something that has happened and what you will do about it. You can write in whatever style comes naturally to you, bullet points or prose, whatever feels right for you.

Worry dolls

This is a more abstract, internalised process, but again it helps to think things through. Worry dolls are very small dolls that were originally made in Guatemala. The idea is that before you go to bed, you tell each doll a worry and put them under your pillow before you go to sleep. According to folklore, the dolls solve your worries while you are asleep. A more scientific approach is the idea of the unconscious mind continuing to work through problems while we sleep (Tallis, 2012). In reflective thinking processes, the idea is similar in that you tell each doll part of the story you are reflecting on and in the morning, with a fresh mind, you begin to analyse and make changes.

Critical incident analysis

A critical incident is anything that we interpret as a problem or a challenge in a particular context, rather than something that happens routinely (Moon, 2006). As such, these can often form the basis of our reflection. We need to explore these incidents to understand them better and find alternative ways of reacting and responding to them. It is important that you approach this exploration in a structured manner, and this is best done with a trusted colleague. Begin by describing the incident, when and where it happened, what happened and how you felt about it. Go on to ask yourself the next layer of questions and begin to interpret the incident: why did it stand out, did you bring a particular point of view to it, could it be seen differently and what would you do differently the next time around. In the next step, find a friend or colleague and share both your account and your interpretation. Let them repeat it back to you in exactly the way you described it, without giving advice or suggesting what they would do, but noting any time you sounded angry, upset, relieved, etc. Conclude by reflecting on how it sounded when it was fed back to you and your emotions were interpreted; would you do anything differently now?

Talking

For some of you, none of the above suggestions will work, and you simply need to think, reflect and talk. Again, it is important to slow the brain down, work things through and take time. Choosing who you will talk to and when is crucial here. You certainly don't want to have the conversation with your best friend in the staff room over lunch, and you don't want someone who will tell you that everything you say is right. Instead, choose someone who you know will challenge your thinking and help to move your reflection on. It may well best be done in the context of supervision. Remember that talking is easily forgotten, or the meaning can change and be misinterpreted at any time. Unlike other forms of reflective practice, it cannot be re-visited at a much later stage.

Reflection

Think about all the methods that have been described. Which one appeals to you most? Which one are you going to try first? Make a conscious decision about how you will start and when.

All the methods that you have read about will aid the process of reflection, but remember that navel gazing is not sufficient. Think about the next stage in the reflective process; we need to be able to review and analyse every aspect of our practice, but we also need to do so honestly and to be open to making changes in the way we do things. Reflection is only purposeful if it is accompanied by analysis and changes your practice. One way of ensuring this analysis takes place is to keep a reflective journal.

CASE STUDY

Shona is in the second year of her Foundation Degree and has a placement in a children's centre. As part of her course, she has been asked to record how she is feeling about her placement, and at that point of her training, she is not feeling very positive. She is based in a room with twenty 3- and 4-year-olds and feels she is struggling to relate to the teacher and nursery nurse. She is finding the practice is very different to her first placement in a small private setting where she worked in the baby room.

Shona decides to record her experiences on a daily basis over a two-week period, being careful to record both the highs and the lows of each day. In the third week she goes over her diary and is able to see that what is actually upsetting her is working with groups of the children for art activities and story. It has nothing to do with the staff.

Shona is able to talk through the challenges with the teacher and nursery nurse and asks them to give her some feedback and some suggestions to improve her practice. Having had these discussions, she begins to feel very differently about her placement.

Keeping a reflective journal

Journaling has become one of the most popular forms of reflective practice and is a requirement for many academic courses and qualifications. Etherington (2004) states that a journal is a private document that is used by the writer to document their thoughts and feelings about any number of issues that seem important to them, while Moon (2006: 1) describes it as 'vehicle for reflection'. Both of these are true if you keep your journal appropriately.

Keeping a journal can feel like a very daunting prospect. It can bring back memories of starting a new exercise book and being afraid you will make a mistake on the first page. For some practitioners it will always be hard work, yet for many experienced journal writers, it becomes their closest friend that accompanies them everywhere. My best advice is to give it a try and persevere, you might be surprised at how habit forming it can become. It does not have to be a beautiful book that you spend hours choosing, although for some this is all part of the exercise. Again, you might find it easiest to write with a fountain pen, a biro or a pencil. It really is up to you. You can keep it electronically, within a loose-leaf file or on post-it notes that you file systematically. Similarly, it does not even need to done on paper; some practitioners choose to use hand-held tape recorders. Again, it is a case of what works for you, which may be decided by when and where you journal.

An immediate question is how does journaling differ from free-flow writing, and the important point here is that it is systematic, it is kept regularly and it is something you can return to for deeper reflection and analysis at a later date. For this reason, a bound book can often be best. More of this later.

Actually starting a journal can be the hardest step. Bolton (2005: 145) suggests the following tips: 'choose a comfortable uninterrupted place and time; make sure you have everything you need to hand; be able to time yourself to write without stopping for about six minutes; allow another 30–40 minutes or so after the six, in order to do the next bit'. The next issue is, of course, what to write about. Some people find it useful to begin by having a list of questions. If you are writing about something that happened during the day, these might include: what happened; who was involved; why are you still reflecting on it; what was your role; what could you have done differently; what do you wish you had done differently; what have you learnt about yourself or others; how has your thinking changed; have you gained any new ideas, questions or insights? Once you have started, you will be surprised at how quickly the words flow, and remember, it is personal, your spelling or grammar won't be checked by anyone.

A useful tip when starting a journal is to use only the right-hand side of your journal for recording your thoughts and feelings, leaving the left side blank. At a later date, you can revisit your writing as part of a deeper analysis and you can begin to ask yourself questions or look for patterns in your behaviour – these can be recorded on the left-hand side of the page. Highlighter pens can be useful in the analysis of your journal. Decide on a colour for different aspects of your writing, for example blue for staffing issues or green for conflict. Go through your journal highlighting extracts using your colour coding system. This will help you to identify any patterns emerging in your behaviour and responses to situations.

It is this analysis and the drawing together of themes that is so important. Although you will gain some insight as you write and slow your thoughts down, there are massive benefits to reading your journal through every couple of months and looking for themes and recurring patterns of thoughts and actions which you might otherwise have missed. Is there something you do that triggers a response from others? Thoughtful reflection on these points will help you to change and improve your practice, which is the whole point of systematically keeping your journal. Remember to write these insights down, make the changes and return to them again after another couple of months.

Reflection

Having read about keeping a journal, take a few moments to note down your feelings. Are you excited by the idea or do you feel daunted? Why do you feel that way? What sort of journal would suit you best? Make a decision about when you are going to begin.

The reflective team

Earlier in this chapter I referred to the fact that professional reflection might also be a process you undertake consciously with your colleagues through your daily evaluations of provision and practice. A natural element of working as, and in, a team is sharing ideas, planning, and in time developing a group understanding of individual strengths and challenges, so that together there is a unified whole. This in itself is valuable, but the concept of a reflective team goes deeper than our daily conversations. It is important to set aside the time to reflect together and improve all aspects of provision, teamwork and outcomes for children and families. Reflective practice within a team does not just happen because one person says it should. For reflection to be meaningful, it must begin with the team agreeing together that they value deeper discussions as personal and professional development. These discussions can help to affirm your values and what you believe in at a time when you are surrounded by change. Whilst this implies that discussions should take place on a 'room' level, there is an added bonus when a whole staff team comes together.

In early years settings, a reflective team is one where individuals take the time to reflect on the team as a whole, and on their role within the team. It is one that considers feedback from children, families and other external partners. A reflective team thinks about their current practice and makes links with new theories and practice. As with any reflective process, having talked about and shared ideas, it is crucial to look for ways of improving and acting on anything that has been discovered. This needs to become part of the cycles discussed earlier in this chapter, where any changes are discussed by the team, reflected on and further changes made in the light of those discoveries. Reflective practice is one of the keys to improving the quality of the setting where strengths and weaknesses are identified and plans put in place.

One of the Ofsted requirements (Ofsted, 2012) for many early years settings is the completion of a Self-Evaluation Form (SEF). Although this can be viewed as an onerous, administrative task, it can be a useful starting point for a team reflection discussion.

The SEF is in three parts: the details of the setting and the views of those who use it; the quality and standards of the provision; and the compliance with the statutory requirements of the Early Years Foundation Stage (DfES, 2012). If the staff team considers the questions within each area, it helps everyone to understand their role and their contribution to the setting as a whole.

CASE STUDY

Alice is the manager of a small private day nursery. She has several new members of staff and is keen to build and develop the team, but is struggling as to where to begin. She decides that thinking about what they need to do in the case of an Ofsted visit would be a helpful starting point as it is something that concerns every practitioner, regardless of their experience or the length of time they have been working in a particular setting.

Alice uses the Self-Evaluation Form as a starting point. Through focusing initially on the details about the setting and the views of those who use it, she is able to use some feedback from the children and their families to launch ideas about communication, displays, information sharing and the environment. By the second meeting, the staff team are enthused and brimming with ideas to take their practice forward.

The practitioner as a researcher

This chapter has concentrated on the idea of early years' practitioners developing their practice and professionalism through reflecting on analysing the daily incidents that continually surround us. However, there is another viewpoint of reflective practice that considers it to be a valid research tool that can create new real-world knowledge. The days when research into early childhood practice was seen solely as the province of academics in universities are thankfully behind us, but it is not unusual for there still to be some trepidation at the term 'research'. However, it is a powerful tool for change and findings can provide solid evidence of quality provision if practice is questioned by those outside the setting. Whilst research can help to create new knowledge and understanding, the additional aspect and purpose of practitioner research is that you are in the best position to put that knowledge into practice. It may seem strange to think about yourself as both a researcher and the subject of your research, but this is increasingly being recognised as a legitimate and important aspect of research.

Robert-Holmes (2011: 3) points out that research is simply a tool, and 'like any other tool, when you learn what it does, why it was invented and how to use it, it becomes beneficial to you'. He goes on to point out that the 'real world knowledge produced by early childhood practitioners is as good as that within the "established" academic community' (2011: 7). However, if you are extending your professional reflections into something that you wish to share with others, there are several factors that you need to think about. Keeping a personal journal which includes your thoughts and reflections on events, children and colleagues alongside yourself is very different to making it public. It can feel a little like sharing your diary, and there may be many elements that you don't want to share. You may want to think through some of these issues if you want your reflective thinking and your journal to enter the world of research.

One of the most important issues is ethics, which needs to underpin all aspects of research. If you have not carried out any research previously, you may have come across the term in relation to on-going debates in areas such as experiments on animals or whether individuals should have the right to choose to die. Ethics are the principles that help us to uphold the things we value. The British Education Research Association has a set of ethical guidelines which can be downloaded from http://www.bera.ac.uk/publications. Their key points are that research should be conducted within an ethical framework of respect for: the person; knowledge; democratic values; the quality of educational research; and academic freedom (2011: 4). A principle of research is that it should be beneficial – in this instance to the children, your setting and you. This means that you need to think through in advance whether you will be harming anyone or anything, and how you are going to prevent this happening. A second equally important consideration is that of voluntary participation and confidentiality. Do not forget that children, as well as adults, can be actively involved in your research and although you need to seek the permission of their parents, you also need to talk to the children themselves and respect their views.

This is the idea of 'informed consent', and means that everyone involved has to principally understand the purpose of the research and how they will be involved. Running alongside it are the promises you need to make as the researcher, such as anonymity, how you will record and store information, who will read it and what you will use the information for. These are obviously quite difficult concepts for children to understand, and will be beyond babies and the very youngest children, which is why involving parents is so important; but do not underestimate the understanding of the 3- and 4-year-olds you may be working with. If you explain what you are going to be doing clearly and use words they understand, most will be able to voice their opinion. It can also make it easier if you are making notes while you are working and continually ask the question 'what are you doing?'

Another consideration in being a practitioner researcher is that of the power you hold. As a professional practitioner you need to be aware that you are in a very powerful position when it comes to meetings with children, parents and possibly colleagues. You need to remember that they may say or do things to try and please you rather than just being themselves. They may even give their consent just because they are afraid of saying no, so you need to think very carefully about how you explain what you want to do and why. Remember to stress that there will be no repercussions if they say no. It is always good practice to have a discussion, put things in writing and then talk to people again after they have had a chance to think it through and maybe have come up with more questions. Another important issue around the notion of power is how you interpret anything you find out – it is your point of view, which again, puts you in a powerful position.

There are no simple solutions to these problems, but part of being a reflective practitioner is your awareness of the issues and the approaches you use to maintain a balance. Remember, ethically speaking, the practitioner-researcher loses the ability to remain anonymous, which may raise issues for you.

Reflection

You have developed your ability to keep a reflective journal, and on reading it through and analysing it after three months, you realise that you are gaining some strong insights into not only your practice, but also the way the team is working. How are you going to share this with them in an ethical way?

Of course, as with any research tool, there are limitations in using a journal as the principle research tool. Mukherji and Albon (2010: 166) identify these as the time it takes to maintain a journal systematically, the need to analyse and ask questions rather than simply describe, and, lastly, the fact that it could be viewed as 'narcissistic or overly self-indulgent'. However, as they acknowledge 'journaling is a tool that has possibilities as well as limitations for the researcher'.

Action research

Using your reflections as a research tool is one method, but another approach which is also relevant to the reflective skills you have been developing is action research. This is another way of improving your personal practice and that of your setting, which in turn will improve outcomes for children and families. It is less about creating new knowledge, although this may be one element of your findings, and more about looking at the impact of change. Put simply, action research is learning by doing, but a more detailed description is that it is a qualitative research approach that involves working through a repetitive cycle of planning, acting and observing, then reflecting on outcomes which lead you to make changes. The cycle begins again as you observe the effect of change, reflect on the outcomes and so on (Clough and Nutbrown, 2012).

Action research is a good way to involve your team or the whole staff. There are two models, proactive and responsive. Proactive action research begins with passion and inspiration, the desire to try something new. This may be from a course you have attended, something you have read or something you have seen in another setting. You begin by listing your hopes and your concerns, making a hypothesis. You then make the change and collect information (data) on the difference that it has made. The next step is to reflect on what you have learned, fine tune the practice you have changed and begin the cycle again. Responsive action research begins with collecting information on something. It may be an observation of practice or behaviour that has unsettled you. You reflect on this and decide on a change that you think might improve things, again, making your hypotheses. You then make the change and begin collecting data, ready to reflect and start again. In this way, action research becomes a continuous cycle of improvement. You can see that the two models rapidly follow the same cycle, the only difference being in how they are initiated (McNiff, 2013).

Reflection

Think about an aspect of the provision in your room that you are unhappy with. How might you go about changing it? Would it be useful to take an action research approach, or are you happy just to make a change and live with the consequences? What do you think would be the benefits or challenges of your decision?

Action research raises the same ethical concerns as already highlighted, and, again, it is important that you consider the ethics of your research from all angles. In the case of a proactive model, it is somewhat easier as you can ensure you have everyone's consent before you actually begin your research and reflection.

As already stated, action research is an approach to research and not a method in itself. There are a range of tools you could use to look at the impact of any change you decide to make. For example, you could continue to record things you observe in your journal, but you may decide that you want a more systematic way of analysing not only how you feel about the changes, but also, depending on what you have changed, of recording the views of the children, the team and/or families. You may decide you want to read more about questionnaires, interviews and document analysis if you decide to go down this path.

Shaping your practice through research

This chapter has primarily focused on two approaches to research, using your reflective journal or carrying out an action research cycle. Of course, although worthy activities in themselves, they are pointless unless they inform and develop your practice with children, families, your team and your work with other professionals. As already highlighted, research has traditionally been associated with creating knowledge in the field you work in, and your research is no less valid because it is about you and your practice, and the knowledge it creates is still important to you and to others. However, it is also very powerful if you work with others to reflect on your practice.

A community of reflective practitioners can do much to change the way you perceive your own situation, but also the way that society views your work as a profession. Wenger (1999) describes this idea as being a community of practice, a group of people who come together and evolve because they share a particular interest or passion, or a group specifically formed with the aim of gaining knowledge about a particular subject, learning from each other and developing themselves personally and professionally. This community of reflective professionals can bring together a range of perspectives from practice, theory, cultural and political persuasions. This in turn impacts on the culture, the principles and the values of the setting, and, like a stone dropped in water, the ripples affect a wider pool of practice.

Research can be a significant tool to inform the way you make decisions, make changes and develop your practice. However, as Rodd (2006: 205) points out, it 'does not provide magical answers and there may be no one right answer to the questions asked, or the problems posed'. This does not mean we should ignore research, as both reflection and action research do not necessarily need conclusions; by their very nature, they are on-going and cyclical.

Of course, you can share your discoveries with a far wider audience than those you immediately work with. You might think about the whole of your setting if they have not been included, other nearby settings, the local authority, or even going on to publish a journal article or speak about it at a conference. But initially, it is important to reflect, share, change, and begin the cycle again.

Journal Task

Dockett, S. and Perry, B. (2007) 'Trusting children's accounts in research', *Journal of Early Childhood Research*, 5(1): 47–63.

This article looks at the qualms some researchers hold about the reliability and validity of children's input into research. It considers issues of ethics and research protocols and the importance of listening to children.

Levels 4 & 5

Thinking about the way the researchers suggest you gain the consent of children, how would you approach this now?

(Continued)

(Continued)

Level 6

The authors consider the artefacts (e.g. paintings or drawings) that children produce and we keep as us exerting our power over the children. How do you feel about this notion? How could you redress the balance?

To download this task as well as other useful online resources please visit: **www.sagepub.co.uk/mukherji**

Summary

In this chapter we have considered what we mean when we talk and read about reflective practice, and why it is important in the field of early childhood. We have looked at the importance of being analytical if reflection is to have a true benefit for yourself, your team and the children and families you work with, and have explored the tools that might help you. We looked in particular at keeping a reflective journal and how this might become an element of a research project alongside action research. We have concluded by thinking about how research informs our practice.

Further reading

Levels 4 & 5

Bolton, G. (2005) *Reflective Practice* (2nd edition). London: Sage. A very readable core text that is full of practical suggestions to help those new to reflective practice.

Mukherji, P. and Albon, D. (2010) *Research Methods in Early Childhood*. London: Sage. This is an introductory text in that it covers all aspects of being a researcher. It combines academic theory with practical advice and applications.

Reed, M. and Canning, N. (eds) (2010) *Reflective Practice in the Early Years*. London: Sage. This book is full of essential information for anyone working in or studying early years practice. It supports the reader in developing a critical and reflective approach to their own work.

Robert-Holmes, G. (2011) *Doing Your Early Years Research Project*. London: Sage. This is a step-by-step guide that anyone undertaking research for the first time will find very helpful.

Level 6

Hallet, E. (2012) *The Reflective Early Years Practitioner*. London: Sage. This text is full of case studies and brings together experience, work-based learning and reflective practice.

Linden, J. (2010) *Reflective Practice and Early Years Professionalism: Linking Theory and Practice*. London: Hodder Education. This text explores the nature of reflective practice with key concepts and practical advice on developing reflective practice on both a personal level and within teams.

MacNaughton, G., Rolfe, S. and Siraj-Blatchford, I. (eds) (2010) *Doing Early Childhood Research*. Maidenhead: McGraw Hill. This book takes a very practical approach and considers both qualitative and quantitative methods. It suggests how to select a topic, review the literature, design their research project, analyse data and produce a report.

References

Bolton, G. (2005) *Reflective Practice* (2nd edition). London: Sage.

Cable, C., Goodliff, G. and Miller, L. (2007) 'Developing reflective early years practitioners within a regulatory framework', *Malaysian Journal of Distance Education*, 9(2): 1–19.

Clough, P. and Nutbrown, C. (2012) *A Student's Guide To Methodology* (3rd edition). London: Sage.

Dewey, J. (1933) *How We Think: A Restatement of the Relation of Reflective Thinking to the Educative Process*. Chicago: Henry Regnery Co.

DfES (2012) *Statutory Framework For The Early Years Foundation Stage*. London: TSO.

DfE (2013) *More Great Childcare*. London: TSO.

Ekebergh, M. (2007) 'Lifeworld-based reflection and learning: A contribution to the reflective practice in nursing and nursing education', *Reflective Practice*, 8(3): 331–43.

Etherington, K. (2004) *Becoming a Reflexive Researcher: Using Our Selves in Research*. London: Jessica Kingsley Publishers.

Gardner, H. (2006) *Five Minds For The Future*. Boston: Harvard Business School Press.

Hallet, E. (2012) *The Reflective Early Years Practitioner*. London: Sage.

Kolb, D.A. (1984) *Experiential Learning: Experience as a Source of Learning and Development*. New Jersey: Prentice Hall.

Linden, J. (2010) *Reflective Practice and Early Years Professionalism: Linking Theory and Practice*. London: Hodder Education.

MacNaughton, G., Rolfe, S. and Siraj-Blatchford, I. (eds) (2010) *Doing Early Childhood Research*. Maidenhead: McGraw Hill.

McNiff, J. (2013) *Action Research: Principles and Practice*. Abingdon: Routledge.

Moon, J. (1999) *Reflection in Learning and Professional Development: Theory and Practice*. London: Kogan Page.

Moon, J. (2006) *Learning Journals*. Abingdon: Routledge.

Mukherji, P. and Albon, D. (2010) *Research Methods in Early Childhood: An Introductory Guide*. London: Sage.

Nutbrown, C. (2012) *Foundations For Quality*. London: DfES.

Ofsted (2012) *Framework for the Regulation of Provision on the Early Years Register*. Ofsted: Manchester.

Reed, M. and Canning, N. (2010) *Reflective Practice in the Early Years*. London: Sage.

Robert-Holmes, G. (2011) *Doing Your Early Years Research Project*. London: Sage.

Rodd, J. (2006) *Leadership in Early Childhood* (3rd edition). Maidenhead: McGraw Hill.

Schön, D. (1983) *The Reflective Practitioner: How Professionals Think in Action*. Aldershot: Ashgate.

Tallis, F. (2012) *Hidden Minds: A History of the Unconscious*. London: Arcade.

Wenger, E. (1999) *Communities of Practice: Learning, Meaning, and Identity*. Cambridge: Cambridge University Press.

4

Observation and Assessment

Jonathan Glazzard

This chapter will:

- Explore the processes of assessment in the Early Years Foundation Stage
- Consider the role of parents and children as partners in assessment
- Identify the challenges of implementing effective assessment in the early years.

The policy context

The Early Years Foundation Stage Framework (DfE, 2012) in England emphasises the importance of assessment as an integral part of the learning and development process. Skilled practitioners are able to use their knowledge of children's achievements, learning styles and interests to plan subsequent learning experiences. Effective assessment is on-going and informal and is used to identify what children know and can do (Howard et al., 2013). This understanding then enables practitioners to scaffold children's learning in order to help them reach the next developmental level (Bruner, 1970). Daily observations can be used to identify next steps in learning and to modify existing provision to more effectively meet the needs of children. This is known as *formative assessment*.

The Early Years Foundation Stage Framework (DfE, 2012) stresses the importance of practitioners' interactions with children. Although you will be expected to compile documentary evidence of children's achievements there is no need to produce extensive, detailed records for the purposes of moderation and assessment. The new Early Years Foundation Stage Framework (DfE, 2012) explicitly states that assessment should not entail prolonged breaks from children. You are only required to document what is absolutely necessary to promote successful learning and development. The Tickell Review (2011) highlighted that practitioners had become frustrated with the amount of documentary evidence they were required to compile to support their judgements about children's achievements. As an early years practitioner you will have a greater impact on children's learning and development if you spend time interacting with them rather than observing what they can do and spending time writing observations. Tickell (2011) emphasised that it is only necessary to record children's key achievements rather than documenting everything you know about a child.

As you get to know the children in your setting you will quickly develop knowledge of what they know and what they can and cannot yet do. Key person systems enable you to focus your attention on a small group of children and this enables you to develop detailed knowledge of learners as individuals. There is little value in spending precious time observing aspects of children's learning and development in which you have already formulated secure judgements. Effective practitioners know their learners well. They are able to talk confidently about their strengths and targets without the need to refer back to assessment evidence. Much of this assessment information will be kept in your head. It is more effective to spend your time focusing on the aspects of children's learning and development that you are less certain about. You should observe them in a variety of contexts while focusing on these aspects in order to develop a more complete picture of each child as a learner.

Your knowledge of each child will increase substantially as a result of your interactions with them. Playing with children, talking to them and their parents and observing them in a variety of contexts will enable you to develop detailed knowledge of each child's holistic development. Whilst you will need to allocate specific time for carrying out observations it is important that the majority of your time is spent directly interacting with children. It is through these interactions that you will really get to know your learners, their strengths and areas for development. In this way *teaching* and *assessment* cannot be divorced.

Observations

Observations should be an integral part of your daily routine. They enable you to identify what stage children have reached in their development and they help you to identify children's next steps. This knowledge should then inform the planning process. To facilitate progress your planning should take account of children's prior achievements and build upon these. Observations enable you to identify what children know and can do. They provide you with an opportunity to celebrate children's achievements in a positive way and they provide you with a means of sharing these achievements with others.

Assessment in the early years should always be a positive process. It should capture children's achievements by stating what they can do rather than what they cannot do. Assessment is a process of 'gathering a range of evidence about children's learning and behaviours so that judgements can be made about their progress' (Howard et al., 2013: 101). This enables practitioners to identify their next steps in order to facilitate improvements in their knowledge, skills and understanding (Black and Wiliam, 1998a, 1998b; Harrison and Howard, 2009). Observations can highlight areas where specific intervention is needed for groups of learners and individuals. Additionally, observations provide you with an opportunity to identify children's interests and this knowledge can subsequently lead to adaptations to classroom provision and planning. Carr and Lee (2012) provide some rich case studies to illustrate ways in which assessment can be built around children's interests through the use of photographs and documented conversations. Developing topics, role play, reading or writing areas around children's interests can result in higher levels of engagement and improved outcomes for learners.

Capturing children's interests through assessment provides the foundation for planning subsequent learning experiences (Sadler, 2008). You can also use your observations as a basis for evaluating your own practice. If your observations indicate that a specific area of the classroom is not well used by the children you can subsequently make adaptations to the provision to increase learner participation in this area. Additionally, if progress in specific areas of learning is slow, this can provide you with a useful opportunity to reflect on how you can make adaptations in order to accelerate progress.

In England practitioners assess children's learning and development against the seven prime and specific areas of learning identified in the Early Years Foundation Stage Framework (DfE, 2012). Your observations should capture children's holistic development. As an early years practitioner you will not only be concerned about children's academic development in areas such as literacy and mathematics, you will be interested in children's development holistically, and you will also need to focus on their social and emotional development, their dispositions, attitudes and relationships with others. Capturing children's achievements across all seven areas of learning will enable you to form a well-rounded picture of each child. Children are individuals and have different strengths, interests and needs. Your observations will demonstrate how children are progressing within each area of learning and this will provide you with a basis for subsequent planning for groups and individuals.

Children's development in the prime areas is critical to their development in the specific areas of learning. Children with poor dispositions and attitudes towards learning will struggle to make progress in all areas of the curriculum. Theorists including Vygotsky (1986), Piaget (1951) and Bandura (1977) have all emphasised the correlation between social interaction and brain development, and Davison et al. (2009) have discussed the relationship between personal, social and emotional development and future academic success. Additionally, children who struggle to listen, hold attention and communicate are at risk of achieving poor outcomes in areas such as reading, writing and mathematics. Observing children in the prime areas will initially enable you to identify a clear focus for each child. Whilst it is important not to neglect any aspect of learning, fundamentally it is important to ensure that children are making good progress in the prime areas. Without this, progress in the specific areas will almost certainly be impeded. Your observations will indicate if children need further interventions in the prime areas before they can be expected to make significant progress in the specific areas.

Interpreting observations

The Development Matters statements in the Early Years Foundation Stage framework (Early Education, 2012) will help you to interpret or make sense of your observations. These statements chart typical development for children at different ages. However, children are unique and progress at different rates. Additionally, each child may not demonstrate consistent stages of development in different areas of learning. There is a danger that the statements might be used to label children as underachievers, particularly in cases where children do not appear to be progressing in line with age-related expectations. You should guard against this and instead try to focus on what children have achieved. The Development Matters statements (Early Education, 2012) can help you to identify children's next steps but sometimes children need to take smaller steps than those which are identified in the framework. Effective practitioners use the documentation as guidance but you should use your own professional judgement when identifying what children need to do next.

The Early Learning Goals (Early Education, 2012) provide descriptors of what children typically should be able to achieve at the end of the Early Years Foundation Stage. The descriptors are helpful in that you will be able to make 'best fit' judgements about children's achievements across each of the areas of learning. The judgements that you make in relation to the Development Matters statements and the Early Learning Goals (Early Education, 2012) should be supported by your observations of children in different contexts. However, there is no requirement to keep copious amounts of documentary evidence for each child. Practitioners have in recent years received mixed messages in relation to this point and some local authorities have demanded that practitioners produce extensive evidence to support their assessment judgements. The current EYFS Framework explicitly states that there is no requirement for practitioners to produce excessive paperwork and the Tickell Review (Tickell, 2011) emphasises that it is only necessary to keep evidence of children's key achievements. This should liberate practitioners from the bureaucratic demands of assessment so that they can focus on spending their time interacting with and supporting children.

You will need to reflect back on your observations to identify children's achievements in relation to the Development Matters statements (Early Education, 2012) and the Early Learning Goals (Early Education, 2012). You should link your observations back to these statements for the relevant areas of learning. This will enable you to see how children are progressing and what their next steps are. One observation of a child in the role play area might provide you with indications about their achievements in several areas of learning. You might have commented on their persistence, ability to share and take turns and their confidence (Personal, Social and Emotional Development). You might have made a comment about their ability to listen to others and understand language (Communication and Language). Additionally, with older children, you might have noted down something about their reading and writing abilities. Children in the early years do not compartmentalise learning into subjects. Learning is integrated into a task and rarely do children ever only learn one thing. You should reflect back on your observations to identify whether it is possible to gain evidence of their achievements in several areas of learning.

Observing a child in their play can provide you with extensive information about their achievements across the curriculum and these observations can be shared out between members of the team. Key persons can focus on specific children in order to make the assessment process more manageable. Bowlby's seminal work on attachment (Bowlby, 1979) has contributed to the development of the 'key person' approach (Elfer et al., 2003), along with the work of Stern (1990), who has emphasised the importance of developing child-centred approaches. Regular assessment meetings provide an opportunity for key persons to share their observations with others so that all members of the team gain as much information about each child as possible. This will enable all practitioners to provide appropriate support to all children. As a team you will need to make decisions about how many long observations you intend to do on each child for the duration of their time in the setting. Long observations of children engaged in child-initiated play for a period of time will need to be limited to make them manageable. One long observation each half-term or term can provide you with extensive information about each child's achievements across the curriculum.

Sometimes you will notice children doing things that you have not seen them do before. These critical incidents can be noted using post-it notes and these can be dated and inserted into each child's assessment profile. Additionally, photographs provide you with a visual means of capturing children's achievements across different areas of learning. These should be annotated to provide the reader with contextual information and a commentary should be provided to indicate what achievements the photograph is demonstrating. These should then be cross-referenced to the Development Matters statements and the Early Learning Goals in the non-statutory guidance (Early Education, 2012). Some photographs, although visually appealing, do not actually evidence specific achievements, so it is important that you select photographs which provide clear evidence of children's achievements in relation to Development Matters or the Early Learning Goals (Early Education, 2012).

Gathering evidence

It is more effective to capture evidence of children's achievements when they are engaged in child-initiated independent learning. Observing children in independent learning will provide you with information in relation to what they can do without adult support. Where possible, when planning activities, you should consider carefully the link between adult-directed learning tasks and the provision of independent learning opportunities. Following on from an adult-directed task on simple two dimensional shapes, these shapes can then be placed in the sand tray for children to access independently. This independent learning provides you with a valuable assessment opportunity as children are interacting with the shapes in their normal play. By standing back and observing them you will quickly be able to ascertain if children are able to use the correct mathematical vocabulary to describe the shapes or if they are able to sort the shapes using different criteria. It is more effective to carry out this assessment some time after the adult-directed task has taken place in order to ascertain if the learning has been internalised.

Sometimes your observations will have a clear focus. You will know exactly what you are looking for in relation to children's achievements. Your focus might be very specific, for example you might be observing to see if they can place a set of numerals in the correct order. The example of the shape activity in the previous paragraph provides a clear example of a tightly defined assessment task. Long observations whereby you observe children for a period of time in their play rarely have a specific focus. In this instance you will observe the child, noting down the context, their words and actions and you will subsequently analyse the observation to identify the child's achievements against particular areas of learning. As you start to build up a picture of each child's achievements you will be able to identify areas where you have limited assessment information for each child. This can then help to shape the focus of subsequent observations.

Current policy

It was with relief that EYFS practitioners were assured that as from September 2012 much of the burdensome paperwork was no longer required to support our assessments of young children. Practitioners have a multitude of roles to perform and can do this most effectively by working with and alongside the children in their care. A competent practitioner knows their children well, and is better placed to observe and assess children's achievements whilst working directly alongside them, rather than following them around with a clipboard to record their actions. Interacting with and observing independent learning, allows the practitioner to engage properly with the children's play and be on hand to witness their successes and make 'mental notes' when something interesting happens. These informal observations enable the adults to identify the children's individual interests and plan more effectively for their learning. Once the children have left, the adults have time to share anecdotes and can record particularly significant achievements. This leads to a smaller collection of recorded evidence to support judgements about individual children, but what has been saved is of much greater importance. Experienced practitioners do not need copious amounts of paperwork in order to confidently talk about each child's accomplishments.

CASE STUDY

Tom joined the nursery soon after his third birthday. He was initially very distressed by this new experience and presented as a very tearful and withdrawn child. He would enter the setting each morning clinging tightly to his father's hand whilst hiding behind him. We encouraged his father to complete early morning routines with Tom but whenever the time came for his father to leave Tom would scream and cry uncontrollably. It was a distressing experience for everyone and, despite all our efforts to support him, this situation continued for several weeks. When his father left, Tom would sit with his head bowed, refusing to interact with the other children or adults.

Our observations of Tom began to focus on his personal, social and emotional development. We noticed that Tom was keen to venture into the outdoor area and we resolved to monitor his responses in this different environment. Within a few days we began to witness very different behaviour – the quiet distressed child we had observed previously, seemingly became a tyrant in the outdoor area. We began to monitor him from a discrete distance. It soon became apparent that the minute Tom felt that he was well away from adult scrutiny his whole demeanour changed. Fearlessly he charged into groups of children, shouting at them and using threatening gestures. It soon became apparent that outdoors his body language changed too. The withdrawn child we observed in the nursery was transformed when outdoors, in an area where he felt less scrutinised. His stature became upright, his eye contact direct and he confidently dominated other children with his voice. We noted that as soon as he became aware of the presence of an adult he would become calm and revert to the withdrawn child we had previously observed. We began to model our expectations of cooperative play, but progress was slow as he quickly reverted to being a very withdrawn child whenever adults were present. Once our concerns had been confirmed, we arranged a meeting with his parents and on the first occasion they seemed genuinely surprised by our concerns. We agreed to meet them on a more frequent basis and hoped that they would work with us to support their son. However, on a subsequent occasion the mother came alone, and with her partner absent, she disclosed that there were problems; she and Tom were fearful of her husband's temper. Our observations enabled us to recognise that the family were in difficulty and we were able to instigate some support for the mother in taking refuge from a violent man.

- After reading about Tom why do you think it is important to observe children in different contexts?
- In relation to safeguarding, what action would you take next regarding the issues identified with Tom's father? Find out about how the Common Assessment Framework could be implemented in this instance.

Children's learning journals

Learning journals give you an opportunity to provide evidence of children's significant achievements during their time in the Early Years Foundation Stage. Typically, they include observational assessments, photographic evidence and samples of children's recorded work. Additionally, they might also include commentaries of discussions with children and parents or carers. Learning journals provide a record of what children know and can do and in this respect they celebrate children's achievements. They should be shared with the children and their parents and they should form a basis for discussions about progress.

Reflection

Practitioners in the early years document observations of children's achievements across all seven areas of learning and children are observed across a range of contexts. However, rarely are children consulted about whether they wish to be observed or provided with the opportunity to agree with the judgements that practitioners make about them. What are the ethical implications of observational assessment? The United Nations Convention on the Rights of the Child (United Nations, 1989) stipulated that children have the right to freely express their views on all matters that concern them, and although this has not been incorporated into legislation in England it has been influential in shaping the pupil voice movement.

Recording evidence

Inspectors and moderation teams from local authorities should not expect to see copious assessment evidence. It is not practical or possible to record everything about a child and it is certainly not practical to provide documentary evidence of achievement in relation to each Development Matters statement (Early Education, 2012). You should be able to provide documentary evidence in relation to children's key achievements rather than attempting to evidence everything. Instead, you should talk to inspectors and moderators about your assessment processes and provide samples of assessments to validate some of your judgements.

All members of the early years team need to be responsible for assessment. Consequently, there needs to be a shared understanding of what good assessment looks like and internal moderation meetings should be planned regularly so that judgements across the team can be checked for consistency. Practitioners across different settings often meet once per term to moderate assessments. This ensures that there is a shared understanding of what constitutes achievement at different levels and aims to increase consistency across a cluster of settings.

CASE STUDY

As a Reception Class teacher I am charged with the responsibility of gathering information for over twenty children in seven areas of learning. This is never more difficult than at the beginning of a school year. The theory is quite simple, I need to gather information from parents, carers and previous settings and make my own observations of the children with the support of one colleague. An on-entry assessment must above all else show an accurate picture of the development of each child against the EYFS development matters.

Children develop rapidly and it is essential that I build a complete picture of each child as quickly as possible. I work in a socially deprived area, in a school with a high percentage of children with special educational needs as well as a high percentage of children with an entitlement to free school meals. The school does not have a nursery and as a result the majority of the young children who begin full-time education with us have had no experiences in nurseries, nor do they enter the setting with previous records.

- When do you think you can start to gather information on children's development?
- What procedures do you think should be put in place to ensure that an accurate assessment is made of these children soon after starting in your setting?
- How might you engage parents in the process?

Record keeping can start even before the children start in a setting. Preliminary visits are an opportunity to gather some initial information by observing the children as they explore the new environment; it is very interesting to observe their confidence levels and their ability to engage in unfamiliar surroundings. It is good practice to meet with parents to discuss their children's development and some establishments are able to release staff to visit the children in their own homes. In other cases parents can be invited in to the placement for a short meeting, which may be combined with the child's preliminary visit. These interviews can help to engage parents in their child's educational experiences and demonstrate that their opinions and knowledge about their child are valued by the staff at the setting. This early engagement can be continued once the child has entered the setting, and parents can be encouraged to maintain contact through daily diaries which share their children's achievements with the practitioners.

Parents as partners in the assessment process

The Early Years Foundation Stage Framework (DfE, 2012) emphasises the importance of involving parents and carers in the assessment process. Research has found that effective home learning environments promote higher intellectual, social and behavioural outcomes for children (Sylva et al., 2003) and effective partnerships help to secure continuity in children's educational experiences (Thompson, 2013). As a practitioner it is important that you recognise that children continue to learn and develop at times when they are not in the setting. This process continues within the home environment as children interact with their parents/carers, siblings, other relatives and friends. As their first educators, parents and carers have a vast knowledge of their children, their interests, strengths, likes and dislikes and next steps. Parents have knowledge about the activities that engage their child for sustained periods of time (Howard et al., 2013). You can 'tap into' this knowledge to enrich the provision within the setting, for example by developing areas or themes based upon children's interests. Additionally, judgements about achievements can only be partial if they are only based on information collected within the setting. A vast amount of information about children's personal, social and emotional development can be collected by consulting parents and carers and it is important to view them as partners in the assessment process. In the early years your assessments will not be limited to children's academic development. As you build up a complete picture of the child you will need to consult those who spend the majority of their time with the child in order to develop a more accurate picture of their achievements.

You can encourage parents and carers to document children's achievements at home by writing short observations. These can be brought into the setting and included into the child's assessment record. It may be necessary to run some training sessions for parents and carers to inform them about the principles of assessment in the Early Years Foundation Stage. You can encourage them to make a note of children's achievements at home or to jot down anything which they feel is significant. Some children may not be confident within the context of a nursery or school but they may be confident within the home environment. This information will enrich your own assessments and form a more rounded perspective of the child's achievements.

You should plan opportunities to consult parents as part of the assessment process. Some practitioners meet regularly with parents to consult them about each child's strengths, interests and areas for development. These informal discussions can be documented and included into each child's assessment record. Practitioners are legally required to formally report to parents on children's progress at the age of 2 and at the end of the Early Years Foundation Stage.

Reflection

Some parents or carers may be reluctant to engage as partners in the assessment process. Why might this be the case? Suggest some ways of addressing this issue.

Some parents or carers may have an inflated view of their child's achievements or they may claim that they have seen evidence of achievements which have not been observed in the setting. In this instance would it be appropriate for the practitioner to ignore the parental assessments? Justify your answer.

Viewing parents and carers as partners in assessment necessitates a power shift away from practitioners. What are the issues in this respect?

Children as part of the assessment process

The notion of children having a voice in their education has gained international support over the last three decades and children are now viewed within policy as individuals with rights. These include the right to express their views and to have their voices listened to and acted upon (United Nations, 1989). The Reggio Emilia approach from Italy and the Te Whāriki approach in New Zealand, both emphasise the importance of listening to children and the role of practitioners as recorders and documenters of children's learning. This makes the learning process visible and enables children to revisit their learning. The Mosaic Approach, developed by Clark and Moss (Clark and Moss, 2001) emphasises the need for practitioners to listen to the perspectives of children using a range of approaches. Children are now viewed as social agents. They are deemed to be confident and capable of making decisions and this is embedded within the Early Years Foundation Stage Framework (DfE, 2012).

Children should be given the opportunity to talk about their achievements and reflect on aspects that they are proud of. Additionally, they should also have the opportunity to talk about their interests as this can inform curriculum planning. You should consult children about their own targets (next steps) and provide them with an opportunity to reflect on how these might be achieved.

Children should be able to freely access their own learning journals. This will give them the opportunity to reflect back on their own achievements and they should have the opportunity to share their journals with their peers. Children should also be afforded the opportunity to decide which pieces of evidence to include in their learning journal by selecting the pieces of evidence which they are proud of.

Young children are generally very enthusiastic and take pride in their achievements, enjoying opportunities to share these successes with the adults who work with them. They also ask incessant questions, and, of course, listening carefully to children is just as important as observing them. The concept of learning journals discussed earlier is a celebration of their achievements and the children should be able to choose what they wish to record, however insignificant it may appear to the adults; if they are proud of a piece of work or something they have made or done they will decide to put it in their journal. Their journals should be readily accessible and they can enjoy looking through them, sometimes alone, to revisit their successes, and at other times sharing the journal with an adult who can acknowledge and celebrate their progress. It is in these comfortable and unthreatening situations that children are frequently able to identify the things they would like to achieve in the immediate future. They are also open to suggestions from the practitioner and in this way significant next steps in learning can be identified. The journals are also an excellent way of engaging the parents' interest. Children may choose to share their journals with their parents informally, or they may become the focus of a discussion during parent consultations.

Reflection

Practitioners are often encouraged to talk to children about their achievements and next steps and to include children's perspectives within their assessment records. However, this represents a significant challenge especially for those practitioners who work with non-verbal children.

- How can children without verbal communication be included as partners in assessment?
- Viewing children as partners in assessment necessitates a power shift away from practitioners. What are the issues in this respect?

International approaches to assessment

In the Reggio Emilia approach from Italy pedagogical documentation is the basis for assessment (Rinaldi, 2006). Evidence of children's experiences is collected through videos, photographs, notes and audio recordings and in this way learning is made visible to children and parents. Practitioners are responsible for documenting children's learning and this process enables learning to be revisited. There is a strong emphasis on listening to children's voices and children lead the learning.

Without doubt the greatest support to any Foundation Stage teacher is the human resources that are deployed to the classroom. Most, but not all Reception Class teachers now have a degree of support from a teaching assistant. A strong teaching assistant or a qualified early childhood practitioner is without doubt the best tool in the tool box. All practitioners working in the early years have experienced first-hand the complexities of working with young children. It is crucial that the people filling these roles have the relevant skills and experience to effectively support the children and help contribute towards the assessment process.

Summative assessment

Progress check at age 2

As from 2012, early education providers in England, including childminders, are required to carry out a progress check which is shared with the child's parents. This check must be carried out between 24 and 36 months, and is applicable to children who receive provision outside the family home. The EYFS Framework (DfE, 2012) requires the practitioners to provide a short written statement, summarising the child's development in the three prime areas of learning, though the parents and the child themselves should ideally contribute to the evidence-gathering process (NCB, 2012). The checks help to promote dialogue between the parents and their child's carers, focusing attention on the child's interests and achievements and helping to identify learning priorities (NCB, 2012: 5). The summary will highlight those areas in which the child's development is beyond expectations, as well as any areas where their progress is slower than expected.

Early years profile

The EYFS profile is a summary of each child's achievements at the end of the Early Years Foundation Stage, and is a summative assessment tool, showing a child's attainment at a specific point in time. The profile documentation, introduced in 2013, is designed to correlate neatly with the EYFS (DfE, 2012) curriculum goals. It identifies children's achievements in relation to each of the 17 Early Learning Goals (Early Education, 2012). There are three levels attributed to each early learning goal – *emerging, expected* and *exceeding* – and these in turn produce a corresponding score of 1, 2 or 3.

Achievement at each Goal at the end of EYFS is defined as:

- Emerging: the child is working below expectations
- Expected: the child is working in line with expectations
- Exceeding: this is consistent with the expectations in the National Curriculum.

Practitioners are required to formally report on each child's progress, in relation to each of the 17 Early Learning Goals, to parents and carers.

Reflection

Many children entering foundation stage settings, especially those from more disadvantaged communities will be classed as 'emerging' in many of the areas of learning. Whilst they will make good progress they may not achieve national expectations and will therefore potentially enter and leave the setting with a score of 1 in many of the early learning goals.

- How do you think young children's achievements should be measured?
- Do you think that national averages/expectations are a useful tool for measuring every child's progress? Which groups do you think may be disadvantaged by this type of policy?

Whilst summative profiles give a good indication of whether a child is achieving the required learning goals, this type of system fails to acknowledge that not all children enter educational settings with the same experiences and skills. In the past, children's progress was assessed in the Reception Class by some form of baseline testing (Nutbrown et al., 2008). Whilst this form of assessment was not favoured by practitioners, nonetheless it helped to focus on how much progress an individual child had made during their first year in school (by assessing their skills at entry and then again at the end of the year). This ensured that the children's individual achievements were recognised, and their personal learning journey was acknowledged. Some children are able to make enormous personal gains in their first year at school, but they may still lag behind some of their more experienced (possibly more socially advantaged) peers. National assessments also disadvantage children who are new to English and who may be unable to express (in English) all that they understand. Similarly, children with a variety of special needs, or summer-born children may also fail to demonstrate all the required goals.

It is children's achievements against the development matters that will best demonstrate the progress they have made. A child who has made good progress will have achieved the expected level of development in the prime areas of learning as well as in the specific areas of mathematics and literacy. The EYFS profile will, however, continue to be a useful document for Year 1 practitioners. Exceeding expectations will be a clear indicator that a child is working within National Curriculum expectations. Until now it has been impossible to make a direct correlation between the EYFS profile and National Curriculum levels.

CASE STUDY

Practitioners are frequently charged with the unenviable task of communicating to parents that their children require additional support to move them towards reaching national expectations. This was not the case with Carmen. She was bright and articulate and ready for the challenges that awaited her each day. In particular we were impressed by her development in early writing and phonics. She engaged enthusiastically in all activities and quickly began to apply her learning in phonics lessons to her independent writing. The progress she made within the first term in school was to be celebrated. I had arranged a meeting with her mother where I looked forward to sharing, in detail, her wonderful progress. My delight was short lived however. Her mother had grave concerns about her daughter. She was equally concerned about our apparent lack of concern about her poor spelling. In reality her spelling was consistently phonetically plausible and within a term she was writing simple sentences with confidence that could be deciphered by any reader. We had noted that when she brought in writing from home her spelling was perfect. It had in fact been corrected by her mother and then copied. Clearly there was a complete misunderstanding of what constituted good achievement in writing.

We invited Carmen's mother to work with us to develop her own understanding of her daughter's achievements. I began by drawing a simple pattern, inviting her to replicate it. She obliged. Then I asked her to explain what she had done. She identified that she had copied my work. I then wrote a sentence containing only non-words. She conceded that she could also copy that. Then I spoke a sentence of non-words and asked her to write it. She acknowledged that doing so was more challenging because she had to think carefully about how to spell the words and wasn't sure if she had done so correctly. She had in fact used her knowledge of phoneme/grapheme correspondence to do so. This was a real revelation to her as she suddenly realised that Carmen did exactly the same when she attempted to write 'new' words. Suddenly the realisation of how her daughter was also applying her own knowledge of phoneme/grapheme correspondences dawned on her. A concerned mother left the meeting beaming with pride. Perfect spellings were no longer evident in homework. They were replaced by phonetically plausible spellings and an extremely proud parent.

- Why was it valuable for the practitioner to spend time with Carmen's mother?
- Why is it important for practitioners and parents to work in collaboration to support children?
- How might you use your record-keeping system's help to illustrate a child's progress (or highlight difficulties) to their parents?

Journal Task

Levels 4 & 5

Carr, M. and Lee, W. (2012) *Learning Stories: Constructing Learner Identities in Early Education*. London: Sage.

Read Chapter 3 of this book and find out about how assessment can be built around children's interests.

Extension to Level 6

Blaiklock, K. (2008) 'A critique of the use of learning stories to assess the learning dispositions of young children', *New Zealand Research in Early Childhood Education*, 11: 77–87.

This article critically reflects on the validity and reliability of learning stories as an approach to assessment. It provides a critique of the approach and this will support you with critical writing at Level 6. Read the article and discuss it with your colleagues. Do you agree with the points that Blaiklock makes?

To download this task as well as other useful online resources please visit:
www.sagepub.co.uk/mukherji

Summary

In summary, this chapter has identified approaches to developing formative and summative assessment with children. It has stressed the importance of involving parents and carers and children within assessment process. Without the involvement of these key stakeholders any assessments carried out by practitioners can only ever be partial. This chapter has emphasised that learning and development takes place in the setting, in the home and in the environment. Consequently, it is important that practitioners develop a holistic knowledge of each child by considering their achievements in a range of contexts.

Further reading

Levels 4 & 5

Jarvis, P., George, J. and Holland, W. (2013) *The Early Years Professional's Complete Companion* (2nd edition). Harlow: Pearson Education Limited. Chapter 5 of this text provides a comprehensive overview of observation in the Early Years Foundation Stage.

Level 6

Harcourt, D., Perry, B. and Waller, T. (eds) (2011) *Researching Young Children's Perspectives: Debating the Ethics and Dilemmas of Educational Research with Children*. Abingdon: Routledge. This text provides an excellent overview of the ethical considerations associated with conducting research with young children. This will be very useful for your research project.

Carr, M. and Lee, W. (2012) *Learning Stories: Constructing Learner Identities in Early Education*. London: Sage. This is an outstanding book. It describes Margaret Carr's seminal work on learning stories and provides plenty of examples of stories which you will enjoy reading. It could form a basis for your own research.

References

Bandura, A. (1977) *Social Learning Theory*. New York: General Learning Press.

Black, P. and Wiliam, D. (1998a) 'Assessment and classroom learning', *Assessment in Education: Principles, Policy and Practice*, 5(91): 7–74.

Black, P. and Wiliam, D. (1998b) *Inside the Black Box: Raising Standards through Classroom Assessment*. London: King's College London, School of Education.

Blaiklock, K. (2008) 'A critique of the use of learning stories to assess the learning dispositions of young children,' *New Zealand Research in Early Childhood Education*, 11: 77–87.

Bowlby, J. (1979) *The Making and Breaking of Affectional Bonds*. Abingdon: Routledge.

Bruner, J.S. (1970) 'The growth and structure of a skill', in K. Connolly (ed.), *Mechanisms of Motor Skill Development*. New York: Academic Press. pp. 62–94.

Carr, M. and Lee, W. (2012) *Learning Stories: Constructing Learner Identities in Early Education*. London: Sage.

Clark, A. and Moss, P. (2001) *Listening to Young Children: The Mosaic Approach*. London: National Children's Bureau.

Davison, J.D., Sherer, K.R. and Goldsmith, H.H. (2009) *Handbook of Affective Sciences*. New York: Oxford University Press.

DfE (2012) *Statutory Framework for the Early Years Foundation Stage: Setting the Standards for Learning, Development and Care for Children from Birth to Five*. Runcorn: DfE.

Early Education (2012) *Development Matters in the Early Years Foundation Stage*. London: DfE.

Elfer, P., Goldschmeid, E. and Selleck, D. (2003) *Key Persons in the Nursery: Building Relationships for Quality Provision*. London: David Fulton.

Harrison, C. and Howard, S. (2009) *Inside the Primary Black Box: Assessment for Learning in Primary and Early Years Classrooms*. The Black Box Assessment for Learning Series. London: GL Assessment.

Howard, S., Harkin, L., Hutchinson, A. and Palaiologou, I. (2013) 'Assessment in the Early Years Foundation Stage', in I. Palaiologou (ed.), *The Early Years Foundation Stage: Theory and Practice* (2nd edition). London: Sage.

NCB (2012) *A Know How Guide: The EYFS Progress Check at Age Two*. DfE/NCB.

Nutbrown, C., Clough, P. and Selbie, P. (2008) *Early Childhood Education: History, Philosophy and Experience*. London: Sage.

Piaget, J. (1951) *Play Dreams and Imitation in Childhood*. London: Routledge and Kegan Paul.

Rinaldi, C. (2006) *In Dialogue with Reggio Emilia: listening, researching and learning*, Abingdon: Routledge.

Sadler, D.R. (2008) 'Formative assessment and the design of instructional systems', republished in W. Harlen (ed.), *Student Assessment and Testing*, Vol. 2. London: Sage. pp. 3–28.

Stern, N.D. (1990) *Diary of a Baby*. New York: Basic Books.

Sylva, K., Melhuish, E., Sammons, P., Siraj-Blatchford, I., Taggart, B. and Elliott, K. (2003) *The Effective Provision of Pre-School Education (EPPE) Project: Findings from the Pre-School Period*, Research Brief No. RBX15–03. London: Department for Education and Skills.

Thompson, W. (2013) 'Meeting EYFS outcomes outside of the early years setting', in I. Palaiologou (ed.), *The Early Years Foundation Stage: Theory and Practice* (2nd edition). London: Sage.

Tickell, C. (2011) *The Early Years: Foundations for Life, Health and Learning. An Independent Report on the Early Years Foundation Stage Framework to Her Majesty's Government.* London: DfE.

United Nations (1989), *Convention on the Rights of the Child,* online http://www.unicef.org/crc/index_understanding.html (accessed 6 August 2013).

Vygotsky, L.S. (1986) *Thought and Language*. London and Cambridge MA: The MIT Press.

Part 2

HOW CHILDREN DEVELOP

A good knowledge of child development is vital for all those working in the field of early childhood. In 2013 this was recognised by UK government when it presented plans to improve the quality of early childhood provision by employing specialist early years teachers who will *specialise* in 'early childhood development' (DfE, 2013: 7). In Part 2 we look at how children learn and develop, drawing on research findings and theory. In a textbook such as this it is impossible to look at child development in detail; rather we look at some of the underpinning themes and approaches to the study of children's development and learning.

There are many good texts that look at child development in detail, such as *The Developing Child* (Bee and Boyd, 2011). You should also look at the *Early Years Learning and Development: Literature Review* (Evangelou et al., 2009) which can be found at the following website: https://www.education.gov.uk/publications/standard/publicationDetail/Page1/DCSF-RR176. This literature review outlines findings from recent research that underpins the Early Years Foundation Stage (DfE, 2012).

Many of the ideas to which you will be introduced in this part of the book are so fundamental to our work with children that you will find them explained in other parts of the book as well. For example in this part of the book, Chapter 5 looks at attachment theory; you will also find it in Chapter 10 which looks at children's health, Chapter 13 which looks at working with parents and Chapter 16 on personal, social and emotional development.

Part 2 starts with Chapter 5 where Penny Mukherji provides an overview of child development theories. Within this chapter you will be introduced to the main ways that 'development' has been conceptualised; from theorists who think that all development is biologically predetermined, to the idea that most of children's development can be explained by the influence of the environment in which a child is raised. You will also be encouraged to reflect upon some of the criticisms of developmental theory.

In Chapter 6 Linda Pound looks at some of the theories relating to how children learn. Looking at children's development in one chapter and children's learning in another is a somewhat artificial divide, as development and learning are inextricably linked, and you will find there is a degree of overlap. Chapter 6 introduces you to the field of cognitive psychology and to some of the well-known theorists such as Piaget, Bruner and Gardener. This chapter helps you make the link between what we know about how children learn, early childhood practice and the requirements of the Early Years Foundation Stage (DfE, 2012).

In Chapter 7 Justine Howard looks at the important contribution that play makes to children's holistic development and learning, linking to the early childhood curriculum. Different types of play are outlined and the adult's role in facilitating children's play is described, in particular the importance of allowing children choice and autonomy. Justine clearly explains the various theories that have been used to explain the purpose of play and how an understanding of the importance of children's play has informed policy and legislation.

References

Bee, H. and Boyd, D. (2011) *The Developing Child*. Cambridge: Pearson.

Department for Education (DfE) (2012) *Statutory Framework for the Early Years Foundation Stage: Setting the Standards for Learning, Development and Care for Children from Birth to Five*. London: DfE.

Department for Education (2013) *More Great Childcare: Raising Quality and Giving Parents More Choice*. London: DfE. https://www.gov.uk/government/publications/more-great-childcare-raising-quality-and-giving-parents-more-choice (accessed 5 August 2013).

Evangelou, M., Sylva, K., Kyriacou, M., Wild, M. and Glenny, G. (2009) *Early Years Learning and Development: Literature Review*. London: DCSF. https://www.education.gov.uk/publications/standard/publicationDetail/Page1/DCSF-RR176 (accessed 3 May 2013).

5

How Children Develop

Penny Mukherji

This chapter will:

- Investigate what is meant by 'child development'
- Discuss why an understanding of child development is essential for early childhood practitioners
- Investigate the main principles and themes used to conceptualise child development
- Outline some of the main theoretical approaches to the study of child development
- Take a critical look at developmental theory.

This is the first chapter in the section on how children develop and is designed to supply you with an overview of some of the different ways that have been used to explain developmental processes in children. Some of you may have studied child development as part of a psychology course, or for an early childhood vocational award and you may be familiar with looking at children's development divided into different areas such as physical development, intellectual development, language development, emotional development and social development. Those of you who are early childhood practitioners will be familiar with thinking about children's development in specific areas, for example the three prime areas of development in the Early Years Foundation Stage: communication and language; physical development; and personal, social and emotional development (DfE, 2012). However, in reality, all these different areas are interrelated and, although it is sometimes convenient to look at specific areas of development in isolation, children's development is holistic, and subject to general principles that govern how they develop. In this chapter we will be looking at some of the ways that have been used to explain these general principles.

What do we mean by 'child development'?

The term 'child development' can mean different things to different people. For example if you ask a mother about her child's development she may talk of how the child has changed from the time he or she was born to becoming the individual that they are now, mentioning how the child has changed physically, the skills the child has acquired and how their personality has developed. A health visitor, however, may look at development in terms of 'milestones of development', which are features of development (such as rolling over or talking) which typically occur at certain ages and indicate that the child is developing as expected.

Reflection

Ask your classmates or, if you work in an early childhood setting, your colleagues, what they mean when they talk about children's development.

I expect that you will find that most of the responses you get will mention change in some form or another. The idea is that from before and after birth children are constantly changing, in their physical growth, the way they think, the way that they interact with the world around them, and the way that they acquire different skills.

Harris (2008) sees developmental change as a process whereby children gradually change from a less mature to a more mature way of thinking and behaving. For Robinson (2008: 3) 'Human development is about anticipation, attainment and assessment'. This encompasses the idea that the process of development is, to some extent, predictable; that we have an idea of changes ahead and once attained, we can evaluate the change. To illustrate this point we can think of parents who have an expectation that children will progress in their movement skills from crawling to walking, and once able to walk parents have an understanding about whether this was 'early', 'about average' or 'late' compared to other children.

Why an understanding of child development is essential for early childhood practitioners

Knowledge of child development is important on many levels. The scientific community is interested in understanding the factors that promote or hinder development and how experiences in childhood impact upon adult psychological processes (Rutherford, 2011). This knowledge is then used by all those involved in promoting the well-being of children and adults to inform policy and practice.

Early childhood practitioners know a great deal about child development; all courses leading to qualifications in the field include a study of child development and practitioners consolidate this learning with everyday, practical experience.

The Statutory Framework for the Early Years Foundation Stage (DfE, 2012) explains that knowledge of child development is needed to be able to recognise where each child is on their developmental pathway in order to supply activities and experiences that will promote and support this development. In addition, practitioners need to be able to make judgements as to whether a child's development is typical of other children of the same age, is delayed, or significantly advanced, so that appropriate support can be arranged. Sharing information about how children are developing, with their parents, is an important aspect of fostering effective partnerships with children's families.

A sound knowledge of child development is one of the foundations of becoming a reflective practitioner, but as you have learned in Chapter 3, more than just knowledge of child development is needed. Practitioners are required to be open minded, willing to see things from other perspectives, and able to see where their own feelings and that of others may influence their judgement (Lindon, 2005).

Thus equipped with a sound understanding of child development and the ability to be reflective, early childhood practitioners are in a unique position to be critical of policy and practice. This may be about practice within their own settings, or about policy decisions made at a national level, such as the responses made by practitioners for the 2011 Tickell Review.

Conceptualising child development

In this section we will investigate some of questions and debates commonly found in the study of child development. We will also be looking at some of the theoretical models and approaches used to help us understand the influences on development.

Are there stages in development?

Traditionally, developmental psychologists have taken a scientific approach, aiming to describe 'normal' pathways of development and to identify key milestones, such as the age children generally start to walk. From this approach arose the question: Is development a smooth process or can one identify different stages?

There are aspects of development, such as physical growth, that appear to be a continuous process until adulthood, albeit with different rates of growth at certain times. However, some aspects of development seem to occur in stages.

Reflection

If you have previously studied child development can you identify theorists who divided children's development into stages?

If you are practitioner, in your experience do you think that children's development is a smooth process or can you identify times when children seem to take a leap forward in their development?

Harris (2008) explains that stage theories are very common in developmental psychology, with Piaget's stage theory of development being one of the most well known, but other theorists such as Freud have also used stages to explain changes in children's development.

How do we identify a developmental stage? Harris (2008) outlines the following criteria:

- A stage involves a qualitative change, not just doing more of something, but doing something differently.
- Transitions between stages involve simultaneous change across more than one domain of development.
- Transitions between stages are rapid.

CASE STUDY

The author's grandson, at 19 months began to acquire new words at a rapid rate. Previously he had learned words at the rate of one or two a week, now he was using several new words everyday. At the same time he started putting words together, informing us that 'Mummy shopping', 'Daddy work' and 'it's a duck'. In his play he started representing 'going away and coming back'; hanging something on his arm to represent a bag, waving and saying 'bye-bye' as he would go into another room. Then he would reappear, waving and saying 'Hiya'. He was fascinated with turning round and round, saying 'round and round' at the same time. In his drawings he would draw spirals, saying 'round and round' as he did so, and one of his favourite finger games was 'round and round the garden'.

1. Analyse the case study using Harris's criteria. Would you say that there is evidence of a transition between stages in development?
2. Which theorists identify the use of symbols as a particular stage of cognitive development? You may find Chapter 6 helpful.
3. Chris Athey (2007) discusses how children use schemas to represent their understanding of the world around them. What schema would you suggest this child is using?

Although 'stages' are part of many theories about children's development, the whole idea that children pass through pre-determined stages has been criticised for being biologically based and ignoring the effects of children's culture and the context in which they are raised (Pound, 2011).

Child development vs lifespan development

Up until the middle of the twentieth century developmental psychology was synonymous with *child* development; there was little recognition that development continues throughout life. Now, however, the perspective has widened to include the study of development across an individual's whole lifespan, with the recognition that 'development' is not just something that happens to children. In addition, the concept of 'development' has widened to include all aspects of change, both the acquisition of skills and mental functions and their decline in old age. Schaffer (2007: 7) identifies the following features of a lifespan perspective:

- Change occurs at all ages.
- Change is not the same as growth.
- Development is holistic.
- Development is multi-directional, that is some aspects of a particular dimension, for example memory, may show stability or even improvement throughout life (long-term memory), whilst other aspects (short-term memory) may decline.
- Some developmental features may disappear altogether, such as the ability shown by infants to discern all the different sounds in human speech, whilst other features remain constant throughout life.

Nature vs nurture

Historically there has long been a discussion about the main influences on development. How much of human development is predetermined by inherited (innate) characteristics already present in a baby, and how much is influenced by the child's environment? This is the 'nature/nurture' debate, which is also known as the 'nativist/empiricist' debate (Brain and Mukherji, 2005).

Reflection

Do you excel at any sports? Have you friends or relatives who are successful sportsmen or women? How much of their success can be attributed to the body they were born with and how much is due to factors such as motivation, support and efficient training? There has been intense debate about this, with some saying that success is mostly to do with inherited characteristics, and others saying that success is due to positive environmental factors.

Hopkins (2001) has written an interesting article which is a good example of the nature/nurture debate applied to sporting prowess. It can be found at: http://www.sportsci.org/jour/0101/wghgene.htm

From this exercise it should be clear that development depends upon an interaction between innate characteristics and environmental factors.

The National Scientific Council on the Developing Child (2010) explains that an individual's genetic make-up is not 'fixed' as was once thought. Early experiences determine whether some genes are turned on or off, and can also have a direct effect on the developing architecture of a baby's brain. These experiences can have an effect both before and after birth.

Evolutionary developmental theory

In psychology there has been a movement that explains human behaviour in evolutionary terms. We have already seen how environmental influence can alter gene expression and that a permanent change can be made to an individual's genetic make-up because of experiences that happen to them. In evolutionary developmental psychology the principles of evolution are used to explain features of human behaviour, arguing that humans possess psychological mechanisms which have evolved to deal with recurrent problems faced by our ancestors (Bjorklund and Pellegrini, 2000). Among other things, evolutionary developmental psychology explains some aspects of human parenting, the role of play in children's development, the extended period of childhood in humans and the role of social structures in cognitive development. Because the modern environment in which we live now is so different from the one in which our ancestors evolved, some behaviours that helped us survive in the past are no longer helpful. For example, our natural inclination to eat sweet, fatty food, when it is available, is helpful when the food supply is erratic but maladaptive in today's society (Bjorklund and Blasi, 2005).

Journal Task

Bjorklund, D.F. and Pellegrini, A.D. (2000) 'Child development and evolutionary psychology', *Child Development*, 71(6): 1687–708.

This is an article about how evolutionary psychology can be a useful 'lens' through which to investigate children's development.

Levels 4 & 5

Read the abstract and conclusion to this article (you may need to have a dictionary at your side) and consider the following:

1. What is evolutionary psychology?
2. Give one example of an aspect of children's development that may have evolved over the generations.
3. Are all evolutionary adaptations beneficial?

Level 6

1. Read the whole paper. Take your time; it is not an easy read.
2. Evaluate the usefulness of the evolutionary developmental psychology approach for early childhood practitioners.

To download this task as well as other useful online resources please visit: **www.sagepub.co.uk/mukherji**

Evolutionary theorists are not without their critics because of their failure to emphasise how much of human behaviour is passed down through the generations, not by the influence of changes to genetic material, but through all the other ways that knowledge and attitudes are passed from one generation to the other. Our behaviour and the contexts in which we live change so rapidly that it is difficult to see how this can be accommodated in the relatively slow process of genetic change (Pound, 2011).

Ecological systems theory

The ecological systems model sets out to look at the effects of children's culture and environment on their development. One of the main advocates for this model was Bronfenbrenner (Underdown, 2007) who suggested that children's development is influenced not just by the immediate environment of their home or school, but also by the wider environments of their community and the cultural and political context in which they live. Because, as discussed earlier in the chapter, there is an interaction between children's immediate context and biological processes, the model is also known as the bio-ecological systems model (Swick and Williams, 2006). The environment of children is represented diagrammatically by four nested circles:

The *microsystem* represents the closest relationships to the child. For very young children this may just be the family, but for older children it may involve relationships formed in early childhood settings or school. The child is seen to be an active agent within these microsystems, both influencing and being influenced by the environment. (Underdown, 2007).

The *mesosystem* consists of the interconnections between the child's microsystems, for example the way that an early childhood setting relates to the child's family and aspects of social support within the child's local community (Underdown, 2007).

The *exosystem* consists of people and places with which children may have no direct contact, but which may have a direct influence on their lives (Pound, 2011) – for example the local council that makes decisions about early childhood services.

The *macrosystem* consists of the laws, policies, values and culture of the society in which children live and the way in which children and childhood is conceptualised and valued by society (Underdown, 2007). The macrosystem may be influenced by global factors. For example, at the time of writing, the global downturn in the economies of Europe and the US has had a direct effect on the amount of money available for early childhood services in England.

The *chronosystem* is not represented by a circle in the model, but is a recognition of the

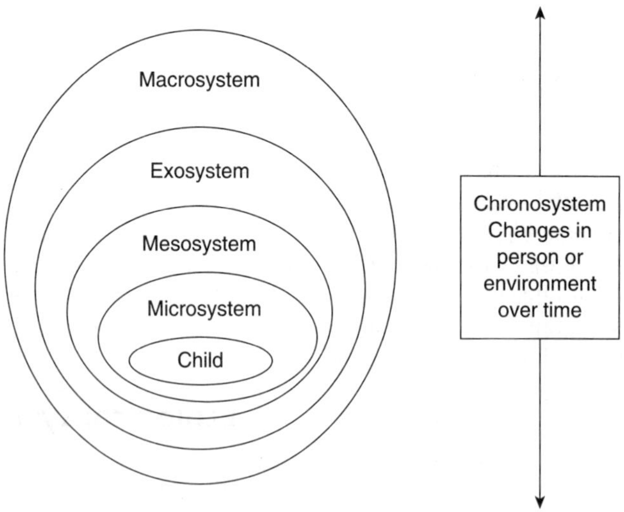

Figure 5.1 Bronfenbrenner's ecological systems theory (Polfuss and Fenn, 2012)

impact that the passage of time has upon the individual. Pound (2011) uses the illustration of divorce, the impact of which may not be felt immediately but later on in a child's life.

The transactional model of development

We have seen how both biological factors and environmental factors can influence children's development. This complex interaction has given rise to the transactional model of development. Davies (2011) describes this model as one which sees development as being the result of transactions made between children and their environment. Transactions are dynamic interactions between children and experiences provided by their immediate family and the social context in which they live. In an infant's first year of life, sensory stimulation and social interaction have a direct effect on brain growth. These are examples of transactions, and as the child grows older they are exposed to an ever-widening circle of experiences, so that transactions are influenced by the cultural and historical context in which the child lives.

The transactional model sees the infant as being an active agent in organising their environment: 'rather than being a passive "container" in which experience is poured; the child creates their own environment' (Davies, 2011: 4). For example, interaction between babies and their caregivers is not a one-way process; the child's behaviour alters the behaviour of the caregiver and vice versa.

Within this model, developmental pathways are not fixed, and transactions at key or critical times can open up alternative pathways. Davies (2011) explains that children can move off the developmental path on which they are 'travelling' onto an alternative path due to positive or negative experiences. For example, an infant who is exposed to parental neglect may move onto a maladaptive pathway, whereas a child who previously had little in the way of stimulation may be moved onto a more adaptive pathway if they start to attend high-quality early childhood provision that enriches his or her life.

As children get older developmental pathways are less flexible, so that a child who has had positive experiences in early childhood is less likely to move onto a maladaptive pathway because of negative experiences later on. Conversely, the older a child is, the less likely it is that positive experiences will move a child onto an adaptive pathway. It is within the first five years of life that pathways are at their most flexible and it is because of this that early childhood is seen as the most effective time to focus interventions directed at supporting children who otherwise may be at risk.

Theoretical approaches in child development

In this section we will look at some of the most influential theories in the field of child development and examine their relevance to early childhood practice today.

Behaviourist theories

Behaviourist theories take an extreme position in the 'nature versus nurture' debate, in that they argue that practically all human behaviour is the result of environmental influence.

One of the most well-known behaviourists was B.F. Skinner (Brain and Mukherji, 2005), who worked in the mid-twentieth century and developed the theory of operant conditioning. Skinner worked with animals and devised a piece of equipment called the Skinner Box (basically a cage) to conduct his research. He discovered that animals would repeat an action if they were rewarded. For example he would put a rat in a Skinner Box and at some point the rat would, by accident, press a lever with its foot. Once pressed, a food pellet would be delivered into the cage. Rats quickly learned that whenever they pressed the lever they would get food. Skinner described their behaviour as being reinforced (strengthened). After undertaking a series of experiments, using a variety of animals, Skinner was able to devise a series of principles that he believed underpinned learning.

1. Any behaviour that is rewarded with something pleasant will be strengthened. Skinner called this positive reinforcement.
2. Learning will also take place if behaviour is rewarded by something unpleasant being removed. For example, a rat in a cage will learn to press a lever if the lever stops a loud unpleasant noise. This is called negative reinforcement.
3. Once learned, if the reward is taken away, the behaviour will gradually decrease. This is called extinction.
4. The strongest and longest-lasting learning is achieved if the learned behaviour is rewarded only some of the time. For example, if pressing the lever is rewarded at random, a rat will go on pressing almost indefinitely on the off chance they will get food. This is called partial reinforcement (Skinner, 1974).

These principles have been used in modifying children's behaviour and underpin positive behaviour management programmes.

Although useful in some situations, the theory is very limited as it cannot really explain how children learn by watching others or the role of instruction. Pound (2011) explains that human behaviour is far too complex to be explained by such a simple theory.

Behaviourist theories neglect to look at the role of imitation and cognition in the learning process. Bandura, working in the 1960s and 1970s, introduced three additions to behaviourist theory. Firstly, he recognised that learning can occur by watching others. Secondly, he suggested that rewards need not be external to the individual, that internal feelings of happiness or satisfaction are rewarding. Finally, Bandura recognised that thoughts have a part to play in the learning process (Bandura, 1977).

Constructivist theories

Constructivist theories of development recognise that children are active agents in their learning and that they use internal processes such as attention, memory, motivation and reasoning to help them make sense of the world.

Piaget was a biologist who was influenced by Darwin's evolutionary theories and developed his theories during the middle years of the twentieth century. He became interested in children's development, especially in the way they developed their abilities to think. His theories are based on the idea that children are predisposed to learn in a certain way, and that learning is an interaction between inherent cognitive structures and experience (Mukherji, 2001).

Piaget saw children's thinking as being very different from adults' thinking, and that children's cognitive abilities developed over time. He described learning as following a series of stages that are linked to the age of the child (Pound, 2011). Piaget believed that the order of these stages was fixed, that all children pass through these stages in the same order, at roughly the same ages. Piaget described learning as an active process where children explore and experiment with objects and people in their environment. The information taken in by the child's senses is assimilated and compared with concepts (schemas) that the child already holds about the nature of the world around them. This new information either confirms what they already know, when they are said to be in a state of equilibrium, or is incompatible with the ideas that they already hold. This is a state of disequilibrium and results in the child adjusting their previously held ideas (accommodating the new information), which results in a change of behaviour (adaptation) (Piaget, 2001).

Piaget's theories emphasised the active role that children take in their own learning. Other theorists, such as Vygotsky and Bruner, looked at the social influences on children's learning, especially the influence of adults.

Vygotsky believed that social relationships have a key role to play in children's learning; that although they could learn through interacting with the environment, they could be helped to reach more advanced levels of understanding with the help of an adult or a more competent friend. Working with children to extend their understanding in this way was described by Vygotsky as working in the child's zone of proximal development. This is a social constructivist theory (Vygotsky, 1978).

Another social constructivist, Bruner, described the way that adults help children with their learning as 'scaffolding', a process where adults often break down tasks to make them more manageable or supply support at critical stages, which is gradually removed as children become more competent. For example, we can help children learn how to dress themselves by giving them articles of clothing in the right order and by holding the articles in a way that makes it easier for the child to put them on (Robson, 2006).

Reflection

If you have experience working with very young children what examples can you give where children appear to be learning on their own? What examples can you think about where children appear to learn better with the help of an adult?

Psychodynamic theories

These theories look at children's development in terms of underlying psychological processes. In particular, psychodynamic theories suggest that events in the past, especially relationships with our parents, can have a lasting effect on our emotional and social development as we get older (Brain and Mukherji, 2005). In this section we will look particularly at the work of Freud, Erikson and Bowlby.

Freud

Freud proposed that our personalities are composed of three parts that develop throughout childhood and are influenced by relationships and experiences that we encounter.

- The Id is the most primitive part of our personality, present at birth and concerned with our survival. The Id demands the instant gratification of our basic needs and desires. It is largely unconscious and is that part of our personality that is present at birth.
- The Ego develops as babies grow older and is that part of the personality that helps us understand that the demands of the Id cannot always be met immediately. Children use skills such as planning and negotiating to help them balance the demands of the Id and the knowledge of what is 'allowed'.
- The Super Ego is the part of the personality that tells us what we should or should not do, that is, 'what is allowed'. The Super Ego is formed by us internalizing the teaching from parents and others in authority over us. The Super Ego is influenced by our conscience and moral values (Pound, 2011).

Freud described how children pass through stages in social and emotional development and that children who encounter painful experiences may become 'stuck' at a particular stage of development. Freud's theories led to the practice of psychoanalysis, a talking therapy with the aim of putting individuals in touch with previously unconscious emotions and internal conflicts which have exerted a negative influence on their feelings and behaviour. His theories have also led to the development of play therapy where children are encouraged to use play and creative activities to express emotions that they may be unable to put into words (Mukherji, 2001)

Erikson

Erikson was profoundly influenced by the work of Freud; he also proposed that individuals pass through different stages. Erikson saw development as a lifelong search for a sense of identity during which individuals have to face a series of challenges or problems (Pound, 2011). For example, in the first year of life babies face the challenge of developing trust in their caregivers. Children who are looked after by unresponsive adults may fail to develop this sense of trust, which may negatively affect their ability to form relationships when they are older (Mukherji, 2001). This idea is very similar to the ideas of Bowlby (Lindon, 2005).

Bowlby and attachment theory

Attachment theory exerts a powerful influence on early childhood policy and practice. Because of this you will find it discussed in several different chapters in this book, for example it is looked at in Chapter 10 where children's health and well-being is discussed and in Chapter 16 when we look at children's personal, social and emotional development. For many years it has been recognised that secure attachment relationships to their main carers is vital for children's emotional development and well-being. However, it has become increasingly clear that secure attachment relationships may be the basis for almost all aspects of development. Attachment is a two-way process of bonding between an infant and their main caregiver, so that the infant develops a close and secure relationship with their attachment figure and has a safe base from which to explore (Bowlby, 2005).

Bowlby, and subsequently his research assistant Ainsworth, described the various stages that babies go through in developing attachment relationships with their main carers. At birth babies show that they can tell their mother from other people but exhibit no distress if the mother is not there. By three months babies start to smile at their caregivers and over the next few months begin to show a preference for people they know. True attachment behaviour is shown from about seven months when babies begin to show separation anxiety. Other attachment behaviours involve children in trying to keep in close contact with their attachment figure (proximity seeking) and using the attachment figure as a safe base, which allows the infant to go off and explore on their own as long as the attachment figure is within sight. From about 10 months old babies begin to show social referencing, that is they look to their attachment figure to see if a new situation is safe, and fear of strangers may be shown. It is usual for infants to become securely attached to one or two adults at first, usually their mothers and fathers, but the number of attachment relationships increases as children get to form close relationships with other family members and, perhaps, their key person in childcare settings (Mukherji, 2001).

Secure attachments are developed over time and are the result of a two-way process of interaction with the baby and the caregiver. The process has been described as 'serve and return' by the Center on the Developing Child (n.d.) because it involves the baby initiating contact, for example by smiling or vocalising, and the adult picking up on this and responding. For attachment relationships to develop there needs to be time and opportunity for the baby and caregiver to get to know each other and to develop the way that they respond to each other, which is why babies develop best when they are cared for by a limited number of people. Sensitive and responsive parenting will support the development of secure attachment relationships.

Secure attachment relationships not only foster a sense of security for babies, but are also the root of social and emotional development. It is through these attachment relationships that babies are supported in their cognitive and linguistic development, begin to develop a sense of identity and are encouraged to use their developing physical skills.

Caregivers who are ill, depressed or stressed may have difficulty in maintaining the consistent, sensitive and responsive relationship that is needed to promote effective attachments. Babies who do not form effective attachment relationships are at risk of developing long-term difficulties with both physical and mental health that persist into adulthood (Robinson, 2008). Because of this, supporting parents in forming and maintaining sensitive and responsive attachment relationships with their children has become an important part of the work of early childhood services in the UK and is a key role of the Healthy Child Programme (DoH, 2009). Attachment theory has informed and guided practice in early childhood settings where the importance of every child having a key person is emphasised. The key person relationship is discussed in more detail in Chapter 16.

The importance of early brain development (0–3)

So far in this chapter we have looked at historical attempts to explain how children develop. In this section we will look at what up-to-date research on brain development has to tell us and the implications that this may have for practice, especially for the 0–3-year-olds.

The Center on the Developing Child (n.d.) outlines the following features of children's development based on the findings of brain research.

1. Experiences build brain architecture; genes provide a basic blueprint for how children develop, but exactly how the brain develops depends upon the experiences an infant encounters (starting from experiences within the womb). The quality of an infant's experiences influences whether or not the child has a strong foundation for learning, health and behaviour, or a fragile foundation.
2. Interaction between genes and experience shapes the brain. An important mediator of this process is the 'serve and return' relationship between infants and their main caregivers. Babies and infants naturally reach out to those around them by

smiling and babbling. If caregivers do not respond sensitively to these initiatives then the brain's architecture does not develop as expected which can lead to future difficulties in learning and behaviour.

3. The brain is at its most flexible early in life, but as children grow older they are less able to adapt.
4. Emotional well-being and social competence are the foundation of all human learning.
5. Chronic stress in early childhood, due to extreme poverty, abuse or maternal depression is toxic to the developing brain and can lead to lifelong problems relating to learning, behaviour and physical and mental health.

Reflection

The Center on the Developing Child, Harvard University has an excellent website full of up-to-date information on children's development. It can be found at: http://developingchild.harvard.edu/#

Investigate this site, look at some of the videos and read some of the research papers. You will find information here that you will find useful throughout your degree course.

1. Write a paragraph on how babies' brains are shaped by experience.
2. What are the implications for early childhood practitioners of this new understanding?
3. How have research findings from brain studies influenced early childhood policy?

There are, however, words of caution about misinterpreting exactly what brain research is telling us (Shonkoff and Bales, 2011). One widely held misconception is that brain development is effectively closed by the age of 3 years, whereas research shows us that, although it responds much more rapidly in early childhood, the brain retains a degree of plasticity throughout life. Other misguided applications of the theory have led to parents 'hot housing' their infants in an effort to give maximum stimulation to the brain. Shonkoff and Bales (2011) give the example of parents of newborn babies being given tapes of Mozart to play to them in an effort to boost their babies' IQs.

Neuroscientific findings have been very influential in guiding policy. Much of the emphasis on early childhood provision has been driven by the understanding that the early years are vital years.

A critical look at developmental theory

The study of child development arose out of the scientific discipline of psychology at the turn of the last century in America. Kehily (2004: 7) describes developmental psychology as identifying the stages and transitions of childhood (in the Western world). Childhood is seen as an 'apprenticeship for adulthood' where 'the progression from child to adult involves children in a developmental process wherein they embark upon a path to rational subjectivity'.

Developmental psychology has, undoubtedly, made a huge contribution to our understanding of childhood and the importance of the early years for our future success and well-being as adults. Research findings have had a profound effect on policy makers and practitioners in the fields of childcare, education, health and social work, as well as influencing our ideas about what it means to be an effective parent. It is, however, important to recognise that some theorists, for a variety of reasons, are critical of developmental theory.

Is the concept of childhood universal?

The study of child development assumes that there is a universally-held idea that a period in life, called 'childhood' exists.

James and Prout (199.7), whilst acknowledging that children are different from adults in that they are biologically immature, suggest that the psychological approach to studying children should be replaced by one that takes a more sociological approach. They suggest an alternative view of children and childhood, which Kehily (2004) summarises in the following way:

- The idea of 'childhood' is socially constructed.
- 'Childhood' is one of many variables that can be used in social analysis (like gender or class).
- Children's relationships and cultures are worthy of study 'in their own right', not just as a stage towards maturity.
- Children are active social agents, affecting as well as being affected by the world around them.
- The best method to study children is not the scientific quantitative approach, but ethnography, a qualitative approach that seeks to get an in-depth understanding of children within the context of their 'normal' lives.
- Studying childhood requires researchers to engage in the process of reconstructing conceptions of childhood in society. (Kehily, 2004: 8)

Reflection

What do you understand by the phrase 'childhood is socially constructed'?

Child psychology is based on western research

From the onset of the discipline of developmental psychology, most research was undertaken either in the United States or in Europe. The social, cultural and political context in which the research was conducted led to the findings not being applicable to children from other parts of the world and for other cultures (Burman, 2008).

Aldgate et al. (2006) explain that there may be very different expectations for children's social development across cultures. For example, in western culture, independence is a prized goal for children. Children are encouraged to feed themselves and dress themselves at an early age. In other cultures, a climate of dependency is encouraged and it is not unusual for children to be fed by their mothers long after this would be 'normal' for western children (Dwivedi, 2002).

Developmental psychology imposes a concept of 'normality'

One of the aims of early researchers such as Gesell (Harris, 2008), was to describe the pathways of development in children. His research led him to test and measure hundreds of children and publish descriptions of how children develop, which are often referred to as 'developmental schedules' or 'developmental norms' (Brain and Mukherji, 2005). Underpinning this research was a belief that healthy children would follow a predictable pattern of development, which was influenced by biological maturational processes. From his research he described norms of development that were used to tell if individual children were developing in the same way as other children, or were advanced or delayed in aspects of their development. Since his work, many other researchers have produced similar 'schedules of development', one of the most famous being Mary Sheridan's book *From Birth to Five* (Sheridan et al., 2008), which is widely used by health professionals for monitoring children's development.

Cannella (1997) suggests that this approach describes development as a linear process and marginalises children who do not follow the same developmental pathway as others, for example children with disabilities or special educational needs. With this approach the emphasis is often on what children can't do rather than what they can do. In addition Cannella points out that the youngest children are seen to be the most 'incompetent', and that children in general are seen to be lacking something, as compared to fully developed adults (Pound, 2011).

Reflection

Extension to Level 6

Erica Burman, in her 2008 book *Deconstructing Developmental Psychology* identifies five themes which she uses to organise her critique of developmental psychology. What is the significance of her analysis on the way developmental psychology is used to guide early childhood policy and practice?

To download this task as well as other useful online resources please visit: **www.sagepub.co.uk/mukherji**

Summary

In this chapter we have investigated various ways that theorists have tried to explain the factors that influence children's development. We have seen that historically there have been attempts to ascribe human development mainly to innate characteristics or to environmental factors. Nowadays we know that there is a complex interaction between the environment and biology, as described in the transactional model of development. We discussed the limitations of developmental psychology and looked at Bronfenbrenner's ecological systems theory, which, whilst recognising the individuality of the child, sees children's development as being influenced by social and economic factors. Three different approaches to looking at children's learning and development were described: behaviourism, constructivist theories and psychodynamic theories. The contribution that brain research has made was discussed. Finally, we looked at some of the criticisms that have been made of developmental psychology.

Further reading

Levels 4 & 5

Lindon, J. (2012) *Understanding Child Development 0–8 Years* (3rd edition). London: Hodder Education. This is a very basic child development text that is a good start for students who are returning to study after a number of years.

Whitebread, D. (2012) *Developmental Psychology and Early Childhood Education*. London. Sage. This is a very clearly written text which gives the latest research findings and relates these to early childhood practice.

Level 6

Harris, M. (2008) *Exploring Developmental Psychology: Understanding Theory and Methods*. London: Sage. This text looks at different theoretical approaches to the study of child development and looks at the methods used when researching in this area.

References

Aldgate, J., Rose, W. and Jeffery, C. (2006) *The Developing World of the Child*. London. Jessica Kingsley.

Athey, C. (2007) *Extending Thought in Young Children* (2nd edition). London: Sage.

Bandura, A. (1977) *Social Learning Theory*. New York: General Learning Press.

Bjorklund, D. and Blasi, C. (2005) 'Evolutionary and developmental psychology', in D. Buss (ed.) (2005) *The Handbook of Evolutionary Psychology*. New Jersey: Wiley.

Bjorklund, D.F. and Pellegrini, A.D. (2000) 'Child development and evolutionary psychology', *Child Development*, 71(6): 1687–708.

Bowlby, J. (2005) *The Making and Breaking of Affectional Bonds*. London: Routledge Classics.

Brain, C. and Mukherji, P. (2005) *Understanding Child Psychology*. Cheltenham: Nelson Thornes.

Burman, E. (2008) *Deconstructing Developmental Psychology* (2nd edition). Abingdon: Routledge.

Cannella, G. (1997) *Deconstructing Early Childhood Education: Social Justice and Revolution*. New York. Peter Lange Publishing Inc.

Center on the Developing Child. Harvard University (n.d.). Available at: http://developingchild.harvard.edu/# (accessed 30 September 2012).

Davies, D. (2011) *Child Development: A Practitioner's Guide*. New York: Guilford Publications.

Department for Education (DfE) (2012) *Statutory Framework for the Early Years Foundation Stage: Setting the Standards for Learning, Development and Care for Children from Birth to Five*. London: DfE.

Department of Health (DoH) (2009) *Healthy Child Programme*. Available at: https://www.gov.uk/government/uploads/attachment_data/file/167998/Health_Child_Programme.pdf (accessed 5 August 2013).

Dwivedi, K.(2002) 'Culture and personality', in K. Dwivedi (ed.), *Meeting the Needs of Ethnic Minority Children* (2nd edition). London: Jessica Kingsley.

Harris, M. (2008) *Exploring Developmental Psychology: Understanding Theory and Methods*. London: Sage.

Hopkins, W. (2001) 'Genes and training for athletic performance', *Sports Science*, 5(1). Available at: http://www.sportsci.org/jour/0101/wghgene.htm

James, A. and Prout, A. (eds) (1997) *Constructing and Reconstructing Childhood*. London: Falmer Press.

Kehily, M. (2004) 'Understanding childhood: An introduction to some key themes and issues', in M. Kehily (ed.), *An Introduction to Childhood Studies*. Maidenhead: Open University Press/McGraw Hill.

Lindon, J. (2005) *Understanding Child Development: Linking Theory and Practice*. London: Hodder Arnold.

Lindon, J. (2012) *Understanding Child Development 0–8 Years* (3rd edition). London: Hodder Education.

Mukherji, P. (2001) *Understanding Children's Challenging Behaviour*. Cheltenham: Nelson Thornes.

National Scientific Council on the Developing Child (2010) *Early Experiences Can Alter Gene Expression and Affect Long-Term Development: Working Paper No. 10*. Available at: http://developingchild.harvard.edu/ (accessed 24 September 2012).

Piaget, J. (2001) *The Psychology of Intelligence*. London: Routledge Classics.

Polfuss, M. and Fenn, M. (2012) 'Parenting behaviors of African American and Caucasian families: Parent and child perceptions, associations with child weight, and ability to identify abnormal weight status', *Journal of Pediatric Nursing*, 27(3): 195–205.

Pound, L. (2011) *Influencing Early Childhood Education: Key Figures, Philosophies and Ideas*. Maidenhead: Open University Press.

Robinson, M. (2008) *Child Development From Birth to Eight*. Maidenhead: Open University Press.

Robson, S. (2006) *Developing Thinking in Young Children: An Introduction for Students*. London: Routledge.

Rutherford, M. (2011) *Child Development: Perspectives in Developmental Psychology*. Toronto: Oxford University Press.

Schaffer, R. (2007) *Key Concepts in Developmental Psychology*. London: Sage.

Sheridan, M., Sharma, A. and Cokerill, H. (2008) *From Birth to Five: Children's Developmental Progress* (3rd edition). Abingdon: Routledge.

Shonkoff, J. and Bales, S. (2011) 'Science does not speak for itself: Translating child development research for the public and its policymakers', *Child Development*, 82(1): 17–32.

Skinner, B. (1974) *About Behaviourism*. New York: Random House, INC.

Swick, K. and Williams, R. (2006) 'An analysis of Bronfenbrenner's bio-ecological perspective for early childhood educators: Implications for Working with families experiencing stress', *Early Childhood Education Journal*, 33(5): 371–8.

Tickell, C. (2011) *The Early Years: Foundations for Life, Health and Learning: An Independent Report on the Early Years Foundation Stage to Her Majesty's Government*. London: DfE.

Underdown, A. (2007) *Young Children's Health and Wellbeing*. Maidenhead: Open University Press.

Vygotsky, L. (1978) *Mind in Society: The Development of Higher Psychological Processes*. Cambridge MA: Harvard University Press.

Whitebread, D. (2012) *Developmental Psychology and Early Childhood Education*. London: Sage.

6

How Children Learn

Linda Pound

This chapter will:

- Help you to consider the power and wonder that surrounds human learning and thinking
- Explore theories relating to the development of cognition
- Support your understanding by focusing on children's learning as it is presented in the EYFS (DfE, 2012)
- Discuss children's right to learn in ways which correspond to their ways of knowing and understanding.

Human learning is a fascinating subject. Our magnificent brains have, over thousands of years, enabled us to change, grow and adapt to a vast array of contexts and conditions. Humans are frequently described as the architects of their own brains and this is recognition of the flexibility or plasticity of our minds. It is increasingly clear that learning goes way beyond cognition and involves movement, relationships with others, feelings and communication – now described within the EYFS (DfE, 2012) as prime areas of learning and development. There is also recent research and understanding about the vital role of music in learning. This is interesting since it has long been considered fundamental to practice within many approaches to early childhood education. Some writers (see e.g. Bresler, 2004; Claxton, 1997) describe a holistic approach to learning as involving a variety of 'ways of knowing' (including physical and affective), which continue to underpin learning throughout life – not just before school.

New theories from old

Our understanding of how people, not just children but humans in general, learn has been constantly evolving – although as will be discussed in Chapter 8, those who have worked with children, observed them carefully and know them well have had some remarkably keen insights into the processes of learning and development. The pioneers of early education achieved this without benefit of current research techniques or neuro-imaging.

Psychology as a discipline in its own right emerged during the latter part of the nineteenth century. Its early history reflects its roots, in physiology, statistics and philosophy – elements which remain evident today (see Pound, 2013a). The first psychology textbook was published in 1874 by Wilhelm Wundt, a German physiologist. Wundt also opened the first laboratory devoted to psychology in 1879, and two years later published the first psychology research journal.

Francis Galton, Charles Darwin's cousin, published the first journal devoted to the subject in 1876, and opened his anthropometric laboratory in 1884. Galton's interest was in human differences, including those to be found in levels of intelligence. It is he who is considered responsible both for the development of the use of statistics in psychology and for identifying the tension between nature and nurture in human intelligence, a debate which continues to rage today. The third element in the birth of psychology is represented by the publication of the philosopher William James's book *Principles of Psychology* in 1890. Since that time, key developments have arisen out of dissatisfaction with existing theories or approaches to understanding the way our minds work. As Millar's words (1968: 18) remind us, 'theory does not have to be correct to be of use'.

The aim of the sections that follow is to demonstrate the way in which theories of learning evolve – as theorists build on other people's ideas, rejecting some aspects and substituting others. Gardner (1993: 25) suggests that 'theories do not die because they are deficient; they fade away when other, more appealing, more compelling, and more comprehensive views come to the fore'. Within education, theories of learning are often thought of in terms of movements such as behaviourism, psychoanalytical theories, constructivism and social constructivism, and so on. Sometimes it is addressed in terms of key figures such as Piaget, Vygotsky, Bruner or Freud, for example. In this chapter, three movements or approaches which have arisen out of criticisms of other theories have been identified and are explored in this chapter. In some cases, as with multiple intelligence theory a single theorist is involved, in this case Howard Gardner. In other cases, such as behaviourism and psychoanalytical theory, a large number of theorists have been involved in creating and modifying an approach.

A word of caution: behaviourist theories of learning are widely referred to as Learning Theory but you need to differentiate between these and other theories of learning, or learning theories – of which there are many. Learning Theory refers only to behaviourist approaches (as described in Chapter 5).

Reflection

As you read the sections that follow, consider in what ways the emerging theories are more appealing, compelling or comprehensive than the ones they seek to replace. (If you are not familiar with any of the theories or theorists mentioned look them up, either online or in a standard textbook so that you have some background understanding.)

Humanistic psychology

In the 1940s, Carl Rogers, Charlotte Buhler and Abraham Maslow established a new movement which they called humanistic psychology. They described it as a third force in psychology, creating a bridge between behaviourism and psychoanalytic theory. The best known of the behaviourists is Burrhus Skinner, while Sigmund Freud is without doubt the most famous psychoanalyst, perhaps even the single most famous figure in psychology. Humanistic psychology sought to establish recognition of the role that emotions and feelings play in behaviour and learning – something denied by behaviourists. Psychoanalysis on the other hand believes that feelings cannot be ignored. Freud's approach, which Rogers believed belittled the client, was rejected by humanistic psychology in favour of what Rogers termed client-centred therapy. This aimed to help clients to become fully functioning persons (Rogers, 2004), or in Maslow's terms to develop self-actualisation (Maslow, 2011).

This approach has impacted on education and understandings of learning in a number of ways. Rogers's work (Rogers and Freiberg, 1994) led to the increased popularity of child-centred learning – subsequently redefined as child-initiated or learner-centred education. In line with his thinking about therapists, it emphasised the role of the teacher as a facilitator. The focus of humanistic psychology as a whole has also supported the growth of understanding of the importance of factors within education such as learning dispositions (Dowling, 2010), emotional intelligence (Goleman, 1996) and involvement and well-being (Laevers and Heylen, 2003).

One further factor is worth considering. Rogers emphasises a sense of excitement as a factor in supporting learning. This is echoed by theorists such as Egan (1991) who refers to the importance of the 'ecstatic responses' of young children. More recently, excitement has been identified by neuroscientists (see e.g. Eliot,

1999) as important in changing the chemistry of the brain, thus making learning more effective.

Cognitive psychology

Ulric Neisser (n.d.) is widely known as the father of cognitive psychology, which was the title of his first book published in 1967. Unhappy, like the humanistic psychologists, with the focus of both psychoanalysis and behaviourism, he proposed a different alternative. Despite coming from totally different disciplines, the early psychologists such as Wundt and James were all interested in the internal workings of the mind, using an approach they termed introspection. They were interested in aspects of cognition such as attention and perception and they 'reported on the activities of their own conscious minds' (Neisser, 1976: 2). Wundt, for example, developed glasses with lenses which inverted all he saw. He meticulously recorded what he saw, how he felt and his surprise that he was able to report that after a short period of use he no longer saw things upside down. His brain interpreted what he saw.

Behaviourism, which emerged from the work of Ivan Pavlov, John Watson and most famously Burrhus Skinner, rejected the idea of mind – because it could not be seen. Instead, behaviourism focused on actions that could be observed. This contrasts sharply with psychoanalytic theory which focuses on internal motivations. Neither, as far as Neisser was concerned, seemed to recognise the importance of finding out how humans come to know and understand the world around them. Paradoxically, he seems to have ignored the work of Piaget, who had been working on *epistemology* (or the nature of knowledge) since the 1930s. This underlines the gap both between European and American psychologists and between those engaged in psychological research and those, such as Piaget, working in the field of early cognitive development.

Gopnik et al. (1990: vii) describe cognitive psychology as having 'united psychology, philosophy, linguistics, computer science and neuroscience'. It is suggested that the use of computer models to explain human behaviour (cognitive science) and the use of computer programs to reproduce human thinking (artificial intelligence or AI) (Fleck, 1982) have provided a major boost to our understanding of human learning. However, despite their enthusiasm for thinking of the brain as a computer, Gopnik et al. (1990: 21) admit that they 'don't know just what kind of computer the brain is' and that the thinking of 'babies and children look(s) very different from the computers we have now' (1999: 148).

Other writers (see e.g. Cohen, 2002) are less enthusiastic about the idea of the brain as a computer. Bruner started out as a cognitive psychologist. Together with George Miller, Bruner established the Center for Cognitive Studies, at Harvard in 1960. Miller had trained in behaviourism, but was among the first to challenge its scientific principles. Miller and Bruner's choice of the word 'cognitive' was an act of defiance, signalling an interest in the mind – rather than just actions (Vitello, 2012). By the 1990s, Bruner had rejected the suggested links between human thought and learning and the artificial intelligence found in computers. What such theories ignore, he believes, is the human and cultural elements of cognition. Since that time his focus has been largely on the relationship between learning, culture and narrative (see e.g. Bruner, 1996, 2003).

The impact of cognitive psychology has been immense. Covering topics such as visual perception, memory, thinking, attention, language, reasoning, judgement, decision making, problem solving, emotion and consciousness, a vast number of approaches has come to be included within cognitive psychology. Described by Pinker (Kahneman, 2011: cover) as 'the most important psychologist alive today', Kahneman suggests that cognitive psychology has applications in every walk of personal and professional life. Within early childhood education the most high-profile areas are probably cognitive neuroscience and developmental cognitive psychology which continue to proliferate.

Multiple intelligence theory (MIT)

MIT is widely applied to education. In developing his theory of multiple intelligences, Howard Gardner (1993) considers a number of theorists who have in a variety of ways influenced his thinking – both for positive and negative reasons. Referring to the publication of Darwin's observations of his son William's development in 1877, Gardner describes Darwin as having done 'more than any other figure to stimulate scientific study of the mind of the child' (1993: 24). Two very distinct branches of psychology – Gesell's maturationist theory of development and the behaviourism or Learning Theory of Watson and Skinner – claimed to have their roots in Darwin's observations. Gesell believed that development was a matter of nature, or maturing, and meticulously detailed the milestones of early development. The behaviourists, on the other hand, believed that all learning and development was due to upbringing.

It has been suggested that Gesell's painstaking documentation of developmental stages paved the way for Piaget's stage theory of development. Gardner (1993: 26) praises Piaget's efforts 'to understand the nature of knowledge and children's mechanisms for learning'. However, he makes four major criticisms of Piagetian theories:

- Piaget argued that development consists of a series of qualitative shifts (for example from the sensori-motor to the pre-operational stage of development; and from the pre-operational to the concrete operational). This view is likened to taking a snapshot – rather than continuous observation – and as such leads to a view that there has been a giant leap, while the development in fact maybe nothing more than a series of tiny steps.

- Piaget believed that moving from one stage to another involved the same qualitative shift in all areas of learning – whereas current thinking and research, and even straightforward observation, show that this is not the case. A child may remain at a sensori-motor stage of development in some areas while performing at an operational stage in others. Bruner rejected this yoked view of development and proposed (see Bruce, 2011) that we all revert to enactive or iconic modes of thinking and learning when tackling something new or difficult – even though we may be operating symbolically most of the time.
- Although Piaget claimed that his theories covered all aspects of knowledge, Gardner believes that he placed too great an emphasis on mathematics and logic.
- His fourth criticism is linked to the second. Gardner (1993: 29) argues that:

> Piaget made a fundamental error in his contention that the older child's more sophisticated ways of knowing eradicate her earlier forms of knowing the world. ... Rather than being eradicated or transformed, they simply travel underground; like repressed memories of early childhood, they reassert themselves in settings where they seem to be appropriate.

This echoes Bruner's view that earlier stages of development do not disappear and work on creativity, which suggests that to be creative requires a child-like approach.

Defining MIT

MIT arose from dissatisfaction not merely with existing theories of learning but in particular with existing theories of intelligence. The first intelligence test, which was devised by Binet and Gardner, highlights the way in which the measurement of intelligence has come to underpin so much of society's approaches to learning.

Reflection

Gardner raises three questions, his answers to which lead him to reject any idea of measured intelligence:

- Is there just one general intelligence or are there different more specific intelligences?
- Is intelligence inherited or is it the result of personal effort or experience?
- Are intelligence tests biased?

Consider your answers to these questions and identify some reasons that support your view.

Gardner identifies a number of intelligences – which White (2008) criticises on a number of counts, but tellingly describes as reflecting Gardner's biography (see Gardner, 1999). It is true to say that the rationale Gardner offers for his selection does closely mirror his professional career. Originally, the intelligences identified were: linguistic; musical; logical-mathematical; spatial; bodily-kinaesthetic; and interpersonal and intrapersonal intelligences. He subsequently added naturalist intelligence. He further proposed an existential intelligence – concerned with spiritual and philosophical awareness. Gardner claims (1999) that his rationale for selecting intelligences has been based on:

- Brain research (which has helped to identify areas of the brain linked to particular aspects of learning and development).
- Developmental journeys, as exemplified by language development.
- Cross-cultural comparisons – music, for example, is found in all cultures.
- Evolutionary psychology.
- Identifiable components of the intelligences known as sub-intelligences. In the case of spatial intelligence, for example, the sub-intelligences might be 'sensitivity to large-scale, local, three-dimensional and two-dimensional spaces' (1999: 37).
- The possibility of being encoded in a symbol system. Language, music, dance and mathematics all have their own symbol systems (although it is less clear how the personal intelligences are encoded).
- Savants or prodigies having singular exceptional qualities indicate the existence of one or other of Gardner's intelligences.
- Experimental psychological tasks which require subjects to do two things at once. If they have difficulty it is likely that the tasks fall within the same intelligence. If not, like walking and talking, then they are likely to belong to different intelligences.
- Results of intelligence tests – despite his rejection of intelligence testing Gardner has used some of their results in an effort to find out whether there are any connections between aspects of measured intelligence (1999). This helps to determine whether intelligence tests actually measure what they claim or whether they are simply measuring general abilities such as speed or logic, for example.

Effective early learning

Development Matters in the Early Years Foundation Stage (Early Education, 2012) and the *Statutory Framework for the Early Years Foundation Stage* (DfE, 2012) highlight the characteristics of effective learning. Three areas of learning and development are to be regarded as prime areas, namely: communication and language; physical development; and personal, social and emotional development. Moylett and Stewart (2012) compare these prime areas to what have been termed specific areas of learning and development, namely: literacy; mathematics; understanding of the world; and expressive arts and design. They suggest that development within the prime areas is 'time sensitive'.

This means that if not acquired early, their acquisition may be more difficult and may make other learning more difficult. They go on to argue that the prime areas are important in all cultures and that development in these areas is not dependent on other learning. This, they claim, is unlike learning in the specific areas where learning is dependent on communicative, physical and personal development.

In this section, these aspects of current policy will be considered alongside a range of theoretical views about children's learning. In addition, there will be exploration of the role of music in all three of the prime areas of development, since there is persuasive and increasing evidence of the way in which it underpins early development (see e.g. Malloch and Trevarthen, 2009).

What is involved in effective learning?

The characteristics of effective learning highlighted in the EYFS (DfE, 2012) provide a helpful starting point. Moylett and Stewart (2012: 9) point out that the publication of the EYFS 'now makes it mandatory for practitioners to respond not just to **what** children learn, but also **how** they learn' (emphasis in original). Tables 6.1, 6.2 and 6.3 explore some of the theoretical underpinnings employed in the identification of these characteristics.

Table 6.1 Theoretical underpinnings of playing and exploring (left-hand column based on Moylett and Stewart, 2012: 10)

Finding out & exploring	
Showing curiosity about objects, events and people	Children are born curious – seeking to make sense of everything going on around them, beginning with the people that surround them (see e.g. Reddy, 2008; Trevarthen, 2011).
Using senses to explore the world around them	Sensory experiences are of vital importance in early learning. Eliot (1999: 123) suggests that 'early experiences at touching and being touched are incredibly important – not only for molding later tactile sensitivity, motor skills and understanding of the physical world but also for ... health and well-being'. Greenfield (2007: 25) argues that 'it is when senses are activated together – the sound of a voice in synchronisation with the movement of a person's lips – that brain cells fire more strongly than when stimuli are received apart'. Blakemore (2001) suggests that in the early years the right side of the brain predominates, making touch and social contact of prime importance.
Engaging in open-ended activity	When Margaret Donaldson (1978) developed a critique of Piaget's work, she placed emphasis on the fact that 'children seem more concerned to discover what a *person* means than to determine precisely what his *words* mean' (Donaldson et al., 1983: 4). This is of particular importance when children are being told what to do – rather than an adult building on what they are doing. Donaldson (1978) drew attention to the way in which children have to set their minds to interpreting what the adult is asking of them – a task which she suggests requires considerable self-control on the part of the young child.
Showing particular interests	Open-ended activity has the added advantage of demonstrating to adults more of what children are able to do and are interested in. This in turn allows adults to tune into children – supporting their learning more effectively.

Playing with what they know	
Pretending objects are things from their experience	Children generally begin to do this in the second year of life – pulling a potato on a string, in place of a longed-for dog; pretending to eat or use a phone. Steiner practice emphasises the importance of materials which allow children to improvise and transform – a piece of wood may be a credit card or a sandwich or it may suddenly be transformed into a boat or a book (see e.g. Nicol and Taplin, 2012).
Representing their experiences in play Taking on a role in their play	Vivian Gussin Paley (see e.g. 1990) writes eloquently of the value of children's play. In the many books she has written she explores the impact that re-presenting ideas and experiences in play can have on children (and the adults who work with them). Like Paley, Haven (2007) argues for the power of story. Imaginative play enables children both to develop an understanding of narrative and of other minds, which is the key to learning (Hobson, 2002; Siegel, 1999; Trevarthen, 2011).
Acting out experiences with other people	The discovery of mirror neurons (see e.g. Ramachandran, 2011) has underlined the vital importance of imitation in learning.
Being willing to 'have a go'	
Initiating activities	This willingness is closely linked to the characteristics of well-being identified by Laevers (1997). He argues that for children aspects such as acting spontaneously, being open to the world around them and showing vitality and self-confidence indicate a sense of well-being which makes learning more possible.
Seeking challenge	Dweck (2006) suggests that mindset is of great importance for learning and achievement. Much of her writing has focused on the importance of recognising that success is the result of effort. Children who believe that cleverness is fixed and that nothing they do will change their achievements, do much less well than those who understand that effort is the crucial factor.
Showing a 'can do' attitude	Practitioners will be aware of the way in which, when they have the opportunity, young children constantly challenge themselves.
Taking a risk, engaging in new experiences, and learning from failure	Space does not allow a proper discussion of the importance of risk-taking. However, it is clear that there are widespread concerns about the lack of opportunity for children to learn to manage risk (Little and Wyver, 2008; Palmer, 2006). Ken Robinson (http://www.ted.com/talks/lang/en/ken_robinson_says_schools_kill_creativity.html) suggests that 'if you're not prepared to be wrong, you'll never come up with anything original'. There is evidence (see Eliot, 2010) that parents are more cautious with girl babies, even though boys are known to be more physically vulnerable and young baby girls equally ready to tackle risky situations (Pound, 2013b).

Reflection

Look at the characteristics of playing and exploring outlined in Table 6.1 and try to identify some examples from your own practice. The case study below might also help you to think of some further examples.

CASE STUDY

Fifteen-month-old Isabel, with the art of walking firmly under her belt, set out to challenge herself. Over several days she first walked a path over gravel, grass, stepping stones set unevenly in the grass and a textured manhole cover. Having tried that and succeeded in completing her obstacle course she began to master it while pushing her doll's buggy. The next challenge involved loading the buggy – at first with dolls, then with bags of mixed objects, large and small – working up to a scooter which hung over the edges and unbalanced the buggy.

Table 6.2 Theoretical underpinnings of active learning (left-hand column based on Moylett and Stewart, 2012: 13)

Being involved & concentrating	
Maintaining focus on their activity for a period of time	Active learning is a phrase often associated with Piaget. This connection is echoed in the fact that he wrote about a stage of sensori-motor development. Piagetian theory suggests that this physical approach to learning is something we grow out of. However, Bruner (1966) termed his first stage of development *enactive* and put forward the theory that we, as learners, constantly return to that stage when we meet new or complex ideas. But active learning is not confined to the physical – it also implies active seeking out of understanding and knowledge as well as taking responsibility for learning.
Showing high levels of energy and fascination Not easily distracted Paying attention to details	Concentration; energy; complexity and precision; and persistence are among the characteristics of involvement highlighted by Laevers (1997). For Laevers 'deep-level-learning' is only possible when there are high levels of well-being and involvement in learners. His rating scales for both are widely used in many settings (see Pascal and Bertram, 1997). High energy or excitement has already been seen to be regarded as an important factor in learning (see section on humanistic psychology).
Keep on trying	
Persisting with activity when challenges occur Showing a belief that more effort or a different approach will pay off Bouncing back after difficulties	Dweck's work underlines the importance of the mindset of the learner – persistence is a learning disposition (Dowling, 2010) and is more likely to occur where children are able to demonstrate and follow their own interests. Dweck reminds practitioners that 'praise can lead students to fear failure, avoid risks, doubt themselves ... and cope poorly with setbacks' (2000: 2). Adults have a vital role to play in promoting persistence and resilience. Vygotsky's theory of the Zone of Proximal Development (ZPD) is relevant here. Adults observing children can often pinpoint an appropriate moment to step in and help. If too early, children may give up and feel that they can't do whatever they are attempting; too late and the child may give up in a torrent of frustration. Time it just right and the child can be helped to achieve with adult support what he or she would not be able to achieve alone.
Enjoying achieving what they set out to do	
Showing satisfaction in meeting their own goals	Kohn (1999) has written a seminal text on the importance of intrinsic rather than extrinsic rewards. Kohn criticises behaviourist approaches as undermining children's ability or willingness to meet challenges for their own sake.

Being proud of how they accomplished something – not just the end result Enjoying meeting challenges for their own sake rather than external rewards or praise	Related research has been conducted into willpower or cognitive control (see Mischel et al., 2011) since it looks at learning dispositions. You may have seen references to experiments in which young children were promised two marshmallows if they could resist eating one while the researcher is out of the room. If you are not familiar with these experiments you can view a short film on http://www.eatmedaily.com/2009/09/psychological-experiments-in-self-control-the-marshmallow-test/ which describes the technique. Mischel et al. (2011) claim that children who are able to demonstrate cognitive control subsequently show higher levels of achievement.

Reflection

Look at the characteristics of active learning outlined in Table 6.2 and try to identify some examples from your own practice. The case study below might also help you to think of some further examples.

CASE STUDY

Twelve-month-old Zac drops a small toy into his mother's wellington boot. He can see it but not reach it; his arm is just too short. For several minutes he persists in attempting to reach it – also experimenting with the other boot. Two or three times he picks up the relevant boot and starts to turn it upside down but at the last minute returns it to the upright position. This may be because the boot is too heavy but whatever the reason he doesn't quite manage to tip the toy out. Finally, after a great deal of persistence, he signals that he needs his mother's help and she turns the boot upside down. This allows him to see the solution to his problem and how close he was to solving it.

Table 6.3 Theoretical underpinnings of creating and thinking critically (left-hand column based on Moylett and Stewart, 2012: 14)

Having their own ideas	
Thinking of ideas Finding ways to solve problems	Young children have little difficulty in coming up with ideas (Gardner, 1993). These ideas, however, need to be nurtured rather than smothered (Robinson, 2011). Problem solving requires experience and opportunities to observe how others solve problems.
Finding new ways to do things	There is evidence that when children are engaged in problems of their own finding they are more likely to be actively engaged and more likely to identify a broad range of strategies for solving the problem (Robson, 2006).

(continued)

Table 6.3 *(Continued)*

Making links	
Making links and noticing patterns in their experience	Making connections is essential to all learning. The links made in play, exploration and conversation, which may arise from interests or from function, create connections in the brain (Eliot, 1999). Brains love pattern (Lucas, 2001): we seek them out and impose patterns where others might see none. This is both an important part of everyday life and a particular feature of mathematical understanding (Pound and Lee, 2011). Other important links arise from family, community and culture. The work of Bronfenbrenner (1979) has been an important factor in raising awareness of the ways in which children are influenced by those around them. Rogoff (2002) has been called the guardian of Vygotsky's theories and has closely studied cultural practices in offering children guided participation to bring them into the culture of the home.
Making predictions/ Testing their ideas	Patterns enable us to predict. Estimating or guessing is a vital part of everyday life. If you had to calculate the time needed to cross a road we'd never make it home each day – but because we guess, based on experience and on our brains' remarkable capacity for estimation, we can cross a number of roads with little conscious thought. Prediction involves risk-taking – there's a chance that we could get it wrong so it is essential to establish a climate of trust (http://www.ted.com/talks/lang/en/tim_brown_on_creativity_and_play.html). Again, Laevers (1997) speaks of feeling at ease, expressing inner relaxation, self-confidence and being in touch with one's feelings as vital ingredients of well-being. In relation to trust, we should not underestimate the impact of psychoanalytical theory. Susan Isaacs was a trained psychoanalysis and this is evident in her writing about young children (e.g. Isaacs, 1930). This is also true of John Bowlby. For many years Bowlby's work was criticised as over-stating the importance of attachment, but more recently his theories have gained renewed interest as the impact of cortisol on brain development is studied (see e.g. Elfer et al., 2003; Gerhardt, 2004; Palmer, 2006).
Developing ideas of grouping, sequences, cause and effect	Piaget was interested in the factors in young children's thinking and learning which he believed limit their abilities. He identified the fact that for young children simultaneous events are believed to have a cause and effect link (or transduction). He offers the example of the wind, which, for example, is commonly believed by young children to be caused by the trees waving. He also wrote about juxtaposition reasoning – asked to group similar objects, Piaget observed that children placed things together with no understanding of why they did so (Singer and Singer, 1990). More recent interest in narrative (see e.g. Haven, 2007) has shown that if asked children will often explain their groupings in narrative terms. This may explain why children have difficulty in tidying up or sorting objects. Their reasons for putting things together differ from those of adults!
Choosing ways to do things	
Planning, making decisions about how to approach a task, solve a problem and reach a goal Monitoring how effectively their activities are going Changing strategy as needed Reviewing how well the approach worked	These learning strategies closely reflect the points made about creativity in the NACCCE report (1999). Robinson (2011) highlights the fact that creativity involves doing, imagining, originality and valuing – which relates to the emphasis in Moylett and Stewart (2012) on monitoring, changing strategy and reviewing. The work of Guy Claxton on 'learnacy' (2008) is also relevant here. He argues that there are 4Rs – resilience, reflection, resourcefulness and reciprocity (by which he means the ability to work alone and with others).

Reflection

Look at the characteristics of active learning outlined in Table 6.3 and try to identify some examples from your own practice. The case study below might also help you to think of some further examples.

CASE STUDY

Context: Colin (2:9) (a boy), Flora (4:1) and Ingrid (6:1) (both girls) are playing in the garden on a hot sunny day.

Observation: Flora and Ingrid are on the swing in the shade. Colin collects unripe walnuts that have fallen from a tree. He finds a bucket to put them in and begins to throw them one by one into the paddling pool. He gets into the paddling pool, gathers them up and begins to throw them into the bucket which is on the grass. He notices that grass clippings have stuck to him, gets out of the paddling pool and spreads soil and clippings over his body. He runs over to the swing and begins 'being' a monster. The girls leave the swing and begin to chase – all three sometimes being monsters and sometimes victims. They all get into the paddling pool. Monsters begin 'eating' walnuts. Ingrid proposes a shop but when she puts the bucket into the paddling pool it topples over. She finds a large flat stone which, when placed in the bucket, makes it stand. She finds some smaller stones for money. Flora gets out of paddling pool and tips the bucket of stones out onto the grass. She retrieves the large stone and puts it into the paddling pool with a big splash. All three begin to jump in and out making bigger and bigger splashes. They become repeatedly covered in mud and wash it off as they jump into the water. They accompany this with a return to the monster theme, with shouts of 'I'm a monster – now I'm all clean'. Ingrid takes the stone out of the water, completely covers herself in mud and stands on the stone being a statue. Flora brings one of the small stones and presses it into Ingrid's outstretched hand, whereupon the statue begins to dance. She clasps Flora to her and twirls her around, deftly placing her on the plinth to be a statue. Flora obliges. Ingrid presses a coin into her hand and the dancing begins again.

This observation demonstrates many aspects of play and exploration. Consider how these children are developing their cognition and make a list.

(Continued)

(Continued)

Does your list include any of the following?

- Showing curiosity. They explore the stones and nuts, and they had recently visited London's South Bank where there are a number of living statues.
- Exploring properties of materials such as floating and sinking. Using the large stone to prevent the bucket toppling over requires experience and problem-solving capacities.
- Demonstrating interests.
- Pretending that objects are something else and in the process allowing them to transform into different objects – money, food, children into statues, stone into plinth, children into monsters, and so on.
- Representing experiences and imagining and acting out situations they have never seen, such as dancing statues.

Alternative views of learning and development in the early years

The EYFS (DfE, 2012) has broadly maintained the areas of learning and development outlined in previous versions of the English curriculum framework for the early years. This is in marked contrast to *Birth to Three Matters* (DfES, 2003: 5), which stated that it took 'as its focus **the child** and steers away from subjects, specific areas of experience and distinct curriculum headings' (emphasis in original). It identifies four aspects 'which celebrate the skill and competence of babies and young children: namely a strong child; a skilful communicator; a competent learner; and a healthy child'. The framework for children up to the age of 3 in Scotland (Trevarthen and Marwick, 2002) is of an entirely different character. The framework lists requirements for 'out-of-home' provision for under one, under two and under three year olds. The focus is on relationships; responsive care and respect.

The renowned provision of Reggio Emilia has no set curriculum. It is based on an underpinning philosophy which focuses on the child as a strong and competent learner and places a strong emphasis on parents and community. The development of symbolic representation is a vital element of practice, with every setting employing an *atelierista* or artist to lead learning. Like the Montessori and HighScope approaches the learning environment is seen as being of fundamental importance.

Te Whāriki, the New Zealand early years curriculum framework, brings yet another perspective to learning. The five strands are linked to what are termed children's voice questions (drawn from Podmore, 2004: 153):

Strand: Children's voice questions:

- Belonging: Do you know me?
- Well-being: Can I trust you?
- Exploration: Do you let me fly?
- Communication: Do you hear me?
- Contribution: Is this place fair for us?

A musical note

Contributors to Malloch and Trevarthen's (2009) weighty book make clear their belief in the power of music and in its role in:

- The development of human characteristics and understandings as a species. Mithen (2005) outlines the elemental role of music in the development of human capabilities. Music or rhythmic movement is highlighted as being the starting point of language (Mithen, 2005) and mathematics (Brandt, 2009). Davies (2003) suggests that 'all human activity is dynamically and rhythmically charged and structured'.
- The development of individual babies. Papousek (1994) describes the voice as the first toy, while Goddard Blythe (2005) suggests that movement is our first language and music our second. What cannot be denied is that movement and music are intrinsically linked, especially in young children who cannot control the urge to move rhythmically to music. As in babies, it seems likely that in human development, dance preceded music and singing preceded spoken language (Pound and Harrison, 2003). Blakemore (2001) underlines the importance of music in the early years as it is during this period that the right side of the brain is particularly active and alert in garnering sensory experience and coming to understand human emotion and interaction.

The growing evidence that supports the elemental importance of music makes it particularly sad that music has not been given a more explicit role in the EYFS. But the fact that it is not easily found in the relevant documentation does not mean that practitioners should not give it a high profile in practice – especially as it involves so many of the listed characteristics of effective learning.

Journal Task

Lowenstein, A. (2011) 'Early care and education as educational panacea: What do we really know about its effectiveness?', *Educational Policy*, 25(1): 92–114.

(Continued)

(Continued)

Levels 4 & 5

This article questions the extent to which policies advocating early intervention in order to support learning and development make a difference.

1. Consider the model of learners and learning which underpin the studies described. Are the characteristics identified ones that you would support?
2. If, as Lowenstein suggests, the quality of primary school education affects the impact of early childhood education, what implications does this have for your work with children and families?

Level 6

Is *school readiness* enough to expect from early interventions? What is needed to make a difference to children's lives in the long term? What changes do you think could be made to practice and policy in the early years to ensure that the impact of early intervention is more long lasting?

To download this task as well as other useful online resources please visit: **www.sagepub.co.uk/mukherji**

Summary

In summary, this chapter has considered the way in which theories of learning have evolved from one another, building on some elements and discarding others. It raises questions about the kind of learning and learners sought in a range of countries inviting critical reflection on current frameworks for learning.

Further reading

Levels 4 & 5

Gray, C. and MacBlain, S. (2012) *Learning Theories in Childhood*. London: Sage. This book provides a useful overview of theories about how children learn, and is succinct and readable.

Stewart, N. (2012) *How Children Learn: The Characteristics of Effective Early Learning*. London: Early Education. The focus of this book is the importance of young children's disposition to learn. The author emphasises self-regulated learning and highlights three strands, namely: playing and exploring; active learning; and creating and thinking critically.

Level 6

House, R. (ed.) (2011) *Too Much, Too Soon?* Stroud, UK: Hawthorn Press. Chapters have been contributed by a wide range of well-respected authors, researchers and theorists, each challenging the status quo of early childhood care and education. You may not agree with everything you read but the text will offer thought-provoking ideas about young children's learning.

Kohn, A. (1999) *Punished by Rewards*. New York: Houghton Mifflin Company. To read more about the problems associated with behaviourist approaches and effective learning in the long term, try Kohn's book. It sets out in detail the negative effects that rewards (or punishments) can have on learning.

Pound, L. (2011) *Influencing Early Childhood Education*. Maidenhead: Open University Press. The author provides a chronological overview of the influences, both pedagogical and theoretical, which have shaped, and continue to shape, our views of young children's learning.

References

Blakemore, C. (2001) 'Early learning and the brain', *RSA Journal*, 148/9 Issue 5491/5504.

Brandt, P. (2009) 'Music and how we became human', in S. Malloch and C. Trevarthen (eds), *Communicative Musicality*. Oxford: Oxford University Press.

Bresler, L. (2004) *Knowing Bodies, Moving Minds: Towards Embodied Teaching and Learning*. London: Kluwer Academic Publishers.

Bronfenbrenner, U. (1979) *The Ecology of Human Development*. London: Harvard University Press.

Bruce, T. (2011) *Early Childhood Education* (4th edition). London: Hodder.

Bruner, J. (1966) *Towards a Theory of Instruction*. Cambridge, MA: Belknap Press of Harvard University Press.

Bruner, J. (1996) *The Culture of Education*. Cambridge, MA: Harvard University Press.

Bruner, J. (2003) *Making Stories: Law, Literature and Life*. Cambridge, MA: Harvard University Press.

Claxton, G. (1997) *Hare Brain: Tortoise Mind*. London: Fourth Estate.

Claxton, G. (2008) *What's the Point of School?* Oxford: Oneworld Publications.

Cohen, D. (2002) *How the Child's Mind Develops*. London: Routledge.

Davies, M. (2003) *Movement and Dance in Early Childhood* (2nd edition). London: Paul Chapman Publishing (Kindle edition).

Department for Education (DfE) (2012) *Statutory Framework for the Early Years Foundation Stage: Setting the Standards for Learning, Development and Care for Children from Birth to Five*. London: DfE. http://www.foundationyears.org.uk/ or https://www.education.gov.uk/

Department for Education and Skills (DfES) (2003) *Birth to Three Matters*. London: DfES.

Donaldson, M. (1978) *Children's Minds*. London: Fontana.

Donaldson, M., Grieve, R. and Pratt, C. (1983) *Early Childhood Development and Education*. Oxford: Basil Blackwell.

Dowling, M. (2010) *Young Children's Personal, Social and Emotional Development* (3rd edition). London: Sage.

Dweck, C. (2000) *Self-theories: Their Role in Motivation, Personality and Development*. Hove: Psychology Press.

Dweck, C. (2006) *Mindset: The New Psychology of Success*. New York: Ballantine Books.

Early Education (2012) *Development Matters in the Early Years Foundation Stage*. http://www.early-education.org.uk/

Egan, K. (1991) *Primary Understanding*. London: Routledge.

Elfer, P., Goldschmeid, E. and Selleck, D. (2003) *Key Persons in the Nursery*. London: David Fulton.

Eliot, L. (1999) *Early Intelligence*. London: Penguin Books Ltd.

Eliot, L. (2010) *Pink Brain, Blue Brain*. Oxford: Oneworld Publications.

Fleck, J. (1982) 'Development and establishment in artificial intelligence', in N. Elias, H. Martins and R. Whitley (eds), *Scientific Establishments and Hierarchies*. Holland: D. Reidel.

Gardner, H. (1993) *The Unschooled Mind*. London: Fontana.

Gardner, H. (1999) *Intelligence Reframed*. New York: Basic Books.

Gerhardt, S. (2004) *Why Love Matters*. Hove, E. Sussex: Brunner-Routledge.

Goddard Blythe, S. (2005) *The Well-balanced Child*. Stroud: Hawthorn Press.

Goleman, D. (1996) *Emotional Intelligence*. London: Bloomsbury Publishing.

Gopnik, A., Melttzoff, A. and Kuhl, P. (1990) *How Babies Think*. London: Weidenfeld and Nicolson.

Greenfield, S. (2007) 'Style without substance', *Times Educational Supplement*, 27 July.

Haven, K. (2007) *Story Proof*. Westport, CT: Libraries Unlimited.

Hobson, P. (2002) *The Cradle of Thought*. London: Macmillan.

Isaacs, S. (1930) *Intellectual Growth in Young Children*. London: Routledge.

James, W. (1890) *Principles of Psychology*. London: MacMillan.

Kahneman, D. (2011) *Thinking Fast and Slow*. London: Allen Lane.

Kohn, A. (1999) *Punished by Rewards*. New York: Houghton Mifflin Company.

Laevers, F. (1997) *A Process-oriented Child Monitoring System for Young Children*. Belgium: Leuven University.

Laevers, F. and Heylen, L. (2003) *Involvement of Teacher and Children Style: Insights from an International Study on Experiential Education*. Leuven: Leuven University Press.

Little, H. and Wyver, S. (2008) 'Outdoor play: Does avoiding the risks reduce the benefits?', *Australian Journal of Early Childhood*, 33(2): 33–40.

Lucas, B. (2001) *Power Up Your Mind*. London: Nicholas Brealey.

Malloch, S. and Trevarthen, C. (2009) *Communicative Musicality*. Oxford: Oxford University Press.

Maslow, A. (2011) *Towards a Psychology of Being* (3rd edition). New York: John Wiley & Sons (first published 1968).

Millar, S. (1968) *The Psychology of Play*. Harmondsworth: Penguin Press.

Mischel, W., Ayduk, O., Berman, M., Casey, B., Gotlib, I., Jonides, J., Kross, E., Teslovich, T., Wilson, N., Zayas, V. and Shoda, Y. (2011) '"Willpower" over the life span: Decomposing self-regulation', *Social Cognitive and Affective Neuroscience*, 6(2): 252–6. http://scan.oxfordjournals.org/content/6/2/252.short (accessed 31May 2012).

Mithen, S. (2005) *The Singing Neanderthals*. London: Weidenfeld and Nicolson.

Moylett, H. and Stewart, N. (2012) *Understanding the Revised Early Years Foundation Stage*. London: Early Education.

NACCCE (1999) *All our Futures: Creativity, Culture and Education*. Sudbury: DfEE Publications.

Neisser, U. (1967) *Cognitive Psychology*. New York: Appletone-Century-Crofts. Cited in: http://www.psychologicalscience.org/index.php/publications/observer/2012/may-june-12/remembering-the-father-of-cognitive-psychology.html

Neisser, U. (1976) *Cognition and Reality*. Reading: WH Freeman and Co.

Nicol, J. and Taplin, J. (2012) *Understanding the Steiner-Waldorf Approach: Early Years Education in Practice*. London: David Fulton.

Paley, V.G. (1990) *The Boy Who Would be a Helicopter*. London: Harvard University Press.

Palmer, S. (2006) *Toxic Childhood*. London: Orion Books Ltd.

Papousek, H. (1994) 'To the evolution of human musicality and musical education', in I. Deliège (ed.), *Proceedings of the 3rd International Conference on Music Perception and Cognition*. Liège: ESCOM.

Pascal, C. and Bertram, T. (1997) *Effective Early Learning: Case Studies in Improvement*. London: Sage.

Podmore, V. (2004) 'Questioning evaluation quality in early childhood', in A. Anning, J. Cullen and M. Fleer (eds), *Early Childhood Education: Society and Culture*. London: Sage.

Pound, L. (2013a) *Cognitive Development*. London: Hodder.

Pound, L. (2013b) *Physical Development*. London: Hodder.

Pound, L. and Harrison, C. (2003) *Supporting Musical Development in the Early Years*. Buckingham: Open University Press.

Pound, L. and Lee, T. (2011) *Teaching Mathematics Creatively*. London: Routledge.

Ramachandran, V.S. (2011) *The Tell-tale Brain: Unlocking the Mystery of Human Nature*. London: William Heinemann.

Reddy, V. (2008) *How Infants Know Minds*. London: Harvard University Press.

Robinson, K. (2011) *Out of Our Minds*. Chichester: Capstone Publishing Ltd.

Robson, S. (2006) *Developing Thinking and Understanding in Young Children*. Abingdon: Routledge.

Rogers, C. (2004) *On Becoming a Person*. London: Constable and Robinson Ltd (first published 1961).

Rogers, C. and Freiberg, H.J. (1994) *Freedom to Learn* (3rd edition). Princeton: Prentice Hall (first published 1969).

Rogoff, B. (2002) *Learning Together: Children and Adults in a School Community*. Oxford: Oxford University Press.

Siegel, D. (1999) *The Developing Mind*. New York: The Guilford Press.

Singer, D. and Singer, J. (1990) *The House of Make-believe*. London: Harvard University Press.

Trevarthen, C. (2011) 'What is it like to be a person who knows nothing? Defining the active intersubjective mind of a newborn human being', *Infant and Child Development*, 20(1): 119–35.

Trevarthen, C. and Marwick, H. (2002) *Review of Childcare and the Development of Children aged 0–3: Research Evidence and Implications for Out-of-home Provision*. Edinburgh: Scottish Executive.

Vitello, P. (2012) 'George A. Miller, a pioneer in cognitive psychology, is dead at 92', *New York Times*, 1 August. http://www.nytimes.com/2012/08/02/us/george-a-miller-cognitive-psychology-pioneer-dies-at-92.html?pagewanted=all (accessed 13 September 2012).

White, J. (2008) 'Illusory intelligences', *Journal of Philosophy of Education*, 42(3–4): 611–30.

7

The Importance of Play

Justine Howard

This chapter will:

- Outline the status of play from a policy and legislative perspective
- Explore the distinction between play as observable behaviour and playfulness as a particular way of thinking about how children approach their activities (as well as the significance of this distinction for children's development)
- Consider how children's play and development are inextricably linked.
- Explore evidence for particular features of play that support children's health, emotional well-being and holistic development
- Outline the important role you have as an early years practitioner in facilitating children's development through providing optimum play experiences.

When you become an early years practitioner, you also become a *play professional*. Understanding the importance of play in the lives of children and young people, and facilitating appropriate play experiences, is one of the most important things that you will do in your career. Central to understanding the importance of play is recognising that children's emotional health lays the foundation for their happy and healthy development.

As you have seen in Chapters 5 and 6, although psychologists talk about children's development in relation to Social, Physical, Intellectual, Communication and Emotional domains (SPICE), in reality, development in all of these areas is intricately linked. These chapters also explain the ways in which children learn and develop from a psychological perspective, for example with reference to: social learning theory (learning by modelling and imitation); psychosocial perspectives (the importance of early experiences); behavioural theory (learning by association and reinforcement); cognitive approaches (the way in which we independently accrue new intellectual skills); and socio-cultural approaches (the importance of other people in shaping our learning and development).

The status of play from a policy and legislative perspective

The value of children's play for their healthy development is now widely recognised in various policies and forms of legislation throughout the United Kingdom and beyond. Children's right to play is also recognised in the United Nations Convention on the Rights of the Child (UN, 1989). Lester and Russell (2010: 12) argue that 'Play is not a luxury to be considered after other rights; it is an essential and integral component underpinning the four principles of the UNCRC'.

King and Howard (2012) describe the development of play policies in Wales, England, Scotland and Ireland, which all emphasise the need for children to have the opportunity to experience high-quality, developmentally appropriate play provision from emotional, health and well-being, educational and recreational perspectives. Play features in the Special Educational Needs and Disability Act (2001), Every Child Matters (DfES, 2004b) and the Disability Discrimination Act (2005), as well as the Children's Plan (DCSF, 2007).

The Play Policy, as part of the Children's plan (DCSF, 2007) had wide-ranging aims including:

- A variety of places for play, free of charge, supervised and unsupervised in every residential area.
- Local neighbourhoods are, and feel like, safe, interesting places to play.
- Routes to children's play space are safe and accessible for all children and young people.
- Parks and open spaces are attractive and welcoming to children and young people, are well maintained and well used.
- Children and young people have a clear stake in public space and their play is accepted by their neighbours.
- Children and young people behave in a way that respects other people and property.
- Children, young people and their families take an active role in the development of local play spaces.

- Play places are attractive, welcoming, engaging and accessible for *all* local children and young people, including disabled children, children of both genders, and children from minority groups.

Although the Play Policy (DCSF, 2007) is no longer in place because of changes made by the new coalition government, much had already been done to ensure children's right to play was recognised. For example:

- The Foundation Phase in Wales and Foundation Stage in England centralise play as a vehicle for learning in early years curricula and practitioners have received training in play.
- Children's centres increasingly support play by involving play therapists, family service co-ordinators, language and play officers, play-workers, play development officers, filial therapists and portage workers.
- There is additional support for play in schools, including improving play facilities on school sites.
- Children and young people have more opportunities for physical activity, physical education and sport.
- The need for creativity in play has been emphasised by involving partnerships between creative art professionals and children's services.
- Play provision is supported for children visiting parents in prison.
- The links between play-based activities and other provision for young people has been emphasised, for example in residential care settings, domestic violence teams, and hospice care.
- Provision emphasises how play must support the inclusion of disabled children.

What exactly is play and how does it contribute to development?

As discussed earlier, children learn and develop in many different ways, so why is play so important?

Reflection

Think about a particular play activity (for example, a group of children in an early years setting playing in the sand). Make a list of all of the things you think children are learning whilst they participate in the activity (consider all the developmental domains – 'SPICE').

Go through your list and identify any learning which you think could not be achieved unless the child was engaged in play. Is there any skill or developmental outcome that *couldn't* be achieved in another way?

Here is an example of what you might come up with.

The scenario

Three children aged 4, are playing in the sand. They have funnels, small containers and shovels. As they dig they are finding leaves, fir cones and conkers. Once they find something they put it into a container. They have made up rules so that each child is in charge of one particular object. One child is collecting the leaves, another, the cones and another, the conkers. Sometimes things are put into the wrong place. Sometimes the children want to keep the items they have found for themselves.

Table 7.1 Identifying the learning opportunities in a play scenario

Learning opportunity	Developmental domain	Could this be learned in other ways and not through play?
Making up and sticking to the rules	Cognitive/social	Yes
Turn taking	Social	Yes
Sorting and learning about the properties of objects	Cognitive	Yes
Learning new words	Language/communication	Yes
Using the spade	Physical (fine motor)	Yes
Picking up items and placing in the container	Physical (fine motor)	Yes

How do your ideas compare with those in Table 7.1? I have run this activity many times with students, and they usually end up with no areas of learning that are unique to play. There are many learning opportunities in play, but children can develop these skills in many others ways. The activity helps us think about what is really special about the way in which children learn through play. Let's take a look at that now.

Play and development

Play offers children the opportunity to develop key skills across domains. Some particular skills associated with each developmental domain are listed below.

Social development

- Gaining the attention of adults and other children
- Learning about social influence
- Co-operation and copying
- Sharing and turn taking
- Social interaction, reciprocity and mutuality
- Organisation of the world
- Culture and societal rules
- Learning about roles and gender.

Physical development

- Develops sensory awareness
- Gross motor activity (e.g. movement and dance)
- Fine motor activity (e.g. threading, drawing)
- Learning about size, shape, gravity
- Learning about our own body (boundaries, limits)
- Balance and muscular strength
- Spatial awareness and co-ordination.

Intellectual development

- Development of memory
- Opportunities for exploration and experimentation
- Develops concentration and attention span
- Learning about predictability and expectations
- Developing reasoning skills
- Problem solving (both confidence and ability)
- Linking cause and effect
- Promotes changes in cognition relating to theory of mind and perspective taking.

Communication/language development

- Provokes a need to communicate
- Is an interactive process (internal and external)
- Non-verbal communication (NVC), gestures and vocalisation can be practised in play
- Acts as 'proto conversation' through turn taking
- Facilitates labelling and the naming of objects
- Develops organisational skills (e.g. narratives for the play)
- Learning about acceptable and unacceptable language (pragmatics)
- Children can play with language (making sounds, learning rhymes).

Emotional development

- Love, security, relationships
- Physical contact and intimacy
- Reading non-verbal cues and recognising emotion
- Regulation of feelings
- Developing a concept of self, self-awareness and self-esteem
- Facilitates the growth of emotional vocabulary and the ability to express feelings
- Provides situations where trust, independence and initiative can emerge
- Develops empathic understanding and a recognition of the needs of others.

Reflection

Consider the developmental domains above, and match them to the core and specific areas in the EYFS (DfE, 2012).

Theories of play

Although children learn in lots of different ways, they have a predisposition toward play. Over the years various theories about the value of play have been proposed – see Table 7.2.

Table 7.2 Theories about the value of play

Surplus energy theory (Schiller, 1873; Spencer, 1875)	Play is a means of releasing excess energy. Here, play is seen as aimless exuberant activity.
Relaxation theory (Lazarus, 1883; Patrick, 1916)	Play replenishes energy supplies in preparation for more important cognitive tasks and prevents cognitive fatigue.
Pre-exercise theory (Groos, 1898)	Play provides children with opportunities to practice survival skills.
Recapitulation theory (Stanley Hall, 1906)	Play is a primitive behaviour which is no longer needed for survival but has remained through evolution.
Cathartic theory (Freud, 1908)	Children play to resolve conflicts and fulfil basic drives.
The psychoanalytic tradition (Buhler, 1930; Freud, 1937)	Play helps cope with anxiety.

These early ideas were largely philosophical with no real evidence to support them, however, they resonate with newer evidence-based theories. For example, arousal modulation theories propose that play provides an optimum means of self-regulation. Over-stimulating environments require exploration to reduce nervous activity, while under-stimulating environments require play to increase nervous activity (Berlyne, 1968). Similarly, more recent evidence-based bio-cultural accounts of play propose that limited opportunities for free play negatively influence the development of social skills which could explain increased anti-social behaviour in modern society (Jarvis, 2007).

Anna Freud (1895–1982) and Erik Erikson (1902–1994) developed early psychoanalytical ideas about play which were very influential in therapeutic work with children and in playwork. Erikson also contributed to our understanding as to how play contributes to emotional health from a developmental perspective.

Later, theorists began to consider the way in which play contributed to development more systematically. Piaget (1951) suggested that the type of play children engaged in was concordant with their cognitive ability, for example practice play during the sensorimotor stage, symbolic play in the pre-operational stage and games with rules emerging at the stages of formal and concrete operations. For Piaget, play was not a major learning activity, but rather served to consolidate ideas learned elsewhere. In contrast, for Vygotsky (1978) play was a leading activity and acted as its own zone of proximal development, enhancing children's development across domains. For Vygotsky, the symbolism demonstrated in play was children's first form of language. Bruner (1972) and Sutton-Smith (1997) propose that play is important for children's development, providing an environment where children are free to experiment with ideas. This view is supported by animal studies such as that of Fagan (1984) who found that rats reared in an enriched environment had denser and more complex brain structures. Siviy (1998) proposes that this is because play activity stimulates the production of proteins responsible for the development and nourishment of brain cells. These theories suggest that there is something special about play that contributes to development.

Types of play and their development over time

Several theorists have attempted to categorise children's play behaviour and a variety of typologies have been proposed. Hughes (2006) suggests that there are 16 play types:

- Rough and tumble play – close encounter play which might involve touching, tickling, gauging strength and discovering physical flexibility.
- Socio-dramatic play – the enactment of real and potential experiences of an intense personal, social, domestic or interpersonal nature.
- Social play – where the rules and criteria for social engagement and interaction can be revealed, explored and amended.
- Creative play – that facilitates novel responses, the transformation of information, awareness of new connections or an element of surprise.
- Communication play – using words or gestures (e.g. mime, jokes, play acting, singing, rhymes, poetry).
- Dramatic play – that dramatises events in which the child does not or has not participated.
- Symbolic play – that allows control, gradual exploration and increased understanding about objects.
- Deep play – that allows children to encounter risky experiences, to evaluate risk and to conquer fear.

- Exploratory play – with factual information consisting of manipulative behaviours such as handling, throwing, banging or mouthing objects.
- Fantasy play – that rearranges the real world and in ways that are never likely to really occur.
- Imaginative play – where the conventional rules that normally regulate behaviour do not apply.
- Loco-motor play – movement in any or every direction for its own sake.
- Mastery play – control of the physical and affective ingredients of the environment.
- Object play – that uses infinite and interesting sequences of hand–eye manipulations and movements.
- Role play – that explores different ways of being, although not normally of an intense personal, social, domestic or interpersonal nature.
- Recapitulative play – that allows children to explore ancestry, history, rituals, stories, rhymes, fire and darkness, enabling children to access play of earlier human evolutionary stages.

Whitebread (2012) suggests that children's play can be divided into five different types and that children benefit from a balance of each of these. The five types are: physical play; play with objects; symbolic play; pretence/socio-dramatic play; and games with rules. These different play types emerge over time, each influencing and being influenced by children's growing repertoire of skills and development. Theorists have documented the way in which children's play develops over time from a social, emotional and cognitive perspective (see Table 7.3).

Table 7.3 The development of play

Social development	Emotional development	Cognitive development
Parten (1932): Children gradually develop social skills over time and they progress through the following types of social behaviour: 1. Unoccupied behaviour (watches but with no sign of engagement) 2. Onlooker behaviour (watches and comments but does not take part) 3. Solitary play (plays alone) 4. Parallel play (plays alongside but does not interact with others) 5. Associative play (interested in the play of others but does not engage in co-operative activity) 6. Co-operative play (interacts and negotiates) 7. Organised play (increasingly complex social rules)	Erikson (1978): Play serves the development of children's emotional health and progresses as follows: 1. Autocosmic play (play focusing on the child's own body) 2. Microspheric play (small world play as child learns to master objects and early symbolism) 3. Macrospheric play (using fantasy play to explore understanding of others and the wider society)	Piaget (1951): Children's play largely reflects their cognitive development and progresses as follows: 1. Practice play (largely sensory in nature as children explore the world around them) 2. Symbolic play/pretence (reflecting children's ability to allow one thing to stand for another) 3. Games with rules (reflecting children's increasingly sophisticated thinking and reasoning skills)

Jennings (1999) highlights the importance of developmental progress in play in her Embodiment Projection Role paradigm (EPR). She suggests that each stage of play is essential to the development of the other and offers important and unique developmental potential. The **E**mbodiment stage involves physical and sensory play where the child learns about their physical self. Once a sense of self has been established, children learn of things outside of the body and engage in **P**rojective play with objects. Finally, when children understand the perspectives of others they begin to act out **R**oles in dramatic play. Jennings suggests that children will develop a full spectrum of play abilities by the age of 7 years and that the full repertoire is important because:

- It creates the core of attachment between mother and infant
- It forms a basis for the growth of identity and independence
- It establishes the 'dramatised body', i.e. the body which can create
- It strengthens and further develops the imagination
- It contributes to a child's resilience through 'ritual and risk'
- It enables a child to move from 'everyday reality' to 'dramatic reality' and back again, appropriately
- It facilitates problem solving and conflict resolution
- It provides role play and dramatic play which in turn create flexibility
- It gives a child the experience and skills to be part of the social world.

Jennings usefully brings together the theoretical ideas of Parten, Erikson and Piaget and convincingly argues that stages must initially occur in sequence but can be returned to throughout childhood, and even adulthood as we deal with the challenges of our daily lives. That the different play types initially emerge in a developmental sequence (each one facilitating the development of the next), is important as it has implications for children who face the challenge of different or adverse circumstances. Children with disabilities involving sensory impairment may need encouragement and support in developing the skills associated with early types of play in order to move forward into pretend and role-play experiences. As the content of play is often shaped by life experience and context, individual differences in play from the perspective of culture are also important. Children of all cultures develop the skills necessary to progress through the different play types, however the content of their play is likely to reflect the norms and values of their culture, including culturally specific toys and play materials, and the nature of the parenting style they have experienced (Sheridan et al., 2011). More detailed information about how difference and diversity may impact on play, along with related professional practice issues, including those related to SEN, are described by Howard and McInnes (2013, see Further reading).

Play as an approach to task – playfulness

Play means different things to different people at different times (Spodek and Saracho, 1987). Activities which 'look like play' may not necessarily feel like play for the person taking part (Howard, 2002). Take a look at the following example of a real scenario I once observed in a nursery classroom in which I was working.

CASE STUDY

Mrs Fraser has been reading 'Mrs Pepperpot' to the children in her Reception Class. The children have really enjoyed listening to the story and some activities extending the book have been planned throughout the week. Today, Mrs Fraser has put out an exciting array of materials in the centre of the craft table. There is air-dry clay in various colours, buttons, lollypop sticks and pipe cleaners. The children are excited to hear that they are going to be making a finger puppet of Mrs Pepperpot. In the centre of the table, Mrs Fraser has put an example of a Mrs Pepperpot puppet she made earlier as a model for the children. She organises the children to work three at a time to complete the task and sits with them as they do so.

Jessica: Look Mrs Fraser, I have done my body [holds up clay shape pressed onto her finger].

Mrs Fraser: Wow, is that the right colour though Jess?

Jessica: I like pink.

Mrs Fraser: Do you remember from the book? Have a look [points at the model in the centre of the table].

Jessica: oh ... [slowly peels off the pink, carefully places it to one side and picks up the 'correct' blue clay and starts again].

Paul: Just the buttons left now, pass me the buttons Jess.

[Mrs Fraser watches as Paul selects four buttons and sticks them onto his model.]

Mrs Fraser: One, two, three, four buttons Paul, is that how many she has? Count again [Paul counts his buttons and takes one off].

Joel: Woooooh woooooh [Joel stands up and 'flies' his Mrs Pepperpot puppet on his finger through the air] she is flying, off we go.

Mrs Fraser: Shush now Joel and sit down, let me take a look. Oh yes, you're done. Put her on the side and off you go to the sand now. Send Ben for his turn.

Joel: [Looks sad to have to stop playing with what he has made.] Can I take it with me?

Mrs Fraser: No, put her on the side now, she'll get spoiled over there and we want to put them all on display.

(Continued)

(Continued)

Joel: [Looks at the puppet on his finger for a few seconds before carefully taking her off.] ...oh ok.

Jessica: Can I go now Miss? [Her model is not finished but she is not keen to carry on.]

Mrs Fraser: No, come on Jess, you have the buttons left [passes her the three correct buttons]. Put these on, then you can go.

- What do you notice about the interactions which took place during this 'play' activity?
- Do you think the activity was 'play'? Why? Why not?
- How do you think the children felt about this activity?
- Have you ever observed a similar 'play' situation?
- How do you think the children's experience could have been improved?

Although we frequently refer to play as 'children's work', young children are clearly able to distinguish play from other types of activity, particularly when they enter nursery and primary school. Children know the difference between contrived play experiences, activities which are designed to look like play (Walsh et al., 2011) and authentic play experiences, activities that children really feel are play (Howard and McInnes, 2013). Children learn in many different ways and whilst they almost certainly do learn through contrived play activity (such as that described above), the experience does not maximise the characteristics of play that can enhance their learning and development.

A key feature of authentic play activity, separating it from other learning experiences, is that it facilitates a way of thinking (or an approach to task) that motivates and encourages children to try out a variety of new behaviours in a safe environment. It protects children's sense of self and allows them to face emotional and intellectual challenge without the fear of failure (Fearn and Howard, 2012). Basically, we must offer children the opportunity to engage in activities which they themselves see as being playful (Howard and McInnes, 2013). To do this, we need to understand what children themselves see as the defining characteristics of play (Smith et al., 1986). Research has demonstrated that for children, a key characteristic of play is a feeling of control and autonomy (Howard, 2002; Wing, 1995). Even if a task is not entirely self-chosen, children need to feel they are directing the course of the activity and any end product. They also learn to distinguish play from other types of activity according to where and with whom it takes place. For example, if children always do their work at a table and their play on the floor or other areas of the classroom, table-top activity will come to be associated with work and not play. Similarly, if adults mainly attend to children during formal directed activities, children will learn to associate them with these activities and not accept them into their play as a play-partner.

Research has used these cues to manipulate experimental conditions to measure the impact of children seeing an activity as play or not play. McInnes, Howard, Miles and Crowley (2009) studied how children behaved when they practised a jigsaw puzzle activity. All children were initially timed to see how quickly they could complete a puzzle. Following this the children practised doing some more puzzles for 10 minutes in either a 'play' or 'not like play' condition. In the 'play' condition, children were told there were some puzzles on the carpet if they would like to have a go. No adult was present. In the 'not like play' condition, children were asked if they would like to sit at the table and do some more puzzles. The adult remained with them but pretended to complete some writing and did not interact with the child. After they had done the puzzles for 10 minutes, they were timed on the initial puzzle again. Children who had practised in the 'play' condition did significantly better in this second trial than children who had practised in the 'not like play' condition. Analysis of the video recordings of children whilst they practised with the puzzles also revealed some interesting differences. In the play-like condition, the children were more involved, less distracted and tried out various ways of solving the jigsaw. They rotated the pieces and organised them into piles of pieces they had tried and not tried out. They talked to themselves as they tried to fit each piece into its correct position. In the 'not like play' condition, however, the children were less engaged, more easily distracted and were less systematic in their attempts to problem solve, often trying the same incorrect piece in a position over and over again.

Research by Whitebread (2010) also found that in activities where characteristics of play are present, children demonstrate higher levels of self-regulation and meta-cognition. Importantly, a study of 139 children participating in an activity they either saw as play or not play (based on choice, adult presence and activity location) has demonstrated that children show significantly higher levels of emotional well-being in play activity (Howard and McInnes, 2012). This supports theories which suggest that approaching an activity as though it were play, protects self-esteem and enables learning and exploration in a safe environment. The following is an extract from Howard and McInnes, 2013: 134–7:

Playfulness as a key factor in facilitating authentic play experiences

Howard and McInnes (2013) propose that research evidence demonstrates how children's perception of playfulness (i.e. approaching an activity as though it were play rather than not play) offers a unique contribution to development in seven particular ways.

Attachment and other social relationships

Play contributes to the healthy development of early attachment bonds, for example in games like 'peek-a-boo'. These warm, trusting relationships provide the child with a secure base from which they develop the confidence to explore the world around them and also play a vital role in the development of what Bowlby (1997) describes as the Internal Working Model (IWM – an internal system which the child uses to shape their growing relationships with others). Play provides valuable opportunities for the development of these new relationships (Panksepp, 2007), and also, where attachments are insecure or have been broken, it can function to restore and rebuild confidence and trust. Positive playful experiences where children feel autonomous and in control of their activities, can serve to remodel the IWM and contribute to many therapeutic techniques for children who have attachment difficulties.

Effective communication

Vygotsky (1978) argued that play was one of the first ways that children explore symbols and through pretence learn that one thing can stand for (symbolise) another, contributing to their future language development. Play offers a wealth of opportunities for children to develop verbal and non-verbal communication skills. They learn about turn taking, negotiation and behavioural adjustments according to context or company. Children may use play as a means of communicating their thoughts and feelings, sometimes playing out difficult or painful experiences (McMahon, 2009). In a playful environment where children feel safe and in control of events, they may be more likely to talk about any issues that are worrying them (Li and Lopez, 2008) as well as talking about their lives in general. This contributes to the growth and development of existing and new relationships. Engaging with children as a play partner enables us to get to know them and communicates to them that we value what they say and do. During play we are able to model actions and emotions, and because of the increased attention associated with activities children perceive to be play (i.e. playfulness), these are more likely to be repeated.

Independence and self-regulation

An important element of children's development is their growing independence and ability to manage their behaviour and emotions. Even during early sensory play, babies learn about their physical self and that their actions impact on the environment and those around them. Gradually, as behaviour becomes more purposeful, cause and effect are recognised. Being able to manage and control our behaviour (to self-regulate) develops over time. In early childhood, self-regulation occurs externally, children think out loud when faced with new or challenging situations. The development of self-regulatory skills is vital to development across domains and children use more self-regulatory language in activities they see as play rather than not play, activities which they approach with a playful mindset (Whitebread, 2010).

Confidence and esteem

Resilient children are those who have a balanced outlook on life and a positive sense of self (Masten and Coatsworth, 1998). When children are engaged in play they are provided with opportunities to develop confidence in their abilities since goals are self set. This reduces the impact of failure but still enables children to learn about their strengths and limitations. Children learn to master skills through play, and a sense of mastery and achievement contributes to the development of self-esteem and the ability to approach new challenges with confidence. Indicators of involvement include: deep concentration, strong motivation, satisfaction and positive energy (Laevers et al., 1997). These indicators overlap with those used in children's self-reports of self-esteem and well-being (Fattore et al., 2007).

Strategies for dealing with conflict and anxiety

Play can be a useful medium for children to communicate their thoughts and feelings. The 'unreal' aspect of play is particularly important. Sutton-Smith (2003) proposes that play enables us to experience primary emotions that could otherwise threaten to overwhelm us. It can provide distance, enabling children to cope with difficult emotions within the safety of their own play space, for example through playing out a scenario with small world toys. Play can act as a cue to both positive and negative emotions. Jennings (1999) proposes that dramatic distance paradoxically brings children closer to being able to deal with trauma and anxiety, and playful experiences offer opportunities to create positive memories which contribute to our life stories. Whilst engaged in play, children can become desensitised to particular fears or phobias, and therapists may use focused play techniques to encourage children to access repressed or unresolved issues that may be stored in the unconscious mind. Play can act as a cue for remembering, enabling children to retrieve information more effectively (Schaefer, 2011).

Flexible and adaptive thinking

Theories of play which centralise the freedom, choice and control children have in play activities, emphasise its role in promoting flexible thinking skills. The ability to adapt and be flexible is a further characteristic of the resilient child (Masten, 2001). When children approach an activity playfully, they are able to make novel connections, express individuality and creativity, and develop their imaginations. Observing children at play we are able to see progression in the way children think about objects they encounter, The pattern of 'What is this?', 'What does this do?', 'What can I do with this?' and 'What could I do with this?' continues through the lifespan (Craft, 2005).

Motivation and attention

High levels of attention and motivation can be observed when children approach an activity as though it is play and they are less distracted in activities that afford them choice and control. There is a significant difference in the amount of time an adult can sustain a child's attention during a directed task at 2 years of age compared with a child of 6 years (five minutes compared with 50 minutes). What is noticeable, however, is that children are able to concentrate for long periods in their self-directed play from a very early age. Several studies report children's increased level of motivation and enthusiasm during play (Howard and McInnes, 2012). If children are in control over what they play, where, with whom and for how long (cues they associate with playfulness), then their attention is more easily maintained.

Extract from Howard and McInnes, 2013: 134–7.

How can early years practitioners facilitate optimum play experiences?

As a professional in children's services, you will have a key role in supporting children's play experiences. Important to this is that we remember how activities must 'feel like play', that they must encourage all children to engage in a playful manner. To do this we must consider play as a process, our aim being to support children in maintaining play flow. When children are deeply engaged in their play, this is where we see maximum developmental benefit across developmental domains. Our interactions must be sensitive to children's needs and we must guard against imposing our own goals and outcomes on children's play wherever possible. In this respect we can learn much from the principles of non-directive play therapy (Axline, 1989) and the Playwork Principles. Both emphasise the need for children to be supported and kept safe in their play while guarding against any adult drive to impose power or make judgements about the quality of what is going on. This can be difficult, particularly if children choose to engage in play which follows a theme which is cynical or dark (Wood, 2010). When supporting children's play, we must carefully balance the following roles, whilst at the same time facilitating child-directed play flow:

- Play partner
- Observer
- Admirer
- Facilitator
- Model
- Mediator
- Safety officer.

To support children and to show them that we really value their play, we must become accepted as a play partner; this requires us to recognise and respond sensitively to children's play cues. Research has demonstrated that adults are more likely to be accepted as play partners, facilitating and supporting children's development to best effect, when they: use open questions, listen carefully and respond sensitively to children's responses, and offer children the opportunity to make real choices in relation to their activities (McInnes et al., 2011).

This means we must be aware of the forces that might shape our interactions, such as pressure to ensure academic achievement and meet curriculum requirements or fears in relation to health and safety. These types of pressures can result in an emphasis on direct teaching or a managing or monitoring role (Howard, 2010). Pressure towards accountability often means we strive to provide concrete evidence of achievements. In authentic play activities, children naturally perform at their best, so play offers an excellent opportunity for observation and assessment. Rather than setting children tasks related to targeted developmental outcomes, consider how you can glean the information whilst observing the children's development in naturally occurring activities. These are likely to be far more fruitful and meaningful. Whilst we have a responsibility to keep children safe, we must ensure that a drive towards safety is not overly restrictive. As is argued by Tovey (2007) it can be useful to reflect on our professional practice and ask if we are striving towards the children in our care being safe enough or as safe as possible.

Journal Task

Little, H. (2010) 'The relationship between parents' beliefs and their responses to children's risk-taking behaviour during outdoor play', *Journal of Early Childhood Research*, 8(3): 315–30.

This article looks at how parental beliefs impact on children's risk-taking behaviours during outdoor play.

Levels 4 & 5

Read the paper and summarise the key findings.

What kinds of factors impacted on whether, or to what extent, parents were likely to allow their children to take risks? What level of 'risk' do you think you would allow in children's outdoor play activity?

How do you think you would score on an attitude towards risk questionnaire? See if you can locate a copy of Franken's Attitude Toward Risk Questionnaire or one that is similar. How do you actually score? How might this impact on your practice as an early years professional?

Extension to Level 6

Outdoor play is an important part of the early years curricula in the UK and beyond. How might parental perceptions of risk-taking behaviour impact on your practice as an early years professional? How might you manage or reduce this impact?

Look carefully at the Categories of Risk Taking Behaviour (Table 1) in the article. How might this be useful in your practice as an early years childhood practitioner?

To download this task as well as other useful online resources please visit:
www.sagepub.co.uk/mukherji

Summary

This chapter has outlined the status of play from a policy and legislative perspective. It has explored the distinction between play as an observable behaviour and playfulness as a particular way of thinking about how children approach their activities (as well as the significance of this distinction for children's development). It has emphasised the importance of ensuring that children see their activities as play in order for opportunities for learning and development to be maximised. Key to this is affording children autonomy, choice and control, and ensuring that as professionals we work as equal play partners when involved in children's play activity.

The chapter has considered how play supports children's development across domains with reference to seven evidenced features of play that support children's health, emotional well-being and holistic development in both the short and long term.

Finally, the chapter has outlined key points as to how you might fulfil your important role as an early years practitioner when facilitating children's development through play.

Further reading

Levels 4 & 5

Lester, S. and Russell, W. (2010) 'Children's right to play: An examination of the importance of play in the lives of children worldwide', Working Papers in Early Childhood Development (57), Netherlands, Bernard Van Leer Foundation. This document provides a comprehensive review of the literature surrounding the role and status of play in contemporary society.

Howard, J. and McInnes, K. (2013) *The Essence of Play: A Practice Companion for Professionals Working with Children and Young People*. Abingdon: Routledge. This text considers how children's play develops and how children develop through their play. It also considers difference and diversity with a wealth of case studies and points for reflection.

Level 6

Whitebread, D. (2012) *Developmental Psychology and Early Childhood Education*. London: Sage. Provides a comprehensive evaluation of key ideas in developmental psychology and their relationship to early years practice – an accessible and invaluable resource.

Fearn, M. and Howard, J. (2012) 'Play as a resource for children facing adversity: An exploration of indicative case studies', *Children and Society*, 26(6): 456–88. This article considers the invaluable role of play for children faced with diverse situations.

Howard, J. and McInnes, K. (2012) 'The impact of children's perception of an activity as play rather than not play on emotional well-being', *Child Health Care and Development*. doi:10.1111/j.1365–2214.2012.01405.x. This article describes a study which adopts an experimental approach to demonstrate the value to emotional well-being of children approaching an activity as though it were play.

References

Axline, V. (1989) *Play Therapy*. Boston: Houghton Mifflin.

Berlyne, D. (1968) 'Laughter, humour and play' in L. Gardner and E. Aronson (eds.), *The Handbook of Social Psychology*, 2nd edition. Reading, Mass: Addison-Wesley Pub. Co.

Bowlby, J. (1997) *Attachment and Loss*. London: Pimlico.

Bruner, J.S. (1972) 'Nature and uses of immaturity', *American Psychologist*, 27(8): 687–708.

Craft, A. (2005) *Creativity in Schools: Tensions and Dilemmas*. Abingdon: Routledge.

DCSF (2007) *The Children's Plan: Building Brighter Futures*. London: DCSF Publications.

DfE (2012) *Statutory Framework for the Early Years Framework Foundation Stage: Setting the standards for Learing. Development of Care of Children from Birth to Five*. Runcorn: DfE.

DfES (2004a) The Children Act [online] HMSO2004 (c.31). Available from: http://www.legislation.gov.uk/

DfES (2004b) *Every Child Matters: Change for Children*. Nottingham: DfES Publications.

Disability Discrimination Act (2005) [online] HMSO2005 (c.13). Available from: http://www.legislation.gov.uk/

Fagan, R.M. (1984) 'Play and behavioural flexibility', in P.K. Smith (ed.), *Play in Animals and Humans*. Oxford: Blackwell.

Fattore, T., Mason, J. and Watson, E. (2007) 'Children's conceptualisation(s) of their well-being', *Social Indicators Research*, 80: 5–29.

Fearn, M. and Howard, J. (2012) 'Play as a resource for children facing adversity: An exploration of indicative case studies', *Children and Society*, 26(6): 456–88.

Howard, J. (2002) 'Eliciting young children's perceptions of play, work and learning using the activity apperception story procedure', *Early Child Development and Care*, 172(5): 489–502.

Howard, J. (2010) 'Early years practitioners' perceptions of play: An exploration of theoretical understanding, planning and involvement, confidence and barriers to practice', *Child and Educational Psychology*, 27(4): 91–112.

Howard, J. and McInnes, K. (2012) 'The impact of children's perception of an activity as play rather than not play on emotional well-being', *Child Health Care and Development*. doi:10.1111/j.1365–2214.2012.01405.x.

Howard, J. and McInnes, K. (2013) *The Essence of Play: A Practice Companion for Professionals Working with Children and Young People*. Abingdon: Routledge.

Hughes, B. (2006) *Play Types: Speculations and Possibilities*. London: Centre for Playwork Education and Training.

Jarvis, P. (2007) 'Rough and tumble play: Lessons in life'. *Evolutionary Psychology,* 4: 330–46.

Jennings, S. (1999) *Introduction to Developmental Playtherapy*. London: Jessica Kingsley Press.

King, P. and Howard, J. (2012) 'Children's perceptions of choice in relation to their play at home, in the school playground and at the out-of-school club', *Children & Society*, doi:10.1111/j.1099–0860.2012.00455.x.

Laevers, F., Bogarts, M. And Moon, J. (1997) *Experiential Education at work, Centre for Experiential Education, Commission of the European Communities SOCRATES*. Leuven: Belgium.

Lester, S. and Russell, W. (2010) 'Children's right to play: An examination of the importance of play in the lives of children worldwide', Working Papers in Early Childhood Development (57). Netherlands: Bernard Van Leer Foundation.

Li, W. and Lopez, V. (2008) 'Effectiveness and appropriateness of therapeutic play intervention in preparing children for surgery: A randomized controlled trial study', *Journal for Specialists in Pediatric Nursing*, 13(2): 63–73.

Masten, A. (2001) 'Ordinary magic: Resilience processes in development', *American Psychologist*, 56(3): 227–38.

Masten, A. and Coatsworth, J. (1998) 'The development of competence in favourable and unfavourable environments', *American Psychologist*, 53(2): 205–20.

McInnes, K., Howard, J., Miles, G.E. and Crowley, K. (2009) 'Behavioural differences exhibited by children when practising a task under formal and playful conditions', *Educational & Child Psychology*, 26(2): 31–9.

McInnes, K., Howard, J., Miles, G.E. and Crowley, K. (2011) 'Differences in practitioners' understanding of play and how this influences pedagogy and children's perceptions of play', *Early Years: An International Journal of Research and Development*, 31(2): 121–33.

McMahon, L. (2009) *The Handbook of Play Therapy and Therapeutic Play* (2nd edition). Hove: Routledge.

Panksepp, J. (2007) 'Can play diminish ADHD and facilitate the development of the social brain?', *Journal of the Canadian Academy of Child and Adolescent Psychiatry*, 16(2): 57–66.

Piaget, J. (1951) *Play, Dreams and Imitation in Childhood*. London: William Heinemann Ltd.

Schaefer, C. (2011) *Foundations of Play Therapy*. New Jersey: John Wiley.

Sheridan, M., Howard, J. and Alderson, D. (2011) *Play in Early Childhood* (3rd edition). Abingdon: Routledge.

Siviy, S.M. (1998) 'Neurobiological substrates of play behavior: Glimpses into the structure and function of mammalian playfulness', in M. Bekoff and J. Byers (eds), *Animal Play: Evolutionary, Comparative, and Ecological Perspectives*. New York: Cambridge University Press.

Smith, P. K., Takhvar, M., Gore, N. and Vollstedt, R. (1986) 'Play in young children: problems of definition, categorisation and measurement', in P.K. Smith (ed.), *Children's Play: Research Developments and Practical Applications*. London: Gordon and Breach Science Publishers. pp. 39–55.

Special Needs and Disability Act (2001) [online] HMSO2001 (c.10). Available from: http://www.legislation.gov.uk/

Spodek, B. and Saracho, O. (1987) 'The challenge of educational play,' in D. Bergen (ed), *Play as a Medium for Learning and Development*. Portsmouth, NH: Heinemann.

Sutton-Smith, B. (1997) *The Ambiguity of Play*. Cambridge, MA: Harvard University Press.

Tovey, H. (2007) *Playing Outdoors: Spaces and Places, Risk and Challenge*. Maidenhead: Open University Press.

United Nations (1989) *United Nations Convention on the Rights of the Child (UNCRC)*. Geneva: United Nations.

Vygotsky, L.S. (1978) *Mind and Society: The Development of Higher Psychological Processes*. Cambridge, MA: Harvard University Press.

Walsh, G., Sproule, L., McGuinesss, C. and Trew, K. (2011) 'Playful structure: A novel image of early years pedagogy for primary school classrooms', *Early Years*, 31(2): 107–19.

Whitebread, D. (2010) 'Play, metacognition and self regulation', in P. Broadhead, J. Howard and E. Wood (eds), *Play and Learning in the Early Years*. London: Sage.

Whitebread, D. (2012) *Developmental Psychology and Early Childhood Education*. London: Sage.

Wing, L. (1995) 'Play is not the work of the child: Young children's perceptions of work and play', *Early Childhood Research Quarterly*, 10: 223–47.

Wood, E. (2010) 'Reconceptualizing the play–pedagogy relationship: From control to complexity', in E. Brooker and S. Edwards (ed.), *Engaging Play*. Maidenhead: McGraw-Hill.

Part 3

INFLUENCING FACTORS

In the words of the Marmot review (2010: 160):

> The foundations for virtually every aspect of human development – physical, intellectual and emotional are laid in early childhood. What happens during these early years (starting in the womb) has lifelong effects on many aspects of health and well-being from obesity, heart disease and mental health, to educational achievement and economic status.

In Part 3 of *Foundations of Early Childhood* we begin to look at some of the main factors that affect children's development in their earliest years, building on the knowledge and understanding that you have acquired from reading Part 2. In Part 2 we looked at how children develop and learn, and a number of different theories were described which attempted to explain the processes involved. We saw that children's development depends upon a complex interaction between the environment in which children live and biological factors. In particular we looked at Bronfenbrenner's ecological systems theory, which sees children's development as being influenced by social and economic factors.

In Chapter 8, Linda Pound investigates the historical background to children's care and education in the UK and Europe. She demonstrates how early childhood education and care have been shaped by society's attitudes towards children, historical events and an emerging understanding of how children learn and develop.

In Chapter 9 Gianna Knowles and Penny Mukherji describe how social inequalities can have a profound effect on children's learning and development. In particular they identify how race, poverty and gender can all act as barriers to children's achievements. Knowles and Mukherji explain how, through upholding the principle of 'inclusive practice', early childhood settings are ideally placed to promote equality and counteract discrimination. The chapter investigates policies and practice which are designed to ensure that all children are given the opportunity to achieve.

Social inequality is a theme that recurs in Chapter 10 where Penny Mukherji looks at how children's health and well-being can affect their learning and development. Within the chapter the importance of positive relationships, supportive physical environments and good nutrition is emphasised. The Healthy Child Programme is identified as having a key role in mitigating against health inequalities, and the role of early childhood settings in promoting children's health is explained.

Finally, in Chapter 11, Tricia Johnson looks at recent legislation and policy initiatives that have been designed to raise the quality of care and education for very young children in the UK. Tricia explains that the Government's aim to reduce the number of children living in poverty was inherent within all the policy initiatives. The rapid changes in legislation and policy are described, together with the effect these changes have had upon the early childhood profession, the children and their parents. The field of early childhood care and education is never static, it is always evolving and change is a constant feature of our lives. By the time this book is published, there will, undoubtedly, be more legislation and policy change that will affect your professional lives. Tricia explains how important it is that early childhood practitioners have a good knowledge of legislation and effective practice so that they can provide the quality care and education that our very youngest children deserve.

Reference

Marmot, M. (2010) *Post-2010 Strategic Review of Health Inequalities: Fair Society, Healthy Lives. The Marmot Review.* London: University College London.

8

The Historical Background of Early Childhood Care and Education: influencing factors

Linda Pound

This chapter will:

- Focus on a range of theorists and thinkers who have helped to shape early childhood care and education
- Explore the historical context, including the views held of children and learning current at the time
- Examine how theorists were influenced by the ideas of others.

This chapter will focus, in broadly chronological order, on a range of theorists and thinkers who have helped to shape early childhood care and education. The historical context of their ideas, including views of children and learning current at the time, as well as other factors, including other theorists who influenced their ideas will be examined.

Early childhood care and education has a long and interesting history. Its history is interconnected with events in society, contemporary thinking about children and ideas about learning. It is also apparent that the pioneers of early education built on the ideas and philosophies of others. We can, for example, trace a chain of development between Rousseau, Pestalozzi and Owen and Froebel, Margaret McMillan and Susan Isaacs, alongside Freud and Piaget.

In analysing the historical roots of early childhood care and education it is also possible to identify some interesting themes. These include the theme of social class.

Outdoor provision permeates much of the pioneering provision. Holistic development is a third category or theme, meaning that early provision for young children was concerned with the whole child. Froebel may have placed an emphasis on the garden but this was by no means his only focus. The McMillans' provision put health in the foreground and Isaacs emphasised opportunities for exploration and risk-taking, but in all cases the motivation was the education of the whole child – physical, intellectual, emotional, social, moral and, in many cases, spiritual. And, of course, for most pioneering theorists, play and imagination were key themes.

Where did it all begin? The care and education of young children in the seventeenth and eighteenth centuries

The name most closely associated with defining children and childhood throughout history is probably Ariès (1962). He suggests that until the mid-eighteenth century, childhood as a concept did not exist. Archard (1993: 20) rejects that view, arguing that although Ariès claims that earlier societies lacked a concept of childhood, 'at most it shows that they lacked our concept'. James et al. (1998: 12) claim that the prevalent view of children in the sixteenth century had been as evil, and that it was this which led to the practice of coddling, in an effort to constrain babies' 'supposed propensity to wilfulness'. In the mid-eighteenth century, Jean-Jacques Rousseau's (1712–1778) contrasting view of the child as innocent began to take hold. For him, according to James et al. (1998: 13), children had 'a natural goodness and a clarity of vision'. Despite Rousseau's undoubted influence on thinking about children and childhood in the eighteenth century, it is someone who predated him who is often referred to as 'the father of modern education'.

John Comenius (1592–1670)

Piaget (1957: 1), writing about Comenius, suggests that 'nothing is easier, or more dangerous, than to treat an author of 300 years ago as modern and claim to find in him the origins of contemporary or recent trends of thought', but it is difficult to avoid the conclusion that Comenius did indeed influence the future of early education. In a similar vein, Peltzman (1991: 79) describes Comenius as 'a man ahead of his time and the first to develop a special system of education for very young children. All those who followed built their ideas around his work'. However, like many of those who were to follow him in pioneering new approaches to education, his ideas were not limited to the early years.

Comenius proposed, in terms now not seen as remarkable but at that time regarded as revolutionary, a complete system of education which would begin in early childhood. Arguing against rote learning, he believed that education should be in keeping with children's development and therefore should, in the early years, be holistic and should have a strong reliance on sensory experience. Even more remarkable is his insistence that all should have equal access to education, regardless of gender, class or ability. He argued that:

> the slower and the weaker the disposition of any man, the more he needs assistance. ... Nor can any good reason be given why the weaker sex ... should be altogether excluded from the pursuit of knowledge (whether in Latin or in their mother-tongue). ...They are endowed with equal sharpness of mind and capacity for knowledge (often with more than the opposite sex) and they are able to attain the highest positions, since they have often been called by God Himself to rule over nations ... to the study of medicine and of other things which benefit the human race. ... Why, therefore, should we admit them to the alphabet, and afterwards drive them away from books? (Comenius, 1896: 219–20)

Comenius was also known as 'the teacher of nations'. He was born in Moravia, now part of the Czech Republic, but was widely known and respected internationally. He undertook the task of reforming both the Hungarian and Swedish education systems. In 1636 he had been offered the post of the first president of Harvard University. He was also invited to reform English education – but in both cases political and religious unrest prevented him taking up the posts (Nutbrown et al., 2008). Perhaps it was his international experience which led him to understand the importance of illustrated texts for children and the use of the child's home language as the starting point for learning another language, notably at that time Latin. Again, although today these seem obvious aids to learning, they were, at that time, seen as highly innovative.

The roots of 'modern educational theory and practice'

It is Johann Pestalozzi (1746–1827) who has been described as 'the starting point for modern educational theory and practice' (Green and Collie, 1916: 1). He had one foot in the eighteenth century and the other in the nineteenth. He was strongly influenced by the work of the eighteenth-century figure, Rousseau, naming his son Jean-Jacques in Rousseau's honour. In the nineteenth century he himself influenced the work of key figures such as Robert Owen and Friedrich Froebel.

Pestalozzi's career in education really took off with the opening of a school in Yverdun, Switzerland in 1805. While Rousseau had been highly influential, he had not really lived his life according to his philosophy – his own five children, for example, were placed in orphanages shortly after their birth (Jimack, 1974). Pestalozzi, on the other hand, strove to put his beliefs into action. Like Comenius he was committed to providing education for rich and poor alike. Robert Owen sent some of his own children to one of Pestalozzi's schools since he believed that all children should be brought up to be self-sufficient and he admired Pestalozzi's focus on learning and practical activity (Donnachie, 2000). Froebel too came under Pestalozzi's influence, working with him for a time and sharing the conviction of both Pestalozzi and Rousseau that children's nature unfolds over time.

Owen also visited Johann Oberlin, known as 'founder of the nursery school movement' who opened the first nursery school, in Germany, in 1779. This was what today might be termed a workplace nursery, catering for the children of mothers engaged in agricultural work. His teaching methods included educational visits, play and story. It is, however, in the nineteenth century with the opening in 1816 of both Robert Owen's workplace nursery in Scotland and Froebel's educational institute in Germany that the story of nursery education in Britain really begins.

Robert Owen (1771–1858)

Owen's work is firmly rooted in the impact of the Industrial Revolution. In 1815 he opened a mill in New Lanark, not far from Glasgow. Many of his workers were refugees from the brutal land clearances occurring in Scotland at that time. Described by a biographer as 'one of the most important and controversial figures of his generation' (Donnachie, 2000: ix) and as just plain 'mad' by another, Owen was very much a lone voice in nineteenth-century industry. He adopted the 'economics of high wages' (van der Eyken, 1967), paying his workers what seemed to be high wages, and providing homes and education for all – children and adults alike. He refused to employ children under the age of 10 and was instrumental in reforms to child labour laws, the spread of socialist values and the growth of trade unions. He believed that by treating his workers fairly his profits would improve. He undoubtedly also had some more altruistic motives for his actions. Van der Eyken (1967: 63) argues that Owen regarded co-operation, equality and respect as the best preparation for the world of work but 'was a lonely voice in an England convulsed with a search for power and quick wealth'.

Hendrick (1997) throws an interesting light on changing views of childhood around this time. He argues that child labour became increasingly unacceptable partly as a result of Rousseauian views of children and partly because:

- Child labour with its long hours, harsh discipline and polluted environments, damaged children's bodies and morals since they were unable to attend school or church and that this in some way threatened society (Cunningham, 1991). Owen was not immune to this idea – indeed his first school was named Institution for the Formation of Character.
- There was a growing recognition that 'child labour was not free labour' (Hendrick, 1997: 41). Children were unable to make their own contracts with employers and 'it followed that child labour was different in kind from adult labour' (Hendrick, 1997: 41) – a fact well understood by Owen.
- Child labour became associated with slavery, particularly in relation to children working in textile factories, since the production of cotton was dependent on slavery. Although abolished in 1833 in Britain, slavery was not abolished in America until 1865.

- Alongside the natural view of childhood there had arisen an evangelical view of children (Hendrick, 1997). Hannah More (1745–1833) was a rather controversial figure who set up the Sunday School Movement – where children were taught to read and to study the catechism but not to write. A member of the evangelical movement, More rejected the views of childhood put forward by Romantic thinkers such as Wordsworth and of those, like Rousseau, who favoured a natural view of the child. Hendrick (1997: 38) cites More as writing:

> Is it not a fundamental error to consider children as innocent beings, whose little weaknesses may, perhaps, want some correction, rather than as beings who bring into the world a corrupt nature and evil dispositions, which it should be the great end of education to rectify?

In this view, children were seen as part of a domestic ideal with a natural order of 'patriarchal domesticity' (Hendrick, 1997: 41–2), within which, it was believed, 'the neglect of children could easily lead not only to the damnation of souls, but also result in social revolution'.

Owen shows evidence both of the influence of the evangelical point of view in his stated wish to save the poor from 'vicious habits' and from 'things that are vile and degrading' (Donnachie, 2000) and of the gentler views of the Romantics and followers of Rousseau. Blackstone (1971: 17) is clear that:

> He was not concerned with breaking wills and creating individuals satisfied with their station. Nor was he concerned with saving souls, or even teaching the principles of Christianity. He wished with the aid of informal teaching and physical activity to create an individual who would be a useful citizen later on.

Teaching at New Lanark has been described as anticipating 'modern psychological theory' (Blackstone, 1971: 17), by insisting on 'real affection, and full confidence between the teachers and the taught'. Whitbread (1972: 10) underlines this, writing that teachers 'were always to speak to [children] with a pleasant countenance, and in a kind manner and tone of voice'. Owen's intention was that children's curiosity and interest should be fed by images, objects and animated conversation (Whitbread, 1972). There was to be an absence of books but a wealth of sensory experiences. Singing, dancing and marching indoors and out were part of the vibrant provision Owen believed children deserved.

Owen's work, though rarely mentioned in the twenty-first century was influential in the nineteenth century. His work led to the creation of what were then called infant schools, catering for children up to the age of 6. Whitbread (1972) pinpoints the work of David Stow who set up two infant schools in Glasgow in the 1820s. There was a focus on outdoor play and the use of wooden blocks. Stow emphasised the importance of understanding over formal instruction. He is said by Whitbread (1972: 12) to have preceded Froebel in favouring free play and to have 'understood Owen's aims better than the various English exponents of infant teaching'.

Friedrich Froebel (1782–1852)

It may seem odd to herald the opening of a school in Germany in 1816 as contributing to the development of nursery education in Britain, but Froebel's influence has been (and continues to be) immense (see e.g. McCormick, 2012; Ouvry, 2012). In fact the school at Griesheim that Froebel opened in 1816 did not even cater for young children. Two decades of working with older children convinced Froebel that:

> The children who came to him at the age of nine or ten often had bad habits of both conduct and methods of learning so ingrained that it was difficult to eradicate them; and his thoughts turned more and more to the importance of the early years of childhood and the way in which children should be treated during those early years. (Woodham-Smith, 2012a: 22)

In 1837 Froebel opened the first kindergarten at Bad Blankenburg. Weston (1998: 15) describes the development of the term 'kindergarten', which, although universally used, is closely linked to Froebel's work: 'the word cleverly describes the human (kinder) with the natural (garten) and can mean both garden of children, and garden for children'. Nicol (2007: 5) adds a third meaning: '"garden" in German is connected with the word that means "to bend" (transform, metamorphose). Froebel used this concept as inspiration for the child's environment, namely a "paradise garden"'. Woodham-Smith (2012a: 22) describes the importance Froebel himself placed on finding the right name:

> He rejected the term 'infant school' because it was not to be a school; children were not to be schooled but freely developed. He rejected various other names including 'Nursery Schools for Little Children'; finally he hit upon the name with a shout – 'Eureka! I have found it, kindergarten it shall be called'.

The first kindergarten was not opened in England until 1851, coincidentally the same year that kindergartens were closed in Prussia, as being agents of socialist propaganda. Woodham-Smith (2012b) indicates that in fact this was due to a misunderstanding, since it was Froebel's nephew who had been advocating both atheist and socialist values. She asserts, however, that this ban did the Froebelian movement no harm. The repressive regime, of which this ban was just one manifestation, drove many German residents to leave their homeland. Many came to Britain where there were other factors which made Froebelian approaches attractive. Infant schools (or as we would now understand them, nursery schools) already had a long history in this country. The pioneering approaches of radical thinkers like Robert Owen favoured a more child-centred approach and raised awareness of the need for a different approach to the education of young children from that favoured for older children. Indeed, in 1837 the Home and Colonial Society had been set up with the express aim of training teachers according to the theory and practice of Pestalozzi.

Froebel believed equally in training for teachers and in child-centred education, declaring that 'my teachers are the children themselves with their purity and innocence, their unconsciousness and their irresistible claims and I follow them like a faithful, trustful scholar' (Woodham-Smith, 2012a: 23). Froebel's philosophy is often linked to that of the Romantics, such as Wordsworth whose 'perception of childhood was of a special (genderless) time of life, filled with childlike qualities, which was lost at the time of its completion – it becomes "a lost realm" since "growing up becomes synonymous with the loss of paradise"' (Hendrick, 1997: 37). James et al. (1998: 16) consider a philosophy which combines the naturally developing child of Rousseau's theory with one 'innately charged with reason … that will develop given the appropriate environment'. But they also link Froebel's views to Locke's philosophy. This is surprising since it is Locke who is renowned for likening children to the empty vessel or blank sheet of paper. For Locke children have no innate qualities, 'the drives and dispositions that children possess are on a gradient of becoming, moving towards reason' (James et al., 1998: 16). Rather than being innately capable of reason, according to Locke, children become capable of reason 'if we provide the right environment' (James et al., 1998: 16). This mix of nature and nurture is said by James et al. (1998) to be the essence of child-centred education.

And yet, Froebel himself, probably the one name most associated with child-centred education, would have rejected the comparison. He favoured the view that it is nature that determines development, arguing that:

> We grant time and space to young plants and animals because we know that, in accordance with the laws that live in them, they will develop properly and grow well; young animals and plants are given rest, and arbitrary interference with their growth is avoided, because it is known that the opposite practice would disturb their pure unfolding and sound development; but the young human being is looked upon as a piece of wax, a lump of clay which man can mold into what he pleases. (Froebel, 2009: 8)

Issues of class

Robert Owen and Friedrich Froebel have come to be seen as both representing and catering for two distinct elements of society. The children attending Owen's institution were children of the industrial revolution, children of working-class parents. His provision was intended both to protect children from the exploitation that accompanied the industrial revolution and the impact of poverty. The first kindergarten in London, set up by Johann and Bertha Ronge in 1851 (who had previously set up kindergartens in Germany) catered for the German children of German émigrés who had travelled to England to escape political persecution. These were not working-class children but children of privileged homes whose families sought extended learning for them outside the home. Whitbread (1972: 31) suggests that 'Froebelians who came here after the prohibition of the Kindergarten in Prussia in 1851, found the English upper and middle classes were immediately interested in their methods of teaching young children'. Blackstone (1971: 14) supports this view, arguing that Froebel's approach 'appealed to a small section of the liberal-minded bourgeoisie and a sprinkling of intellectuals'. They, she suggests, began to think about the importance of social interaction and organised play in their children's development.

Bruce (2011) rejects this view, arguing that from its inception Froebelian provision had catered for poor children. She cites Weston (1998: 15) who suggests that at Bad Blankenburg 'there were nearly 50 children registered in 1839, many of whom had first to be washed in the fountain in the market place before starting school'. However, Singer (1992: 60) supports the view that Froebelian education did not really take off amongst working-class children in Britain. She argues that around 1855:

> conditions seemed favourable for a new wave of pedagogic innovations, but this did not materialize. The steps taken to lower the rising cost of national education were disastrous for the quality of education for young children. There was also resistance to Froebel's learning through play. ... But in the end it was the unwillingness to spend money on young children from the working class which decided the matter. A kindergarten required smaller classes, well-trained teachers and sufficient toys and play material. Another reason was that this freer form of education was thought to be less suitable for children from the lower social classes.

Woodham-Smith (2012a: 60) identifies two distinct arguments about early education which sadly are still all too familiar today. On one hand is the view that children should be taught 'their prescribed tasks before they are legally required to repeat them; by mere reiteration the tasks will become familiar'; while the other side of the argument suggests 'develop the infant's powers; teach him to attend, to construct, and "change" the standards'.

Paradoxically, while arguments raged about the best form of education for young children, Froebelian philosophy, which emphasised the role of the mother in nurturing children, was to impact on school attendance. Although the number of mothers in work declined during the latter part of the nineteenth century, the number of children in school increased, so that by 1900, 43 per cent of 3- and 4-year-old children were attending school. After 1900 numbers fell rapidly:

> The education offered to young children fell into disrepute. The reasons for this were the catastrophic defeats in the Boer War, and the soldiers' poor general health. ... [which] was associated with mothers working outside the home in the working classes. (Singer, 1992: 61–2)

Whitbread (1972: 44) also describes this change in numbers of children in school. She writes of the increased numbers of very young children, below the statutory age of schooling, who began to attend with older brothers and sisters once compulsory schooling was introduced in 1870:

> Nursery accommodation was what was really needed for the youngest of these children, but a babies' classroom was what was provided. There they were often penned into their seats to keep them from mischief. Continually rising numbers meant permanent

> overcrowding. ... A typical example was in Leicester where a new infant building was added to an elementary school in 1893, but the baby room which had been planned for forty was accommodating an average of eighty only five years later.

Despite repeated lobbying by Froebelians and others concerned about their plight, there was little or no progress towards more appropriate education for the youngest children. Whitbread (1972) highlights the constraints, which included: class sizes (which were three times the number of 24 advocated by Froebel); fixed, tiered and galleried accommodation; inappropriately trained or unqualified teachers; and pressure to teach basic skills. In 1875 more than 111,000 children under the age of three were in elementary schools, but this number then began to drop as the school leaving age was raised to 11, meaning that there was less available space. Whitbread (1972: 50) concludes that:

> [al]though Pestalozzi and Froebel thought that their infant pedagogy was applicable to all social classes ... neither had to face up to the exigencies of mass infant education in the conditions prevailing in industrial towns. Teachers with experience of these realities did not begin to develop an appropriate theory of infant education until the next century.

Twentieth-century developments

The poor did not have the luxury of choice that affected middle-class decisions about the education of their young children. The widespread view that education for working-class children was likely to lead to social revolution had contributed to inappropriate provision. The Boer War (1899–1902) acted as a catalyst for changing public opinion. The recruitment of soldiers for that conflict underlined the poor health and fitness of members of the working classes. Children came to be viewed as the nation's resource, 'children of the nation' (Hendrick, 1997) but it was clear that many were more in the realms of 'sickly survival' than close to realising their potential (Baistow, 1995). Concern was reflected in a series of legislative acts regulating many aspects of children's welfare, including the prevention of cruelty and neglect of children (1889), the provision of school meals for the needy (1906) and establishing school medicals (1907). A contemporary public health activist and medical journalist, Kelynack (quoted by Hendrick, 1997: 42), described the prevalent mood at the beginning of the twentieth century: 'The child is a new discovery ... and in all sections of society eagerness is being manifested to understand and serve the child'. Hendrick (1997: 51) concludes that in an age of fundamental change around the start of the twentieth century 'children were being reconstructed as material investments in national progress'.

Rachel (1859–1817) and Margaret (1860–1931) McMillan were leading activists in the struggle to nurture and protect children. It was they who had led the way in promoting school meals and school medicals. Pound (2011: 27) describes their early work:

> The sisters' combination of astuteness and determination enabled them to persuade a reluctant London County Council and a philanthropic American industrialist to join with

> them in establishing the first school clinic in 1908. However, they quickly realised that although they could provide some remedies for endemic poor health, their work was not preventing disease. Their curative approach included vast numbers of tonsillectomies and a remedial gym which was seen to improve children's health and strength. But, in 1911, they set up a night camp in a churchyard in Deptford which they believed would help to minimise the spread of tuberculosis. More than 50 children slept in open air shelters for nine months of the year.

While their motivation was health, a major element of the drive that led to the establishment of the first Montessori school in Rome in 1907 was the work of Edouard Seguin (1812–1880) in Paris. Seguin studied mental deficiency, regarding it as 'a pedagogical problem rather than a medical one' (Bradley et al., 2011: 72). In addition to studying the work of Seguin, Maria Montessori (1870–1952) was influenced by the work of Rousseau, Pestalozzi and Froebel. In 1900 she became the director of a demonstration school for 'retarded children': her methods were highly successful, raising achievement amongst the pupils often to that found in mainstream schools, 'which led her to question the quality of the education provided to such establishments' (Bradley et al., 2011: 72). Montessori (1919: 33) wrote that 'I became convinced that similar methods applied to normal children would develop or set free their personality in a marvellous and surprising way'.

The nurseries, or Case dei Bambini, which Montessori established, catered for children of the slums, the children of poor working mothers. A decade later this was to be reflected in the work of Steiner. The first Montessori nursery was set up in America in 1911, and in England in 1912. This is of particular interest since it was set up by Bertram Hawker with the support of Edmond Holmes. Holmes had become Chief Inspector of Elementary Schools in 1905 but was forced to resign in 1911 when a confidential memorandum in which he criticised school inspectors who had previously been elementary school teachers was made public. A subsequent publication, *What Is and What Might Be*, is said to have marked the beginning of progressive educational thinking in England (Selleck, 1972). Holmes was deeply influenced by Montessori's work and his influence spread. In 1916 a London borough provided Montessori-trained teachers and equipment to all its schools catering for young children (Bradley et al., 2011).

Inter-war progressivism

During the years between the end of the First World War and the beginning of the second, there was a burgeoning of progressive education. The names most commonly associated with innovation in early childhood education at that time include Margaret McMillan, Rudolf Steiner, Maria Montessori and Susan Isaacs. In the Table 8.1 an overview of some aspects of their approaches are outlined.

However, these four were by no means the only progressive figures in the field. Some initiatives, such as the first forest school, established in 1929, and the Little

Table 8.1 Comparison of progressive approaches to early childhood care and education

Approach	Key features	Aspects of development emphasised	Role of play & imagination	Issues of class	Theoretical influences
Margaret McMillan (1860–1931)	Emphasis on outdoor provision, music and free play Stressed the importance of space and time	Health and physical fitness was seen as the key to total well-being and to be a necessary precursor to intellectual development	Seen as the means to unlock the whole personality by allowing the expression of feelings and emotions otherwise constrained by inappropriate pedagogy, the pressures of industry and adverse social conditions	Focused entirely on the needs of children living in poverty. Built on socialist ideals	Pestalozzi Froebel Active link with Steiner
Rudolf Steiner (1861–1925)	Imitation Movement Imagination Rhythm and repetition Respect for the child	Believed there to be three seven-year cycles of development. From birth to 7 the emphasis is on being active. No formal instruction is given within this period	Described imagination as 'the real driving power of the soul' (1923: 142) Play and imagination are of fundamental importance, not to be hampered by formality	Developed as an educational system for factory workers	Developed philosophy of *anthroposophy* Admired McMillan's work and visited her school
Maria Montessori (1870–1952)	Independence including daily living Developing concentration Prepared environment	From conception to the age of 6 is described as a period of self-creation	Work and play are seen as synonymous. Play is often regarded by others as being undervalued by Montessori practitioners. They, however, insist that this is simply a misunderstanding about the similar characteristics of work and play – both of which develop engagement and concentration	Had its roots in the education of children regarded as subnormal and developed for normal but poor children	Seguin Froebel Pestalozzi Rousseau
Susan Isaacs (1885–1948)	Renowned for the challenging nature of the outdoor provision Curiosity Talk to promote thinking Emphasis on emotional needs	Isaacs became the first head of the Department of Child Development in 1933 (now London Institute of Education) Although having an undoubtedly holistic view of education, she emphasised the emotional aspects	Play regarded as an essential means of making sense of the world. In keeping with psycho-analytical ideals, phantasy was valued as opening up to the child 'all the things he cannot do and may not be in real life' (Isaacs, 1929: 10–11)	The Malting House School catered for a small number of highly privileged children, mainly boys	Anna Freud Melanie Klein Froebel Dewey Argued with Piaget about stages of development

To download this table as well as other useful online resources please visit: **www.sagepub.co.uk/mukherji**

Commonwealth, described as 'a co-educational learning community for difficult children' (Pound, 2011: 24), were very successful but short lived. Others, such as Bedales, Summerhill and Dartington, survive today. One long-term development which survives is Chelsea Open Air Nursery, 'set up in 1929 for children whose lives were regarded as too advantaged and sheltered' (Pound, 2011: 32). It is said that the children were given the nickname 'Kensington cripples' (Whitbread, 1972) or 'cripples of Chelsea' (Pound, 1986) because of their lack of independence. They were, in other words, disabled by not having learnt to care for themselves, having been pampered by nannies.

Reflection

It is clear that many of the approaches designed to cater for children brought up in poverty have become very popular with families with far greater socio-economic advantages. And yet, as we have seen, in the nineteenth century, Froebelian approaches, which were developed within the middle classes were regarded as inappropriate for working-class children. What reasons might there be for this shift?

Developing theories

Alongside the development of philosophies relating to the care and education of young children, many theoretical influences were emerging. Isaacs was influenced by the work of psychoanalytical thinkers Melanie Klein (1882–1960) and Anna Freud (1895–1982). Freudian theories have had an immense impact. That might be because of the sheer readability of his work (Bullig, 2006), but whatever the reason it was not until the 1950s and 1960s that his work was challenged by both cognitive and humanistic psychologists (see Chapter 6). Rock and Fonagy (2006: 535) describe the influence of Sigmund Freud (1856–1939):

> Admired or ridiculed, idealised or pilloried, Freud was a gigantic intellect. His credentials as a psychologist, indicated by his commitment to studying the mind, are beyond question. Also beyond doubt is Freud's influence on 20th-century thought inspired by and inspiring scientific, cultural and social endeavours across continents. For many years Freud represented a universal reference point in scientific psychology. For or against him, historical figures in our field often identified themselves by the position they took in relation to his corpus.

Isaacs also had contact with Piaget, who visited the Malting House School in 1927. They did not always agree but did in fact have a shared interest in development. However, Isaacs believed that Piaget placed insufficient emphasis on the social and emotional aspects of learning and that his view that development moved in stages, marking qualitative shifts in thinking was wrong. Lev Vygotsky was also writing in this inter-war period. Although his work would not become known in the west until decades later, he was aware of the work of Piaget. Another incipient set of theories emerging at this time was behaviourism. The work on classical conditioning by Ivan Pavlov (1849–1936) influenced Burrhus Skinner (1904–1990) in the late 1920s. The full impact of Skinner's work was not felt until after the Second World War but nonetheless in 1928 when he began his studies at Harvard, 'Skinner discovered replicable and universal laws of behaviour that still hold true today' (Slater, 2004: 12).

Post-war optimism?

Just as the Boer War had influenced public opinion at the turn of the century, so the Second World War shaped policy and practice in interesting ways in the second half of the century. The evacuation of something in excess of one million children, described as 'a cruel psychological experiment on a large scale' (Hendrick, 1997: 54), 'shone a torchlight into the darkest corners of urban Britain, and what was revealed was both shocking and frightening in its implications for racial efficiency, emotional stability and post-war democracy'. Hendrick (1997: 56) argues that from this period there emerged a dual view of children, both as 'an individual citizen in a welfare democracy and as a member of a family'. He argues that this post-war child is 'the child of the welfare state'.

Researchers such as Susan Isaacs (1941) who edited the *Cambridge Evacuation Survey* highlighted the vital importance of family connections. Similarly, John Bowlby undertook a study of children separated from their parents which was to lead to the development of his attachment theory. It is difficult to underestimate the influence of these ideas (see e.g. Bowlby, 1953). The journal task below considers the relative impact of risk and resilience factors in young children's well-being and development.

Journal Task

Schaffer, H.R. (2000) 'The early experience assumption: Past, present and future', *International Journal of Behavioral Development*, 24(1): 5–14.

This article considers a wide range of views about the importance of early experience.

Levels 4 & 5

1. Schaffer suggests that research has shown that children are not passive recipients of experiences and that few, if any, effects are irreversible. Read the examples he gives to support this argument and outline some examples from your own experience which either support or challenge his view.

(Continued)

(Continued)

2. Schaffer also argues that children are more affected by apparently negative experiences. Look at some work on resilience, such as that cited in the article by Rutter and Rutter (1993) or Pugh (2002) and consider what actions you might take to help to promote resilience in young children.

Level 6

John Bruer (1999) has a different stance on this debate but arrives at some similar conclusions. Consider how you might help parents and colleagues to make sense of diverse and sometimes contradictory arguments about early experience. Outline your own viewpoint and give reasons for your conclusions.

To download this task as well as other useful online resources please visit: **www.sagepub.co.uk/mukherji**

The end of World War II brought with it:

> post-war social idealism [which] in Britain had produced a successful scheme to provide medical care for everyone. The intention to provide secondary education for all children had not proved so successful, however, for it was becoming only too clear that among working class families academic success was effectively being limited to a disproportionately small number of children. (Nicholls and Wells, 1985: 1)

At the same time, Bowlby's theories of attachment had paved the way for a reorganisation of nursery education. During the war, nursery provision had included a mixture of care and education to meet the needs of the many mothers who were working long hours as part of the war effort. The end of the war brought the return to civilian employment for many men, the loss of employment opportunities for many women, and a rise in the birth-rate. Arguments about the need for early attachment led to a change in the provision for young children. Day nurseries gradually came to cater for a ghetto group of needy families while most nursery education provision was reduced to part-time. Riley (1983) describes these changes and the accompanying rationale, which used political, social, psychological and psychiatric arguments.

It is interesting to contrast what happened in England to nursery provision in Reggio Emilia where parents determined that they would maintain and extend the nursery provision set up during the war in their 'devastated town, rich only in mourning and poverty' (Malaguzzi cited by Drummond 2008, and that this would be achieved through 'the sale of an abandoned war tank, a few trucks, and some horses left behind by the retreating Germans' (Malaguzzi, 1993: 42). Moreover, it was decided that 'people who conformed and obeyed were dangerous' and that therefore the aim should be to 'nurture a vision of children who can think and act for themselves' (Moss, 2001: 136).

The period since the end of the Second World War has seen the emergence of numerous other models of curricula. MacNaughton (2003) categorises approaches according to the extent which she believes they enable children to:

(a) *Conform to society*. In this category, curricula seek to 'reproduce the skills needed to achieve national economic, social and political goals' and 'the understandings and values that enable society to reproduce itself' (MacNaughton, 2003: 121). MacNaughton sees Montessori education and the New Zealand curriculum, Te Whāriki, as conforming approaches. The first is perhaps not surprising since Montessori was attempting to help children of the slums conform through independence and daily living skills. The second is perhaps more questionable since it is widely valued as representing a good model of integrated provision. However, alongside EYFS in England (DfE, 2012), MacNaughton regards it as conforming since it sets a large number of learning goals.

(b) *Reform society*. Both HighScope and Reggio Emilia are categorised as offering reforming approaches. These seek to 'reform the individual from a dependent and developing child to a self-realized, autonomous, adult, "free" thinker' and 'reform society and its values so that freedom, truth and justice can prevail' (MacNaughton, 2003: 155). Again this holds some surprise. It is clear that the residents of Reggio Emilia were seeking to transform their society. It could be argued that HighScope along with other Headstart programmes wanted to transform the life chances of children living in socio-economically disadvantaged conditions. Long-term studies of children participating in the research study show that some transformation has been achieved, saving the state a great deal of money (Schweinhart et al., 2005). However, it could equally be argued that the programme sought to ensure that children conformed to societal norms such as employment and the age of parenthood.

(c) *Transform society*. For MacNaughton (2003: 182) 'a "transforming society" position rests on the belief that educators can work with children and their families to create a better world'. Citing Giroux (1990) she suggests that transformation involves both the individual and society as a whole. Privileged groups, she argues, should learn how to develop a less unjust society while less advantaged groups might be given critical literacy and numeracy skills.

Reflection

While one may have a great deal of sympathy with MacNaughton's emphasis on anti-discriminatory transformative aims, her solutions seem simplistic. They link to the earlier discussion of class. Reflect on the class issues she identifies and on her categories of provision. How would you set out to transform society? In addressing these ideas you might want to consider some postmodern theories (see e.g. Albon, 2011).

Summary

In summary, this chapter has considered the ways in which early childhood education and care has been shaped by historical events, society's attitudes to children and to social justice. The influence of the ideas of seventeenth- and eighteenth-century thinkers on nineteenth-century reformers has been considered. These in turn influenced the wave of progressive approaches to education which emerged during the first half of the twentieth century, which were further shaped by the emergence of new understandings and perceptions of children and their learning and development. The second half of the twentieth century has seen yet more change – but with many of the same questions about social class and access to provision re-emerging.

Further reading

Levels 4 & 5

Pound, L. (2011) *Influencing Early Childhood Education*. Maidenhead: Open University Press. This book offers an overview of the way in which early childhood education developed, with its interconnectedness between theorists and with social and political events.

Miller, L. and Pound, L. (eds) (2011) *Theories and Approaches to Learning in the Early Years*. London: Sage. Part 2 of this book offers chapters written by advocates of Froebelian approaches, Montessori education and Steiner Waldorf education – approaches which the editors term 'foundational'.

Level 6

Penn, H. (2011) 'Gambling on the market: The role of for-profit provision in early childhood education and care', *Journal of Early Childhood* Research, 9(2): 150–61. This journal article look at some current political concerns. Consider the link between historical perspectives and political decisions, looking at parallels between current and past provision.

References

Albon, D. (2011) 'Postmodern and post-structuralist perspectives on early childhood education', in L. Miller and L. Pound (eds), *Theories and Approaches to Learning in the Early Years*. London: Sage.

Ariès, P. (1962) *Centuries of Childhood*. London: Jonathan Cape.

Archard, R. (1993) *Children: Rights and Childhood*. London: Routledge.

Baistow, K. (1995) 'From sickly survival to the realisation of potential: Child health as a social project', *Children Society*, 9: 20–35.

Blackstone, T. (1971) *A Fair Start: The Provision of Pre-school Education*. London: Allen Lane/ LSE.

Bowlby, J. (1953) *Child Care and the Growth of Love*. Harmondsworth: Penguin Books Ltd.

Bradley, M., Isaacs, B., Livingston, L., Nasser, D., True, A.M. and Dillane, M. (2011) 'Maria Montessori in the United Kingdom: 100 years on', in L. Miller and L. Pound (eds), *Theories and Approaches to Learning in the Early Years*. London: Sage.

Bruce, T. (2011) 'Froebel today', in L. Miller and L. Pound (eds), *Theories and Approaches to Learning in the Early Years*. London: Sage.

Bruer, J. (1999) *The Myth of the First Three Years*. New York: The Free Press.

Bullig, M. (2006) 'The persistence of Freud', *The Psychologist*, 19(9): 540–1.

Comenius, J. (1896) *The Great Didactic*. London: Adam & Charles Black (first published 1657).

Cunningham, H. (1991) *The Children of the Poor: Representations of Childhood Since the Seventeenth Century*. Oxford: Blackwell.

Department for Education (DfE) (2012) *Statutory Framework for the Early Years Foundation Stage: Setting the Standards for Learning, Development and Care for Children from Birth to Five*. London: DfE. http://www.foundationyears.org.uk/ or http://www.education.gov.uk/

Donnachie, I. (2000) *Robert Owen: Owen of New Lanark and New Harmony*. East Lothian: Tuckwell Press.

Drummond, M.J. (2008) *Learning Partners*. Available at: http://www.tes.co.uk/article.aspx? storycode=398895 (accessed 20 November 2013).

Froebel, F. (2009) *The Education of Man*. New York: Dover Publications Inc. (first published 1826).

Giroux, H. (1990) *Curriculum Discourse as Postmodern Critical Practice*. Geelong, Victoria: Deakin University.

Green, J. and Collie, F. (1916) *Pestalozzi's Educational Writings*. London: Edward Arnold.

Hendrick, H. (1997) 'Constructions and reconstructions of British childhood: An interpretative survey, 1800 to the present', in A. James and A. Prout (eds), *Constructing and Reconstructing Childhood*. London: Falmer Press.

Isaacs, S. (1929) *The Nursery Years*. London: Routledge & Kegan Paul

Isaacs, S. (1941) (ed.) *Cambridge Evacuation Survey*. London: Methuen.

James, A., Jenks, C. and Prout, A. (1998) *Theorizing Childhood*. Cambridge: Polity Press.

Jimack, P. (1974) 'Introduction' to *Emile* by J-J. Rousseau. London: Dent and Sons (first published 1762).

MacNaughton, G. (2003) *Shaping Early Childhood*. Maidenhead: Open University Press.

Malaguzzi, L. (1993) 'History, ideas and basic philosophy', in C. Edwards, L. Gandini and G. Forman (eds), *The Hundred Languages of Children*. Westport, CT: Ablex Publishing.

McCormick, C. (2012) 'Froebelian methods in the modern world: A case of cooking', in T. Bruce (ed.), *Early Childhood Practice: Froebel Today*. London: Sage.

Montessori, M. (1919) *The Montessori Method: Scientific Pedagogy as Applied to Child Education in 'The Children's Houses'*. London: Heinemann.

Moss, P. (2001) 'The otherness of Reggio', in L. Abbott and C. Nutbrown (eds), *Experiencing Reggio Emilia*. Buckingham: Open University Press.

Nicholls, J. and Wells, G. (1985) 'Editors' introduction', in G. Wells and J. Nicholls (eds), *Language and Learning: An Interactional Perspective*. Lewes, E. Sussex: Falmer Press.

Nicol, J. (2007) *Bringing the Steiner Waldorf Approach to Your Early Years Practice*. London: David Fulton.

Nutbrown, C., Clough, P. and Selbie, P. (2008) *Early Childhood Education: History, Philosophy and Experience*. London: Sage.

Ouvry, M. (2012) 'Froebel's mother songs today', in T. Bruce (ed.), *Early Childhood Practice: Froebel Today*. London: Sage.

Peltzman, B. (1991) 'Origins of early childhood education', in P. Persky and L. Golubchick (eds), *Early Childhood Education* (2nd edition). Lanham, MD: University Press of America.

Piaget, J. (1957) 'Jan Amos Comenius (1592–1670)', *Prospects* (1993) XXIII(1/2): 173–96. UNESCO: International Bureau of Education http://www.ibe.unesco.org/publications/ThinkersPdf/comeniuse.PDF (accessed 20 August 2012).

Pound, L. (1986) 'Perceptions of nursery practice: an exploration of nursery teachers' view of the curriculum' (unpublished MA (ed) thesis). Roehampton Institute/Survey University.

Pound, L. (2011) *Influencing Early Childhood*. Maidenhead: McGraw-Hill.

Pugh, G. (2002) 'The consequences of inadequate investment in the early years', in J. Fisher (ed.), *The Foundations of Learning*. Buckingham: Open University Press.

Riley, D. (1983) *War in the Nursery*. London: Virago.

Rock, B. and Fonagy, P. (2006) 'Freud's influence: Personal and professional perspectives', *The Psychologist*, 19(9): 535.

Rutter, M. and Rutter, M. (1993) *Developing Minds*. Harmondsworth: Penguin.

Schweinhart, L., Montie, J., Xiang, Z., Barnett, W., Belfield, C. and Nores, M. (2005) *Lifetime Effects: The HighScope Perry Preschool Study through Age 40*. Ypsilanti, MI: HighScope Press.

Selleck, R. (1972) *English Primary Education and the Progressives 1914–1939*. London: Routledge & Kegan Paul.

Singer, E. (1992) *Child-care and the Psychology of Development*. London: Routledge.

Slater, L. (2004) *Opening Skinner's Box*. London: Bloomsbury Publishing.

Steiner, R. (1923) 'Margaret McMillan and her work', *Anthroposophy*, II(11): 141–3.

van der Eyken, W. (1967) *The Pre-school Years*. Harmondsworth: Penguin Press Ltd.

Weston, P. (1998) *Friedrich Froebel: His Life, Times and Significance*. London: Roehampton Institute.

Whitbread, N. (1972) *The Evolution of the Nursery-infant School*. London: Routledge & Kegan Paul.

Woodham-Smith, P. (2012a) 'The origins of the kindergarten', in E. Lawrence (ed.), *Friedrich Froebel and English Education*. Abingdon: Routledge (first published 1952).

Woodham-Smith, P. (2012b) 'History of the Froebel movement in England', in E. Lawrence (ed.), *Friedrich Froebel and English Education*. Abingdon: Routledge (first published 1952).

9

Social Inequalities

Gianna Knowles and Penny Mukherji

This chapter will:

- Discuss why we should be concerned about inequalities in terms of children's achievements, life chances and social justice
- Investigate barriers to equality and social justice, looking at:
    - The effects of discrimination
    - How adults' attitudes affect children's learning
    - How children's attitudes about themselves affect their progress.
- Investigate how to promote equality, looking at:
    - Policies and practice designed to counteract the effect of disadvantage
    - Special educational needs and inclusion
    - Anti-discriminative practice
    - Gender conscious practice.

One of the most fundamental principles that has underpinned the UK's education system since 1947 is the notion that it is a system that provides free education, with 'equal opportunities and social mobility' being core values (Brighouse et al., 2010: 20). There is a sense that the UK is a society that rewards educational success; that is to say, if you do well at school and possibly later at university you are more likely to gain stable employment that is both potentially rewarding personally and financially, which in turn will provide you with greater social mobility. In this way you will have fulfilled your personal potential and have a greater capacity to achieve both personal and financial well-being. The UK education system also recognises that educational potential is not special to any one group of children. All children have the potential to be successful and achieve in their learning, whatever background they come from, whatever their ethnicity, income group, gender or ability. However, while this may be the belief about and intention for the education system in the UK, there remains the problem that at as early as 5 years old differences in attainment between groups are observed. Results for how well children achieve in the Foundation Stage Profile show that girls do better than boys, white children do better than children from other ethnic groups, and children from families with relatively higher incomes do better than children from poor families (DfE, 2012a). This chapter investigates some of the issues around social inequality and aims to help you reflect upon the role of early childhood practitioners in promoting equality.

Why are we concerned with equality?

Children's achievements

The Statutory Framework for the Early Years Foundation Stage (DfE, 2012b) explains in its introduction that for children to fulfil the potential they are born with, one of the most important elements that needs to be in place in the first five years of a child's life is access to 'high quality early learning' (DfE, 2012b: 2). The document goes on to explore how high quality learning includes 'equality of opportunity and anti-discriminatory practice, ensuring that every child is included and supported'.

Generally, everyone who works with young children is committed to providing the best educational opportunities for children that they can, and *all* children should have access to free pre-school early years settings where they can enjoy play and learning experiences. However, as we have noted, research shows that while successive governments have sought to provide all young children with the equal opportunity to attend pre-school settings, by the age of 5 there are significant differences between different groups.

Reflection

Look at this document: Department for Education (2012a) *Statistical First Release: Early Years Foundation Stage Profile Attainment by Pupil Characteristics, England 2011/12*. London: DfE. http://www.education.gov.uk/rsgateway/DB/SFR/s001098/sfr30-2012.pdf

- What do the statistics tell you about how different groups of children achieve?
- What factors do you think are at work to produce these results?

The government states that: 'research has shown that a gap between high achievers and low achievers in the educational system starts to appear at 22 months of age' (DfE, 2010: 31).That is, by the age of 2 some children, are already falling behind other children because of a range of environmental factors in the lives of these children. The life factors that make this difference can be that the child:

- has a disability or special educational need (SEN)
- has English as an additional language
- comes from a low-income home
- lives in a deprived area
- comes from particular minority ethnic groups
- has been, or is in care. (DfE, 2010: 30)

Equality and gender

We have looked at how certain groups of children appear to be achieving less well than others by the end of the foundation stage. We noted that girls outperform boys, and continue to do so throughout their time in education. However, women experience a lack of opportunity when they are older, in that women, on average, earn less than their male counterparts and are underrepresented in certain occupations and among higher paid managers and directors (EHRC, 2013). In the field of early childhood there are also barriers for men, who are severely underrepresented in the workforce.

Equality and social justice

For many the idea of equality is closely linked to their notion of justice. In Europe what is meant by justice has been debated for thousands of years. Plato (424–347 BCE) in exploring what is meant by justice was also explaining a way that all people might live together and enjoy 'the good life' (Evans, 2010: 9), or what Maslow (1943) described as self-actualisation. Justice, therefore, could include the idea that *everyone* should be given the opportunity to flourish, to achieve a sense of well-being or fulfil their potential and that living in a *just* society is one way of enabling this to happen.

Maslow put forward the idea that we all have needs that have to be met for us to be able to achieve the best we can out of life. He arranged these needs in a hierarchy (Figure 9.1), which showed that basic physiological needs (food, warmth, shelter) have to be met before an individual can seek to meet 'higher level' needs such as a safe environment, love, the need to be held in high esteem and finally, 'self actualisation' which is the need to do and be what we know we can do and be (Maslow, 1943).

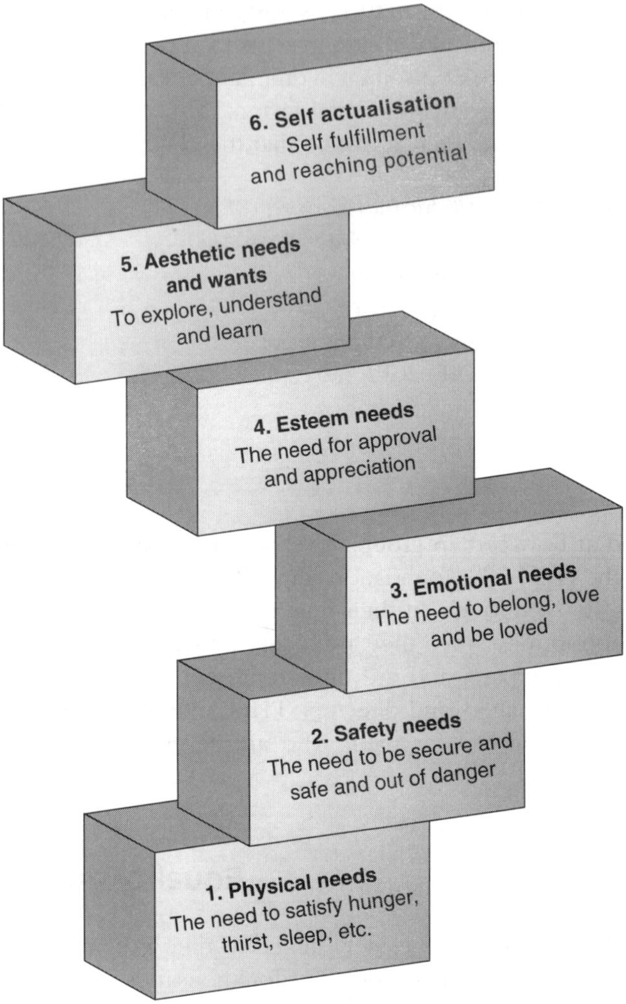

Figure 9.1 **Maslow's hierarchy of needs (adapted from Dukes and Smith, 2009)**

John Rawls (1921–2002), the American political philosopher (cited in Lovett, 2010), is often credited with developing Plato's ideas about justice into our contemporary understanding of social justice. Rawls was interested in how 'luck' plays a part in how good a life we lead (Hinman, 2003). He thought that it often seems to be just 'luck' that determines the family and circumstances into which a child is born – something over which a child has no control. However, it is the family into which the child is born and their personal circumstances that often shape the long-term outcomes for that child and later that adult. For example, a child born into poverty will, more often than not, go on to be a poor adult (Field, 2010). Whereas, a child born into an even slightly more wealthy family will, very likely, go on to have a wealthier and healthier life and possibly more fulfilled life.

Reflection

Read the following document: Field, F. (2010) *The Foundation Years: Preventing Poor Children Becoming Poor Adults.* London: Cabinet Office http://webarchive.nationalarchives.gov.uk/20110120090128/http:/povertyreview.independent.gov.uk/media/20254/poverty-report.pdf

- What factors influence the life chances of children? You will find page 39 useful. In addition, Chapter 10 of this book will give you additional insight.
- What is the evidence that good quality early childhood services can have a positive impact on the lives of children from disadvantaged families?

Rawls's work explores further how inequalities of birth, such as variations in family income, impact on life chances and seem to perpetuate an unjust and unequal rather than a just and equal society. He was concerned to develop a just society so that inequalities occasioned by birth might be overcome to create a just society in which luck plays a minimal role in enabling children to achieve good long-term life chances (Hinman, 2003: 245). In particular, he explored how a society might develop a *mutually beneficial system of cooperation* (Lovett, 2010: 18) which would provide everyone with an equal chance of achieving long-term well-being and self-actualisation, whatever their starting point; that is, a society that is based on the principle of social justice.

As Brighouse et al. (2010) discuss, if we want to live in a society that is concerned with the long-term well-being of all members of society:

> if it is not possible to avoid a situation in which some are worse off than others, then at least ... it is only fair that society should be arranged in such a way as to improve the condition of the worst off so far as possible. (Brighouse et al., 2010: 24)

Many would argue that the UK does just this. That is to say the benefits and welfare system, the National Health Service and the compulsory education system provide the opportunity for everyone to thrive and flourish. However, having the opportunity to do something is not the same as being able to take advantage of that opportunity. It can be argued that there are barriers that prevent children and adults from being able to make the best of opportunities that seem to be on offer and move towards self-actualisation.

Barriers to equality and social justice

CASE STUDY

Alisha is 4. She has cerebral palsy and is in a wheelchair. Alisha's mother says:

> We were very keen that Alisha attended an early years setting and could make friends in the way that all children want to. While the law says that children like Alisha have an equal opportunity to do this, equal to that of all children, in practice it didn't work out like that. We approached a number of settings; some said that they would take Alisha, but that they hadn't yet had their premises modified to accommodate wheelchairs, or that they didn't have staff who knew how best to deal with a child like Alisha. When we did find a place that could accommodate a child in a wheelchair we found that the staff hadn't really thought about how some activities would need to be adapted so that Alisha could be included and fully access all areas of the curriculum (especially some of the outside activities). We found that some staff tended to overcompensate and didn't let Alisha do the things that she could! The other children were great and Alisha made lots of friends – it was the parents who were a problem. When Alisha invited children to play at our house, and to come to her birthday party we found that some parents were really 'funny' and made it quite clear that they didn't want their child to be friends with Alisha.

Alisha was not given the same opportunities as the other children to be fully included in all the activities provided by the setting and did not have equal access to the curriculum.

- Identify the possible barriers that may have prevented Alisha from full participation.

Discrimination and inequality

This case study about Alisha shows how children can be prevented from taking advantage of the opportunities available because of others' acts of discrimination. For example, the parents who did not want their children to be friends with Alisha were overtly or deliberately discriminating against Alisha. The staff were also displaying discrimination. They probably were not deliberately seeking to discriminate against Alisha, but they had failed to understand the need to think through the activities they had planned to ensure Alisha could be included.

This example of unwitting discrimination is also an example of institutional discrimination. In this case the early childhood setting as an institution has, over time developed its own way of doing things and while those working in the institution know that they should not discriminate and, indeed will have various policies to that effect, bad practice has been allowed to get by unnoticed.

Adams et al. (2007) explore the notion of how some groups in society have more power than others and how the values, beliefs and attitudes of those in power can, deliberately or unwittingly, prevent some children from being able to realise opportunities that may be available to them. Adams et al. (2007) discuss how 'bias, prejudice, or bigotry perpetuates the pervasive nature of social inequality woven throughout social institutions as well as ... within individual consciousness' (Adams et al., 2007: 3).

It may seem challenging to think of different groups in society as having power over other groups. However, throughout our everyday life we experience others having power over us and, in turn, there are situations where we are the ones who have the power. We are not thinking here of situations where someone is forcing or coercing us to do things that we do not want to do – although these situations may happen in your life. We are thinking more of those hour-by-hour social interactions where we have to respond to someone else's rules, wishes or expectations.

In early childhood settings and school classrooms it is usually the adults who make decisions and have power over children (and parents), although, increasingly, early childhood settings and schools are involving children in making decisions. Listening to the views and opinions of children and incorporating these views into decision making is an important way of helping redress the power imbalance. Chapter 2 looks at ways in which children can be involved in decision making.

Children's learning is affected by the attitudes of adults

As we have discussed, the reasons why race, class and gender have such an impact on how a child may achieve at school has much to do with the values, attitudes and beliefs held by the powerful adults around them and the unwitting effect these attitudes may have on the children they work with. Jensen (2009) undertook research with early years practitioners in Denmark and found that some practitioners hold a deficit model about particular groups of children, especially those brought up in poverty, those with special needs, and children from 'minority' ethnic groups and cultures. A 'deficit model' can lead practitioners to *expect* some children to achieve less well than other children. This expectation can lead to adults unconsciously behaving in a way that fulfils these expectations. Classic research undertaken by Rosenthal and Jacobson (1968) found that if teachers were told a certain group of children would make dramatic strides in their school work, then these children achieved much better results than the other children in their class, even if (unknown to the teachers) these children were chosen at random from the class and there should have been no difference in the way they performed.

Reflection

It is the beginning of a school year and nursery staff are discussing the new children who will be starting that term. One is heard to comment that they can expect trouble from a particular child because he comes from the local traveller's camp, commenting that 'you know what that can mean'.

- What negative attitudes may the practitioner hold about gypsy and traveller children?
- How may this affect the way the child is treated and what effect may this have on the child's progress in the setting?
- How may this affect the relationship between the setting and the parents?
- If you heard a colleague make such comments, how would you deal with the situation?

The way children 'see' themselves can affect the way they learn

We all have ideas about the kind of person we are, for example whether we are shy or bold, attractive or plain, good at our job or not. The ideas we hold about ourselves make up our 'self concept' or 'self image' (Mukherji, 2001) and are formed, in part, from the reactions of others around us. If the ideas we hold about ourselves are positive, that is, we feel loved and able to achieve what we want to achieve, then it is said that we have high self-esteem or a positive self image. If, however, we hold predominately negative ideas about ourselves, for example that we are ugly, unlovable and unintelligent, then it is said that we have low self-esteem or a negative self image (Brain and Mukherji, 2005).

If children feel secure and loved, and the adults around them have high but realistic expectations of them, then children's self-esteem will be high. Conversely, if children are unloved, neglected or are led to believe that they are failures, then it is likely that they will develop feelings of low self-esteem (Mukherji, 2012). There is a relationship between what a child thinks about themselves and the way that they learn (Humphrey, 2004). The literature on what is meant by self-esteem and the self concept is complex; Humphrey points out that a child's 'global' self concept may not be directly related to achievement, but that certain components may influence learning. Recently Dweck (2010) has looked at one particular component of a child's self concept, that is the ideas that children hold about their learning capabilities. She explains that some children have fixed 'mindsets', believing that they are born with a fixed level of intelligence that will not change, whereas other children have a 'growth' mindset, whereby they believe that intelligence is not fixed, but grows over time. Dweck suggests that children who have a fixed mindset value looking 'smart' and will not put themselves in situations that could lead to failure, whereas children with a growth mindset relish challenges, and even failure, as they can see that there are opportunities to learn from these experiences. This has implications for educators; when tackling a new task or attempting a challenge, children should be helped to look at the strategies that have worked and those that have not, rather than praising success.

It is not just parents and family that contribute to a child's self concept; children will be affected by the way they see people like themselves treated by society in general, including how they are represented by the media. For example, if boys and girls are treated differently in the home, with girls being encouraged to help in domestic chores while the boys are encouraged to help their father with DIY, and these roles are reinforced by the way that men and women are portrayed in the media, then these ideas become internalised by children. This will influence the way that children behave and the choices they make as they grow older. Children who belong to a particular cultural or ethnic group will, likewise, absorb ideas and attitudes about themselves from those around them and their experience of how people like themselves are treated and represented by the media. If children encounter negative, racist, attitudes, these attitudes may be incorporated into their self concept. For example, young black men are often portrayed as being more likely to be in trouble with the law and less likely than others to get a job after school (Mukherji, 2012). These negative views may not only influence children to think that there is no point in working hard, but may also affect teachers' expectations as to their likely achievement in the school system.

Promoting equality in early childhood settings

In this section of the chapter we will look at some of the ways that early childhood practitioners can promote equality and social justice. Practice needs to be underpinned by a thorough understanding of children's rights and a recognition of the imperative placed upon early childhood practitioners to uphold these rights.

> For early childhood practitioners 'equality' entails valuing all children as individuals, recognising that children have individual needs and that their rights as individuals need to be respected and upheld. (Mukherji, 2012: 239)

If you have not already done so it is suggested that you read the chapter on children's rights (Chapter 2) to help you understand the relationship between upholding children's rights and the promotion of equality in early childhood settings.

The role of early childhood services in counteracting the effect of disadvantage and poverty

At the start of the chapter we noted that one of the main factors influencing children's attainment at age 5 is poverty and disadvantage (DfE, 2012a). In 2012 it was estimated that one in three children in the UK live in poverty (Child Poverty Action Group [CPAG], 2012).

The CPAG points out that there is a direct link between poverty and inequality. Children from impoverished households have poorer health and are more likely to go hungry than their peers. When they leave school they are more likely to have gained fewer qualifications than their contemporaries and if they do find employment they are likely to earn less than their peers (CPAG, 2012). Not only that, poor children are more likely to experience discrimination and negative language (Mukherji, 2012). Previous and current governments have emphasised that the best way to help children from impoverished backgrounds is to give them access to high quality early childhood provision, and to target resources to the most disadvantaged children in the first five years of their life (DWP and DfE, 2011). In 2011 the Department of Education published the Government's response to various reports that outlined the effects of poverty and disadvantage on children's life chances. The document laid down the Government's commitment to providing support and intervention early on in the lives of disadvantaged children, taking a multidisciplinary and cross-governmental approach.

Reflection

Read the following document: DfE (2011) *Supporting Families in the Foundation Years* http://www.education.gov.uk/childrenandyoungpeople/earlylearningandchildcare/early/a00192398/supporting-families-in-the-foundation-years

- Outline the main policy initiatives proposed in this document.
- Looking back on what was proposed in 2011, how many of these initiatives have come to pass?
- What role do early childhood practitioners have in promoting equality for impoverished and disadvantaged children?
- What are the implications for leaders within the sector?

Inclusive practice and special educational needs

By reading the case study about Alisha earlier on in this chapter it should be clear that 'equality' does not mean treating all children exactly the same. Alisha has the opportunity to attend an early childhood setting, just as other children do, but other factors act as a barrier to her enjoying the opportunity in a way equal to other children. Some of the factors that mean that Alisha's experience is not equal to that of other children are due to external physical issues, such as ramps not being in place and staff not being trained. In some ways it could be argued these are quite straightforward problems to solve. However, the more challenging barriers that prevent Alisha from having the same opportunities are the attitudes of other people; for example, staff not thinking through the need to ensure that all the activities they plan can be accessed by all the children, or the parents of some of the other children not wanting to foster a friendship between their children and Alisha.

The struggle for the right for children with special educational needs and disabilities to be educated together with their peers in mainstream schools has had a long history, and in 1978 Baroness Warnock recommended that children with special educational needs or disabilities should be integrated into mainstream school as far as possible (DfES, 1978). Internationally, the need for all children to be given the right to be taught together in ordinary schools, with support to access all areas of the curriculum (inclusion) was recognised in the 1994 Salamanca Statement (UNESCO) where 92 countries signed an agreement that inclusion should be the norm. The right for inclusive education has been strengthened by subsequent legislation in England, for instance the 2001 Special Needs and Disability Act which made it against the law to discriminate against disabled children in the provision of services. In practice this means that children with disabilities should not be treated less favourably than other children and that reasonable adjustments for disabled children should be made.

Journal Task

S.L. Odom, V. Buysse and E. Soukakou (2011) 'Inclusion for young children with disabilities: A quarter century of research perspectives', *Journal of Early Intervention*, 33(4): 344–56.

This article discusses how the inclusion of children with disabilities has been developing over the past 25 years. While the article focuses on the USA education system the principles that are discussed mirror the principles that underpin the approach to inclusion in the UK.

Levels 4 & 5

Consider the different approaches to inclusion discussed in the article, which ones do you think are the most beneficial for the children? What reasons can you give to support your ideas?

What do you think it means when the authors discuss the idea that where a school or setting is truly inclusive all the children benefit, not only those who have a special educational need or disability?

Level 6

On page 347 the authors discuss how the most successful inclusion experiences in terms of outcomes for children are where the inclusion programmes are set within 'a large ecological systems context'.

(Continued)

(Continued)

What do you think this means and why would 'a large ecological system context' that supported inclusion be so beneficial? You will find an explanation of ecological systems theory in this book in Chapter 5.

To download this task as well as other useful online resources please visit: **www.sagepub.co.uk/mukherji**

Completing the journal task will help you understand that the concept of 'inclusion' relates to all children, not only those with special educational needs or disabilities. Inclusive education involves provision that values all children, regardless of their circumstances and background. The Early Childhood Forum (2003) describes inclusion as a process, rather than a state, that includes the processes of identification and understanding and removing barriers to full participation and belonging.

Reflection

At the time of writing, in England, there are changes in the way that children with special educational needs will be assessed and supported, moving from the 2001 Special Educational Needs Code of Practice (DfES, 2001) to new legislation due to come into operation in 2014 (DfE, 2012c).

- Investigate the SEN and disability policy in your setting. Ask the person with special responsibility for this area how children are supported and what procedures are in place.
- In 2005 Ofsted produced a report that outlined aspects of good practice in the area: *Removing Barriers: A Can-do Attitude* http://www.ofsted.gov.uk/resources/removing-barriers-can-do-attitude. Identify aspects of good practice from this report that you could share with your colleagues.

Reducing racism and discrimination in early childhood settings

The population of Britain is very diverse. The Office for National Statistics (ONS, 2011) identified that approximately one in six of the population in England and Wales are non-white, with some areas, such as London, having a larger proportion of non-white residents. People from 'black and minority ethnic backgrounds' can often be the targets for racist and discriminatory behaviour.

There have been a number of laws passed in the UK that have sought to ensure the UK is a place where people are treated equally in all situations, and early childhood settings have to comply with these laws. The most recent piece of legislation, the Equality Act 2010, seeks to bring together all aspects of previous laws and establish clear guidance with regard to the equal treatment of all persons. As the Government states, the Equality Act 2010 'bans unfair treatment and helps achieve equal opportunities'. The Act covers nine protected characteristics which cannot be used as a reason to treat people unfairly. These protected characteristics are: age, disability, gender reassignment, marriage and civil partnership, pregnancy and maternity, race, religion and belief, sex and sexual orientation (Home Office website, 2013).

All courses leading to early childhood qualifications are designed to produce a workforce who understand about inequalities and who can promote equality in their practice. Settings are expected to have policies and procedures in place to promote anti-discriminative practice. Consequently, it is possible to think that racism and discrimination are no longer 'problems' in early childhood settings. However, often racism is very subtle, and Lane (2008) considers that practitioners may not be aware of the extent to which racism pervades society and directly affects the lives of very young children and their families. In recent years Britain has seen a rise in Islamophobia and anti-Semitism (Weller, 2011), together with negative attitudes being openly expressed about recent immigrant groups such as Poles and Eastern Europeans. Lane (2008) suggests that to become aware of the extent to which racism effects the lives of children and families, practitioners need to both *know* and *understand* about racism. Historically, anti-racist training had a reputation of being confrontational; some practitioners are apprehensive and fear using the 'wrong words', however, Lane (2008) suggests that if practitioners know what racism is, know how to recognise it and understand its origins, then the worry and guilt that sometimes surrounds the subject will be removed and practitioners will be in a better position to notice when practices and policies in early childhood settings are discriminatory. From this we can see that there is a need for everyone working in early childhood settings to participate in high quality training and that there should be a whole team approach, with everyone taking individual and collective responsibility for promoting anti-discriminative practice.

Reflection

Read Jane Lane's 2006 document, *Right from the Start: A Commissioned Study of Antiracism, Learning and the Early Years*, published by Focus First UK. http://www.focus-consultancy.co.uk/pdfs/first4.pdf

This document discusses the role of the early childhood sector in tackling racism and examines the benefits to society as a whole, together with the barriers that need to be overcome.

(Continued)

(Continued)

- Look at the section on priorities for action at a setting level. What suggestions are there for promoting anti-discriminative practice?
- If you are involved in an early childhood setting, review the policies, procedures and practices of the setting in the light of this document and produce an action plan to improve the quality of work in this area.

Your reflections may have led you to conclude that anti-discriminative practice involves helping children, parents and staff recognise when they are holding discriminatory attitudes towards members of other groups. Mukherji (2012) points out that it is not just members of black or minority ethnic groups who may experience negative attitudes and prejudice. Gay and lesbian parents, teenage parents, older parents, and those with special needs or traveller families may all experience prejudice and discrimination from other parents, staff and, occasionally, children. We have a responsibility for ensuring that all those who use early childhood settings feel included and 'safe', and staff teams should discuss how this can be achieved. This discussion should evaluate the experiences of parents and children from first contact with the setting, the home visit (if there is one) and the settling-in process, as well as the day-to-day life of the setting. This may involve relooking at the literature that parents receive from the setting to ensure that specific groups are included. For example, is all written communication translated into community languages? Is inclusive language used; for example, is it recognised that children may have same sex parents? If illustrations are used do they show parents from different ethnic minorities and very young mothers? When entering the setting are there images and resources that reflect the background of the families using the facilities and are all parents included in the life of the setting, and not just the parents we feel comfortable with?

Early childhood settings are ideally placed to help reduce prejudice. Dhont et al. (2011: 514) point out that 'frequent positive contact between members of different groups has been considered one of the most powerful strategies to promote positive intergroup attitudes and reduce intergroup bias'. The more activities that are arranged for *all* those involved in the setting to meet, either socially or with a shared purpose such as a work party, then the more likely it is that negative attitudes will be reduced.

Reflection

Gypsy, Roma and Traveller children and families are groups that are victims of negative attitudes and discrimination both in society as a whole and within early childhood settings due to the lack of knowledge of practitioners.

Read this document: DCSF (2009) *Building Futures: Developing Trust. A Focus on Provision for Children from Gypsy, Roma and Traveller Backgrounds in the Early Years Foundation Stage.* Nottingham. DCSF Publications. http://www.foundationyears.org.uk/wp-content/uploads/2011/10/Developing_Trust.pdf

- Reflect upon your own attitudes towards children and families from these groups then discuss your reflections with your colleagues on the same course as you or colleagues you work with.
- In what ways can the principles of the Early Years Foundation Stage help you in establishing quality provision?
- If you are connected with an early childhood setting, evaluate the setting's practice in relation to this document.

Reflective practice will help us identify when our practice fails to include all children. We will look at a specific example of how this may happen when planning to deliver aspects of the curriculum. Most early childhood settings use traditional tales and nursery rhymes as starting points for literacy learning. Often we draw on stories and rhymes that are familiar to us and reflect our ethnic and cultural background. However, sometimes the material we use, although very familiar to us, may be outside the experience of the children we are working with, particularly if they have a different ethnic, cultural or socio-economic background to us. This is not a problem, as long as we ensure all the children are familiar with the stories and rhymes we are using and similarly make sure we do some research to extend our knowledge and understanding of the stories and rhymes the children we are working with know. However, if children are presented with literature that derives from *only* one cultural background, the children who are not familiar with that literature may be disadvantaged compared to those children who know the stories well. Similarly, such situations can unwittingly pass on the message that in this setting we only value particular stories and rhymes and that other stories and rhymes have no place in our setting. Garner (2007: 79) describes this as *invisibility and visibility norms.* Bourdieu (Knowles and Lander, 2011) discusses how society can behave as if some forms of literature, music, ways of dressing and certain aspects of behaviour are seen as being more acceptable than others; even *better* or more desirable than others. In particular he relates this idea to notions of class and low income. Generally speaking, early childhood settings and schools give visibility to books, stories, clothes and ways of behaving that can be associated with middle-class attitudes and values.

Gender conscious practice

At the beginning of the chapter we noted how there are equality issues surrounding an individual's gender, with boys consistently underachieving within the education system (DfE, 2012a) and women affected by inequalities in the workplace as they grow older (EHRC, 2013). Early childhood practitioners, therefore, need to bear both these issues in mind when planning to promote gender equality, a process that has been called gender conscious practice (Abril et al., 2008).

Reflection

In 2008 Abril et al. published the results of a two-year international study into how to introduce gender conscious practice into the early childhood curriculum and into vocational training for early childhood practitioners. The report called *Gender Loops* can be found here: http://www.genderloops.eu/docs/toolbox.pdf

- What is meant by 'gender conscious practice'? In what ways may it help redress gender inequality?
- Read through the document and decide what actions may be appropriate for you as an individual to implement and what actions need to be implemented by the whole team.
- Most of the suggested activities are for children over 3 – reflect upon what you can do with younger children to help them avoid developing stereotypical attitudes.

The *Gender Loops* initiative starts with a section where practitioners are asked to reflect upon their own attitudes and beliefs, which should be the starting point for *any* initiative designed to promote equality within early childhood settings. Our attitudes are especially important when we think about our practice where boys are concerned. Often boys' natural exuberance is seen to be something that has to be contained within early childhood settings and the curriculum has a tendency to be slanted towards meeting the needs of girls. Indeed, early childhood settings are predominantly 'female' spaces, with the vast majority of practitioners being women. Intuitively it may seem that the 'feminising' of education may have a direct effect on the achievement of boys within the education system. However, the issue is very complex and may, itself, reveal stereotypical ideas about the roles of men and women (Skelton, 2002).

Reflection

Look at the following document: DCSF (2007) *Confident, Capable and Creative: Supporting Boys' Achievements: Guidance for Practitioners in the Early Years Foundation Stage.* http://www.foundationyears.org.uk/wp-content/uploads/2011/10/Confident_Capable_Boys.pdf

- Make a list of 'good practice' points.
- If you are involved in an early childhood setting, share these points with your colleagues and evaluate your practice.

Summary

In this chapter we have explored how there can be barriers to children's achievement because of issues relating to disability, race, poverty and gender. We have investigated the barriers to equality, looking at how poverty and disadvantage and the attitudes of adults and children can lead to stereotypical thinking and discriminatory behaviour. Early childhood services and settings are ideally placed to promote equality and counteract discrimination and we discussed policies and practice which are designed to ensure all children are given the opportunity to achieve. We discussed the importance of reflecting upon our own experiences, knowledge and beliefs which can have a profound effect upon the way we interact with children and their families.

Further reading

Levels 4 & 5

Baldock, P. (2010) *Understanding Cultural Diversity in the Early Years*. London. Sage. This text gives students and practitioners an understanding of theoretical concepts whilst giving sound practical advice. It has a very useful chapter on supporting diversity in settings where most of the children are white British.

Casey, T. (2010) *Inclusive Play: Practical Strategies for Children from Birth to Eight* (2nd edition). London. Sage. Although aimed at provision for children with disabilities, the rights-based approach taken in this text makes it invaluable for all those working with young children.

Knowles, G. and Lander, V. (2011) *Diversity, Equality and Achievement in Education*. London: Sage. Although not specifically aimed at early childhood, this text gives comprehensive coverage of the subject area. It will help those working in early childhood put their practice within a wider context.

Wall, K. (2011) *Special Needs and Early Years* (3rd edition). London: Sage. This text supplies a clear, practical account of working with children and their families in early childhood settings.

Level 6

McNaughton, G. and Davis, K. (eds) (2009) *'Race' and Early Childhood Education: An International Approach to Identity, Politics and Pedagogy*. Basingstoke: Palgrave Macmillan. This text investigates topics from a variety of different theoretical perspectives and will help you reflect more deeply about the issues outlined within this chapter.

References

Abril, A., Cremers, M., Duncan, N., Golubevaite, L., Krabel, J., Lilaite, A., Bredesen Nordfjell, O., Raudonyte, J. and Romero, A. (2008) *Gender Loops Toolbox for Gender-conscious and Equitable Early Childhood Centres.* http://www.genderloops.eu/docs/toolbox.pdf (accessed 14 March 2013).

Adams, M., Bell, L.A. and Griffin, P. (ed.) (2007) *Teaching for Diversity and Social Justice* (2nd edition). London: Routledge.

Baldock, P. (2010) *Understanding Cultural Diversity in the Early Years.* London: Sage.

Brain, C. and Mukherji, P. (2005) *Understanding Child Psychology.* Cheltenham: Nelson Thornes.

Brighouse, H., Haydon, G. and Tooley, J. (2010) *Educational Equality* (2nd edition). London: Continuum International Publishing.

Casey, T. (2010) *Inclusive Play: Practical Strategies for Children from Birth to Eight* (2nd edition). London: Sage.

Child Poverty Action Group (2012) *End Child Poverty.* http://www.endchildpoverty.org.uk/ (accessed 16 March 2013).

Department for Children, Schools and Families (DCSF) (2007) *Confident, Capable and Creative: Supporting Boys' Achievements.* London: DCSF. Available at: earlyarts.co.uk/wp-content/uploads/Confident_Capable_Boys.pdf (accessed 22 November 2013).

Department for Children, Schools and Families (DCSF) (2009) *Building Futures: Developing Trust. A Focus on Provision for Children from Gypsy, Roma and Traveller Backgrounds in the Early Years Foundation Stage.* Nottingham: DCSF Publications. http://www.foundationyears.org.uk/wp-content/uploads/2011/10/Developing_Trust.pdf (accessed 21 March 2013).

Department for Education (2010) *Achievement of Children in the Early Years Foundation Stage Profile.* London: DfE.

Department for Education (2011) *Supporting Families in the Foundation Years.* http://www.education.gov.uk/childrenandyoungpeople/earlylearningandchildcare/early/a00192398/supporting-families-in-the-foundation-years (accessed 17 March 2013).

Department for Education (2012a) *Statistical First Release: Early Years Foundation Stage Profile Attainment by Pupil Characteristics, England 2011/12.* London. HMSO.

Department for Education (2012b) *Statutory Framework for the Early Years Foundation Stage.* London: DfE.

Department for Education (2012c) *Statutory Framework for the Early Years Foundation Stage: Setting the Standards for Learning, Development and Care for Children from Birth to Five.* London: DfE. https://www.media.education.gov.uk/assets/files/pdf/eyfs%20statutory%20framework%20march%202012.pdf (accessed 6 August 2013).

Department of Education and Science (1978) *The Report of the Committee of Enquiry into the Education of Handicapped Children and Young People* (Warnock Report). London: HMSO.

Department for Education and Skills (2001) *The Special Educational Needs Code of Practice.* London: DfES.

Department for Work and Pensions and the Department for Education (2011) *A New Approach to Child Poverty: Tackling the Causes of Disadvantage and Transforming Families' Lives.* London: HMSO.

Dhont, K., Roets, A. and Van Hiel, A. (2011) 'Opening closed minds: The combined effects of intergroup contact and need for closure on prejudice', *Personality and Social Psychology Bulletin*, 37(4): 514–28.

Dukes, C. and Smith, M. (2009) *Building Better Behaviour in the Early Years.* London: Sage.

Dweck, C. (2010) 'Even geniuses work hard', *Educational Leadership*, 68(1): 16–21.

Early Childhood Forum (2003) *Policy Statement: Definition of Inclusion.* London: HMSO.

Equality Act 2010 London: HMSO. http://www.homeoffice.gov.uk/equalities/equality-act/ (accessed 4 March 2013).

EHRC (2013) *Equality and Human Rights Commission Submission to the Equal Opportunities Committee Women and Work Inquiry*. http://www.equalityhumanrights.com/ (accessed 16 March 2013).

Evans, J.D.G. (2010) *Plato Primer*. Durham: Acumen.

Field, F. (2010) *The Foundation Years: Preventing Poor Children Becoming Poor Adults*. London: Cabinet Office. http://webarchive.nationalarchives.gov.uk/20110120090128/http:/povertyreview.independent.gov.uk/media/20254/poverty-report.pdf (accessed 4 March 2013).

Garner, S. (2007) *Whiteness: An Introduction*. Abingdon: Routledge.

Hinman, L.M. (2003) *Ethics: A Pluralistic Approach to Moral Theory*. Boston, MA: Wadsworth.

Humphrey, N. (2004) 'The death of the feel-good factor? Self-esteem in the educational context', *School Psychology International*, 25(3): 347–60.

Jensen, B. (2009) 'A Nordic approach to Early Childhood Education (ECE) and socially endangered children', *European Early Childhood Education Research Journal*, 17(1): 7–21.

Knowles, G. and Lander, V. (2011) *Diversity, Equality and Achievement in Education*. London: Sage.

Lane, J. (2006) *Right From the Start: A Commissioned Study of Antiracism, Learning and the Early Years*. http://www.focus-consultancy.co.uk/pdfs/first4.pdf (accessed 15 March 2013).

Lane, J. (2008) *Young Children and Racial Justice – Taking Action for Racial Equality in the Early Years – Understanding the Past, Thinking About the Present, Planning for the Future*. London: The National Children's Bureau.

Lovett, F. (2010) *Rawls's 'A Theory of Justice': A Reader's Guide*. London: Continuum International Publishing.

Maslow, A. (1943) 'A theory of human motivation', originally published in *Psychological Review*, 50: 370–96. http://www.psychclassics.yorku.ca/Maslow/motivation.htm (accessed 6 August 2013).

McNaughton, G. and Davis, K. (eds) (2009) *'Race' and Early Childhood Education: An International Approach to Identity, Politics and Pedagogy*. Basingstoke: Palgrave.

Mukherji, P. (2001) *Understanding Children's Challenging Behaviour*. Cheltenham: Nelson Thornes.

Mukherji, P. (2012) 'Equality and inclusion', in F. Veal (ed.), *Early Years for Levels 4+5 and the Foundation Degree*. London: Hodder Education.

Office for National Statistics (ONS) (2011) *Population Estimates by Ethnic Group 2006–2009*. Cardiff: ONS.

Office for Standards in Education, Children's Services and Skills (2005) *Removing Barriers: A 'Can Do' Attitude*. http://www.ofsted.gov.uk/resources/removing-barriers-can-do-attitude (accessed 14 March 2013).

Rosenthal, R. and Jacobson, L. (1968) *Pygmalion in the Classroom: Teacher Expectation and Pupils' Intellectual Development*. New York, NY, US: Holt, Rinehart & Winston.

Skelton, C. (2002) 'The "feminisation of schooling" or "remasculinising" of primary education', *International Studies in Sociology of Education*, 12(1): 7–96.

Special Educational Needs and Disability Act 2001. London: HMSO.

UNESCO (1994) *The Salamanca Statement and Framework for Action on Special Needs Education*. Paris: UNESCO.

Wall, K. (2011) *Special Needs and Early Years* (3rd edition). London: Sage.

Weller, P. (2011) *Religious Discrimination in Britain: A Review of Research Evidence, 2000–10. Equality and Human Rights Commission Research Report 73*. Manchester: EHRC.

10

Health and Well-being

Penny Mukherji

This chapter will:

- Look at the concept of health and well-being as it applies to children and their families
- Investigate the factors that influence the physical health and emotional well-being of children from pre-conception onwards
- Investigate how social inequality has a direct effect on the health of children
- Look at the child health programme
- Examine the role of early childhood settings in promoting children's health.

The importance of promoting the health of children in their early years cannot be overstated. According to the Marmot review (2010: 160):

> The foundations for virtually every aspect of human development – physical, intellectual and emotional are laid in early childhood. What happens during these early years (starting in the womb) has lifelong effects on many aspects of health and well-being from obesity, heart disease and mental health, to educational achievement and economic status.

Compared with children living at the turn of the twentieth century, 'Children and young people are healthier today than they have ever been' (DCSF and DoH,

2009: 3). In 1900 the infant mortality rate for children born in the UK was 140 per thousand live births, (Hicks and Allen, 1999), whilst in 2012 the infant mortality rate for children born in the UK was 4.1 (CIA, 2013). In the era before antibiotics and immunisations, very many children failed to survive childhood, succumbing to infections such as measles, small pox, diphtheria and TB. Poor sanitation, overcrowded living conditions and a lack of medical care all contributed to high levels of illness and ill health.

During the twentieth century huge strides were made in the provision of healthy living conditions, with the demolition of overcrowded slums, the provision of clean water and the establishment of an effective refuse and sewerage system. These improvements, taken together with the development of a universal childhood immunisation programme, led to improvements in children's health. The development of the welfare state, which raised families out of absolute poverty and the establishment of the National Health Service further contributed to this steady improvement.

However, it has become clear that although the health of *all* children has improved, the health of children from disadvantaged families has not improved as fast as that of children from more advantaged families (Marmot, 2010). This gap is widening year on year and is an indictment on our society today.

How are health and well-being defined?

There are no fixed definitions of 'health' or 'well-being'; these terms are very subjective and depend upon factors such as where you live, your social class, age and education. There are two main approaches to defining health and well-being. One approach is to look at the views of different groups of the population and another is a more formal approach where academics and organisations try to define health in a way that is helpful for policy makers.

The views of parents and practitioners

In a study conducted in 2010 by London Metropolitan University and the National Children's Bureau (in press) parents and early childhood practitioners viewed 'health' as being part of the wider concept of 'well-being'. Parents and practitioners described the concept of well-being as complex and holistic in nature. Participants in the study used words such as 'net', 'mesh', 'jigsaw' and 'Russian Doll' to explain this complexity. Furthermore, the concept was seen to be dynamic (in that an individual's state of well-being can fluctuate over time), and subjective. Participants in the project saw health as being an aspect of well-being, but not synonymous with it. Health was seen as a prerequisite for, but not a guarantee of, an individual's well-being.

Formal definitions

There have been many attempts to devise a 'formal' definition of 'health', all of which have faced criticisms of some kind. The most widely quoted definition of 'health' was devised in 1946 by the World Health Organization (WHO) in which health was defined as 'a state of complete physical, mental and social well-being and not merely the absence of disease or infirmity' (Grad, 2002: 1). This definition appears to equate health with well-being, in that to be healthy one has to be in a state of well-being. It has been criticised because of the inclusion of the word 'complete' since under this definition almost all of us would be defined as unhealthy (Underdown, 2007). Since 1946, others have added emotional, spiritual and social aspects of health to the concept, so that now 'health' is defined in holistic terms. In 1984 the WHO extended its definition to include the idea that health is a resource, related to how well an individual can adapt to change. Health is now defined as:

> The extent to which an individual or group is able on the one hand to realise aspirations and satisfy needs; and, on the other hand to change or cope with the environment; health is, therefore, seen as a resource for everyday life. Not the objective for living; it is a positive concept emphasising social and personal resources as well as physical capacities. (WHO, 2009a: 29)

The importance of children's health

> A vital and productive society with a prosperous and sustainable future is built on a foundation of healthy child development. Health in the earliest years – actually beginning with the future mother's health before she becomes pregnant – lays the groundwork for a lifetime of well-being. (Center on the Developing Child, Harvard University, 2010: 2)

Blair (2008) outlines why it is so important that resources are allocated to maximising the health of children in the first five years of life:

- It is a basic human right: working towards achieving the best health for all children is enshrined in Article 24 of the UNICEF Rights of the Child.
- Evidence from neurobiological studies indicates that what happens in early childhood is crucial in terms of future physical and emotional health.
- Allocating resources to support vulnerable children and families will increase their resilience to negative economic and societal forces and reduce inequalities in health.
- There is a cost benefit to the nation. If resources are used to support families and children in the early years, they will be less likely to need hospital services, less likely to be involved in criminal activity and more likely to continue in education and become productive members of society (Blair, 2008: 3).

Factors that influence children's health

The Center on the Developing Child (2010) identifies four interrelated dimensions to health. The first dimension describes how an individual's health can be influenced by an interaction between genetic predispositions and the environment. For example, a child exposed to alcohol in the womb may have permanent ill health as a result. The adverse and permanent effect of stress on children's developing brains is another example of genetic/environmental interaction.

The second dimension affecting children's health is described by the Centre as 'Foundations of Health', and describes three conditions needed for children to thrive.

- Children need to be raised within stable, responsive relationships.
- Children need to be raised within safe and supportive physical environments.
- Children need to be given the best possible nutrition from pre-conception and pregnancy (via the mother) and after birth.

The third dimension focuses on the capacities of both the children's caregivers and the communities in which they are raised to promote health and prevent disease. Finally, the fourth dimension focuses on public and private sector policies and programmes that are designed to promote the health of children.

Reflection

Look at the following documents:

Center on the Developing Child, Harvard University (2010) *The Foundations of Lifelong Health Are Built in Early Childhood.* Harvard University. http://developingchild.harvard.edu/resources/reports_and_working_papers/foundations-of-lifelong-health/

Department of Children, Schools and Families and Department of Health (DCSF/DoH) (2009) *Healthy Lives, Brighter Futures: The strategy for Children and Young People's Health*. London: DCSF/DoH. https://www.education.gov.uk/publications/eOrderingDownload/285374a.pdf

Using information from both of these documents identify why it is important to focus on the health of young children and the factors that affect children's health.

Factors affecting children's health before they are born

In the previous section we noted that children's health is affected by the interaction of both genetic and environmental factors. In this section we will look at some of these genetic and environmental factors in more detail, specifically as they apply in pregnancy.

Genetic influences on development and health

Sometimes, within the cells of the developing foetus, there are abnormalities or changes in chromosomes or genes and these changes can adversely affect the way children develop. One in 200 babies have a chromosomal abnormality such as Down syndrome. Some conditions are due to changes on single genes, for example sickle cell disease. Although some abnormalities appear spontaneously, many are passed on from parents to their children, for example cystic fibrosis (Mukherji, 2005).

It is possible to identify some conditions such as Down syndrome by screening during pregnancy and the mother will be given counselling to help her and her partner decide whether or not to continue with the pregnancy (Liptack, 2008).

Environmental factors

Environmental factors can have an influence before conception. Some environmental toxins such as radiation or chemicals can cause abnormalities in the chromosomes or genes. An example of this is the pesticide 'agent orange' that was used as a defoliant in the Vietnam War. The children of fathers returning from the war were found to have a higher risk than usual of birth defects (Mekdeci, 2012).

Once a baby is conceived, drugs or chemicals can affect the foetus if they cross the placental barrier. The most dangerous time is the first three months when the main body structures are being formed. Pregnant women are advised to stop drinking and smoking during pregnancy because of the adverse effects on the baby. Infections can also affect the developing foetus. Some infections, for example Rubella (German measles) can have a devastating effect early on in pregnancy but have fewer ill effects in late pregnancy (DoH, 2009a).

Maternal age and nutritional state can all have an adverse effect on the health of a foetus. Very young mothers who are still growing and those with a poor diet are likely to give birth to small babies and be at risk of premature delivery (Spencer and Logan, 2002).

Complications at birth, including problems with the placenta, can lead to a baby being born with disabilities. In addition, immediately after birth, poor medical care, poor social conditions and poor nutrition of mother and infant can all lead to adverse effects on the baby (DoH, 2009a).

Nutrition and children's health

There is a direct link between children's nutritional status and their health. In the majority world approximately 30 per cent of children suffer from malnutrition because they do not receive enough to eat (Albon and Mukherji, 2008). Some children will perish because of lack of food, whilst others will survive to become intellectually and physically stunted. An example of this is in India, where in 2009 48 per cent of children were considered to be stunted and 43 per cent underweight, with 20 per cent of all children categorised as wasted (World Bank, 2012). In the UK there is growing concern that, because of the economic downturn, there is an increasing number of children who regularly go hungry. In November 2012 the charity Action for Children, who work with vulnerable children and families, reported that many of the 50,000 children whom they support do not know where their next meal is coming from and that 83 per cent of their project managers reported an increase in the number of families struggling to make ends meet. However, the majority of children in the UK do not lack food, but they too can suffer malnutrition if they are given too much food to eat, leading to obesity, or anaemia and dental problems if they are given the wrong type of food.

Reflection

Read Chapter 2 in Albon, D. and Mukherji, P. (2008) *Food and Health in Early Childhood.* London: Sage. (This is an ebook.)

1. What percentage of morbidity (death) and mortality (illness) can be attributed to poor diet in the UK?
2. The most common conditions in children, related to malnutrition, in the UK are obesity, oral diseases, iron deficiency anaemia and vitamin D deficiency.
   - What effects do the conditions have on children's health and development? (Page 31 looks at obesity.)
   - How can they be prevented?
3. What evidence is there that a lack of micronutrients can effect children's intellectual development and behaviour?

Breastfeeding

Breastfeeding is the natural way to feed babies and the guidelines state that all babies should be exclusively breastfed until they are six months of age (WHO, 2012).

Reflection

Levels 4 & 5

Look at this NHS website: Your pregnancy and baby guide (newborn section) http://www.nhs.uk/conditions/pregnancy-and-baby/pages/pregnancy-and-baby-care.aspx (accessed 16 April 2013).

(Continued)

(Continued)

1. What are the advantages and disadvantages to the baby and mother of breastfeeding?
2. What is meant by 'exclusive breastfeeding' and how long should it continue?
3. Thinking about the mothers you know personally or with whom you come into contact in your professional work, how many mothers start breastfeeding their children and how many are exclusively feeding by six months? What reasons do they give for their decisions?

Extension to Level 6

Look at the following document: WHO World Health Organization (2009) *Infant and Young Child Feeding: Model Chapter for Textbooks for Medical Students and Allied Health Professionals.* http://whqlibdoc.who.int/publications/2009/9789241597494_eng.pdf (accessed 12 September 2012).

This document gives the evidence upon which the recommendation that all babies should be exclusively breastfed is based. Analyse the evidence and evaluate how relevant the recommendations are for mothers living in the minority world, where food shortages and hygiene may not be important factors.

In 2010, 81 per cent of mothers breastfed their babies immediately after birth (The NHS information Centre, 2011). However, not all these mothers continued to breastfeed until six months. Bolling et al. (2007) report that in 2005, although 78 per cent of mothers initiated breastfeeding, by six weeks only 50 per cent were still breastfeeding and that by six months only 26 per cent of babies were being breastfed. If we look at the figures for exclusive breastfeeding, then the statistics are much lower; by six weeks only 21 per cent of babies were fed on breast milk alone and by the age of six months the rate of exclusive breastfeeding is negligible (Albon and Mukherji, 2008).

Why is it that mothers are not conforming to the current guidelines? Albon and Mukherji (2008) suggest that factors such as a mother's socio-economic group and ethnicity play a part, with breastfeeding rates being higher in higher socio-economic groups and among Black and Asian mothers. They also suggest that other factors such as cost, convenience, mother's health, employment status and the wishes of her family all have a part to play in the decision to continue breastfeeding.

The universal application of breastfeeding guidelines, for both the majority and minority worlds has caused controversy. Fewtrell et al. (2007) acknowledge that the guidelines are appropriate for children from the majority world, but that there is insufficient evidence to show that, in the minority world, exclusive breastfeeding until six months of age meets the nutritional needs of the average baby. They recommend that randomised controlled studies are needed before we know for certain if exclusive breastfeeding until six months is best for babies in the minority world.

If babies are not being exclusively breastfed, on what are they being fed? Most children will have been introduced to bottle feeding using infant formula and for many weaning onto solid food is started around four months. As early childhood professionals it is important that we recognise that the majority of mothers do not follow health guidelines regarding feeding. Whilst informing mothers of the guidelines, it is our role to support mothers in their decisions about breast or bottle feeding and to help them keep their babies safe.

Weaning

According to guidelines, babies should not normally be weaned (introduced to solid food) until six months of age (DoH, 2009b). However, Bolling et al. (2007) state that 51 per cent of mothers have introduced solids before the age of four months.

Albon and Mukherji (2008) identify a number of factors that influence mothers' decisions to start introducing babies to solid food, the most common reason being that parents are worried that babies are hungry. Another strong influence on mothers' decisions to introduce babies to solid food are the opinions of their immediate family and the cultural customs of the community in which the family live.

Reflection

It is important that early childhood practitioners keep up to date on the current recommendations for weaning infants onto solid food.

Look at this NHS website: Your pregnancy and baby guide (weaning in babies and toddler section) http://www.nhs.uk/conditions/pregnancy-and-baby/pages/pregnancy-and-baby-care.aspx

1. As an early childhood practitioner, what do you consider to be your role if you see a mother feeding chocolate to her three-month-old baby?
2. What advice would you give to a mother who has a baby of four months old who is being breastfed, but who is no longer sleeping through the night? The mother is convinced that the baby is hungry.

Early childhood practitioners can find themselves in difficult positions when they see a mother doing something that may be harmful for her baby. Very occasionally the situation could be interpreted as a child protection issue. More usually the baby is not at immediate risk of harm and the practitioner will have time to be reflective. Good early childhood practice is built upon effective relationships with parents and such situations need to be handled sensitively and in a non-judgemental way.

Feeding the older child

By the time a baby is one year old they should be eating more or less the same food as the family, having three main meals with nutritious snacks in-between. Some mothers may still be breastfeeding; the decision to stop feeding often depends on factors such as the mother's return to work, the birth of a sibling and family/cultural practices.

There are differences in nutritional requirements for children under 5 compared to older children. Young children need proportionally more fat in their diet than older children and adults and they have smaller stomachs. This means that they should have small, frequent meals with only moderate amounts of fibre. The NHS Choices website (pregnancy and baby guide) is a good source of information about providing food and drink for children of this age.

Providing food and drink for children in early childhood settings

For many children who attend early childhood settings full-time, most of their food and drink will be provided by the setting. This is a tremendous responsibility as we have already seen how important adequate nutrition is for children's health. There are two aspects to meeting children's nutritional needs in settings. One is making sure that the food is healthy and nutritious; the other involves the social and emotional aspects of food and drink provision.

Although various local authorities and organisations have provided guidance for early childhood settings, it was not until 2012 that the Government (through the auspices of the School Food Trust) issued guidelines for settings in England. These guidelines have been well thought through and cover not only nutritional aspects of food, but the wider context of the importance of food and mealtimes in the holistic development of children.

Reflection

1. Think back to when you were a child. Do you remember how food and special meals were a central part of family and cultural life? You may remember birthday parties and the importance of the birthday cake or the role food played in celebrations such as Eid or Christmas.

Look at The School Food Trust (2012) *Eat Better, Start Better: Voluntary Food and Drink Guidelines for Early Years Settings in England – A Practical Guide.* http://www.childrensfoodtrust.org.uk/assets/eat-better-start-better/CFT%20Early%20Years%20Guide_Interactive_Sept%2012.pdf

What suggestions are made within the document for providing food for special celebrations? Some settings have a total ban on birthday cakes being brought into the setting by parents. Reading the guidelines, what might be a compromise situation?

(Continued)

2. If you are involved with an early childhood setting look at the guidelines and evaluate the food and drink provision in the setting.
    - Does current provision meet the guidelines?
    - Is the policy up to date?
    - How are mealtimes arranged? Do staff sit and eat with the children?
    - Are there any changes to be made?

Childhood obesity

There has been growing concern that the obesity rates for adults and children in the UK are increasing. However, there are signs that the rate of childhood obesity may be levelling off (Dinsdale et al., 2012). Children who are overweight or obese may be compromising their future health, as obesity can lead to cardiovascular disease, diabetes and psychological difficulties (Albon and Mukherji, 2008).

Obesity is caused when children consume foods that contain more calories (a unit of energy) than they need. The excess energy is stored as fat. However, Albon and Mukherji (2008) explain that the diets of children actually contain fewer calories than they used to, with the difference that the proportion of saturated fat in the diet has risen. There is evidence to suggest that physical activity has a role to play, in that children who are less active are more at risk of becoming obese (Swinburn and Egger, 2002).

There is a social gradient in the incidence of obesity, in that children from lower socio-economic groups tend to have higher rates of obesity (Albon and Mukherji, 2008), indicating that there are social and cultural factors that influence food choices both for children and their parents.

Journal Task

DeMattia, L. and Lee Denney, S. (2008) 'Childhood obesity prevention: Successful community-based efforts', *The Annals of the American Academy of Political and Social Science*, 615: 83–99.

Levels 4 & 5

This American article looks at childhood obesity from an ecological approach or model.

1. Ecological models are derived from ecological systems theory (Bronfenbrenner, 1986). Describe, in general terms, what an ecological model is and how it has been used to help us understand influences on both child development (Chapter 5 looks at this in some detail) and childhood obesity.
2. Looking at the ecological model of childhood obesity (Davison and Birch, 2001) consider what actions early childhood practitioners could initiate that may contribute to the prevention of childhood obesity.

(Continued)

(Continued)

Level 6

Much of the press coverage of childhood obesity has focused on parents and implies that if parents gave children the 'right food' their children would not be obese. This is a deficit model. Chapter 13 looks at various models of how early childhood practitioners work with parents. Explain why a deficit model of parenting is not helpful in understanding childhood obesity and suggest more appropriate models/approaches.

To download this task as well as other useful online resources please visit: **www.sagepub.co.uk/mukherji**

The physical environment and children's health

Compared to adults, children are more at risk from environmental hazards because their bodies are still developing, and, because of their small size, they have relatively higher exposure to hazards than adults. As with many health issues, there is a social gradient in ill health related to environmental hazards; children from lower socio-economic groups are more at risk than children from more privileged backgrounds. This is because poorer families tend to live in more run-down areas where the risk of accident and pollution is high. In addition, parents may lack the physical and emotional resources to keep their children safe (Environment Agency, 2012).

The Health Protection Agency identify the main causes of environmental disease as being:

- Water and sanitation
- Accident and injury
- Obesity and lack of physical activity
- Indoor and outdoor air pollution, such as smoke reduction
- Physical hazards such as excessive noise and biological hazards (HPA, 2009: 6).

A healthy environment also includes issues of sustainability and climate change.

Reflection

Look at the UK's strategy for environmental health for children: Health Protection Agency (2009) *A Children's Environment and Health Strategy for the United Kingdom.* Oxford: Health Protection Agency. http://www.hpa.org.uk/webc/HPAwebFile/HPAweb_C/1237889522947

1. If you are involved in an early childhood setting, how can you and your colleagues help ensure that you are providing a clean and safe environment for the children and families in your care?
2. Children have a right to be educated about environmental issues, and concepts can be introduced within the Early Years Foundation Stage Curriculum to help them understand. Eco-schools in Scotland have produced guidance for early childhood settings on how to undertake an 'Eco-audit' and how to introduce environmental topics to very young children. (http://www.ecoschoolsscotland.org/earlyyears/Guide/Intro.html)

Emotional health and well-being

When we looked at definitions of health we saw that health and well-being are interlinked. In this section we will look at the emotional health of young children and see how it relates to overall well-being.

CASE STUDY

In the LMU/NCB well-being study children emphasised the importance of relationships, especially with their mothers, food and playing outdoors.

This is an excerpt of a conversation with three young children in an early childhood setting:

Adult: What things make you feel a little bit happy?

Child J: You [to his Grandmother].

Adult: Do you have any special friends at home M?

Child M: Mummy 'cos she makes me happy.

I ask child P what his favourite place at home is. He replies 'Mummy'.

In another setting there was the following conversation:

Adult: Are you smiling? What makes you smile?

Child A: Sweeties.

(Continued)

(Continued)

Adult: What makes you feel happy?

Child B: Chicken, chicken – it's my favourite dinner.

Chapter 2 looks at the importance of listening to children. How might you find out from very young children what gives them a feeling of well-being?

The LMU/NCB study found that the well-being of children is strongly related to relationships, especially with their mothers, and is confirmation that one of the foundations of health is stable relationships (Center on the Developing Child, 2010).

Anything that disrupts healthy relationships between infants and their main carers can have permanent negative effects on children's development. This is especially true if very young children are exposed to high levels of stress. The National Scientific Council on the Developing Child (2010) explains that there is a link between high levels of stress in early childhood and mental illness later in life. It is thought that this is mediated by the stress hormone cortisol that has an adverse effect on brain development. This can affect all areas of development and increases the risk that, as an adult, the individual may be at risk of asthma, hypertension, heart disease and diabetes.

To develop healthily, children need to experience secure attachment relationships with their main caregivers. These secure attachments can act as a protective factor, reducing the adverse effects of a stressful environment. However, poor attachment relationships or separation from main attachment figures can have serious consequences for children's development (Oates, 2007).

Reflection

> Good parenting is at the heart of a child's well-being and development. And parents' and carers' well-being is key to their ability to raise their children. When mothers and fathers have poor well-being, they are less able to be good parents to their children. (Roberts et al., 2009: 11)

1. What circumstances may lead parents to be in a negative state of well-being which may adversely affect their ability to parent effectively?
2. How may these situations adversely affect parents' abilities to form effective attachment relationships?

(Continued)

3. How can parents be supported in their role and what part do early childhood settings have in providing this support?

You will find Chapters 13 and 16 helpful.

As we have seen, there is a link between stressful events in early childhood and later mental illness. The charity, Young Minds (2013) estimates that there are approximately 850,000 children in the UK who have mental health problems that include anxiety, depression, conduct disorders and severe hyperactivity disorders. The charity identifies the difficulties that some children face which can lead to future mental ill health such as illness in the family, divorce and parental drug or alcohol problems within the family. These are known as 'risk factors', but experience tells us that not all children who experience difficult circumstances will go on to become mentally ill. There has been considerable research into the factors that protect children from the adverse effects of challenging events. Protective factors that increase children's resilience include being in good health, strong attachment relationships, and coming from an economically secure family.

Reflection

This document looks at the risk and resilience factors affecting children's emotional health: Smith, R. (2002) *Research Review: Promoting Children's Emotional Health*. http://www.barnardos.org.uk/promoting_children_s_emotional_health_a_research_review.pdf

- Read the document and identify how early years settings can help protect children from emotional ill health.
- If you are involved with a setting evaluate how effectively you support children and families who are facing challenging situations.

Health inequalities

(It is suggested that you read this section in tandem with Chapter 9 on social inequalities.)

In the introduction we discovered that although the health of all children in the UK has improved dramatically since the beginning of the twentieth century, there is a social gradient in that children from disadvantaged homes are less healthy than children from more privileged backgrounds.

Reflection

Look at the following site: Child and Maternal Health Observatory: http://www.chimat.org.uk/profiles

This site gives you the latest statistics about the health of children in the area you live or work.

Look at the profiles for the London Borough of Bromley and the London Borough of Hackney. Bromley is a relatively affluent area in south London. Hackney is a poor, relatively deprived, inner city area. What do the statistics tell you about the relationship between children's health and the area in which they live? What reasons can you think of to explain the differences that you see?

The social gradient in health was noted by Douglas Black in 1980, and in 1997 Sir Donald Acheson confirmed that not only was the health of people in lower socio-economic groups worse than that of those in higher socio-economic groups, but that the gap was widening (Mukherji, 2005).

In February 2010 the Marmot review was published. The review:

- Acknowledged that the social gradient in health exists and is widening. It emphasised that health inequalities result from social inequalities and that tackling social inequalities will reduce inequalities in health.
- Introduced the concept of 'proportionate universalism'. Actions to improve health must be targeted for everyone, but resources should be targeted in proportion to levels of need/disadvantage.
- Stated that reducing health inequalities will require action on six policy objectives:

1. Give every child the best start in life.
2. Enable all children, young people and adults to maximise their capabilities and have control over their lives.
3. Create fair employment and good work for all.
4. Ensure a healthy standard of living for all.
5. Create and develop healthy and sustainable places and communities.
6. Strengthen the role and impact of illness prevention. (Marmot, 2010: 9)

Marmot clearly considers that policies designed to help give children the best start in life are key to minimising social inequalities and reducing health inequalities. He recommended that the Government should increase expenditure in the early years, make more support available for parents and provide good quality early years childcare and education.

In February 2012 the Marmot review team published figures that indicate that whilst the general health of people living in England and Wales had improved, health inequalities between the richest and poorest areas actually continue to rise (UCL Institute of Health Equity, 2012).

There are multiple and interrelated factors that contribute to the social gradient in health, some of which have already been highlighted in this chapter. Mukherji (2005) identifies that lack of resources, education and social support can lead to children's health being compromised even before birth; with higher instances of teenage pregnancy, and increased rates of smoking, alcohol and drugs in disadvantaged families. Once children are born, those from impoverished backgrounds are more likely to have poor nutrition, suffer from higher rates of accidents and live in an environment that is more polluted than children from wealthier families.

Marmot (2010) emphasised that resources should be targeted on children in their earliest years because interventions later on in life are less effective. In the next section we will look at the Healthy Child Programme (DoH, 2009c) which is one of the main policy initiatives that, it is hoped, will have a direct effect on reducing social inequality, as well as health inequality.

Promoting children's health through the Healthy Child Programme

Most of us are familiar with baby clinics where mothers bring their babies for health check-ups, growth monitoring and immunisations. The emphasis on the 'old style' of baby clinic was the physical health of the baby. There was a fixed schedule of check-ups, with all babies being given the same check-ups at the same age. This is known as 'universal' provision. The Healthy Child Programme has moved away from this towards a system whereby every child is given 'core' services and check-ups, with extra provision being targeted at children and families identified as being at risk. This is known as 'proportionate universalism', and is one of the principles suggested by the Marmot Review (2010).

The Healthy Child Programme schedule is composed of various elements:

- Health check-ups, where the child's growth is monitored and development checked. This system of monitoring used to be known as child health surveillance. As part of these check-ups children may be given screening tests to identify specific conditions. For example, every child will have their hearing tested at birth and blood will be taken from their heel to see if they have conditions such as hypothyroidism (low levels of thyroid hormone).
- Depending on the age of the child there will be discussions about feeding, sleep, play, safety and sensitive parenting. As children get older, there is less emphasis on physical growth (except for a continuing emphasis on obesity prevention) and

more emphasis on sensitive parenting and the social and emotional development of children.

- As part of the Healthy Child Programme children are offered vaccinations against common illnesses. This is one of the success stories in child health, and, according to the NHS vaccination website, vaccinations have saved more lives than any other medical procedure. The Healthy Child Programme offers a programme of vaccinations against an increasing number of diseases. The vaccination schedule constantly changes as more vaccines are produced.

Reflection

Look at the Healthy Child Programme: https://www.gov.uk/government/uploads/system/uploads/attachment_data/file/167998/Health_Child_Programme.pdf

Read through the Healthy Child Programme schedule (from page 31) and note:

- The schedule that is used in pregnancy
- The schedule that is used once the baby is born
- The difference between 'core' provision and the additional support offered to children and families in need.

Parents are given a personal child health record to keep – The Personal Child Health Record. Here is a link: http://shop.healthforallchildren.co.uk/pro.epl?DO=IMAGE&ID=pchr_alts_jun03

Investigate this link. Note how the record contains both medical information and the results of tests, etc. and advice for parents about 'normal' development. Parents are encouraged to note developmental changes in their baby as their observations will form the basis of developmental check-ups.

Investigate the NHS Vaccination website: http://www.nhs.uk/Planners/vaccinations/Pages/aboutvaccinationhub.aspx

If a mother asked your advice about immunising her child against measles, mumps and rubella, what advice would you give her?

Promoting children's health in early childhood settings

In England, early childhood practice is guided by the requirements of the Early Years Foundation Stage (DfE, 2012). The concept of health and well-being is holistic in nature and practically every aspect of the EYFS will relate to the promotion of children's health and well-being in some way. However, two of the three prime areas of the curriculum particularly relate to children's health: physical development and personal, social and emotional development.

Reflection

Look at the Department for Education (DfE) (2012) *Statutory Framework for the Early Years Foundation Stage*. http://media.education.gov.uk/assets/files/pdf/e/eyfs%20statutory%20framework%20march%202012.pdf

Identify the aspects of the document that relate to children's health and note how settings are expected to work with both parents and health professionals such as health visitors in promoting children's health and well-being.

Fostering stable and responsive relationships in early childhood settings

The key person relationship in early childhood settings is fundamental to helping children form stable relationships with practitioners and provides the basis for fostering quality, supportive relationships with parents (Manning-Morton and Thorp, 2003). Early childhood settings which have effective policies and procedures in place to support key person relationships and good parental partnerships will be in a good position to support parent–child relationships within the home.

Some parents may need extra support with forming effective relationships with their children and the key person is in a good situation to identify these parents and to refer them to parenting support programmes or to other professionals such as health visitors or family support workers. Chapters 13 and 16 look at these topics in more detail.

Fostering safe and supportive physical environments within early childhood settings

It goes without saying that early childhood settings should provide a safe and hygienic environment for children. However, a supportive physical environment goes beyond the removal of hazards. It involves the arranging of an environment that is developmentally appropriate, fosters identity and motivates children to explore, experiment and take risks. For example, a supportive environment for a child who is just crawling would involve putting mirrors and family photos at their eye level, providing stable rails and furniture so they are motivated to pull themselves up to stand, and organising the environment so they can move around the room by 'cruising' when they are ready. A supportive physical environment involves the provision of free access to a stimulating outside area, and areas for rest and quiet play. A supportive physical environment also involves paying attention to lighting, heating and ventilation (Manning-Morton and Thorp, 2003).

Fostering children's nutrition in early childhood settings

Earlier on in this chapter we looked at providing food and drink in settings and we investigated the voluntary guidelines produced by The School Food Trust (2012). The provision of a healthy diet is only part of the responsibilities of the setting as children's identity is inextricably linked to the food they eat and the way they eat it. It is important that decisions about menus are taken in partnership with parents so that the menus reflect the culture of the children. Parents should also be involved in policy decisions about food and drink that is brought in from home.

Summary

In this chapter we have investigated why it is vital to promote the health of very young children. We have identified the conditions needed for children to develop healthily and have looked at factors that affect their health both before and after birth. The importance of positive relationships, supportive physical environments and good nutrition was emphasised. The social gradient in health was discussed and the key role that the Healthy Child Programme plays in mitigating against health inequalities was investigated. Finally, the role of early childhood settings in promoting children's health was explored.

Further reading

Levels 4 & 5

Albon, D. and Mukherji, P. (2008) *Food and Health in Early Childhood*. London: Sage. This text was written for early childhood practitioners and looks at food and drink provision in a holistic way; from scientific information on nutrition, to issues of food and identity and emotional aspects of eating.

Underdown, A. (2007) *Young Children's Health and Well-being*. Maidenhead: Open University Press. This book looks at the factors that affect the health of very young children, looking in more depth at the topics covered in this chapter.

Level 6 (Honours)

Hall, D. and Elliman, D. (2003) *Health for All Children*. Oxford: Oxford University Press. This was the book on which the Healthy Child Programme was based and will deepen your understanding of some of the issues underpinning the programme.

References

Action for Children (2010) 'UK children will go hungry this Christmas'. http://www.actionforchildren.org.uk/news/archive/2012/november/uk-children-will-go-hungry-this-christmas (accessed 9 January 2013).

Albon, D. and Mukherji, P. (2008) *Food and Health in Early Childhood*. London: Sage.

Black, D., Morris, J., Smith, C. and Townsend, P. (1980) *Inequalities in Health: Report of a Research Working Group*. London: Department of Health and Social Security.

Blair, M. (2008) *Optimising Health in the Early Years*. Child Public Health Interest Group, Community Practitioners and Health Visitors Association, British Association of Community Child Health. London: Early Childhood Forum, National Children's Bureau.

Bolling, K., Grant, C., Hamlyn, B. and Thornton, A. (2007) *Infant Feeding Survey 2005*. London: The Information Centre for Health and Social Care. http://www.dhsspsni.gov.uk/pchr_final_version.pdf (accessed 6 August 2013).

Bronfenbrenner, U. (1986) 'Ecology of the family as a context for human development: Research perspectives', *Developmental Psychology*, 22: 723–42.

Center on the Developing Child, Harvard University (2010) *The Foundations of Lifelong Health are Built in Early Childhood*. http://developingchild.harvard.edu/resources/reports_and_working_papers/foundations-of-lifelong-health/ (accessed 11 September 2012).

Central Intelligence Agency (CIA) (2013) *United Kingdom Infant Mortality Rate*. http: //www.indexmundi.com/united_kingdom/infant_mortality_rate.html (accessed 20 November 2013).

Child and Maternal Health Observatory (n.d.) *Child Health Profiles*. http://www.chimat.org.uk/profiles (accessed 16 September 2012).

Davison, K. and Birch, L. (2001) 'Childhood overweight: A contextual model and recommendations for future research', *Obesity Reviews*, 2(3): 159–71.

DeMattia, L. and Lee Denney, S. (2008) 'Childhood obesity prevention: Successful community-based efforts', *The Annals of the American Academy of Political and Social Science*, 615: 83–99.

Department for Children, Schools and Families (DCSF) and Department of Health (DoH) (2009) *Healthy Lives, Brighter Futures: The Strategy for Children and Young People's Health*. https://www.education.gov.uk/publications/eOrderingDownload/285374a.pdf (accessed 16 March 2013).

Department for Education (DfE) (2012) *Statutory Framework for the Early Years Foundation Stage*. London: DfE. http://media.education.gov.uk/assets/files/pdf/e/eyfs%20statutory%20framework%20march%202012.pdf (accessed 17 September 2012).

Department of Health (DoH) (2009a) *The Pregnancy Book*. London: DoH Publications.

Department of Health (DoH) (2009b) *Birth to Five*. London: DoH Publications.

Department of Health (DoH) (2009c) *Healthy Child Programme*. London: DoH Publications. https://www.gov.uk/government/uploads/system/uploads/attachment_data/file/167998/Health_Child_Programme.pdf (accessed 16 March 2013).

Dinsdale, H., Rider, C. and Rutter, H. (2012) *National Child Measurement Programme: Changes in Children's Body Mass Index between 2006/07 and 2010/11*. Oxford: National Obesity Observatory.

Environment Agency (2012) Addressing Environmental Inequalities. http://www.environment-agency.gov.uk/research/library/position/41189.aspx (accessed 14 September 2012).

Fewtrell, M., Morgan, J., Duggan, C., Gunnlaugsson, G., Hibberd, P., Lucas, A. and Kleinman, R. (2007) 'Optimal duration of exclusive breastfeeding: What is the evidence to support current recommendations? 1, 2, 3', *American Journal of Clinical Nutrition*, 85(2): 635S–638S.

Grad, F. (2002) 'The preamble of the Constitution of the World Health Organization', *Bulletin of the World Health Organization*, 80(12): 981–2.

Hall, D. and Elliman, D. (2003) *Health for All Children*. Oxford: Oxford University Press.

Hicks, J. and Allen, G. (1999) *A Century of Change: Trends in UK Statistics Since 1900*. Social and general statistics section, House of Commons Library, London.

Health Protection Agency (HPA) (2009) *A Children's Environment and Health Strategy for the UK*. London: Health Protection Agency.

Liptack, G. (2008) Overview of Chromosomal Disorders. http://www.merckmanuals.com/home/childrens_health_issues/chromosomal_and_genetic_abnormalities/overview_of_chromosomal_disorders.html (accessed 11 September 2012).

London Metropolitan University and the National Children's Bureau (in press) *2010 Well-Being Project*.

Marmot, M. (2010) *Post-2010 Strategic Review of Health Inequalities. Fair Society, Healthy Lives: The Marmot Review*. London: University College London.

Manning-Morton, J. and Thorp, M. (2003) *Key Times for Play: The First Three Years*. Maidenhead: Open University Press.

Mekdeci, B. (2012) 'Agent Orange & birth defects'. http://www.vva.org/veteran/1207/agent_orange_feature.html (accessed 11 September 2012).

Mukherji, P. (2005) 'The importance of health', in L. Dryden, R. Forbes, P. Mukherji and L. Pound (eds), *Essential Early Years*. London: Hodder.

National Health Service (NHS) (n.d.) *The Personal Child Health Record*. http://www.dhsspsni.gov.uk/pchr_final_version.pdf (accessed 6 August 2013).

National Scientific Council on the Developing Child (2010) *Early Experiences Can Alter Gene Expression and Affect Long-Term Development: Working Paper No. 10*. http://www.developingchild.net (accessed 16 March 2013).

NHS website: Your pregnancy and baby guide (newborn section) http://www.nhs.uk/conditions/pregnancy-and-baby/pages/pregnancy-and-baby-care.aspx (accessed 16 April 2013).

Oates, J. (ed.) (2007) *Attachment Relationships: Quality of Care for Young Children. Early Childhood in Focus, 1*. Milton Keynes, UK: The Open University.

Oates, J. (2007) 'Attachment matters', *Early Childhood Matters*, 109: 17–20.

Roberts, Y., Brophy, M. and Bacon, N. (2009) *Parenting and Well-being: Knitting Families Together*. London: The Young Foundation.

Smith, R. (2002) *Research Review: Promoting Children's Emotional Health*. http://www.barnardos.org.uk/promoting_children_s_emotional_health_a_research_review.pdf (accessed 16 March 2013).

Spencer, N. and Logan, S. (2002) 'Social influences on birth weight', *Journal of Epidemiology and Community Health*, 56: 326–7.

Swinburn, B. and Egger, G. (2002) 'Preventative strategies against weight gain and obesity', *Obesity Reviews*, 3(4): 289–301.

The NHS Information Centre, IFF Research (2011) *Infant Feeding Survey 2010: Early Results*. London. The NHS Information Centre for Health and Social Care. https://www.catalogue.ic.nhs.uk/publications/public-health/surveys/infa-feed-serv-2010-earl-resu/infa-seed-serv-2010-earl-resu-rep.pdf (accessed 6 August 2013).

The School Food Trust (2012) *Eat Better, Start Better: Voluntary Food and Drink Guidelines for Early Years Settings in England – A Practical Guide*. http://www.childrensfoodtrust.org.uk/assets/eat-better-start-better/CFT%20Early%20Years%20Guide_Interactive_Sept%2012.pdf (accessed 16 April 2013).

UCL Institute of Health Equity (2012) *Marmot Review: 'Two Years On' Data*. http://www.instituteofhealthequity.org/media/press-releases/two-years-on-data (accessed 24 August 2012).

Underdown, A. (2007) *Young Children's Health and Well-being*. Maidenhead: Open University Press.

World Bank (2012) *Nutrition at a Glance, India*. PDF.

World Health Organization (WHO) (1986) *The Ottawa Charter on Health Promotion*. http://www.who.int/healthpromotion/conferences/previous/ottawa/en/ (accessed 17 July 2012).

World Health Organization (WHO) (2009a) *Milestones in Health Promotion Statements from Global Conferences*. http://www.who.int/healthpromotion/Milestones_Health_Promotion_05022010.pdf (accessed 16 April 2012).

World Health Organization (WHO) (2009b) *Infant and Young Child Feeding: Model Chapter for Textbooks for Medical Students and Allied Health Professionals*. http://whqlibdoc.who.int/publications/2009/9789241597494_eng.pdf (accessed 12 September 2012).

World Health Organization (WHO) (2012) 'Breastfeeding'. http://www.who.int/topics/breastfeeding/en/ (accessed 12 September 2012).

Young Minds (2013) http://www.youngminds.org.uk/ (accessed 9 January 2013).

11

Recent Legislation and Policy Initiatives (1997–present)

Tricia Johnson

This chapter will:

- Define legislation and policy
- Provide you with a deeper knowledge and understanding of legislation and policy related to early years provision from 1997 to the present that will enhance your ability to analyse and critique related topics
- Enable you to discuss government legislation and policy in relation to different childcare settings
- Provide you with a knowledge of the related green papers and reports which have informed and influenced policy and legislation in the early years
- Enable you to compare, contrast and critique the Statutory Framework for The Early Years Foundation Stage (EYFS) 2008 with that of 2012 in relation to practice, the Early Learning Goals and Birth to Three Matters.

This chapter will provide you with an outline of the legislation and policy initiatives related to early years practice that have been implemented between 1997 and the present time. The subject material for this chapter is extremely broad, therefore reference will be made to other chapters in the book where you will cover these subjects in more detail. You will be encouraged to use related documents to assist you with your research.

In the UK, the year 1997 marked a change in government; the New Labour government came to power after a landslide victory over the Conservative Party. One of the first initiatives to impact directly on childcare provision was the National Childcare Strategy 1998 which had a strong focus on Early Years Care and Education. This was seen by many early years practitioners as an exciting time because early years was high on the government agenda and focused on raising the quality of care and education for children aged from birth to 5 years. It has, in fact, resulted in many very important changes within early years practice. Many of these changes have resulted in improvements in the quality of provision of childcare and education for children aged from birth to 5 years of age. Eisenstadt (2012) identified the fact that prior to 1997 early years provision had been 'patchy'.

Early years provision has been governed by legislation and policy for many years, for example the Infant Life Protection Act 1872, the Children Act 1908 and the Children Act 1948. These Acts were related to the development of the social state, although the Children Act 1948 was influenced by child psychology, such as the attachment theories of Bowlby and Winnicott (Cameron, 2003). The Children Act 1989 was developed because there were concerns that too many children were being placed in the care of local authorities. It aimed to address the balance of responsibility to protect and care for children between the state/other carers and family, and defined 'parental responsibility'. Current legislation and policy is very closely linked to everyday practice within early years settings. In order to ensure your understanding of the developments in legislation and policy throughout the period from 1997, different aspects of the subject are covered (please refer to the Timeline [Table 11.2] at the end of the chapter). A number of reflective tasks will help you to consider the impact of government initiatives and curriculum changes, and encourage you to research the topic in greater depth.

Legislation and policy

Legislation

Legislation is statutory law, which, when related to Early Years Care and Education, regulates and ensures a minimum standard of education and care across the range of provision available to parents/carers for children aged from birth to 5 years of age.

Legislation has been define as:

> 'the process of making laws'. (*Concise Oxford Dictionary*, 1995: 777)

Policy

Policy is developed to implement legislation and is a written statement that outlines an intent, related to specific legislation, which is, following discussion by all parties involved, adopted by the Government, workplace management or the workforce.

> Policy has been defined as 'a course or principle of action adopted or proposed by a government, party, business or individual'. (*Concise Oxford Dictionary*, 1995: 1057)

What is the purpose of legislation and policy?

While the answer to this question may seem obvious, it is important to consider and understand the processes that result in legislation and policy being developed. Legislation is developed by governments following enquiries, reviews and reports such as the Laming Inquiry (2003) and the Tickell Review (2010) in response to public demand, or unacceptable incidents such as the deaths of Victoria Climbié and Baby P. Legislation resulting from the Laming Inquiry and review (2003) was Every Child Matters (2003) and the Children Act (2004), and legislation following the Tickell Review (2010) of the EYFS (DCSF, 2008a) is the Early Years Foundation Stage (DfE, 2012). Whilst much of the legislation listed in this chapter has impacted profoundly upon the provision of Early Years Childcare and Education, the Laming and Tickell reviews are included because they bring together many of the policies that govern the day-to-day care and education of young children.

Policies, as stated above, are developed from legislation to ensure that all staff in settings are aware of, and implement, the requirements of the law. Policies underpin practice (Jones and Pound, 2008) and are put in place to satisfy the requirements of legislation, ensuring that minimum standards of care and education are maintained. The main policies in Early Years Care and Education are those linked to the health and safety of children, their learning and development, and working in partnership with parents/carers. The policies that legally must be in place, in accordance with the Statutory Framework for the Early Years Foundation Stage (2012: Section 3, pp. 13–15), the Safeguarding and Welfare Requirements, are: Safeguarding/Child Protection, Health and Safety, and Safer Recruitment. Whilst examples of policies are available through organisations/websites such as the Pre-School Learning Alliance, all policies must be tailored to the setting where they are to be implemented.

Therefore, the purpose of legislation and policy for every setting is to ensure that children are safe, healthy, learn and develop, enjoy and achieve (Every Child Matters, HMSO, 2003).

Policies also guide staff to ensure that children are welcomed and fully included in the learning community through strong partnerships with parents/carers and other professionals. Thus legislation and related policies correspond directly to the role of practitioners, that is, to provide for the care, curriculum, health and inclusion, quality of provision, safeguarding and well-being of children who attend your settings.

The main initiatives and legislation from government will now be explored in more detail. The timeline (see Table 11.2), suggests that the agenda for early years was addressed, in some respects, solely by the Labour government. However, the quality of early years education and care has been on the agenda for many years (see Chapter 8). The Rumbold Report (HMSO, 1990) which followed the Inquiry into the Quality of the Educational Experience offered to 3- and 4-year-olds provided many recommendations regarding ratios (Rumbold, 1990: 10–11). The recommendations are similar to those in the Tickell Review (2011), for example: staff ratios of 1:13 for children 3–5 years, involvement of a qualified teacher, continuing professional development, provision of an appropriate curriculum, partnerships with parents, multi-agency working, to name but a few.

Changes involving the level of qualifications for childcare workers and the ratios of qualified to unqualified staff within each setting occurred during the early 1990s. These changes were due to demographic changes in the general workforce. Women were being encouraged by the Government to return to work. There was a resultant need for rapid expansion in childcare provision, particularly private provision of full daycare to respond to the needs of working mothers. There was much debate and many concerns expressed about staffing this rapid expansion, focusing on the qualification levels of staff and in particular the managers. Prior to this rapid expansion many, but not all, held a Level 3 qualification, such as the NNEB.

Reflection

Compare and contrast the recommendations in the Rumbold Report 1990 with those in the Tickell Report 2012 in relation to staff ratios and involvement of qualified teachers. List and critique the similarities and differences.

Gradually, through research within the UK (including the Effective Provision of Preschool Education (EPPE) project 1997–2004) and reports on professional practice in Europe and Scandinavia, the Government recognised the importance of a well-qualified, graduate-led, workforce. The requirement for practitioners to be well qualified and able to provide well-grounded play-based approaches was highlighted. The findings from research along with expert advice from childcare and educational experts and international approaches to care and education (e.g. the Reggio Emilia approach from Italy, and Forest Schools in Scandinavia) were used to support parts of the EYFS (DCSF, 2008a) practice framework – for example, the importance of truly listening to young children (OECD, 2004: 12–15, in EYFS, 2008a: CD). Professional development opportunities were provided for the workforce, though access to such activities can be compromised by locality or lack of funding.

The journey from 1997 to the Early Years Foundation Stage 2012

The deficit in the number of childcare places was addressed, to an extent, through the aim of the National Childcare Strategy 'to deliver affordable, accessible and good quality childcare in every neighbourhood' (DfES, 1998, in Mooney, 2007), and the related funding that was made available by the government. However, at that time, qualification levels were not adequately addressed.

The National Childcare Strategy 1998

The National Childcare Strategy 1998, developed by the Labour government set the target for the 'development and support of high quality, sustainable childcare for 0–14-year-olds (and older where feasible) in every community' (DfEE, 1998).

The implementation of the strategy was led by the local authorities, and, to this end, the Early Years Childcare and Development Partnerships (EYCDPs) were formed in each authority in 1998. Factors considered for new childcare provision were:

- Diversity: voluntary, private and public sector involvement
- Accessibility to rural and disadvantaged families
- Inclusion of special needs and disabled children where possible and appropriate
- Equal opportunities for different cultural, ethnic and religious backgrounds
- Quality, stimulating care with staff who aim to continuously improve their services
- Affordability
- Accessibility to where the children live and the parents work
- Integration of early years education with childcare
- Access to accurate local information for parents, carers, children, employers, and providers (DfEE, 1998).

Having identified 4-year-olds in their area, EYDCPs received funding to provide them with free nursery education for 2.5 hours per day, five days a week from September 1998. The aim was for 66 per cent of 3-year-olds to access free places from 2002. The majority of these places were to be in private and voluntary settings. EYDCPs were also charged with setting up 'Out of School Clubs' in their areas. Many funding streams were available, for example: New Opportunities Fund, Sure Start, Working Families Tax Credits, Childcare Tax Credit, and the Standards Fund for staff training. Millions of pounds were being invested in childcare provision.

Sure Start

The Sure Start programme was developed following recommendations from Glass (1999, in Eisenstadt 2011) for professionals in care and education to identify and work with parents and children in low income/deprived areas in order that these children did not experience disadvantages on entry to school. According to Eisenstadt (2011) the aim was: 'To work with parents and children to promote the physical, intellectual and social development of pre-school children – particularly those who are disadvantaged – to ensure they are ready to thrive when they get to school'. This will be achieved by:

- Improving social and emotional development
- Improving health
- Improving the ability to learn. (Eisenstadt, 2011: 32)

Sure Start Centres received funding and were developed from the Sure Start Programme in order to address child poverty; this funding was provided by two government departments; Health and Education (Eisenstadt, 2011). Sure Start Centres were initially in areas that had been identified as having the worst evidence of child poverty, but the initiative was later extended to provide Children's Centres throughout the country. EYDCPs worked closely with, and within, Sure Start Centres, aiming to reduce the effects of child poverty. Three rounds of funding were provided, and each time local authorities were tasked to submit bids for the funding, including plans, evidence, rationale, and staffing and sustainability assessments for each centre.

Sure Start included professionals from care, education, health, local government and police working in collaboration to identify areas of child deprivation and families with specific needs. These included isolated families, those new to the area, teenage mothers, single mothers, and families with physical and mental-health needs. Each Sure Start Board included parent representatives as well as professionals. The concept was viewed positively, especially working collaboratively with other professionals. Children's Centres began employing staff from across the professions, creating close links between health and education sectors.

Three- and five-year plans were developed by the EYCDPs in each authority, which had to be approved by central government (the departments of Health and Education) before they were adopted. Annual reports were submitted showing progression, for example outlining the number of children attending settings, the number of nurseries, daycare provision, childminders, etc. and information on areas of deprivation and the demographic distribution of early years settings. This enabled identification of further development required in the locality. The timescales set by the Government were very short, and linked future funding to immediate outcomes. This resulted in many settings having their funding reduced because the outcomes were not met or only partly met.

Despite the original aims of Sure Start, the Government's expectations of rapid outcomes resulted in local authorities experiencing funding cuts. The future of the Sure Start Programme was threatened, especially during the 2002 Childcare Review, (Eisenstadt, 2011). The aims of Sure Start changed:

Sure Start aims to achieve better outcomes for children, parents and communities by:

- Increasing the availability of childcare for all children
- Improving the health, education and emotional development for young children
- Supporting parents as parents and in their aspirations towards employment. (DfES, 2002: 7, in Eisenstadt, 2011: 90)

Reflection

Levels 4 & 5

Consider the two sets of aims (as quoted from Eisenstadt) of the Sure Start Programme. Do you consider that they have been implemented? Have they impacted upon reducing child poverty? What is the situation with Sure Start today in relation to the new government? Is the aim of the National Childcare Strategy being met?

Level 6

Analyse the impact of affordable childcare and funding for 3–4-year-olds on private settings. The following documents will help you to consider these points:

The National Childcare Strategy 1998
The National Childcare Strategy Review 2009 – Childcare and Early Years survey of parents
Sure Start Children's Centres Report 2009–2010
National Evaluation of Sure Start Local Programmes 2011

The impact of Sure Start Children's Centres is acknowledged in the 2009–2010 Government report, where it states that: 'Children's Centres are a substantial investment with a sound rationale, and it is vital that this investment is allowed to bear fruit over the long term' (HMSO, 2010: 3).

This statement concedes that very often initiatives, legislation and policy are not given sufficient time to achieve their ultimate goal. Sadly, constant change does not necessarily result in the improvement of provision and outcomes for children and their families, despite the stated aims.

Reflection

Consider the effects that constant change and reduction in funding can have on the morale of staff.

Exploring the National Childcare Strategy and the Sure Start Programme has taken you from 1997 through to 2010. We now return to the year 2000 when the Curriculum Guidance for the Foundation Stage was published.

Curriculum Guidance for the Foundation Stage 2000

The Curriculum Guidance for the Foundation Stage (CGFS) (QCA/DfEE, 2000) was developed and implemented after the Desirable Learning Outcomes (SCAA, 1996) which had been devised for children from 3–5 years. Many professionals raised concerns about the resultant pressures on very young children when expected to achieve the desired goals. One may question the difference between Desirable Learning Outcomes and Early Learning Goals – is this purely semantic? Both are related to the progress of young children by statutory school age, however outcomes can be translated as 'results', whilst goals might be translated as a 'desired destination'. Nutbrown (2011) describes DLOs as 'age-related goals' and ELGs as 'outcomes in the six areas of learning' (Nutbrown, 2011: 169).

The purpose of the new guidance was to enable practitioners to understand the Early Learning Goals. It provided suggested play activities and learning exemplars for children aged 3 to the end of the Reception year, guiding the children's progress towards achieving these goals before entering Key Stage 1. In the Foreword, Margaret Hodge stated that the aim was 'to provide high quality, integrated early education and childcare service for all who want it' (QCA/DfEE, 2000: 2). The areas of learning and early learning goals were divided into six areas in line with those developed for the Desirable Learning Outcomes:

- Personal, social and emotional development
- Communication, language and literacy
- Mathematical development
- Knowledge and understanding of the world
- Physical development
- Creative development (QCA/DfEE, 2000: 4).

This was the first time that there had been a National Curriculum for this age group (Staggs, 2012). 'Well planned play' was identified as the key way that children learn, and was enthusiastically welcomed by practitioners. Staggs (2012) also highlights the inclusion of emotional development and communication within the areas of development in the CGFS that had not been included in the Desirable Learning Outcomes. There were 12 principles for early years education, including employing practitioners who understood and could deliver appropriate curriculum requirements, who understood child development, observed and responded to individual needs, and who worked closely with the parents/carers and provided a safe, stimulating, inclusive environment. The guidance supported practitioners to achieve the principles through the 'stepping stones', with the learning goals describing the ages and stages of development.

Although the CGFS was welcomed, and did help to raise the standards of care and education for 3- to 6-year-olds, there were reservations about its formality and the focus on educational achievement. It provoked professionals to ask whether a curriculum was needed for the youngest children (Pugh, 2010). In addition, others questioned whether care and education for children aged from birth to 5 years were separate entities, arguing that life is a learning experience and practitioners must respond to the changing needs of each child. Practitioners working with children under 3 years often complained that there was a perception that children were born aged 3, with Nutbrown and Page (2008) suggesting that life begins at 5 in the minds of many politicians. This can partly be explained by the fact that most children below 3 had historically been cared for at home. It was not until women with young children began to return to work in the 1990s, causing an increased number of very young children to be cared for outside the home, that this mindset very gradually began to change. Despite demographic changes in our society, and the development of the Birth to Three Matters framework (DfES, 2002) supporting practitioners in providing care and learning needs for the youngest children, Clark and Baylis (2011) identify that the split between care and education does still exist in some settings.

Birth to Three Matters 2002

This framework was intended to 'Support children in their earliest years' (DfES, 2002) and was welcomed by many practitioners working with the youngest children. It was, according to Pugh (2010:9), 'a significant development in the recognition of the particular needs of our youngest children'. It was the first time that there had been any specific national guidance for practitioners working with very young children. The framework had four aspects:

- A Strong Child
- A Skilful Communicator
- A Competent Learner
- A Healthy Child (DfES, 2002).

Each aspect was divided into four components, with relevant information and guidance pertaining to each area of development, observation, effective practice and planning, and resourcing. It was disseminated throughout England to all relevant settings, mostly daycare, caring for children from birth. Training was provided by local Early Years Child Development Advisors and other early years professionals to enable practitioners to interpret and follow the guidelines within the framework. The approach of the Birth to Three Matters Framework was holistic in that it included working with the whole child (Eisenstadt, in Abbott and Langston, 2005), providing care and education as well as healthcare, and demonstrating the importance of working closely with parents/carers. This holistic approach was affirmed in Every Child Matters 2003.

Reflection

Use the aspects from Birth to Three Matters and consider the ways they link to the areas of learning and development and the principles in the Curriculum Guidance for the Foundation Stage. Make notes from your research for use when you have considered the Early Years Foundation Stage 2008.

Every Child Matters 2003 and the Children Act 2004

Every Child Matters 2003 and the Children Act 2004 were published after the Laming Inquiry 2003 into the death of Victoria Climbié (See Chapter 14). Every Child Matters partly informed the development of the Children Act 2004 and also informed childcare provision on becoming part of the legislative framework of the early years. Every Child Matters included five principles which were to enable children to:

- Be healthy
- Stay safe
- Enjoy and achieve
- Make a positive contribution
- Achieve economic well-being.

Settings providing care and education for children from birth to 18 years were charged with linking these five principles to the care and education for each child within lesson plans, individual plans and general daily routines and planning. However, in 2010, the Coalition Government came to power, and although it stated that every child does matter, it removed these five principles and in their place used the phrase, 'help children achieve more', which, it could be argued, does not have the same impact as the original five principles.

The Children Act 2004 is used in conjunction with the Children Act 1989, and the Childcare Act 2006 to regulate early years provision. The Children Act 1989 has not been replaced by the Children Act 2004. In order to put the two acts into context and so that you may appreciate the legislation that is involved in both acts, the introductory statements have been included below.

The Children Act 1989 is:

> An Act to reform the law relating to children; to provide for local authority services for children in need and others; to amend the law with respect to children's homes, community homes, voluntary homes and voluntary organisations; to make provision with respect to fostering, child minding and daycare for young children and adoption; and for connected purposes. (HMSO, 1989 C 41 Introduction)

The Children Act 1989 emphasised the importance of working together with all professionals working with children, to ensure that local authorities provided the care and protection required by children, especially those at risk.

It also clarified the term, 'parental responsibility', which has now been amended to include fathers as well as mothers when two parents are unmarried. This is a section that may impact upon a childcare setting because it is important for the staff to know if the father has been registered as having parental responsibility.

The Children Act 2004 is primarily:

> An Act to make provision for the establishment of a Children's Commissioner ... (HMSO, 2004 C34 Introduction)

A Children's Commissioner was appointed with specific duties and Local Safeguarding Children Boards were formed in each local authority. Childcare provision such as childminders, daycare, pre-school and nurseries are still regulated by Section 10 of the Children Act 1989. Section 1 of the Children Act 1989 stated that 'The welfare of the child shall be court's paramount consideration' (Children Act 1989).

Reflection

Read through the Safeguarding/Child Protection policy at your placement, reflect on the content – is it fit for purpose or should it be reviewed/updated? Analyse the content in relation to the Children Acts 1989 and 2004, the Childcare Act 2006 and the requirements of the EYFS 2012. You will find useful information in Chapter 14.

The Childcare Act 2006

The introduction to the Childcare Act 2006 indicates that it provides support and reinforcement (Pugh, in McAuliffe et al., 2006) to the Children Act 1989 and Children Act 2004. It gives local authorities the powers to improve the well-being of young children, to inform parents and regulate and inspect childcare provision. It is the first act that supports the provision for children aged from birth to 5 years of age. Section 18 explains the term 'childcare', Section 19 the term 'young child' and Section 20 'Early Years Provision'. Sections 39 to 46 set out the requirements that early years settings must meet in order to register and then remain registered.

There are clear requirements within this Act for the provision for welfare, the provision for learning and development, and the importance of professionals working in partnership with parents. These aspects have been included and set out in the Early Years Foundation Stage 2008 and 2012.

The Children's Plan, Building Brighter Futures 2007

In order to support and continue the impetus to improve experiences for children and families, The Children's Plan – Building Brighter Futures was announced in December 2007 with the aim of making England 'the best place in the world for our children and young people to grow up' (DCSF, 2007: 3). Section 4 of the executive summary identifies five principles that underpin the plan, namely:

- government does not bring up children – parents do – so government needs to do more to back parents and families;
- all children have the potential to succeed and should go as far as their talents can take them;
- children and young people need to enjoy their childhood as well as grow up prepared for adult life;
- services need to be shaped by and responsive to children, young people and families, not designed around professional boundaries;
- it is always better to prevent failure than tackle a crisis later. (DCSF, 2007: 5–6)

These principles were addressed through government plans to secure the 'health and wellbeing' (DCSF, 2007) of all children by providing adequate funding for local authorities to provide support to parents, especially those living in areas of poverty and those with a disability or whose children had a disability. It recognised the importance of ensuring children are 'safe and sound' (DCSF, 2007) by providing safe and secure settings, including outdoor playgrounds, with facilities for children with disabilities. The plan requested research into the safety of websites and the impact of videos/media on young children (see e.g. the Byron Review: DCSF, 2008b). 'Excellence and equity' were to be developed within all early years settings to enable children to reach their full potential and children were to be enabled to enjoy their play and learning; all practitioners should be working in partnership with parents from the early years through to secondary education. The plan encourages adults to respond to the 'stage' that a child has reached, rather than their age. It stresses the importance of appointing well-qualified staff in early years settings in order to raise the standards and meet the principles mentioned above.

In order to ensure that early years staff were well qualified, various streams of funding were made available to support early years provision and also to support staff access to Higher Education (HE) programmes (e.g. Foundation Degrees in Early Years/Early Childhood Studies). Latterly the Graduate Leader Fund was available for early years staff to access BA (Hons) Degrees and Early Years Professional Status. This funding provided the opportunity to 'up-skill' the workforce through Continuing Professional Development (CPD) and to work towards achieving the Government aim of employing a graduate in every setting by 2015. The plan also proposed that qualified teachers should all achieve Masters level, stressing the importance of collaboration across the professions to ensure that the needs of all children, in relation to both care and education, were fully responded to.

The Early Years Foundation Stage Framework 2008

The Early Years Foundation Stage was developed in line with the Ten Year Childcare Strategy 2004, to bring together the guidance from Birth to Three Matters 2002 and the CGFS 2000 (Staggs, 2012), along with the five goals of Every Child Matters 2003 (see above). The Early Years Foundation Stage Framework included the statutory requirements for registration (previously the National Standards for under 8s Day Care and Child Minding 2003), health and safety, and a framework for the learning and development needs of all children.

It became mandatory for settings registered with the Office for Standards in Education (Ofsted) to work within the Early Years Foundation Stage Framework. This included maintained, non-maintained and private and voluntary settings providing for children from birth to 5 years, although there were some exemptions (see EYFS 2008, section 4 for guidance and exemptions). Ofsted would now complete the inspections for early years settings; prior to this Ofsted had inspected the learning and development/education provision for the children, and Social Services had inspected the welfare provision.

As stated previously, the purpose of the EYFS was to integrate childcare and education, to ensure inclusion of children from all cultures and those with learning difficulties and disabilities, and to raise standards across the full range of settings. These changes, as identified by Staggs (2012), caused anxieties amongst many practitioners, especially because there had already been so many changes for practitioners to adjust to.

The Statutory Framework for the Early Years Foundation Stage 2008

The purpose and aims were to set the standards, ensure equality of opportunity and anti-discriminatory practice, encourage partnerships with parent/carers and other professionals, improve the quality and consistency of care and education, and provide a secure foundation for future learning. The aims were to be met through four principles: recognising that each child is 'unique', forming 'positive relationships', and providing 'enabling environments' that would promote the 'children's learning and development in different ways and at different rates'.

The learning and development requirements included the following three elements of the Children Act 2006:

- The early learning goals
- The educational programmes
- The assessment arrangements.

The early learning goals were divided into six areas of learning, and educational programmes were to be planned for each child relating to these areas, and to the goals that were expected to be achieved by the end of the Foundation Stage. On-going assessments were to be completed regularly through observation to inform future planning, thus ensuring continuing learning and development. The requirements of the Early Learning Goals, as stated at the beginning of this chapter, promoted strong debates amongst professionals, which in fact are still on-going.

The welfare requirements were divided into three sections: an overview; general welfare requirements; and meeting the welfare requirements (see Table 11.1).

Table 11.1 A comparison of the welfare requirements and how the welfare requirements are met

General welfare requirements	Meeting the welfare requirements
Safeguarding and promoting children's welfare	Overarching general legal requirements
Suitable people	Specific legal duties
Suitable premises, environment and equipment	Statutory guidance
Organisation	
Documentation	

All early years settings were required to comply with the legal requirements as set out in this section of the EYFS 2008, requirements which had previously been covered by the National Standards for Day Care and Child Minding and inspected by Social Services.

Reflection

Levels 4 & 5

Access the National Standards for Day Care and Child Minding (2001) and the Statutory Framework for the Foundation Stage (2008). Compare and contrast the two sets of welfare requirements. List the changes you identify.

Level 6

Analyse the impact of the changes for early years practitioners.

Practice Guidance for the Early Years Foundation Stage 2008

This booklet is divided into three sections which relate to those used in the Statutory Framework: Implementing the EYFS; Learning and Development and Welfare requirements. The document provides guidance for practitioners regarding how to implement the statutory framework, and includes appendices with very detailed information to help practitioners understand and provide for the learning and development of each child. Whilst the EYFS 2008 specifies the requirements for learning and development, it also specifies the welfare requirements of children aged from birth to 5 years, recognising that the well-being of very young children not only relates to their learning and development, but, very importantly, to their general health and well-being. Thus the EYFS supported the theme from Birth to Three Matters that, for very young children, their daily routines provide important learning experiences in all six areas of learning.

The EYFS 2008 was thought to be very helpful by many, but also very prescriptive and regimented by others (Open Eye Campaign, 2009 in House, 2011). There was much criticism of the Early Learning Goals, particularly those relating to literacy and numeracy, which were thought to be unrealistic (Staggs, 2012). This continuing criticism, in part, prompted the new Coalition Government to instigate the already planned EYFS review, by Dame Clare Tickell (2011), (Staggs, 2012).

The Tickell Review 2011

The Tickell Report opens by saying, 'The earliest years in a child's life are absolutely critical' (DfE, 2011: 2). This immediately stresses the importance of the role of all adults working with very young children, parents/carers, early years workers, teachers, doctors, nurses, health visitors, physiotherapists, dentists, educational psychologists, etc. The Tickell Review recognised that the EYFS 2008 had improved the outcomes for children by the end of the Reception year, but identified that 44 per cent had still not achieved the expected outcomes. Although the EYFS was reported to have raised standards, there were points that could be improved upon in helping providers support the care and education of children in their settings. The use of complex language and the complexity of some of the legal requirements within the framework, prompted the Review to recommend that the language be simplified and the number of early learning goals decreased. The simplification of the language would help parents and carers to become more involved with the settings and thus form stronger partnerships. Following the publication of the Tickell Review and Report (2011), the EYFS was revised and published for implementation in September 2012.

Statutory Framework for the Early Years Foundation Stage 2012

The EYFS 2012 is presented in one booklet, with two further publications to support early years practitioners: 'Development Matters in the Early Years Foundation Stage' (Early Education, 2012), and *A Know How Guide: The EYFS Progress Check at Age Two* (NCB, 2012).

The main EYFS document (DfE, 2012) is divided into three sections. The first, on learning and development requirements, defines the role of the setting in providing for the all-round learning and development of each individual child in partnership with parents/carers and other professionals. There are seven areas of learning and three prime areas with guidance that explains the requirements for these areas of learning and development. Staff in settings must complete regular assessments to inform planning in response to the individual needs of each child. Play experiences should be adapted to ensure each child is included, with opportunities for child-led and adult-led play. The framework states that the play must be purposeful and lists three components of effective teaching. It also requires that each child has a 'key person' who liaises closely with the child's parents/carers.

Section 1.12 reflects the findings of the EPPE project 2007 that good quality, effective pre-school provision effects positive outcomes for children to the end of year 5, but just attending pre-school does not have this same effect (DfE, 2012). Both Tickell (2011) and Nutbrown (2012) stress the importance of having good quality, appropriately qualified early years staff in settings, staff who can carry out regular assessments to be used to inform planning.

The second section relates to assessment. A progress check at the age of 2 has been introduced and also the Early Years Foundation Stage Profile has to be completed by the end of the term that the child reaches the age of 5 years. Both of these assessments must include evidence that regular observation and assessment have been completed throughout the child's time at a setting. All records must be shared with the parents/carers and with other professionals (and settings where appropriate).

The third section relates to safeguarding and welfare requirements. As with the EYFS 2008, this section is 'designed to help providers create high quality settings which are welcoming, safe and stimulating, and where children are able to enjoy learning and grow in confidence' (EYFS, 2012 Sec 3.1 p.3). It regulates childcare provision through the statutory requirements for child protection, staffing levels, health and safety, equality of opportunity, management of children's records, complaints procedures, development of relevant policies and working within the requirements of Ofsted. In line with the recommendation of the Tickell Review 2011 for the language within the documentation to be simplified, it is interesting to compare the language in Section 3 'The Welfare Requirements' in the EYFS 2012, with the corresponding welfare requirements to be found in the EYFS 2008.

Reflection

Compare and contrast the EYFS 2008 with the EYFS 2012. Critique the changes in relation to the support for Early Childhood Practitioners and the standards of child-care and education. Does the EYFS 2012 include the recommendations made in the Tickell Report 2011?

Journal Task

Levels 4 & 5

Hübenthal, M. and Ifland, A.M. (2011) 'Risks for children? Recent developments in early childcare policy in Germany', *Childhood*, 18(4): 114–27.

This article discusses the conflicts between investment in childcare and early childcare policy resulting in 'payoffs for the society's economy and the individual child' against possible identified risks for children.

Access the National Childcare Strategy and the full journal article, identify and then describe similarities and differences in the approaches between German policy and UK policy.

Extension to Level 6

Consider the analysis within the article, the aims of the National Childcare Strategy and the Early Years Foundation Stage 2012 and then analyse the possibility of these risks occurring in the UK.

To download this task as well as other useful online resources please visit:
www.sagepub.co.uk/mukherji

Summary

This chapter has included the aims of the legislation, policies, reviews and reports relating to early years provision to provide safe, high quality care and education for children from birth to 5 years of age and beyond. The Government's aim to reduce the percentage of children living in poverty is inherent within all of the policy initiatives.

An outline of the main changes and the expansion of childcare provision that have impacted on early years practitioners from 1997 through to 2012 has been provided. The journey has not necessarily been smooth because it has been rapid and, despite reviews, legislation and policy to raise standards, criticism about early years provision, particularly the outcomes and early learning goals, continues. It must be appreciated that, whilst raising awareness, criticism can raise alarm for practitioners and parents. Therefore, it is important that you and all early years practitioners working within the EYFS framework have a good knowledge of legislation and effective practice to provide for the health, well-being, learning and development of every child within your setting.

This will be achieved through strong partnerships with parents and other professionals within your settings and externally. In this way you will help to ensure that the aims of the National Childcare Strategy 1998, the Children Acts 1989 and 2004, the Childcare Act 2006, and the Early Years Foundation Stage Framework 2012 are embedded in practice. The importance of the Early Childhood Practitioners being well and appropriately qualified remains the key to providing high quality childcare and education (EPPE, 1997; Nutbrown, 2012; Tickell, 2011), within the guidelines of legislation and policy. Always remember to ensure 'the child' is at the centre of your practice and that, 'Quality is not an act, but a habit' (Aristotle Adapted and acknowledged by Durant 1976, from Nicomachean Ethics. Hackett Publishing Company, 1999)

Table 11.2 Timeline of legislation, policy, reports and reviews directly related to early years provision, 1997 to present

1997	The New Labour Government came to power, one of their first major initiatives was the National Childcare Strategy
1998	1. The National Childcare Strategy was implemented 2. The Early Learning Goals replaced the Desirable Learning Outcomes 3. The introduction and formation of Early Years Development and Childcare Partnerships in each Local Authority 4. The Sure Start Programme was announced in July 1998 following recommendations to the Government by Norman Glass to address the issue of child poverty (Eisenstadt, 2011: 1)
2000	Curriculum guidance for the foundation stage for children aged 3–5 years, to help teachers plan and respond to the diverse needs of children (DfEE/QCA, 2000)
2001	The Day Care and Child Minding (National Standards) (England) Regulations and the Special Educational Needs Code of Practice
2002	Birth to Three Matters was launched in November of this year to support staff working with children from birth to 3 years
2003	1. The Day Care and Child Minding (National Standards) (England) Regulations. These revoked the standards previously set for 2001 2. The Laming report – in response to the death of Victoria Climbié 3. Every Child Matters – green paper which informed the Children Act 2004
2004	The Children Act 2004 which was, and still is, to be used in conjunction with the Children Act 1989
2005	The Disability Discrimination Act 2005
2006	The Childcare Act 2006
2007	The Children's Plan – Building Brighter Futures (2007)
2008	Statutory Framework for the Early Years Foundation Stage (EYFS) 2008 The Byron Review 2008 – Children and New Technology
2009	The Laming report – a progress report following the death of Baby P.

(Continued)

Table 11.2 (Continued)

2010	The Equality Act 2010 The Tickell Review of the EYFS 2010 The Field Report December 2010 – preventing poor children becoming poor adults The Conservative/Liberal Democrat Coalition Government was formed following the general election in May 2010
2011	The Munro Review of Child Protection 2011 – a child-centred system The Allen Report 2011 – Early Intervention – The Next Steps (HM Government, 2011)
2012	The Allen Report 2011 – Early Intervention – Smart Investment, Massive Saving (HM Government, 2011) The Early Years Foundation Stage (EYFS 2012) The Nutbrown Review (2012) – Early Years Qualifications

To download this table as well as other useful online resources please visit: **www.sagepub.co.uk/mukherji**

Further reading

Levels 4 & 5

Department for Education and Department of Health (DfE and DoH) (2011) *Supporting Families in the Foundation Years*. London: DfE. This document sets out the Government's vision for the Foundation Years, from 2011, of prevention, early identification and early intervention through such initiatives as 'Family Nurse Partnerships' in order to improve the outcomes for all very young children. It also includes responses to the Field, Tickell, Marmot, Allen and Monro reports.

House, R. (2011) *Too Much, Too Soon*. Gloucestershire: Hawthorne Press. This book covers many aspects of childcare and education that should possibly be considered when writing policies for early years settings.

Level 6

Barker, R. (2009) *Making Sense of Every Child Matters*. Bristol: Policy Press. Whilst being directly linked to Every Child Matters, this text will assist research and analysis of the roles of all professionals who may be involved in early years settings. It will improve your understanding of different roles, the constraints and benefits of multi-agency working and the ability to analyse policy within practice.

Foley, P., Roche, J. and Tucker, S. (2001) *Children in Society*. Hampshire: Palgrave. This book will provide you with further links between contemporary theory and policy in relation to practice.

References

Abbott, L. and Langstone, A. (2005) *Birth to Three Matters: Supporting the Framework for Effective Practice*. Maidenhead: Open University Press.

Cameron, C. (2003) 'An historical perspective on changing child care policy', in J. Brannon and P. Moss (eds), *Rethinking Children's Care*. Buckingham: Open University Press.

Clark, R. M. and Baylis, S. (2011) '"Wasted down there": Policy and practice with the under-threes', *Early Years, An International Journal of Research and Development*, 32(2): 229–42.

DCSF (2007) *The Children's Plan – Building Brighter Futures*. Nottingham: DCSF Publications.
DCSF (2008a) *The Early Years Foundation Stage* (Revised edition). Nottingham: DCSF Publications.
DCSF (2008b) *Byron Review: Children and New Technology*. Nottingham: DCSF.
DfE (2009) Childcare and Early Years Survey of Parents. London: NatCen.
DfE (2011) The Munro Review of Child Protection: Final Report, *A Child-centred System*. Norwich: DfE/TSO.
DfE (2011) The Tickell Review: *The Early Years: Foundations for Life, Health and Learning*. London: DfE.
DfE (2011) *National Evaluation of Sure Start Local Programmes*. www.gov.uk (Accessed 19 August 2013).
DfE (2012a) *The Statutory Guide to the Early Years Foundation Stage*. Runcorn: DfE.
DfE (2012b) *The Nutbrown Review – Foundations for Quality*. Runcorn: DfE.
DfEE (1996) *Nursery Education: Desirable Learning Outcomes for Children's Learning on Entering Compulsory Education* http://www.pgce.soton.ac.uk/ict/docl/ (accessed 19 August 2013).
DfEE (1998) *UK Childcare. Policy and Legislation*. http://www.uk.childcare.ca/policy/policy.shtml (accessed 7 December 2012).
DfEE (2001) *National Standards for Under Eights Day Care and Childminding*. Nottingham: DfEE.
DfES (2002) *Birth to Three Matters*. London: DfES Publications.
Early Education (2012) *Development Matters in the Early Years Foundation Stage*. London: Early Education.
Eisenstadt, N. (2011) *Providing a Sure Start – How Government Discovered Early Childhood*. Bristol: The Policy Press.
Eisenstadt, N. (2012) 'Poverty, social disadvantage and young children', in L. Miller and D. Hevey (eds), *Policy Issues in the Early Years*. London: Sage.
HM Government (2011) The Allen Report: *Early Intervention; The Next Steps*. London: HMSO.
HMSO (1989) The Children Act 1989. UK: The Stationery Office Publications.
HMSO (1990) The Rumbold Report: *Starting with Quality*. UK: The Stationery Office Publications.
HMSO (2003) Every Child Matters UK: The Stationery Office Publications.
HMSO (2003) The Laming Report: *The Victoria Climbie Inquiry*. UK: The Stationery Office Publications.
HMSO (2004) The Children Act 2004. UK: The Stationery Office Publications.
HMSO (2006) The Childcare Act 2006. UK: The Stationery Office Publications.
HMSO (2010) *Sure Start Children's Centres, 5th Report* (Children, Schools and Families Committee HC 130). UK: The Stationery Office Publications.
HMSO (2010) The Field Report: *The Foundation Years, Preventing Poor Children Becoming Poor Adults*. UK: The Stationery Office Publications.
House, R. (2011) *Too Much, Too Soon*. Gloucestershire: Hawthorne Press.
Jones, C. and Pound, L. (2008) *Leadership and Management in the Early Years*. Maidenhead: Open University Press.
LGA (2010) The Marmot Review: *Fair Society, Healthy Lives*. London: LGA.
McAuliffe, A.M., Linsey, A. and Fowler, J. (2006) *Childcare Act 2006: The Essential Guide*. Slough: NFER.
McAuliffe, A., Linsey, A. and Fowler, J. (2006) *Childcare Act 2006: The Essential Guide*. London: National Children's Bureau.
NCB (2012) *A Know How Guide. The EYFS Progress Check at Age Two*. London: DfE/NCB.
Mooney, A. (2007) *The Effectiveness of Quality Improvement Programmes for Early Childhood Education and Childcare*. London: Thomas Coram Research Unit and Institute of Education, University of London.

Nutbrown, C. (2011) *Key Concepts in Early Childhood Education and Care*. London: Sage.

Nutbrown, C. and Page, J. (2008) *Working with Babies and Children Under Three*. London: Sage.

Pugh, G. (2005) 'Policy matters', in L. Abbott and A. Langston (eds), *Birth to Three Matters*. Maidenhead: Open University Press.

Pugh, G. (2010) *Contemporary Issues in the Early Years*. (5th edition). London: Sage.

QCA/DfEE (2000) *Curriculum Guidance for the Foundation Stage*. London: QCA/DfEE Publications.

School Curriculum Assessment Authority (SCAA). (1996) *Nursery Education: Desirable Outcomes for Children's Learning on Entering Compulsory Education*. London: SCAA and Department for Education and Employment.

Staggs, L. (2012) 'The rhetoric and reality of a national strategy for early education and assessment', in L. Miller and D. Hevey (eds), *Policy Issues in the Early Years*. London: Sage.

Websites

https://www.gov.uk/government/publications?departments%5B%5D=department-for-education

http://webarchive.nationalarchives.gov.uk/20120106144646/education.gov.uk/

UK legislation: http://www.legislation.gov.uk/

Definition of disability under the Equality Act 2010: https://www.gov.uk/definition-of-disability-under-equality-act-2010

Childcare: A Review of What Parents Want: www.equalityhumanrights.com/uploaded_files/research/childcare_what_parents_want.doc (accessed 29 April 2012).

Sure Start Children's Centres Fifth Report of Session 2009–10: http://www.publications.parliament.uk/pa/cm200910/cmselect/cmchilsch/130/130i.pdf

http://www.brainyquote.com/quotes/quotes/a/aristotle379604.html#ffLq8tBimvBUZZz3.9 9 (accessed 18 November 2012).

Part 4

APPROACHES AND PRACTICE

Within the early childhood community of practitioners in the UK there is a generally understood approach to delivering care and education to very young children. That is to say provision is underpinned by a set of principles that are seen as fundamental and guide practice. The Early Years Foundation Stage (DfE, 2012: 3) is based upon the following principles:

- Every child is a unique child, who is constantly learning and can be resilient, capable, confident and self-assured
- Children learn to be strong and independent through positive relationships
- Children learn and develop well in enabling environments, in which their experiences respond to their individual needs and there is a strong partnership between practitioners and parents and/or carers
- Children develop and learn in different ways and at different rates. The framework covers the education and care of all children in early years provision, including children with special educational needs and disabilities.

In this section of the book we look at some of the historical influences that explain how these principles have developed and we look at how these principles underpin our practice today.

In Chapter 12, Edwina Mitchell looks at some of the historical, social and cultural influences on early years curriculum and the pedagogic approach that we take. Edwina investigates examples of different curricula from the UK and around the world, to illustrate how each curriculum reflects the social, political and cultural context in which it was developed.

One of the principles underpinning the EYFS (DfE, 2012) is that of working in partnership with children's parents. In Chapter 13, Penny Mukherji and Vicky Mummery investigate the huge influence that parents have on their children's lives and how important it is that early childhood practitioners establish strong working relationships with parents. Penny and Vicky use evidence from research and theoretical models to suggest practical ways to encourage high quality setting–home partnerships.

For children to thrive they need to be protected from harm. Early childhood practitioners have to place children's welfare at the heart of their practice. Safeguarding children is discussed in Chapter 14, where you will be introduced to some of the issues regarding safeguarding and protecting children. Protecting children is the responsibility of society as a whole and the importance of collaborative and effective working with parents, other agencies and professionals is emphasised. It is important that early childhood practitioners can identify children who may be at risk of abuse and take appropriate action; this chapter will help you feel more confident when dealing with such issues.

Practitioners who are involved in child protection cases need the support of their colleagues and their manager. In Chapter 15 Judy Stevenson looks at management and leadership within early childhood settings. She describes how leaders carry the vision of the setting and are tasked with ensuring that practice reflects the underpinning principles of early childhood care and education. Leadership is not just the role of the head of centre or nursery manager, and Judy encourages all practitioners to think about the leadership role that they play within their teams and to reflect upon their own philosophy and the ways that they interact with their colleagues.

Reference

Department for Education (DfE) (2012) *Statutory Framework for the Early Years Foundation Stage: Setting the Standards for Learning, Development and Care for Children from birth To Five*. London: DfE.

12

Curricula and Pedagogic Principles in the Foundation Stage (0–5)

Edwina Mitchell

This chapter will:

- Introduce you to the underpinning principles of curriculum and pedagogy
- Explore the concept of modernism and postmodernism
- Discuss how society views the child and how children learn
- Investigate a variety of curriculum models or models
- Explore the 'best age' to start compulsory schooling.

What do we mean by 'pedagogy' and 'curriculum'?

Pedagogy

Pedagogy is a word that you will come across in many of your textbooks. Siraj-Blatchford (1999) argues that pedagogy is a term that early years practitioners find intimidating, which means that it is seldom used by them and you may not use it yourself.

Reflection

Think about where you have come across the word 'pedagogy'. Is it a word you use and understand or is it new to you? Undertake an internet search to find out in what circumstances the word is used.

Originating from Ancient Greek, pedagogy literally means 'to lead the child' (McShane, 2007), but in practice the word encompasses the underpinning beliefs and values that guide the way practitioners work to support children's learning. Watkins and Mortimer (1999: 3) describe pedagogy as 'any conscious activity by one person designed to enhance learning in another'. Siraj-Blatchford et al. (2002: 27) see pedagogy as 'all of the knowledge, skills and values that children are meant to learn in educational establishments'. This involves the planned interactions, learning and teaching that take place within your early years setting. It also includes what children learn from the 'hidden curriculum'; those things children learn unintentionally from the messages they receive through their interactions with others and the organisation of the environment. Pedagogy also describes the learning that occurs within the family and the wider community. In Europe pedagogy has a holistic meaning that covers both the education and the care that you provide to ensure young children's well-being and development (Petrie et al., 2009). From a holistic perspective the child is seen as being connected to others yet having their own unique experiences and learning; practice in the UK is now moving towards this more holistic view of pedagogy. In the early years, pedagogy encompasses teaching practice, organisation of the environment and provision of resources that encourage exploration and play to facilitate children's learning. A play-based pedagogy that provides activities based on children's observed interests needs expert pedagogues who can develop children's knowledge, skills and dispositions interactively within the setting and the wider community.

Curriculum

Reflection

When you hear the word 'curriculum' what does it mean to you? Do you think in terms of the subjects that you studied at school or perhaps you are thinking about the Early Years Foundation Stage, or one of the other curriculum frameworks that you might be familiar with? Make a note of everything that comes to mind when you think about the word curriculum. At the end of this chapter return to your notes and see how your ideas have developed.

You might think of curriculum in terms of the development of children's skills or subjects to be learned, but actually the word curriculum covers much more than this. QCA (2000: 2) defines the term 'curriculum' as 'everything children do, see, hear and feel in their setting both planned and unplanned'. Drummond et al. (1989) set out the concept of curriculum by stating that a curriculum for young children encompasses everything the child sees or hears in their environment, everything the adults do with the child and all of the activities the child puts together for him/herself.

Curricula are always politically and socially constructed with the aim of teaching children the subjects, knowledge and skills that politicians, educators and society want children to learn from education (Brock et al., 2009; Laevers, 2005). Miller and Pound (2011) suggest that curricula are shaped by the social context in which they operate so they are not easily transferable to other cultures. There is, however, a difference between what teachers want children to learn and what children think that they have learned in any planned or unplanned curriculum (Brock et al., 2009).

The curriculum and the pedagogical practices that we use are underpinned by both philosophy and psychology, which influence how we view the child and the ways that we work with them. When considering the different views of the child and the curricula that they might experience, two terms which you may have come across in your reading will be used – 'modernism' and 'postmodernism'. Let us now look at what these words mean.

Modernism and postmodernism

Modernity relates to a historical period called the Age of Enlightenment which started in the seventeenth century which reached its height during the industrial revolution of the eighteenth century and declined during the twentieth century (Dalhberg et al., 1999). Before this period many people held superstitious beliefs and seldom questioned the authority of either the church or the state (Cooper and Burrell, 1988). However, during the Enlightenment, a group of intellectuals who wanted people to be independent thinkers, to question their previously held beliefs and ideas, developed a set of ideas we call modernism.

During this period of history there was substantial growth in our understanding of science and mathematical knowledge which led to the technological advances that underpinned the industrial revolution. Thinkers from this time wanted a separation of the concepts of religion and the newly discovered scientific knowledge (Cannella, 1997). Modernist thinkers believed that 'knowledge' was out there waiting to be discovered. They believed that 'knowledge' supplied universal truths applicable to everyone, without having to take social and historical contexts into consideration. Discovery of this 'knowledge', they thought, would lead to an ordered world which would make continuous progress towards social justice and happiness. These historical and philosophical ideas, about universally applicable knowledge helping us to make a perfectly ordered world, are called *grand narratives* or *metanarratives*, which could be described as a set of truths in which everybody believes (Albon, 2011).

You may wonder 'how these ideas relate to early childhood and the curricula designed for young children'. Immanuel Kant believed that when children are born they already have some concepts in their minds, and sensory input from their environment, and the experiences they have help children to refine their ideas (Brook, 2003). For example, children are born with their brains already hardwired so that they hold a concept of 'mother' in mind, such as her voice and her smell. Daily interactions and sensory experiences with their mothers help children refine their innate concepts so they develop a wider concept of 'mother' (Garret, n.d.). These ideas were built upon by Piaget (Packer and Goicoechea, 2000) in developing his theory of how children learn. Piaget believed that children have internal psychological cognitive structures, or ways of putting together information, which are different from an adult. These internal cognitive structures to develop in fixed universal stages, each being qualitatively different from the one before. Learning occurs through children's interactions with the environment. If this is how you view the child then the curriculum that you provide will be related to developmentally appropriate practice designed for the ages and stages of children's learning. The Early Years Foundation Stage (DfE, 2012) curriculum has been strongly influenced by Piagetian ideas of ages and stages of development and so could be described as a modernist curriculum.

However, there was a growing unease among the intellectual community with regards to the ideas associated with modernity (Albon, 2011). The search for universal truths did not allow for the diversity of ideas, people and cultures that exist in the world. Postmodernists argue that the world and knowledge is not predictable and certain but is always changing; there is no universal 'knowledge' out there waiting to be discovered so that it can be applied to everyone (Cooper and Burrell, 1988). Dahlberg et al. (1999: 23) state that 'From a postmodern perspective there is no external position of certainty, no universal understanding that exists outside history or society that can provide foundations for truth, knowledge and ethics'. This means that our understanding about the ages and stages of child development may not apply universally, as we once thought.

Postmodernism does not reject scientific understanding but challenges how that knowledge is arrived at. Science is only one way among others of looking at the world. In postmodernism, knowledge and ideas are culturally and historically constructed through the use of language and conversation, which is influenced by time, space and by the values of the community in which that knowledge is shaped. The knowledge constructed can never be value free and objective, and, as Dahlberg et al. (1999) point out, it is always influenced by those in society who hold the power.

As with modernism, postmodern ideas have an impact on how you view the child and the curriculum that you provide in your setting, which will be discussed after the next section.

Views of the child and how they learn

This is also covered in Chapters 5 and 6 but a brief overview will show how the different perspectives have influenced the pedagogy and the curriculum frameworks that we will be discussing later.

Just like curricula, views of children and childhood are shaped by the historical and cultural context in which those views are formed (Smidt, 2006). These views reflect the political and social concerns of their cultural group (Cannella, 1997; Murphy, 2007).

Bruce (1997) describes three philosophical views of the child:

- Empiricism – sees the child from a deficit perspective where the practitioner provides the skills and knowledge the child does not have. This leads to a mechanistic curriculum in which the knowledge is transmitted to the child and which focuses on measurable, testable outcomes (David, 2001).
- Nativism – argues that humans are pre-programmed by biology to develop into adults in an ordered way, leading to the concept of 'norms of development' (Crain, 2000). Adults determine what the child needs as the child is not seen to be competent enough to know their own needs (Cannella, 1997). This leads to a curriculum that meets the ages and stages criteria and is considered developmentally appropriate.
- Interactionism – argues that the environment and natural biological development work together. Think back to ideas of Kant, where the child refines concepts that they already have in their brain with their sensory experiences in their environment. These views typify the interactionist perspective, leading to a progressive curriculum which focuses on the child fulfilling its own individual potential and where the adult and child co-construct their learning together.

A philosophical postmodern perspective of the child questions the idea of the child as being an adult in waiting, seeing children as beings in their own right rather than in the process of becoming. Children are seen as 'socially competent actors' who are equal participants in society and who have agency, that is, they are able to act for themselves in order to achieve a self-chosen outcome (Johansson, 2012; Smith, 2012: 29). This leads to a curriculum that gives children greater responsibility to make choices and decisions about their learning and to have a voice in society. This viewpoint is exemplified by that way Summerhill School is run.

Reflection

Research A.S. Neill's Summerhill School on the internet to see how this school is run on democratic lines where the children have an equal voice in their community and choose what they want to study.

Developmental psychology has also influenced our views of the child, with the main approaches being:

- Behaviourism – children are seen as 'incomplete people' on the path to adulthood and learn the necessary skills by imitating others; their actions are reinforced by a series of rewards or punishments (Bruner, 1996). The practitioner's role is to act as a role model and provide an environment that emphasises what adults want children to learn (Johansson, 2012).
- Cognitive Theories of Learning – children actively construct their knowledge through exploring their environment which the adult organises to support learning (Miller, 2002).
- Socio-cultural theories of development – hold that learning is a social construction where children and adults or peers form supporting relationships that enable knowledge to be co-constructed (Rogoff, 1990; Vygotsky, 1978). Practitioners scaffold the learning, facilitating problem solving through trial and error.
- Cognitive science – holds that babies' brains are innately driven to learn. Babies' brains are like a powerful computer that comes with a basic programme of knowledge but their experiences within the world allow them to constantly refine their ideas, thus extending their knowledge (Gopnik et al., 1999). Cognitive scientists hold that the formation of close, loving relationships is key to effective learning, which has led to an emphasis on the importance of key person relationships in settings (Lally, 2007, cited in Gammage, 2008; Rushton and Larkin, 2001, cited in OECD, 2002).

Most philosophers and developmental psychologists come from a modernist perspective where early childhood is seen as a unique stage in life where children are perceived as thinking in a different manner from adults and that curricula and learning opportunities are designed with this in mind (Miller, 2002).

A postmodern perspective understands that views of the child as a social construction are impacted by a variety of considerations like gender, class, race and the environment the child grows up in. It argues that children should be valued as unique individuals who are accepted by, and have equal power in, society, leading to a curriculum which MacNaughton (2005) describes as 'transforming'. This curriculum would allow children to fulfil their potential so that they can contribute to the development of society but would also encourage children to be critically reflective, to question the beliefs and values of the society in which they live (MacNaughton, 2005).

Curriculum models

Developmentally Appropriate Practice

In 1987, in the USA, The National Association for the Education of Young Children set out *Developmentally Appropriate Practice in Early Childhood Programs Serving*

Children from Birth Through Age 8 (Bredekamp, 1987). Based on the premise that all children grow and develop in universal predictable sequences, the practitioner's knowledge of child development is crucial to this programme. The practitioner observes individual children's developmental level and interests and prepares the environment to facilitate their exploration, supporting the child's physical, emotional, social and cognitive development through age-appropriate activities. Children choose their activities, which must be concrete and relevant to their lives, and are allowed plenty of time to pursue their enquiries.

For the under 3s there are appropriate and inappropriate examples of both learning and welfare requirements. A separate section for children from 4 to 5 years describes the broad curriculum goals and lays out teaching strategies but gives more detailed goals for physical, cognitive, aesthetic and language and literacy development. A section for the primary grades of schooling sets out that learning should occur through an integrated project-based curriculum.

HighScope

Based on Piagetian principles and developed by Weikart in the early 1970s in the USA (Epstein, 2012), HighScope views children as active learners who learn through first-hand experiences and relationships rather than through direct teaching. An enriched environment organised into learning areas allows children to follow their own interests and goals independently. There are 58 key learning experiences, divided into five learning areas, in which children's achievements are assessed through observation (Weikart, 2004). Primarily, HighScope is renowned for its 'plan, do, review' approach. A consistent routine starts with a 10–15-minute small-group discussion with the practitioner where children plan what activities they wish to pursue. This is followed by a 40–60-minute work period in which children carry out their chosen activities and then they reconvene in their groups with the practitioner for a further 10–15 minutes to review what they have done. There are also small and large group activities and 30 minutes assigned to for outside play. The practitioners are seen as partners who support the children's play and learning through active exploration and problem solving, all designed to help children acquire the skills and abilities considered important for educational achievement.

Early Years Foundation Stage curriculum

The forerunner of today's curriculum in the early years was the 1996 *Desirable Outcomes for Children's Learning on Entering Compulsory Education* (SCAA, 1996), arising from government recognition that children's early experiences impacted their levels of achievement in school. This curriculum applied to children from 4 to 5 years and was divided into six areas of learning: Language, Literacy and Communications; Mathematics; Knowledge and Understanding of the World; Personal and Social;

Creative; and Physical Development (SCAA, 1996). *The Curriculum Guidance for the Foundation Stage* was published in 2000, laying out the curriculum for children over 3 years old to the end of the Reception Class (DFEE, 2000). Its underpinning belief was that 'The early years are critical in children's development' (QCA 2000 foreword). This document laid out the learning goals, divided into the same areas of learning (except 'Mathematics' became 'Problem solving, Reasoning and Numeracy') that children could be expected to achieve during this period, preparing them for Key Stage 1. Expected achievements were set out in stepping stones leading to the final early learning goal. As a guide for practitioners, to facilitate assessment, the stepping stones were illustrated with what children might do to show their learning, with a section on the role of the practitioner in helping children achieve the goals. A guide for practitioners working with younger children, the Birth to Three Matters Framework followed in 2003. This was divided into four developmental aspects, each with four components. Each component showed age-related levels of development, what practitioners should look for and suggestions to guide practice (Sure Start, 2003). In 2008 the two documents were combined into the Early Years Foundation Stage (EYFS) (DCSF, 2008), which set out both the welfare requirements and the learning goals for children from birth to 5 years, including those with additional needs. The learning areas and the presentation were very similar to the previous documents. As a result of a review of the EYFS, a new curriculum, The Statutory Framework for the Early Years Foundation Stage (DfE, 2012), setting the standards for learning, development and care for children from birth to five, came into being in 2012 and is mandatory for all early years providers. It holds that children are active learners who learn best through adult-led and child-initiated play activities with the aim of children becoming creative and critical thinkers. The framework sets out three prime learning areas:

- Communication and Language
- Physical Development
- Personal, Social and Emotional Development.

And four specific areas:

- Literacy
- Mathematics
- Understanding the World
- Expressive Arts and Design.

In each section there are either two or three learning goals that children might be expected to attain by the end of the Reception year. Children will be assessed for progress in the prime areas between the ages of 2 and 3 years, with a developmental report summarising their strengths and weaknesses given to their parents. This should fit into the Healthy Child Programme review for 2-year-olds. In the term the child reaches 5 years of age an EYFS profile will be completed, with children assessed as having emerging goals, or meeting or exceeding them in all the learning areas, and this will be shared with Year 1 teachers and parents.

Welsh curriculum

In 1996 the Welsh Assembly set out *Desirable Learning Outcomes for Children's Education Before Compulsory School Age* (ACCAC, 1996) which valued play and was widely welcomed by those in the field of early years education. Concerns about the provision for children which focused on the early development of reading and writing eventually led to the development of the *Framework for Children's Learning for 3–7-year-olds in Wales* (DCELLS, 2008). The aims of the framework are strongly based on the United Nations Convention on the Rights of the Child.

The framework argues that children learn actively through hands-on experiences in a play-based, holistic, developmentally appropriate curriculum focusing on the development of children's skills and understanding through first-hand experiences and problem solving. There is a strong emphasis on the development of children's personal, social and emotional development which lies at the heart of the curriculum. The curriculum is developed through practitioner-led and child-initiated activities based on the child's existing skills and knowledge.

The seven areas of learning are:

- Personal and Social Development, Well-Being and Cultural Diversity
- Language, Literacy and Communication Skills
- Mathematical Development
- Welsh Language Development
- Knowledge and Understanding of the World
- Physical Development
- Creative Development.

Each learning area lays out the skills children need to acquire and can typically be expected to achieve, and the range of learning opportunities that they should experience in order to develop those skills. At the end of the Foundation Stage practitioners assess each child's levels of attainment, using either English or Welsh, in the first three learning areas. The practitioners are expected to look at the child's achievements in a variety of contexts and consider their strengths and weaknesses. The learning must be matched to the appropriate foundation stage outcome so that it achieves an accurate picture of the child's abilities (DCELLS, 2008).

Reflection

Having read about the English and Welsh curriculum frameworks for the early years, using the internet investigate the Scottish curriculum for early years and make comparisons between the three.

Swedish curriculum

There has been a long history of pre-school provision in Sweden, with daycare for children from 1 to 5 years in which children's learning occurs through adult and child interpersonal relationships, followed by pre-school classes for 6-year-olds (Pramling, 2004). A National Curriculum, which was more about regulation than defining curriculum guidelines, was implemented for children from 1 to 5 in 1998, but this only laid out the learning goals, which covered children's holistic development and focused on the transmission of the values and norms inherent in Swedish culture. These are based on democracy, social justice and equality, as well as inculcating children with the ideas of respect for all creatures and care for the environment. How these goals were to be met was decided democratically at local levels within settings. The Swedes believe that children learn through play and contextual meaning-making, acquiring their knowledge through their interactions with their environment. This means that practitioners must be aware of all the possibilities for learning that the environment has to offer (Alvestad and Pramling-Samuelsson, 1999).

The revised and more prescriptive Swedish curriculum states that the curriculum comprises 'activities within which teaching takes place based on defined goals' (Ministry of Education and Research, 2011). It still has the same underpinning fundamental values and states that 'children assimilate ethical values and norms primarily through their concrete experiences', and also that 'adults serve as important role models' (Läroplan_förskolan, 2010: 4). The curriculum states that the learning should start from what the child already knows and stresses the importance of learning through play, both indoors and out. The curriculum divided into seven sections:

1. Norms and Values
2. Development and Learning
3. Influence of the Child
4. Pre-school and Home
5. Cooperation between the Pre-school Class, the School and the Leisure Time Centre
6. Follow up, Evaluation and Development
7. Responsibilities of the Head of the Pre-school.

The first three sections lay out the learning goals, the practitioner's responsibilities and how these should be met, emphasising that everyone in the team should follow the norms and values. The section on development lays out goals that cover children's holistic development and includes goals for mathematical, science and technological learning, and suggests that the learning can be organised through themes. Children for whom Swedish is not their first language must be supported in maintaining their cultural identity and learning through both their mother tongue and in Swedish. The importance of working with parents and carers is also highlighted. The second three sections contain guidelines and suggestions for meeting these, whilst section 7 details a pre-school head's responsibilities. But the most important message that comes through this document is that 'The preschool should actively and consciously influence and stimulate children into developing their understanding and acceptance of society's democratic values' (Läroplan_förskolan, 2010: 8).

Te Whāriki

Te Whāriki the New Zealand early years curriculum was developed by Carr, May and Reedy in 1993 (Soler and Millar, 2003) in response to concerns that the needs, outlooks and values of the Maori and wider Pacific populations were not being met. The authors of this curriculum wanted to avoid implementing a framework that was based either on developmental psychology or focused on the acquisition of school-based skills and knowledge (May, 2004). They constructed a curriculum coming from a socio-cultural perspective that fostered the values of a bi-cultural society and nurtured children's learning dispositions. The crucial underpinning principle is one of 'empowering children to learn and grow' (May, 2004: 17).

Starting from what the child already knows, learning is understood to occur through a complex intermingling of children's experiences and social interactions with people and their environments. The underpinning principles are based on children's *holistic development (Kotahitanga)* the importance of the *family and community (Whanau Tangata)* and the positive *relationships (Nga Hononga)* that children have with people, places and things in their lives, which leads to *empowerment (Whakamana),* enabling children to learn and grow (New Zealand Ministry of Education, 2012). The Maori language is not a direct translation but holds similar interpretations.

Children's learning is seen as a woven mat upon which everyone can stand where the principles are interwoven with the five strands of learning:

- Mana Atua – well-being
- Mana Tangata – contribution
- Mana whenua – belonging

- Mana reo – communication
- Mana aoturoa – exploration.

Each of the strands has three or four broad learning goals and the curriculum outlines the differences in children's needs and abilities in three age ranges, 0–18 months; 18–36 months and 2.5–5 years, although many settings have mixed age groups and it is the responsibility of the practitioners to decide how this is managed. Unlike the EYFS's linear view of learning, children's development is seen as a spiral that they might go up and down (Soler and Millar, 2003).

To support and extend the learning, practitioners plan activities based on observations of the children's learning. The necessary resources and organisation of the environment is then arranged. The adults in each setting will work out their own philosophies, policies and procedures to meet their own cultural expectations. Practitioners work in partnership with parents and aim to support them and the community.

Assessment occurs through Learning Stories, written and photographic accounts which demonstrate the context of the learning and what the learning shows. Children, practitioners and families contribute to the process (Carr and Lee, 2012).

Experiential curriculum

The experiential curriculum used in Flanders and the Netherlands is based on the work of Ferre Laevers (2004). It is a child-centred curriculum in that it is based on researchers' interpretations of children's educational experiences. The underpinning values of this framework are based on the concept of the child's links between themselves and others, the community and the environment. It aims to produce citizens who become self-confident adults who are connected to their world. Self-organisation is the key that facilitates children's engagement with the learning opportunities. To achieve this children need the determination and commitment to do something, the competence to make choices, the ability to imitate actions, the capacity to develop an investigation, and the time reflect and assess the situation (Laevers et al., 2002).

To achieve a quality learning experience, experiential education looks at children's well-being and involvement, arguing that these are indicators of deep-level learning. Children who have a sense of well-being are open to the experiences on offer, responsive to suggestions and are able to be flexible in their thinking. They have a good sense of self-esteem, have a sense of who they are and what they want, are confident and assertive and full of energy. They have fun in the setting, enjoying their own and others' company. Their holistic needs are being met, which allows the child to fulfil their potential for learning. Children are assessed against indicators of five levels of well-being, ranging from extremely low to extremely high.

Examining children's involvement requires practitioners to assess whether children can select their own activities, are motivated, can concentrate and get a sense of satisfaction from their explorations, in other words they are fully engaged in what they are doing and open to the stimulus that the activity provides. Involvement occurs when the activity matches both the child's current level of development but also fits in to the child's zone of proximal development, to their potential level of development (Vygotsky, 1978), allowing them to learn at the appropriate deep level. Five levels of involvement are measured:

- Little or no activity
- Interrupted/sporadic activity
- Sustained activity that lacks intensity
- Activity that has intense moments
- Sustained intense activity.

The pedagogy covers: organisation of classroom and aesthetics; the provision of experiences and activities; observation to facilitate meeting the child's needs; and providing goals and boundaries. It involves looking at interpersonal relationships, helping the child develop ideas around behaviour, feelings and values, and identifying children with additional emotional or developmental needs. The practitioner offers challenges to children who are engaged or suggestions to a child who is not engaged with activities. The pedagogy allows the child to follow his/her own interests and gives plenty of uninterrupted time for the child to explore and experiment.

Children are screened for progress three times a year, considering the areas of physical development, representation in language and visual arts, understanding of the physical world, social development, maths and logic.

Reggio Emilia

Parents, children, practitioners and politicians led by Loris Malaguzzi worked together after the Second World War to develop their early childhood settings for children from birth to 6 years of age (Rinaldi, 2004). Despite the fact that Reggio Emilia's pedagogy has a world-wide reputation, what happens in this city does not apply to the rest of Italy. Dahlberg et al. (1999) highlight the difficulties of transporting curricula from one social, cultural context to another but acknowledge that investigating other philosophies encourages reflection of the relationships to be found between long-held beliefs, values and practices, a process described as deconstruction.

Reggio's aim is to encourage the development of strong, confident, sociable children who are able to think for themselves, believing that this occurs best through warm shared relationships (Rinaldi, 2004). This perspective ties in with the postmodern view of education as a transforming process where the child is supported in their ability to develop into a critical thinker. In Reggio Emilia the crucial perspective is that education occurs through the interactions and relationships between the child, society and the environment, which is seen as the third teacher. The learning occurs through exchanges of ideas between friends, parents, the community and practitioners, as well as self-reflection, so that meanings and understanding are negotiated through the sharing of ideas.

There is no set curriculum but rather what is called an 'emergent curriculum', which means that the learning programme, based on the interests of the children, is constructed through projects which are put together by both the children and the teachers. Crucially, the philosophical underpinnings of Reggio views the child as a citizen with rights who is an active and capable learner and who wants to explore and test their ideas about their world. They believe that children have an innate ability to express their ideas and communicate them through 'The Hundred Languages of Children', using symbolic representation systems such as painting, drawing, modelling, drama, words, technology, etc. The expression of these languages is supported by the presence of visual-arts specialists or *atelieristas* in every setting. The environments are very carefully organised to be attractive and display children's projects, enhancing their sense of being valued.

Projects may last a week or a year depending upon the interests of the children, whilst practitioners offer children challenges to overcome and organise supporting resources to effectively maintain the interests of the group and the learning opportunities. The practitioner is understood to be a learner alongside the children; therefore, listening to the children is key to the practitioner's role, as is documenting the processes of the children's projects. The documentation is a visible aid to the children's memories and demonstrates to the wider world what happens in the settings. It enables the practitioners/researchers to see what the children do or do not understand about their topics and to extend further the challenges to the children.

Earlier in the section on Reggio you will have come across the word deconstruction. Go back and look at how the meaning of this word was described. You can also think of it in terms of questioning or critiquing what you are reading, as a student, an essential skill if you wish to get good grades in your assignments.

Reflection

Having read about the different curricula used in early years education, do a comparison of them all, relating their ideas to your own practice. Try to deconstruct some of the ideas. Use some of these questions to start you off and then think of your own questions:

- What was the social and political context when these curricula were designed?
- What was the underpinning educational aim driving these educational documents?

- Which theoretical perspectives on children and how they learn influenced the design of these curricula?
- What was the race, gender and class of the theorist in question?
- Who holds the power in these curricula, the adult or the child, or are they considered as partners?
- What assessment instruments are used and for what purpose are the children assessed?

Extension to Level 6: After deconstructing the curricula, consider which could be thought of as coming from a modernist perspective or could be described as a transforming postmodern curriculum.

Journal Task

Edwards, S. (2003) 'New directions: Charting the paths for the role of sociocultural theory in early childhood education and curriculum', *Contemporary Issues in Early Childhood*, 4(3): 251–66.

This article examines the influence of Piaget and Vygotsky's ideas on child development and their impact on early years curricula.

Levels 4 & 5

- Compare the description of curriculum in this article with what you have read in the chapter and with wider reading that you have done. How does it relate to your own practice?
- Examine the criticism of Piaget's theories of child development. Why was a curriculum based on developmental theory questioned? What are your views on this and what reading can you find that will support your ideas?

Level 6

- Compare the differences in Vygotsky and Piaget's view of child development and how they have influenced the curriculum models discussed in this chapter. Compare the three curriculum models in this article with your own practice, supporting your decisions with theory from wider readings.

To download this task as well as other useful online resources please visit:
www.sagepub.co.uk/mukherji

What is the best age to start compulsory schooling?

The school starting age has been a matter for debate for some time, with the focus on whether starting school early is beneficial to children or damaging. In the UK the

1870 Education Act set the school starting age for children as the term after their fifth birthday (Sharp, 2002). In many countries children start compulsory schooling at age 6 and in Sweden it is 7. There are advantages and disadvantages to starting compulsory school later. Professor Brooks argues that later school entry allows children more time to develop their social, language and fine motor skills (Rowan, 2011), whereas early school entry can benefit children from disadvantaged families. However, research by Arnold Lincove and Painter (2006) and Black et al. (2008) shows that the academic advantage of an early school start fades with increasing age. Sharp (2002) suggests that starting academic learning too early can result in children experiencing higher levels of anxiety, lower self-esteem and less motivation to learn.

The early years curricula discussed in this chapter emphasise the importance of learning being play-based and focused on the interests of the child to provide a quality experience that enhances and develops children's positive dispositions to learning. The role of the practitioner is to support the child's individual learning through the provision of resources and organisation of the environment. Curricula for older children focus on the knowledge that society deems it important for children to acquire and is generally more formal and delivered didactically. The subject of children's transition to school-based learning will be discussed in Chapter 20 on transitions.

Summary

This chapter has outlined the concepts of pedagogy and curriculum, arguing that they are influenced by social and historical contexts. It has introduced the ideas of modernism and postmodernism, showing how this links into early childhood. A variety of views on how children learn has been outlined. A variety of early years curricula from around the world has been introduced, in order for you to consider whether each could fit into the modernist perspective or could be thought of as a transforming curriculum. Lastly, the school starting age debate has been discussed briefly.

Further reading

These books will help develop your understanding of curricula and pedagogy.

Level 4

Maybin, J. and Woodhead, M. (2003) 'Shaping early childhood education', in J. Maybin and M. Woodhead (eds), *Childhoods in Context*. Chichester: Wiley/The Open University Press. This text outlines the development of early childhood education in the UK and gives an outline of the EYFS, Te Whāriki and Reggio Emilia approaches.

Level 5

Miller, L. and Pound, L. (2011) *Theories and Approaches to Learning in the Early Years*. London: Sage. Chapter 3 explores postmodern and post-structuralist ideas in early childhood education. Part 2 addresses three thinkers in early childhood education. Chapter 7 discusses the HighScope approach.

Level 6

Pound, L. (2011) *Influencing Early Childhood Education: Key Figures, Philosophies and Ideas*. Maidenhead: Open University Press. This text discusses several of the theorists that underpin early childhood education and development whilst Chapter 5 looks at deconstructing early childhood ideas.

References

ACCAC (Qualifications, Curriculum and Assessment Authority for Wales) (1996) *Desirable Outcomes for Children's Learning before Compulsory School Age*. Cardiff: ACCAC.

Albon, D. (2011) 'Postmodern and post-structuralist perspectives on early childhood education', in L. Miller and L. Pound (eds) *Theories and Approaches to Learning in the Early Years*. London: Sage.

Alvestad, M. and Pramling Samuelsson, I. (1999) *A Comparison of the National Preschool Curricula in Norway and Sweden*, Vol.1 No. 2. ECRP.

Arnold Lincove, J. and Painter, G. (2006) 'Does the age that children start kindergarten matter? Evidence of long-term education and social outcomes', *Journal of Educational Evaluation and Policy Analysis*, 28(2): 153–79.

Black, S., Devereux, P. and Salvanes, K. (2008) *Too Young to Leave the Nest: The Effects of School Starting Age*. Working Paper 13969. Cambridge, MA: National Bureau of Economic Research.

Bredekamp, S. (ed.) (1987) *Developmentally Appropriate Practice in Early Childhood Programs Serving Children from Birth Through Age 8*. Washington, DC: The National Association for the Education of Young Children.

Brock, A., Dodds, S., Jarvis, P. and Olusoga, Y. (2009) *Perspectives on Play: Learning for Life*. Harlow: Pearson Education Limited.

Brook, A. (2003) 'Kant and cognitive science', http://http-server.carleton.ca/~abrook/papers/2003-KantCogSci-Teleskop.pdf

Bruce, T. (1997) *Early Childhood Education* (2nd edition). Abingdon: Hodder & Stoughton.

Bruner, J. (1996) *The Culture of Education*. Cambridge, MA: Harvard University Press.

Cannella, G. (1997) *Deconstructing Early Childhood Education: Social Justice and Revolution*. New York: Peter Lang Publishing.

Carr, M. and Lee, W. (2012) *Learning Stories: Constructing Learner Identities in Early Education*. London: Sage.

Cooper, R. and Burrell, G. (1988) 'Modernism, postmodernism and organisational analysis: An introduction', *Organisation Studies*, 9(1): 91–112.

Crain, W. (2000) *Theories of Development: Concepts and Applications* (4th edition). London: Prentice-Hall.

Dahlberg, G., Moss, P. and Pence, A. (1999) *Beyond Quality in Early Childhood Education and Care: Postmodern Perspectives*. London. Routledge Falmer.

David, T. (2001) 'Curriculum in the early years', in G. Pugh (ed.), *Contemporary Issues in the Early Years*. London: Paul Chapman Publishing.

DCELLS (2008) *Framework for Children's Learning for 3–7-Year-Olds in Wales*. Cardiff: Welsh Assembly Government.

DCSF (2008) *The Early Years Foundation Stage*. Nottingham: DCSF Publications.

DfE (2012) *Statutory Framework for the Early Years Foundation Stage*. London: DfE.

DFEE (2000) *The Curriculum Guidance for the Foundation Stage*. London: DFEE Publications.

DfES (2003) *Birth to Three Matters*. Nottingham: DfES Publications.

Drummond, M.J., Lally, M. and Pugh, G. (1989) *Working with Children: Developing a Curriculum for the Early Years*. London: National Children's Bureau.

Epstein, A. (2012) 'All about HighScope – FAQs', http://www.highscope.org/Content.asp?ContentId=291

Gammage, P. (2008) *The Social Agenda and Early Childhood Care and Education: Can We Really Create a Better World?* Leuven: Bernard Van Leer Foundation.

Garret (n.d.) 'Kant's model of the mind', http://www.calstatela.edu/faculty/jgarret/560/notes-kant.pdf (accessed 17 June 2012).

Gopnik, A., Meltzoff, A. and Kuhl, P. (1999) *How Babies Think*. London: Phoenix.

Johansson, B. (2012) 'Doing adulthood in childhood research', *Childhood*, 19(1): 101–14.

Laevers, F. (2004) 'Experiential education – effective learning through well-being and involvement', in *Starting Strong: Curricula and Pedagogies in Early Childhood Education and Care. Five Curriculum Outlines*. Paris. Directorate of Education, OECD.

Laevers, F. (2005) 'The curriculum as means to raise the quality of early childhood education: Implications for policy', *European Early Childhood Education Research Journal*, 13(1): 17–29.

Laevers, F., Vandenbussche, E., Kog, M. and Depondt, L. (2002) *A Process-Orientated Child Monitoring System for Young Children*. Leuven: Leuven University.

Läroplan_förskolan (2010) *Curriculum for the Preschool Lpfo98. Revised 2010*. Stockholm: Skolverket.

MacNaughton, G. (2005) *Doing Foucault in Early Childhood Studies: Applying Poststructural Ideas*. London: Routledge.

McShane, J. (2007) 'Pedagogy: What does it mean?', Learning and teaching update. http://www.teachingexpertise.com/articles/pedagogy-what-does-it-mean (accessed 5 March 2012).

May, H. (2004) 'Te Whāriki – a woven mat for all to stand on', in *Starting Strong: Curricula and Pedagogies in Early Childhood Education and Care. Five Curriculum Outlines*. Paris: Directorate of Education, OECD.

Miller, L. and Pound, L. (2011) *Theories and Approaches to Learning in the Early Years*. London: Sage.

Miller, P. (2002) *Theories of Developmental Psychology* (4th edition). New York: Worth Publishers.

Ministry of Education and Research (2011) 'Status and pedagogical task of preschool to be strengthened', Fact sheet (Sweden).

Murphy, E. (2007) 'Images of childhood in mothers' accounts of contemporary childrearing', *Childhood*, 14(1): 105–27.

New Zealand Ministry of Education (2012) 'What they learn', http://www.minedu.govt.nz/Parents/EarlyYears/WhatTheyLearn.aspx (accessed 6 August 2012).

OECD (2002) *Understanding the Brain: Towards a New Learning Science*. Paris. OECD Publications.

Packer, M. and Goicoechea, J. (2000) 'Sociocultural and constructivist theories of learning: Ontology not just epistemology', *Educational Psychologist*, 35(4): 227–41.

Petrie, P., Boddy, J., Cameron, C., Heptinstall, E., McQuail, S., Simon, A. and Wigfall, V. (2009) *Pedagogy – a Holistic, Personal Approach to Work with Children and Young People Across*

Services. European Models for Practice, Training, Education and Quality. London: Thomas Coram Research Unit and the Institute of Education, London University.

Pramling, I. (2004) 'The Swedish curriculum – goals for a modern pre-school system', in *Starting Strong: Curricula and Pedagogies in Early Childhood Education and Care. Five Curriculum Outlines.* Paris: Directorate of Education, OECD.

QCA (2000) *Curriculum Guidance for the Foundation Stage.* Nottingham: DFEE.

Rinaldi, C. (2004) 'The Reggio Emilia approach – really listening to children', in *Starting Strong: Curricula and Pedagogies in Early Childhood Education and Care. Five Curriculum Outlines.* Paris: Directorate of Education, OECD.

Rogoff, B. (1990) *Apprenticeship in Thinking.* Oxford: Oxford University Press.

Rowan, A. (2011) 'When is the best age to send your child to school?' *Telegraph*, 28 March.

School Curriculum Assessment Authority (SCAA) (1996) *Nursery Education: Desirable Outcomes for Children's Learning on Entering Compulsory Education.* London: SCAA and Department for Education and Employment.

Sharp, C. (2002) 'School starting age: European policy and recent research', paper presented at the LGA Seminar 'When Should Our Children Start School?' LGA Conference Centre, 1 November.

Siraj-Blatchford, I. (1999) 'Early childhood pedagogy: Practice, principles and research', in P. Mortimer (ed.), *Understanding Pedagogy and its Impact on Learning.* London: Paul Chapman Publishing.

Siraj-Blatchford, I., Sylva, K., Muttock, S., Gilden, R. and Bell, D. (2002) *Researching Effective Pedagogy in the Early Years.* London: DfES.

Smidt, S. (2006) *The Developing Child in the 21st Century: A Global Perspective on Child Development.* London: Routledge.

Smith, K. (2012) 'Producing governable subjects: Images of childhood old & new', *Childhood*, 19(1): 24–37.

Soler, J. and Millar, L. (2003) 'The struggle for early childhood curricula: A comparison of the Early Years Foundation Stage, Te Whāriki and Reggio Emilia', *International Journal of Early Years Education*, 11(1): 57–68.

Sure Start (2003) *Birth to Three Matters: A Framework to Support Children in their Earliest Years.* London: Sure Start.

Vygotsky, L. (1978) *Mind in Society: The Development of Higher Psychological Processes.* Cambridge, MA: Harvard University Press.

Watkins, C. and Mortimer, P. (1999) 'Pedagogy: What do we know?', in P. Mortimer (ed.), *Understanding Pedagogy and its Impact on Learning.* London: Paul Chapman Publishing.

Weikart, D. (2004) 'The HighScope curriculum: active learning through key experiences', in *Starting Strong: Curricula and Pedagogies in Early Childhood Education and Care. Five Curriculum Outlines.* Paris: Directorate of Education, OECD.

13

Working in Partnership with Parents in Early Childhood Settings

Penny Mukherji and Vicky Mummery

This chapter will:

- Explain why it is important that early childhood settings should work effectively with parents
- Investigate how families are changing and what we mean by the term 'parent'
- Explore different models of working with parents and identify the values that underpin a true 'partnership'
- Look at the importance of a child's home learning environment, and how parental partnership can promote this
- Look at how effective partnerships can help with observation, planning and assessment
- Explore practical ways of promoting and maintaining partnerships with parents and identify some of the barriers to effective parental partnership
- Discuss ways in which parents can be supported in their parenting role and the need for a multidisciplinary approach.

Practically every discipline working within the early childhood sector, whether this is health, education, or social services, emphasises the importance of working effectively with children's parents. This has not always been the case. A generation ago the views of parents were not considered important; 'professionals' were deemed to know best.

However, there has been a considerable change of practice, and now effective partnerships with parents are considered to be a key principle for anyone working within the field of early childhood.

In this chapter we will look at some of the reasons why there has been such a change of emphasis. We will investigate some practical ways of supporting parents in their role and of involving parents in the care and education of their children.

Why effective parental partnerships are so important

Traditionally, Margaret McMillan is seen as being a pioneer in recognising the value of working with parents. Fitzgerald (2004) highlights that although her work was influential in the early twentieth century, much of her work with parents focused on them being seen as in need of support as they were perceived to lack the skills or knowledge needed to raise children healthily. This is a deficit model that views parents as being lacking in some way that the professional practitioner can remedy. The Plowden Report (CASE, 1967) was one of the first reports to point out that children progressed better when parents were more involved with the school. Although teachers and practitioners are clearly seen as the experts in their children's progress, the report recognised that parents should be given every opportunity to join in the life of the school, be given regular reports about their children's progress and have the opportunity to contribute their views on matters to do with the running of schools. The Rumbold Report, *Starting with Quality* (DES, 1990) again flagged up the importance of parental involvement in their children's education. This report was responsible for the well-known idea that parents are the child's first educator and recognised that this is why parents should be involved in their child's education (Nutbrown and Clough, 2006). Since the publication of The Rumbold Report, the importance of establishing effective relationships with children's parents has become a feature of government legislation and guidance. However, it was not until Tickell in her 2011 report that the importance of quality parental partnerships and the need for a well-trained knowledgeable workforce to be able to maintain productive partnerships was really seen as essential. Consequently, the need for quality parental partnerships was given a prime position in the Foundation Stage Framework (DfE, 2012a).

Policy initiatives in the UK reflect international policy which has been guided by documents such as the OECD *Starting Strong* reports (2006, 2012) and UNICEF's Innocenti Report Card 8 (2008), which emphasise that parents have a right to be involved in their children's education and that educational settings have an obligation to ensure that this happens.

Why is it that parental partnerships are so important? There is increasing evidence that early home experiences have a profound effect on an individual's life chances. Waldfogel and Washbrook (2008) report that a study of affluent and poorer families in the US found that half of the difference in outcomes for children entering school could be ascribed to parental influence. Parents influence their children through three main mechanisms:

1. The quality of the attachment relationships within the family
2. The parenting style that is adopted within the family
3. The home learning environment.

Effective parental partnerships can support parents in their parenting role and in this chapter we will look at parental partnerships from two different viewpoints. First of all we will look at how working as a team with parents in early childhood settings can help positively influence a child's home learning environment, and then we shall look at how parents can be supported in their parenting role. However, before we start looking at these topics in detail we need to investigate how our understanding of the concept of 'family' has been gradually changing, and what we mean when we use the word 'parent'.

What do we understand by the term 'family'?

There is a traditional view that, in the UK, a family consists of a married couple and two children. However, if we look at current statistics this is no longer the case.

Reflection

Look at: Beaumont, J. (2011) *Social Trends No. 41, 2011 Edition*. Basingstoke: Palgrave Macmillan for the Office for National Statistics. http://www.ons.gov.uk/ons/rel/social-trends-rd/social-trends/social-trends-41/index.html

Access this document and consider the following points:

- What is the most common type of family according to the Office of National Statistics?
- How many families had dependent children in 2010?
- What is the percentage of children born to parents who are married?
- What does the introduction of civil marriages tell us about how family units are evolving?
- Can you find the definition of family in the documentation? Is this definition useful in practice and does it reflect the families you work with?

We all have different ideas as to what 'being family' entails; sometimes very close friends with no biological relationship can be considered 'family'. Robinson and

Diaz (2006) suggest that the definition of family should be fluid so as not to exclude different family structures. They consider that families should be viewed as social spaces and point out that our concept of what a family is is influenced by our personal experiences.

Although it is clear that family structure has changed over the years, Golombock (2000) highlights that the idea that the 'best way' to raise children is within two parent, heterosexual families, is still powerful and is expressed in the media and by politicians. As practitioners we may be unconsciously holding stereotypical views about what sort of family structure is the 'best', and later on in the chapter we will look at how our personal views can come in the way of establishing effective parental partnerships.

Who is a 'parent'?

At first glance this is an easy question to answer; a parent is the biological mother or father of a child. However, we all know children who are being raised in families where one or both of the 'parents' are not biologically related to them, for example children who are adopted, those in reconstituted families and children being raised within same sex partnerships. Although they may not be biological parents, most adults, who are in a parenting role, have legal 'parental responsibility'. However, some adults who are in a parenting role are not legally accepted as parents.

Reflection

Explore this website, which contains clearly written information on parental responsibility: https://www.gov.uk/parental-rights-responsibilities/what-is-parental-responsibility

1. What is 'parental responsibility'?
2. Who has 'parental responsibility'? Do all biological fathers automatically have parental responsibility?
3. If you don't have 'parental responsibility' can you acquire it?

Some of you may have been surprised to find out that not everyone we would automatically expect has parental responsibility. There is a rise in children born to parents who are cohabiting, and, even though the family may be stable, the father doesn't automatically have parental responsibility, unless he is named on the birth certificate. Step-parents may also not have legal parental responsibility for their stepchildren.

Although practitioners need to know how a family is constructed, and who has parental responsibility, this is not the most important aspect of family life for children. Golombock (2000) stresses that it is what happens within families, not how families are made, that has a psychological impact on children and influences their future achievements.

Models of parental partnership

When you read the literature on working with parents you will find that there are a variety of terms used, such as parental involvement, parental participation and parental partnership. Whereas, at first glance, these terms may seem very similar, they reflect underlying differences in the way that parents are perceived.

Wall (2006) explains that the term 'parental involvement' is used when describing all the ways that parents participate in the life of the setting. For example, in most early years settings it is usual for parents to be invited to stay with their children when they are settling in, help out on trips and attend performances. In 'parental involvement', typically parents and practitioners are not seen as equals within the relationship. The degree of 'involvement' is dictated by the practitioners in the setting and there is an implicit understanding that the practitioner is the 'expert' and holds the power within the relationship.

Parental partnership is seen to be more equal (Kirnan, 2012) in that both parent and practitioner understand and value each other's contribution to the well-being of the child. Both parent and practitioner are seen to be 'experts', the parent being the expert on their own child, and the practitioner being expert in the care and education of young children. An effective partnership is based on the sharing of information; the parents sharing information about the child's learning and development at home, and the practitioner sharing information about the child's learning and development in the setting. Kirnan (2012: 12) uses the term 'educational partnership' to describe 'the process whereby schools, parents and other services support each other in stimulating children's curiosity, motivation and development'.

The nature of power within parent/practitioner relationships is discussed by MacNaughton and Hughes (2003). They identify three different sorts of parental partnerships, those that are:

- *Conforming* to traditional power relationships; where the practitioner is held to be the professional expert and has the most power in the relationship.
- *Reforming* power relationships; where the relationship is more equal and power is shared between practitioner and parent. Parents and practitioners share information and the expertise of both is recognised.
- *Transforming* power relationships; where parents hold the power and are involved in much of the important decision making in a setting. The practitioner's expertise is recognised, but the parents decide on policy, etc.

There are very few settings where power relationships have been totally transformed, but it is clear that parental partnership policies that are based on a conforming model will not facilitate quality outcomes. Indeed, such partnerships have been criticised as being 'classed, gendered and racialised, representing a dominant discourse of white, middleclass motherhood' (Kirnan, 2012: 15).

Reflection

Levels 4 & 5

If you are involved in a setting use the information you have just read to write 250 words analysing the predominant model that underpins practice in this area.

Level 6

In what ways may policies that promote parental involvement be 'classed, gendered and racialised representing a dominant discourse of white, middleclass motherhood'?

The values that underpin a true partnership

It should be clear that the way that we relate to parents on a day-to-day basis and the policies that settings write to guide practice in this area are underpinned by the values and attitudes we hold as individuals and the values and aims of the setting. Wall (2006: 67) states that effective partnerships should be based on 'equality, trust and respect'. In Chapter 3 you will have read about reflective practice. It is particularly important that you use reflective practice to help you analyse the extent to which you are treating parents with 'equality, trust and respect'. MacNaughton and Hughes (2011: xi) suggest that practitioners should be aware of six unfair thinking habits which can lead to unjust relationships between parents and practitioners:

- *Essentialising* is when we expect someone to behave in a particular way because of the group to which they belong. For example, we may hold stereotypes to do with gender, class and ethnicity.
- *Homogenising* is when we try to eradicate differences between individuals of a particular group. We need to reflect that sometimes the differences between people *within* a particular group are bigger than the differences *between* different groups.

- *Othering* is when you see yourself and the group to which you belong as the norm, and everyone else as deviating from this.
- *Privileging* is when we see ourselves or the group to which we belong as more important than anyone else.
- *Silencing* is when we make it difficult for certain individuals or groups to be heard.

Later on in the chapter we will identify some of the barriers that exclude parents from being able to work in full partnership with practitioners and we will investigate how this may relate to unfair thinking habits on the part of practitioners.

Effective parental partnerships and children's learning

Quality partnerships with parents can benefit children's learning in a variety of ways. Principally, effective relationships have a positive effect on children's home learning environments and can facilitate practitioners getting to know the child and family so that appropriate learning experiences for the child can be provided. Harris and Goodall (2006) conclude that it is how involved parents are in learning activities in the home that has the most benefit on children's achievements, especially in early childhood, rather than how involved parents are in their children's setting.

The influence of quality parental partnerships on children's home learning environments

Research indicates that the 'home learning environment' has a powerful influence on a child's educational achievement (Desforges and Aboucher, 2003; Sylva et al., 2004). The 'home learning environment' relates to activities that happen in the home with parents and children, such as playing and reading together and asking the children about what they have done that day in school or nursery. The influence of the family is so powerful that Melhuish et al. (2008) consider the children's home learning environment to have more of an effect on their learning than parental education, income or occupation.

The role that effective parental partnerships have on improving the home learning environment for children is internationally recognised and is explained in documents such as the New Zealand *Teachers, Parents, and Whănau Working Together in Early Childhood Education* (Mitchell et al., 2009) and the document produced for the Netherlands early childhood sector by the Bernard van Leer Foundation: *Parental Involvement in Early Learning* (Kirnan, 2012).

Reflection

Look at the documents *Teachers, Parents, and Whänau Working Together in Early Childhood Education* (Mitchell et al., 2009) (http://www.nzcer.org.nz/pdfs/15120.pdf) and *Parental Involvement in Early Learning* (Kirnan, 2012) (http://bernardvanleer.org/files/Parental_involvement_in_early_learning.pdf).

Levels 4 & 5

1. What do research studies tell us about the benefits of the home learning environment?
2. In what ways can an effective partnership with parents influence the home learning environment?
3. What practical suggestions are made for facilitating effective relationships within settings?
4. If you are involved in an early childhood setting, evaluate to what extent the practice reflects the suggestions made in these documents.

Level 6

To what extent would you consider recommendations made for practice within other countries to be applicable to your practice?

Parental partnerships: observation, planning and assessment

One way to motivate parents to become more involved in their children's learning at home is to involve them in this process within the setting; indeed, without parental input it is difficult to see how this is to be achieved. At a basic level this could involve asking parents about their children's likes and dislikes, abilities and interests before the child starts the setting, either at a home visit or in a meeting at the setting. However, in the EPPE project, Sylva et al. (2004) found that the most effective settings went beyond this, with practitioners sharing information about children and involving parents in decision making about their children's learning.

This way of working with parents has been researched and developed at the Pen Green Centre in Corby, England. Whalley and Dennison (2007) describe a way of working with parents that has come to be known as the 'Pen Green Loop'.

In the Pen Green Loop, parents are asked to share observations they have undertaken of their children, playing and learning at home, with centre staff, who in turn share

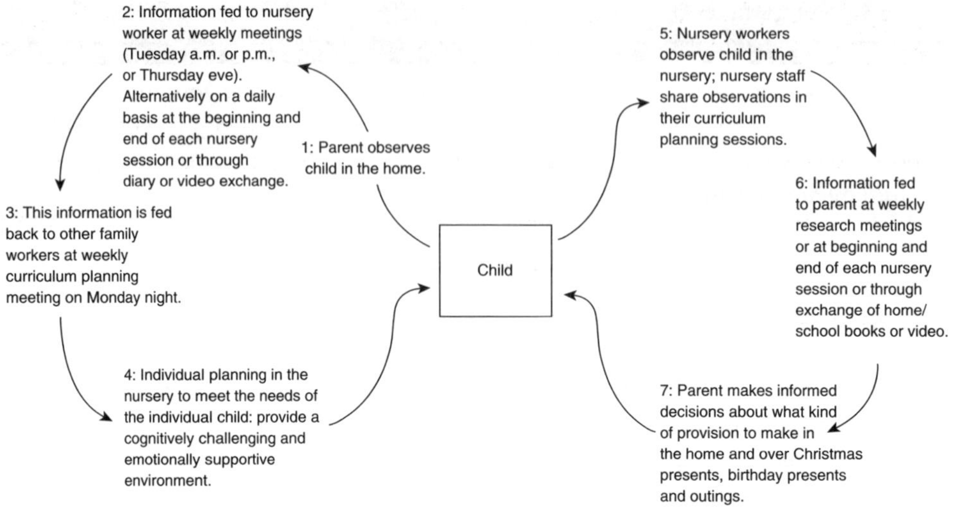

Figure 13.1 The Pen Green Loop (Whalley and Dennison, 2007: 126)

information with them about what children are interested in in the nursery. In the discussions that follow both parents and staff devise plans to build on the children's interests both at nursery and at home. For example, a parent may have recorded a child playing with a cardboard box by getting inside it and closing the lid. They may also report that the child likes making 'dens' under the kitchen table. The setting may have observed the child being fascinated with wrapping up parcels and dressing up. Together, parents and practitioners explore the possibility that the child may have an enveloping schema (Arnold, 1999). At Pen Green planning is undertaken based upon what the parents and practitioners know about the child, using a format called Possible Lines of Development, where activities based on the child's schemas are planned to encompass all areas of the curriculum to be undertaken both at home and in the nursery (Whalley and Dennison, 2007). For example, to further develop personal and social development the child may be encouraged to wrap a parcel and then play 'pass the parcel'. Of course, not every setting has the resources available to them that the Pen Green Centre has, but exchange of information and planning together is a principle that most settings could aim for.

Observation and planning are always linked to some form of assessment. By this we mean that in the planning cycle there is a need to reflect upon the children's learning and to identify 'next steps'. This sort of ongoing formative assessment is implicit in the Pen Green approach where parents and practitioners work together to assess children's achievements and identify 'next steps'.

There are two points within the EYFS where children are to be more formally assessed. From September 2012 all 2-year-old children will be given a progress check. If children are attending an early childhood setting the progress check will be undertaken by the setting. The 2-year-old progress check places a huge emphasis on involving parents with the EYFS statutory framework, stating that 'Practitioners must discuss with parents and/or carers how the summary of development can be used to support learning at home' DfE (2012a: 11).

Reflection

The NCB have produced a useful guide to support practitioners with 2-year-old children, a progress check which can be found at: http://www.foundationyears.org.uk/wp-content/uploads/2012/03/A-Know-How-Guide.pdf

- Why is it so important that parents are involved in this process?
- What sort of model of working with parents underpins this guidance?

In addition to the 2-year-old progress check, under the terms of the EYFS statutory framework (DfE, 2012a), children's attainments are assessed at the end of the foundation stage by means of the EYFS Profile. As with the 2-year-old progress check it is intended that the profile will be based, not only on evidence gathered in the setting, but also using information gathered from parents about children in their home environment (STA, 2013). For both the progress check and the profile it is intended that once all the information has been gathered and written up, the final report is discussed with parents, so that they have an opportunity to discuss their children's progress and to be involved in discussions about future plans.

Sometimes practitioners or parents may have worries about children's progress, to the extent that there are concerns that a child has a special educational need (SEN). Quality parental partnerships are essential if the child and family are to be supported in such circumstances. At the time of writing the guidance for supporting children with special needs and disabilities in England is changing, however, the principles of listening to parents and treating them with 'equality, trust and respect' (Wall, 2006: 67) remains a core value.

Reflection

If you are involved in a setting find out what the procedures are for identifying and supporting children with SEN.

1. How are parents involved in the processes of identification, planning and assessment?
2. If possible talk to parents to find out how supported (or not) they feel and how effective they feel partnerships are between themselves and the setting.

Establishing effective partnerships with parents

First contact

First contact is rarely face to face; for many parents the initial contact may be by email or a telephone call. Staff should take the time to reflect on the image that is portrayed in any material that is to be seen by prospective parents, including information on websites and the setting's brochure. Any information should emphasise the approach the setting takes when working with parents and should include positive images that reflect diversity, provide information in the main community languages and use inclusive language. It may be appropriate for managers to monitor how initial telephone calls and emails from prospective parents are handled and provide training if needed.

Many settings arrange to visit families at home so that they can get to know parents and children in their own environment, and it is during these visits that the conversations can start about what the children are interested in and what the setting can provide. However, many parents view home visits with suspicion and worry that they are being 'checked up on'. There may be class, language and cultural differences that act as barriers to communication. A study by Greenfield (2012) revealed that there were tensions between practitioners and parents around home visits and suggested that practitioners need to be sensitive to the power imbalance between themselves and parents; training and sufficient time is needed for home visits to be successful.

Whether there is a home visit or not, before a child starts nursery there needs to have been the opportunity for parents to meet their children's key person and to pass over all the information about their children's likes and dislikes, their routines at home and how they communicate their needs; practitioners will also have information to relate to parents. It is at this time that the parental partnership policy can be explained. Some parents may find the concept of working in partnership very strange as it may be a different way of interacting with school or nursery than they are used to. This will be an important meeting and due consideration has to be given to providing an interpreter if parents cannot speak the language of the setting.

The key person

It is a requirement of the EYFS (DfE, 2012a: 18) that:

> each child ... be assigned a key person. Their role is to help ensure that every child's care is tailored to meet their individual needs ... to help the child become familiar with the setting, offer a settled relationship for the child and build a relationship with their parents.

Elfer et al. (2003) strongly argue that the key person relationship is integral to quality provision as this promotes individual specialised relationships which support young children's development. In order for the key person to be effective there has to be a strong relationship with parents, and ways to keep parents informed and involved in their children's learning have to be thought through.

The settling-in period is integral to building a key person relationship with the child and their parents/carers as this is the time when, ideally, a secure base is built and the key person should become a trusted adult by the family. Manning-Morton and Thorp (2003) reflect that 'getting the balance right' is something that should be considered from the very beginning. As practitioners you should aim to build the foundations of the partnership on real and manageable expectations. For example, parents should be told the best time in the day to contact their key person and the key person should have realistic expectations about how easy it may be for parents to meet face to face for discussions. For children over 3 and in Reception Class the relationship between children and parents and their key person will be different because each adult will be the key person for more children than when the children are younger. In these circumstances, ways of maintaining effective communication have to be even more carefully thought through.

Settling in

In the majority of settings children are introduced to the life of the nursery with a planned period of 'settling in' when parents are encouraged to stay with their children at first, gradually increasing the amount of time the children spend in the setting on their own.

CASE STUDY

Dylon is seven months old and his mother is returning to work. She has arranged for a settling-in period of a week. Dylon has not been looked after by anyone except his parents before and his mother is very anxious that he won't settle. She is also feeling resentful about having to go back to work and worries that Dylon may come to love his key person more than her.

1. How may Dylon's mother's anxieties affect how Dylon settles into the nursery?
2. What can the key person do and say to alleviate these anxieties?
3. What emotions may the key person be experiencing?
4. What is the role of the manager in helping facilitate a smooth transition?

Settling in can be a difficult time for parents, children and practitioners. Managers need to make sure that a child's key person is not on holiday and that the practitioner has plenty of time to support the parent as well as the child. Parents may have conflicting emotions about leaving their children and practitioners need to be especially sensitive to how parents may be feeling.

Ways of communicating with parents

Although regular face-to-face discussions with parents to share information using a 'Pen Green' model is ideal, in reality this may be difficult to achieve, especially for working parents when time is short. The following methods of communication have all been found to be useful.

- Notice boards: to give information about activities being undertaken in the setting with the children together with news about events such as holiday closures, social events and trips, as well as giving information about support that parents can access. If at all possible, information should be supplied in the main community languages.
- Newsletters: containing information similar to that contained on a notice board.
- Home/setting diaries: for very young children these can include details about food eaten, nappies changes and sleep, as well as activities undertaken. It is possible to maintain a 'Pen Green' type of dialogue in this way, although parents and practitioners will need to be motivated and training will need to be given.
- Documentation: such as children's profile books or 'All about me' books that can be sent home, informing parents of children's achievements in the setting with the expectation that parents will share similar information about what children are doing at home.
- Using technology: many parents have smart phones and use email. These methods have the advantage of both parties being able to respond at a time that suits them.
- Parent–teacher conferences: these are typically face-to-face meetings arranged on an evening after school where a teacher or early childhood practitioner talks to a parent about their child's progress. If parents are unable to attend it may be possible to rearrange the meeting or use technology such as Skype.

Journal Task

Cheatham, G. and Ostrosky, M. (2009) 'Listening for details of talk: Early childhood parent–teacher conference communication facilitators', *Young Exceptional Children,* 13(1): 36–49.

This journal article explains some of the pitfalls encountered in parent–teacher conferences.

Levels 4 & 5

Sometimes parent–practitioner conferences are less than satisfactory:

1. In what ways may the conference go badly?
2. What do Cheatham and Ostrosky suggest will facilitate communication?

Level 6

Read through the description of Mary's meeting with the parent at the beginning of the article. Analyse the meeting in terms of the underpinning model of partnership held by Mary, looking for evidence of 'unfair thinking' (MacNaughton and Hughes, 2011).

To download this task as well as other useful online resources please visit: **www.sagepub.co.uk/mukherji**

Barriers to establishing effective partnerships

Language

It is difficult to establish an effective relationship if parents do not speak the language of the setting. Some settings have staff members or other parents who can act as translators (although one has always to be mindful of issues of privacy, etc.). There may be translation services one can use or the parents themselves may have a partner who can translate. Similar issues may arise if parents are deaf. If no one in the setting can sign then often conversations have to be written. When selecting staff, consideration should be given to making the ability to sign or speak a community language one of the selection criteria. Any written material should be translated into the main community languages of the setting.

Gender

Another group who are reported as being less involved in settings is fathers. Based on research findings, Kahn (2006) makes the following recommendations.

1. Ongoing training and professional development is needed to raise staff awareness of the issues.
2. Instead of addressing parents as a group, fathers and mothers need addressing explicitly.
3. If fathers drop off or collect children then every effort must be made for face-to-face communication.
4. Managers need support to enable them to address this issue with staff (Kahn, 2006: 7).

Ethnicity/culture

Some groups of parents are excluded because of their ethnicity or culture. It is easy to become complacent and think that the early childhood sector no longer has a 'problem' with racist attitudes and discrimination, however, Lane (2007) points out that racism can be very subtle and practitioners may fail to realise the extent to which racism pervades society and can affect the children and families they care for. Cemlyn et al. (2009) point out that Gypsies and Travellers still face overt racism and discrimination. Training and reflective practice is key to practitioners being able to recognise when they hold negative attitudes and how these attitudes can impact the relationships that they are trying to build with parents.

Gay and lesbian parents

Fitzgerald (2004) suggests that gay and lesbian parents may feel anxious as they could have worries about whether or not to tell the setting about their relationship, because of possible negative attitudes. Some practitioners may have concerns about gay and lesbian parents' abilities to raise children appropriately; however, research indicates that these concerns are unfounded (Patterson, 2005). Fitzgerald (2004: 73) makes the following suggestions.

- Use inclusive terms in the setting such as parent or parents rather than mummy and daddy. Remember that gay and lesbian parents may not have told you about their family make-up.
- Look at how you communicate with new parents (documents, home visits, one-to-one). Consider how you can make gay and lesbian parents feel comfortable and accepted.
- Review all documentation/policies so that only inclusive language is used.
- Review the resources used in the setting. Are positive images of different family compositions available to parents/children in the setting?
- Are all parents encouraged to become involved, or are staff reluctant to ask gay/lesbian parents?
- Have the staff team decided how they will respond to children's questions in a positive, affirming way?
- Staff teams need the opportunity to discuss such issues. Do not assume all of the team have the same understanding/positive views as you.

The need for training

A number of training initiatives have been developed, both at local and national level, to increase the confidence, knowledge and skills of early childhood practitioners.

These initiatives include PEAL (Parents, Early Years and Learning) and PEEP (Parents Early Education Partnership).

Reflection

PEAL and PEEP both have websites that explain what they do and what their aims are:

http://peal.org.uk/
http://www.peep.org.uk/
For both programmes:

- What are the underpinning principles upon which the training is based?
- What are the aims of the programmes?
- What underlying model of parental partnership is reflected by these programmes?
- For whom is training intended?
- What is the research upon which the training is based?
- What evaluation studies are there, and what have been the main findings?

If you are involved in a setting, are there 'good practice points' that could be used with your staff team?

Parent support programmes

There is a dominant view within society that if only parents looked after their children better then there would be fewer 'problems'. For example, after the August 2011 riots in the UK, the investigative report said:

> We heard from many communities who felt that rioter behaviour could ultimately be ascribed to poor parenting. We need to consider what can be done to ensure that all children get the right support, control and guidance from parents and guardians. (Riots, Communities and Victims Panel, 2012: 1)

However, most research indicates that rather than poor parenting causing social ills, it is social problems related to poverty and disadvantage that have a negative effect on parents' ability to parent effectively (Mukherji, forthcoming).

There has been much research into what is considered to be the 'best' way to parent, however most is culturally specific and is from a western point of view. One well-known study was conducted by Baumrind in 1966 who concluded that the most successful parents were those who were responsive, caring, attentive, warm, and who used age appropriate and child friendly approaches to discipline. This is commonly known as an authoritative style of parenting. Most parenting support programmes in the UK are based on supporting parents in forming effective attachment relationships and helping parents use an authoritative, or positive approach, to disciplining children. The three main programmes that are used in the UK for supporting parents are: Strengthening Families, Strengthening Communities; Triple P; and Webster Stratton.

Reflection

Conduct an internet search and investigate the Strengthening Families, Strengthening Communities; Triple P; and Webster Stratton parenting support programmes.

- Are the programmes based on research findings?
- What are the aims of each programme?
- How is each programme structured?
- How are the facilitators trained?
- Have there been any evaluation studies of the effectiveness of the programmes?
- Can you identify what model of parental partnership underpins each programme?

Multidisciplinary working

Supporting parents in their role is high on the UK Government's agenda, and this involves initiatives across the whole of the early childhood sector, not just early childhood care and education. There is an emphasis on such interventions reaching the families that need it most, with current Government initiatives, outlined in the *Healthy Child Programme* (DoH, 2009), *The Marmot Review* (Marmot, 2010) and *A New Approach to Child Poverty* (DWP and DfE, 2011), all reflecting the concept of targeted support. Much of this support is delivered via Sure Start Children's Centres which have been set up with the aim of improving outcomes for the most disadvantaged children and families (DfE, 2012b). Very many of you will have had the experience of working in partnership with other professionals such as social workers and health professionals to ensure that families are supported; this way of working is referred to as multidisciplinary working, interagency working or integrated practice. Although widely regarded as being beneficial for children and their families this is a very different approach to that previously used in early childhood. Siraj-Blatchford and Siraj-Blatchford (2010) indicate that the whole area of integrated working is complex with many very different models of partnership in place. They conclude that 'there is some way to go before all practitioners and stakeholders develop a clear understanding of the aims, objectives and effective delivery of integrated services' (Siraj-Blatchford and Siraj-Blatchford, 2010: 31).

Summary

In this chapter we examined the influence parents have on future outcomes for their children, through the quality of their relationships, their parenting skills and the quality of the home learning environment. We investigated the concepts of 'family' and 'parent' and how this may impact on the way we support families in early childhood settings. We explored different models of partnership and noted that the way we work with parents reflects our underpinning values. The influence of effective partnerships on the home learning environment was discussed, together with an exploration into the way that parents can work with practitioners to observe children, plan the curriculum and assess children's achievements. Practical ways of communicating with parents were explored together with ways of overcoming barriers to effective communication. Finally, we examined ways in which parents can be supported in their parenting role and the need for multidisciplinary working.

Further reading

Level 4

Fitzgerald, D. (2004) *Parent Partnership in the Early Years*. London: Continuum. This basic text is a useful practical guide that also provides a rationale as to why some approaches are more beneficial than others for children, families and settings.

Levels 4 & 5

Whalley, M. and the Pen Green Team (2007) *Involving Parents in their Children's Learning*. London: Paul Chapman Publishing. This book discusses the different elements that need to be taken into consideration when working with parents.

Golombock, S. (2000) *Parenting: What Really Counts?* London: Routledge. This book is particularly useful when considering the different social contexts of family life.

Level 6

MacNaughton, G. and Hughes, P. (2011) *Parents and Professionals in Early Childhood Settings*. Maidenhead. Open University Press/McGraw Hill. This book looks at the values underpinning effective parental partnerships.

References

Arnold, C. (1999) *Child Development and Learning 2–5 Years: Georgia's Story*. London: Paul Chapman.

Baumrind, D. (1966) 'Effects of authoritative parental control on child behaviour', *Child Development*, 37(4): 887–907.

Beaumont, J. (2011) *Social Trends No.41, 2011 edition*. Basingstoke: Palgrave Macmillan for the Office for National Statistics. http://www.ons.gov.uk/ons/rel/social-trends-rd/social-trends/social-trends-41/index.html (accessed 4 January 2012).

Cemlyn, S., Greenfields, M., Burnett, S., Mathews, Z. and Whitwell, M. (2009) *Inequalities Experienced by Gypsy and Traveller Communities: A Review*. Manchester: Equality and Human Rights Commission.

Central Advisory Council for Education England (1967) *Children and their Primary Schools* [Plowden Report]. London: HMSO.

Cheatham, G. and Ostrosky, M. (2009) 'Listening for details of talk: Early childhood parent–teacher conference communication facilitators', *Young Exceptional Children*, 13(1): 36–49.

DES (1990) *Starting with Quality: The Report of the Committee of Inquiry into the Quality of the Educational Experience Offered to 3 and 4 Year Olds, Chaired by Mrs Angela Rumbold CBE MP*. London: HMSO.

Desforges, C. and Abouchar, A. (2003) *The Impact of Parental Involvement, Parental Support and Family Education on Pupil Achievement and Adjustment: A Literature Review*. London: Department for Education and Skills.

DfE (2012a) *Early Years Foundation Stage (EYFS)*. London: DfE.

DfE (2012b) 'Core purpose of Sure Start Children's Centres'. http://www.education.gov.uk/childrenandyoungpeople/earlylearningandchildcare/a00191780/core-purpose-of-sure-start-childrens-centres (accessed 23 January 2013).

DoH (2009) *Healthy Child Programme*. https://www.gov.uk/government/uploads/system/uploads/attachment_data/file/167998/Health _Child_Programme.pdf (accessed 6 August 2009).

DWP and DfE (2011) *A New Approach to Child Poverty: Tackling the Causes of Disadvantage and Transforming Families' Lives*. London: TSO.

Elfer, P., Goldschmeid, E. and Selleck, D. (2003) *Key Persons in the Nursery*. London: David Fulton Publishers.

Fitzgerald, D. (2004) *Parent Partnership in the Early Years*. London: Continuum.

Golombock, S. (2000) *Parenting: What Really Counts*. London: Routledge.

Gov.UK (2013) *Parental Rights and Responsibilities*. https://www.gov.uk/parental-rights-responsibilities/what-is-parental-responsibility (accessed 15 January 2013).

Greenfield, S. (2012) 'Nursery home visits: Rhetoric and realities', *Journal of Early Childhood Research*, 10(1): 100–12.

Harris, A. and Goodall, J. (2006) *Parental Involvement in Education: An Overview of the Literature*. Coventry: University of Warwick.

Kahn, T. (2006) *Involving Fathers in Early Years Settings: Evaluating Four Models for Effective Practice Development*. London: DfES.

Kirnan, M. (2012) *Parents Involvement in their Children's Learning*. The Hague: International Child Development Initiatives (ICDI) Leiden on behalf of Bernard van Leer Foundation. http://bernardvanleer.org/files/Parental_involvement_in_early_learning.pdf (accessed 17 January 2013).

Lane, J. (2007) 'Culture, ethnicity, language, faith and equal respect in early childhood – does "getting it" matter?', *Education Review*, 20(1): 101–7.

MacNaughton, G. and Hughes, P. (2003) 'Curriculum contexts: Parents and communities', in G. MacNaughton, *Shaping Early Childhood: Learners, Curriculum and Contexts*. Maidenhead: Open University Press.

MacNaughton, G. and Hughes, P. (2011) *Parents and Professionals in Early Childhood Settings*. Maidenhead. Open University Press/McGraw-Hill.

Manning-Morton, J. and Thorp, M. (2003) *Key Times for Play*. Buckingham: Open University Press.

Marmot, M. (2010) *Fair Society, Healthy Lives: The Marmot Review. Strategic Review of Health Inequalities Post 2010. Executive Summary*. London: The Marmot Review.

Melhuish, E.C., Sylva, K., Sammons, P., Siraj-Blatchford, I., Taggart, B. and Phan, M. (2008) 'Effects of the Home Learning Environment and preschool center experience upon literacy and numeracy development in early primary school', *Journal of Social Issues*, 64(1): 157–88.

Mitchell, L., Haggerty, M., Hampton, V. and Pairman, A. (2009) *Teachers, Parents, and Whānau Working Together in Early Childhood Education*. Wellington: New Zealand Council for Educational Research. http://www.nzcer.org.nz/pdfs/15120.pdf (accessed 17 January 2013).

Mukherji, P. (forthcoming) 'The well being of adults living with babies and young children', in J. Manning-Morton (ed.), *Exploring Well-being in Early Childhood*. Maidenhead: Open University Press.

National Children's Bureau (2012) *The Know How Guide: The EYFS Progress Check at Age Two*. London NCB. http://www.foundationyears.org.uk/wp-content/uploads/2012/03/A-Know-How-Guide.pdf (accessed 20 January 2013).

Nutbrown, C. and Clough, P. (2006) *Inclusion in the Early Years*. London: Sage.

OECD (2006) *Starting Strong: Early Childhood Education and Care*. Paris: OECD Publishing. http://www.oecd.org/newsroom/37425999.pdf (accessed 17 January 2013).

OECD Research Brief (2012) *Parental and Community Engagement Matters: Encouraging Quality in Early Childhood Education and Care (ECEC). Starting Strong111 Toolbox* OECD. http://www.oecd.org/edu/school/49360363.pdf (accessed 6 August 2013).

Parents Early Education Partnership (PEEP) http://www.peep.org.uk/ (accessed 23 January 2013).

Parents, Early Years and Learning (PEAL) http://peal.org.uk/ (accessed 23 January 2013).

Patterson, C. (2005) *Lesbian and Gay Parenting*. Washington, DC: American Psychological Association.

Riots, Communities and Victims Panel (2012) *After the Riots: The Final Report of the Riots, Communities and Victims Panel*. London: LCVP.

Robinson, K. and Diaz, C. (2006) *Diversity and Difference in Early Childhood and Education Issues for Theory and Practice*. Maidenhead: Open University Press.

Siraj-Blatchford, I. and Siraj-Blatchford, J. (2010) *Improving Development Outcomes For children through Effective Practice in Integrating Early Years Services*. London: Centre for Excellence and Outcomes in Children and Young People's Services (C4EO).

Standards and Testing Agency (2013) *Early Years Foundation Stage Profile Handbook*. http://www.foundationyears.org.uk/wp-content/uploads/2012/11/2013_eyfs_handbook.pdf (accessed 20 January 2013).

Sylva, K., Melhish, E., Sammons, P., Siraj-Blatchford, I. and Taggart, B. (2004) *The Effective Provision of Pre-School Education (EPPE) Project: Final Report*. London: DfES and Institute of Education, University of London.

Tickell, C. (2011) *The Early Years: Foundations for Life, Health and Learning. An Independent Report on the Early Years Foundation Stage to Her Majesty's Government*. http://media.education.gov.uk/MediaFiles/B/1/5/%7BB15EFF0D-A4DF-4294-93A1-1E1B88C13F68%7DTickell%20review.pdf (accessed 13 January 2013).

UNICEF (2008) *The Child Care Transition*. Innocenti Report Card 8. Florence: UNICEF Innocenti Research Centre.

Waldfogel, J. and Washbrook, E. (2008) 'Early years policy', paper prepared for Sutton Trust-Carnegie Summit: Social Mobility and Education Policy http://www.bristol.ac.uk/ifssoca/outputs/waldfogeleyp.pdf (accessed 23 January 2013).

Wall, K. (2006) *Special Needs and Early Years*. (2nd edition). London: Paul Chapman Publishing.

Whalley, M. and Dennison, M. (2007) 'Dialogue and documentation: Sharing information and developing a rich curriculum', in M. Whalley and the Pen Green Team, *Involving Parents in their Children's Learning*. London: Paul Chapman Publishing.

14

Safeguarding and Protecting Children

Claire M. Richards

This chapter will:

- Provide a theoretical understanding of safeguarding and protecting children within a legislative, policy and multi-agency framework
- Consider the implications for the early childhood practitioner in meeting the needs of a child who has been abused or neglected while sustaining constructive relationships with parents
- Emphasise the importance of the student/practitioner's critical reflective disposition in all aspects of their professional practice in safeguarding and protecting children
- Include strong recognition of the voice of the child towards ensuring that safeguarding and child protection practice is child-focused
- Consider some of the concerns or anxieties students and practitioners may have in the context of their perspectives and experiences of safeguarding and protecting children in an early years setting.

The chapter will focus on some of the key issues and themes affecting policy and practice in relation to safeguarding and protecting children, and the implications for you as a new student or an experienced practitioner. You will see that an emphasis is placed on how you develop and extend your current professional practice as part of your commitment to providing a good quality service for children and their families. It is essential for you to recognise the role of early years settings in responding to the needs of children, and to appreciate the complexities and challenges of safeguarding children. All those working with young children and their families need to develop an awareness of the multitude of issues surrounding children's well-being, and be committed to updating their knowledge and practice.

Lansdown offers an important reminder regarding the vulnerabilities of children: 'Adults need to listen to children in order to gain their insights into the nature of the dangers they face and the type of protection they need' (2011: 154).

Children's welfare

It is a sad fact that a happy and secure childhood is not a universal experience, and that many children in our society suffer neglect and deprivation, and in some cases abuse at the hands of those who should be providing a safe and loving home life for them. As frontline practitioners, staff in early years settings need to be vigilant, constantly assessing the well-being of the children in their care. They also need to recognise those families who may be showing signs of distress, carefully monitoring the situation and assessing whether the situation in a family could escalate, giving rise to concern about the child's needs and welfare.

Table 14.1 explains key terms used when discussing children's safety and well-being:

Table 14.1 Key definitions of terms

Term	Definition
Safeguarding	To protect children from abuse and neglect, preventing the impairment of their physical, mental, emotional and social development and to promote and ensure an environment which is conducive to their health and welfare. The concept of safeguarding children is to promote and maintain a satisfactory level of care and nurturing to sustain their overall development.
Child protection	Is a step up from safeguarding approaches and is a direct response specific to protecting children who are suffering, or at risk of suffering significant harm because of abuse and/ or neglect. The Children Act 1989 introduced the concept of 'significant harm' as the threshold for decisions and compulsory actions to be taken in the best interests of children in order to protect them.
Physical abuse	May involve the hitting, shaking, throwing, scalding, burning, poisoning, suffocating of a child, or any form of physical pain or harm which is likely to cause injury or suffering to a child. Alternatively, a parent or carer may deliberately cause a child to develop the symptoms of illness, this is sometimes known as 'fabricated illness'.

Term	Definition
Emotional abuse	The constant emotional maltreatment of a child which can involve bullying, frightening, belittling or humiliating the child to such an extent that they feel unloved, unwanted or worthless. Emotional abuse can be a part of all types of abuse and neglect though it can be experienced separately from other forms of abuse.
Sexual abuse	This form of abuse, committed by men or women, can involve forcing or coercing the child to take part in sexual acts, whether or not the child is aware of what is happening. It can involve physical contact with the child such as penetration by rape, oral sex or non-penetrative sex such as, kissing, stroking. The abuse may also involve masturbation or forcing or enticing the child to look at pornographic material and imitate sexual acts. The child may also be groomed and influenced by an adult in preparation for penetrative sex or other sexual acts through direct contact or via the internet.
Neglect	Is recognised as persistent failure to meet the child's basic physical and psychological needs which is likely to cause an impairment or delay in the child's development and health. Neglect can also involve a chronic failure to be responsive to the child's emotional needs, failing to protect them from harm and danger, not attending to their health care and medical needs and not providing adequate food, warmth, shelter or supervision.
Child in need	Is a vulnerable child whose physical and psychological well-being and development is likely to be impaired without the provision of support services to meet their needs and/or to support their family. A child is 'in need' if their health will be (further) impaired without the provision of services provided by the local authority, or they need additional support for a disability.
Significant harm	The measure which brings about compulsory intervention by the local authority to assess the risk of harm the child is suffering (or likely to suffer) in the context of abuse and neglect. Significant harm may be due to an isolated incident of abuse or trauma experienced by the child, or persistent patterns of abuse and/or neglect which have or may cause damage to the child's development and well-being.

Source: adapted from DCSF (2010).

Some possible indicators of abuse and neglect

A practitioner's concerns about a child in their setting may arise from observations of the child, their knowledge of the child's family and aspects of their home life. The practitioner should be alert to any changes in a child's behaviour, observing and recording information as part of any forthcoming professional discussion about the child.

Factors which can cause concern about a child's safety and welfare can include: injuries or bruising, weight loss, unkemptness and poor hygiene, behaviour changes in the child, or aspects of their interaction with parents or carers which prompt concern. A child may disclose something to the practitioner which worries them, but staff need to be particularly sensitive to those with communication difficulties and disabilities and babies who cannot communicate their distress verbally.

The following indicators are adapted from *Working Together to Safeguard Children* (DCSF, 2010).

Physical abuse

There may be emotional aspects with any of the indicators of abuse, for example a child may seem generally anxious, fearful or aggressive. In the case of physical abuse, they may wince or move away from any aspect of touch: they may be reluctant to wear certain clothing, or resist getting changed because it is painful or because their injuries may be seen. A child may seem reluctant, or be unable to tell you, how they got their injury or bruise.

Sexual abuse

Babies, toddlers and young children can be victims of rape and other forms of sexual abuse perpetrated by men and women. This form of abuse is more likely to be committed by someone known to the child, such as a parent, older sibling, carer, relative or babysitter. Young children are particularly vulnerable because they are in the trusted care of adults, as are children with disabilities. Early years practitioners should be alert for causes of concern such as: soreness, bleeding or a discharge from the genital or anal area of the child; bite marks, grazing, or scratches to the genital or anal area or breast of the child; and signs of a sexually transmitted disease. The child may also show signs of emotional distress such as being agitated, withdrawn or aggressive. They may be fearful of certain care routines such as nappy changes, potty training, bathing, and they may seem preoccupied with their genitalia or use inappropriate sexual language in their communications, play or drawings.

Emotional abuse

This form of abuse can be more difficult to identify in isolation, as it may appear that the child is well cared for by their family; however, it is also experienced by children suffering other forms of abuse. A child may be told that they are unwanted or unloved by their parent(s). A parent may have limited understanding of how children develop, or how to respond appropriately to their needs; the child may be ignored and have their needs denied. Alternatively, parents can be overprotective, preventing them from participating in activities, or may be obsessive about diet, health or cleanliness, transferring these anxieties to their child. A child may be seen as troublesome or blamed for things going wrong. They may be shouted and sworn at, bullied and threatened and made to feel generally worthless. These experiences of emotional abuse can affect a child's self-esteem, resulting in developmental delays, or they may self-harm, such as hair-pulling or scratching. In these circumstances the child may become silent and withdrawn or aggressive towards other children and adults, or they may be clingy and fearful of new experiences in the setting.

Neglect

It is essential that practitioners are aware of the long-term consequences of chronic neglect on the developing child, and the negative impact on their transitions to adolescence and adulthood. Long-term neglect is a feature of significant harm to a child, and requires practitioners to make professional assessments and judgements about aspects of parenting and a child's home life which they may consider detrimental to their well-being and development. Neglect focuses on children's most basic needs not being met, the absence of appropriate care and supervision. Babies may show signs of an insecure attachment with a parent, which is usually consistent with insensitive and ineffective parenting. A child may not thrive (without medical cause), be underweight, withdrawn, have poor communication skills or be anxious with their peers. Practitioners may notice poor hygiene, a child constantly wearing soiled clothes, or persistent nappy rash, and neglected children may be hungry, displaying a voracious appetite or being overly protective of their food in the setting. A child may seem reluctant to be left alone and seem clingy, or conversely not form bonds with other children or adults in the setting. Children may experience a significant number of accidental injuries, possibly because of poor parental supervision, though this could indicate physical abuse.

The student practitioner voice and experience

Whether you are relatively new to working with young children and their families, or have many years of experience, you will be aware of some of these issues, particularly high-profile cases in the media about the abuse and death of children in their family homes, perpetrated by adults, possibly their parents or carers. These incidents can be disturbing and incomprehensible, particularly as these crimes are against the most vulnerable members of our society. You may find some aspects of this subject distressing, and it may touch on some painful aspects of your own life-history. However, it is important that you have an awareness of these issues so that you are adequately prepared emotionally and professionally to deal with any instances of child neglect or abuse that you may come across in your professional capacity.

Reflection

Take a few moments to consider the four main areas of neglect, and physical, emotional and sexual abuse. What do you already know about these issues, and are there some aspects that you feel uncomfortable addressing?

(Continued)

(Continued)

As a practitioner you need to recognise that the needs of young children must come first, and that your emotional response to any cases you encounter during your career are secondary. You will, over time, develop a set of skills enabling you to remain empathic but professional when dealing with difficult situations. Be assured that as a member of a team, you can share your concerns with others, and you should also have access to other agencies as part of a multidisciplinary approach.

As a starting point for writing this chapter I consulted with a group of Level 5 undergraduate students as they prepared for professional practice placements. I wanted to gain an insight into what they thought would be useful to know and understand regarding safeguarding children and child protection.

The issues and themes raised by the group of student practitioners, who were studying a child protection module, included the following:

- A need to understand their role and responsibilities in safeguarding and protecting children as a student whilst on professional practice placement.
- Guidance on what to do in a setting if they had concerns about a child.
- Guidance on what to do if they felt their concerns were ignored or not taken seriously.
- A need to understand the role of the Designated Safeguarding Officer within a setting.
- An understanding of the referral process to Children's Social Care when there is a concern about a child.
- An understanding of the role of other professionals who may be involved in safeguarding and protecting children.

Some issues raised here may surprise you, though you probably agreed with many of their points. It is clear that preparing for a professional practice placement does provoke anxiety, and that student practitioners need to feel confident and armed with a basic understanding of the issues, in order to prepare for the experiences they may encounter. Early years settings need to be proficient and effective in their safeguarding awareness and practices, ensuring that they pass their knowledge and experience on to less experienced practitioners. This is exemplified by a knowledgeable, skilled staff team whose team-members have open and reflective dispositions, supported by sound policies and procedures. Teams need to engender a culture which promotes and enables the voice of the child, sustains positive partnerships with parents and families, and provides an environment which encourages and supports student participation and learning. The following case study attempts to provide an illustration of a dilemma for a student about safeguarding and protecting a child in practice.

CASE STUDY

Mary is a Level 5 student on an Early Childhood Studies degree and has almost completed her second week of professional practice in a local nursery. Overall, Mary has enjoyed her experience and felt welcomed and part of the team, and she is quite confident that she will receive a good evaluation for her student portfolio from Sue, the setting's manager. However, there has been one incident which has unsettled Mary. She reported a child's disclosure to Sue who also happens to be the Designated Safeguarding Officer of the setting.

Sam is 3 years old and Mary noticed he was struggling to put on his coat. Whilst she gave him some help, Sam complained that he had a very sore arm as his daddy had pulled him whilst putting him to bed. Mary could see that Sam was in pain and felt concerned, so adhering to the settings guidelines, she spoke with Sue. However, Sue did not appear interested; she did not speak with Sam and appeared to dismiss Mary's concern explaining that Sam's father is a respected GP in the village, who would never do such a thing, adding that Sam tends to be a child who worries and is easily upset.

Mary remains concerned for Sam and she records that he complained of a painful arm in his daily profile notes. She reflects on what has occurred and wonders whether she may be overreacting. She does not want to upset Sue, nor Sam's father; she also wants to receive a good evaluation report. Later, when Mary is at home, she still feels worried about Sam.

What do you think Mary should do on her return to the setting tomorrow? How might the university support her?

The balance of reasoned and intuitive practice

Munro (2008) discusses the components of child protection work which are acknowledged as emotionally and intellectually challenging. She refers to the wisdom and ethics of practitioners working with children and families, and the need for a critical balance between intuitive practice and sound reasoning skills. The intuitive aspects relate to human traits, such as sensitivity, astuteness, good listening and communication skills, and a reflective disposition, including professional experience and the day-to-day skills which can be observed in the daily provision of care and education for children. Experienced practitioners are able to respond to and anticipate children's need for routines and boundaries helping them to feel safe in an uncertain world. It would be improper and risky to make professional judgements about a child or their family based on intuition alone, so childcare workers need to acquire knowledge and a set of professional skills enabling them to work effectively. This highlights the criticality of practitioner's observations, assessments and knowledge of children and their families. This goes alongside participation in professional supervision (Richards, 2012), awareness of the setting's Child Protection Policy and discussions with the Designated Officer for Safeguarding. If we consider the implications for Mary, in the case study, it is apparent that she is beginning to develop an appreciation of some of the complexities involved in safeguarding and protecting children, and the importance of following professional guidelines and the need to follow up her concerns. We also need to be aware of the statutory guidance of the Early Years Foundation Stage (DfE, 2012) and the multi-agency procedural guidelines stipulated by the Local Safeguarding Children Board.

Learning lessons from the past

The history and legacy of British child protection history is punctuated with public inquiries following the death of children in circumstances of abuse and neglect. One of the earliest examples concerned the death of 12-year-old Dennis O'Neill in 1945, killed by his foster-father, a case which highlighted the vulnerability of some children in the care of the state. Child protection legislation has been in place since 1889 through the 'Prevention of Cruelty to Children Act' (Powell and Uppal, 2012), and since then many new acts have been introduced. Two of the most significant acts legislating for the protection of children are the Children Act 1989 and the Children Act 2004. Unfortunately, laws do not mean that all children are fully protected from the harm or cruelty of adults (including parents or carers, members of their extended family, foster carers or even adults providing institutional care in children's homes, hospitals or secure accommodation).

The details of public inquiries provide important insight into the types of abuse experienced by some unfortunate children, including recent high-profile inquiries into the deaths of Victoria Climbié (Laming, 2003); Peter Connelly (Laming, 2009) and Kyra Ishaq (Radford, 2010). These notorious cases highlight the need for vigilance in our communities, and particularly within the helping professions. The need for a renewed focus on the welfare of children to protect them from harm was prioritised in the latter part of the twentieth century (Wilkins and Price, 2012). Subsequently, the scrutiny of professional practice through processes of public inquiries and Serious Case Reviews (SCRs) have highlighted: 'concerns about inter-professional practice in relation to communication between professionals and agencies and how professionals work together to assess and support children and families' (Hingley-Jones and Allain, 2011: 44).

The emphasis of a SCR is on a collaboration of openness and transparency between agencies and professionals and an avoidance of a blaming approach. The review is facilitated by an Independent Chair, and is subject to terms of reference. These are seen as the key elements towards ensuring a highly scrutinised process.

'SCRs are not inquiries into how a child died or was seriously harmed, or into who is culpable. These matters are for coroners and criminal courts, respectively, to determine as appropriate' (DCSF, 2010: 234).

Ofsted also has an examination role regarding the adequacy and impact of these reviews (DCSF, 2010), making recommendations for improving practice, including how agencies and professionals communicate with each other, within and beyond their organisation. The role of early years services are receiving greater focus in this process, particularly in light of their intense and frequent contact with the child and family, and their professional commitment to listening to children. There is particular concern about risk assessments where the voice of the child goes unheard (Brandon et al., 2012; Ofsted, 2011), or where decisions and judgements made by professionals are misguided or hampered due to practitioners prioritising the needs of the parent at the expense of the child (Laming, 2009) and colluding with the parents. Ferguson (2005) discusses how staff can be frightened or intimidated by parents and family. Referring back to the case study, Mary might speculate that Sue's reluctance to act may be related to her anxiety about approaching Sam's father who has a prestigious position in the community. So we can see that staff, despite concern for the child, may be influenced by their relationship with the parents; however, this is certainly not in the interests of the child.

Journal Task

Thaller, J. (2012) 'The children are listening: An autoethnographic account of the years leading up to familicide in a quiet, suburban neighborhood', *Qualitative Inquiry*, 18(3): 266–72.

This journal article is based on a personal account of the author's memories about a friend of hers who was a victim of physical abuse and who died at the hands of his step-father.

Levels 4 & 5

- The friends of the victim and their parents were aware that the victim was being abused, yet there was a 'wall of silence'. What may have prevented friends and neighbours from bringing their concerns to the authorities?
- What is the connection between domestic violence and child abuse?
- A parent in your setting confides with you that she is being hit by her partner. You have worries that her children may also be at risk of abuse, but so far have not noticed anything untoward with the children. How should you handle the situation?

(Continued)

(Continued)

Extension to Level 6

- Thaller reports that in the 1970s women who stayed with their abusive partners were considered to be victims of 'Battered Woman Syndrome' a helpless state in which women were seen to be powerless to protect their children. How has this view changed?
- Review the evidence that there is a connection between domestic violence and parenting capacity.

To download this task as well as other useful online resources please visit:
www.sagepub.co.uk/mukherji

An overview of key legislation and policy

As you progress through your course of study, you will have a growing appreciation of the sociological context of childhood, particularly in relation to the way that culture, economics and social concerns such as poverty impacts on the experiences of young children within a family (Field, 2010). The pace and complexity of legislation and policy changes over the last two decades are especially significant in heralding signs of past and present governments' efforts to improve services for children and their families, and to reduce the damaging effects of child abuse and neglect.

The core of child protection legislation is rooted in the principles and values of human rights, where the child is perceived and treated as a citizen, entitled to the same rights as adults (discussed further in Chapter 2). However, the promotion and enforcement of children's rights is problematic, partly due to attitudes towards children, their status in society, and values and beliefs about family life, parenting and adults power over children. The 1989 United Nations Convention on the Rights of the Child (UNCRC, 1989) enshrines the protective rights of children and is evident through the provision of the Children Act 1989. This law is key to the promotion of the voice of the child and is significant in the context of their protection and assessment of their needs.

A child in need assessment

One aspect of safeguarding and early help for a child is through the initiation of an Initial Assessment within the remit of Section 17 of the Children Act 1989. This assessment would be introduced for a child whose development may be delayed or impaired without the provision of appropriate services, or where there is a concern that the child is unlikely to achieve or maintain a satisfactory level of health and development (HM Government, 2013). The process is led by a qualified and experienced social worker collaborating with other key professionals who are known to the child and family, such as the child-minder, and who have a close relationship with the child and family. There is a focus throughout this process on the child's developmental needs, the parents' capacity to care for the child, and other factors such as the wider family and environment.

A child protection inquiry

The promotion of the 'voice of the child' is integral to the Children Act 1989, and local authorities have a duty to hear the 'wishes and feelings' of the child (with due regard to their age and understanding); the parents may be part of this dialogue as long as their presence is consistent with protecting or safeguarding the child.

When it is recognised that a child is suffering (or at risk of suffering) significant harm, Section 47 of the Children Act 1989 is implemented to enable a thorough assessment of the risk to the child. This process is led by a qualified social worker who will invite input from the child's family, the child themselves as appropriate, and other professionals known to the family, including an early years practitioner. A meeting known as a Child Protection Conference will be arranged. This is an important opportunity to share information about the child and their family, including a decision regarding the need to place the child on a Child Protection Plan. This plan should ensure that the child is safe from harm (and potential future harm), promote the developmental needs of the child, and support the parents and the family, if appropriate and safe to do so, in meeting the safeguarding and welfare needs of the child.

A critical difference between a Section 17 child in need assessment, and a Section 47 child protection inquiry, is the higher threshold of assessment and intervention with a Section 47 inquiry. Thus, for a Section 17 assessment, there may be no suspicion or concern about actual or likely significant harm to a child; this assessment may be based on issues relating to a child's overall development without the input of support services. However, during the process a concern may be identified about a child's welfare in the context of significant harm, in which case the assessment would escalate to a Section 47 child protection inquiry.

The revised Early Years Foundation Stage (DfE, 2012) is an example of recent expectations placed on the early years workforce, and is rightly rigorous and non-concessionary, placing emphasis on the culture of safeguarding and child protection practice within early years settings. The language of the statutory guidance is direct about the role and responsibilities of the practitioner in its prescriptions, employing the terms, 'must have' or 'must do', for example: '[Service] Providers must train all staff to understand their safeguarding policy and procedures, and ensure that all staff have up-to-date knowledge of safeguarding issues' (DfE, 2012: 14).

Role of adults in education and care settings

Some families will have come to the attention of various agencies before their children start education or day-care. Background knowledge and inter-agency work-practices enhance the way in which practitioners can monitor vulnerable children and families, and help to promote their welfare and safety. Irrespective of your current level of experience, it is important to understand the various child assessment approaches, and become familiar with aspects requiring you to report in your capacity as a key professional known to the child. The Common Assessment Framework (CAF; HM Government, 2013) offers early identification and help for a child's additional needs. This assessment is based on a holistic child-centred approach, requiring the cooperation of the parents (and the child), and involves other professionals known to the family. The CAF adheres to principles of ethical and effective information sharing, in order to formulate a plan which best meets the needs of the child.

You should research the guidance produced by the Local Safeguarding Children Boards (LSCB) within your Local Authority. Most LSCBs offer a comprehensive website for professionals and members of the public, giving information and guidance about what to do if they are worried about a child, in addition to inter-agency guidance on safeguarding children and training opportunities.

Practical considerations

Earlier in the chapter I mentioned intuitive practice, and how, through your knowledge of individuals, perhaps as their designated keyperson, recognising changes in a child may prompt concern. It is important to reflect on aspects of the child's behaviour: for example, have they become unusually shy or clingy, or do aspects of their appearance or behaviour concern you?

Lynch (2009) posits a number of ideas which can help practitioners to evaluate whether there are true grounds for concern. She emphasises the importance of thinking through the factors which initially prompted the concern, based on information you have about the family, when the issue first became apparent, and including the views of colleagues (in particular the Designated Officer for Safeguarding Children [HM Government, 2013] or senior manager in your setting). Children's Social Care services are another source of support that you can consult without identifying the child or family, as a means of 'checking out' the cause of the concern, and to gather a clearer understanding of the child's needs. A discussion with the Designated Officer could subsequently result in a child referral to Children's Social Care, following a consultation and consent from the parents as required and as appropriate.

As your theoretical understanding develops you will appreciate the crucial role of observations, assessment and careful records to plan for children's needs and provide for appropriate next steps in their development (see Chapter 4). You may need this information when required to provide evidence for CAF meetings or child case conferences.

When starting in a new setting you should ask to see their policy documents, in particular those relating to safeguarding and protecting children, and meet with the Designated Officer for Safeguarding. Whatever your role (permanent or voluntary) you must feel confident that, should you have concerns about a particular child, your views will be heard (Broadhurst et al., 2010). If you are concerned, and have even anecdotal evidence, you should approach other members of the team and discuss the concerns further with the Designated Officer or Manager. Ultimately, you must adhere to the setting's child protection procedural guidelines, as this formal approach assures you that you have taken the appropriate steps. However, if you remain uneasy or you consider that you have not been heard or taken seriously, then you must look to the guidance provided by your college or university. This experience resonates with the case study on p. 271 A proactive response to Mary's continuing concern about Sam should prompt a timely discussion with her personal tutor. Together they could instigate a plan of action in order to address the concern. The critical message for all students and practitioners is to take positive action rather than to do nothing at all.

The child's voice

Listening to children and encouraging their participation in aspects of their day-to-day experiences within an early years setting is undoubtedly a key feature of safeguarding children. Practitioners should be advocates in promoting the rights and interests of the child, since they are more likely to have a trusting relationship with the child who may be subject to a child protection inquiry. Arild Vis et al. (2010) comment that a failure to include a child's perspective as part of safeguarding practice could result in delay in detecting abuse or neglect; indeed, if children are not used to being listened to, they may not even consider disclosing their situation. It is particularly important to be mindful of the risk of overlooking the needs of the non-verbal child. Spyrou (2011) refers to the importance of finding effective ways of representing the 'voice' of the child. This point is especially salient when working with very young children, and highlights the collaborative role of the Special Education Needs Co-ordinator (SENCO) in contributing to the assessment of children with a learning disability who may have limited speech. Cuthbert et al. (2012) state that 45 per cent of Serious Case Reviews in England concern babies of less than one year of age; the vulnerability of these very young children is worrying, and it highlights the important role for staff providing day-care in the safeguarding of such vulnerable children, in terms of early detection and responding to concerns.

Reflection

What personal qualities do you consider to be important for good professional practice to safeguard and protect children? Why do you think reasoning and analytical skills are important in safeguarding and child protection work?

Working constructively with parents

An emphasis on creating trusting and positive partnerships is important (EYFS: DfE, 2012), however, practitioners should ensure that their relationship with parents does not compromise the safety and welfare of a child in their care. Sometimes relationships can be strained by concerns for a child's well-being. Powell and Uppal (2012) describe 'the maintenance of a positive relationship with parents or carers while meeting the needs of the child [as] a delicate exercise' (2012: 152). Tactful diplomacy and professional assertiveness are essential attributes for the practitioner engaging in the complex and challenging world of child protection, and the interests of the child must come first. Whilst we must avoid jumping to conclusions, we should take account of observations and discussions with the parents, record pertinent information, reflect on thoughts and feelings and make good use of professional supervision in assessing the needs of a child. If a child confides in you, subsequently raising a concern about sexual abuse, you may wonder whether to involve the parents. The spirit of the current child protection legislation does encourage this approach unless to do so would place the child at further risk of harm. Nevertheless, staff can feel vulnerable, and managers need to support their staff to help manage their fears about possible hostile reactions from parents whose children are identified as being abused or become the subject of a Child Protection Plan.

The complexities and challenges of parenting need recognition, particularly those experiences which may impact upon the safety and welfare of a child. These factors may include domestic abuse, mental illness, drug or alcohol abuse or parental learning disabilities (Cleaver et al., 2011; Cuthbert et al., 2012). If these issues go undetected there is an increased risk that children may be inadequately cared for and may be at increased risk of significant harm (Cleaver et al., 2011). These authors describe the 'dimensions of parenting capacity' which include the ability to provide basic care for a child, emotional warmth and safety, clear guidance about behaviour and boundaries of acceptable behaviour, and appropriate stimulation to encourage the child's intellectual and social development. Practitioners should be cautious about making assumptions about a parent's capability to meet their child's needs, but an awareness of these factors is critical when providing information to assist professional judgements of the needs of or risk to a child.

The practitioner has a challenging role in maintaining a constructive professional relationship with the parents of the child, based on openness, honesty and respect, whilst keeping the needs of the child keenly in focus as an absolute priority. The needs of the child must never be overlooked or compromised at the risk of being drawn into or distracted by meeting the needs of the parents.

Broadhurst et al. (2010) emphasise the need to continue to engage with parents as a means of assessing continued risk to a child. Practitioners are aware of the challenges of working with hostile, uncooperative or difficult parents, and therefore should have access to supportive supervision. Gardner and Cleaver (2009) describe how involving parents or carers in planning for their children can increase their self-esteem and motivation to improve their parenting skills. The practitioner could involve parents in decision making (no matter how small or seemingly insignificant) about their child in the setting. In explaining the practitioner's role to the parents, the practitioner should clarify what is negotiable or non-negotiable in terms of their professional responsibilities towards the child.

Reflection

You should formulate a clear strategy for working effectively with parents, which identifies key features of a successful working partnership. Make a list of strategies which you would feel comfortable incorporating into your working practices.

Your list might include the following features:

- Being clear with parents about your role and responsibilities to safeguard and protect the child
- Being persistent in your attempts to engage and communicate with parents/carers
- Being explicit about the limits of confidentiality and information sharing with other professionals involved with the child and family
- Involving the parents in decision making and planning for the child as appropriate
- Keeping your feelings in check in order to be safe. Not jeopardising your safety if threatened, while also keeping the protection needs of the child in focus and making sure other professional colleagues are informed of your experiences
- Keeping up-to-date records on developments and progress with the child and your work with parents, including any concerns and actions taken by the setting
- Ensuring that you have access to professional supervision.

Working as a team and multi-agency practice

Current policies and legislation stress the importance of multi-agency working practices. Children's Centres have demonstrated the effectiveness of providing a variety of family support services in one location. This multi-agency working enables professionals to work alongside one another to help support families in crisis. Recent reports have highlighted the importance of intervention and prevention programmes supporting 'at risk families' before problems become difficult to handle. Practitioners should not be working in isolation, but should work collaboratively with other key professionals such as the SENCO, school nurse, social worker or health visitor.

Reflection

As a student practitioner:

- What sort of preparations can you make for professional placements in order to develop your knowledge and understanding of the role of the early years setting to safeguard and protect children?
- What would you do if you were worried about a child in a setting? With whom would you discuss your concerns about the child? Are you familiar with guidance provided by your university or college?

As a more experienced practitioner:

- How do you support students on professional placement in your setting in developing their understanding of good practice in safeguarding and protecting children?
- Can you think of an incident when you were worried about a child? Reflecting on that experience, is there anything that you would have done differently and why?
- If you receive professional supervision, how does or how can this experience help you to improve your practice in safeguarding and protecting children?

Summary

The chapter has considered a range of pertinent themes surrounding safeguarding and protecting children within the early years sector, with an emphasis on the importance of collaborative and effective working with other agencies and professionals. The voice of the student practitioner was identified from the outset of the chapter. There has been an acknowledgement of the commitment to work with parents, and the challenge when dealing with circumstances where parents have abused their baby or young child. There has also been acknowledgement of the voice of the child throughout these themes. I have highlighted the importance of sharing concerns with other professionals and feeling confident to take appropriate action when worried about a child. Sometimes practitioners may feel foolish or worry that they are over-reacting, however history informs us that it is more important for a child's safety and welfare to share your concerns in order to establish good working practices with regard to safeguarding and protecting children.

Further reading

Levels 4 & 5

Powell, J. and Uppal, E.L. (2012) *Safeguarding Babies and Young Children: A guide for Early Years Professionals*. Maidenhead: Open University Press. This is essential reading as it provides a good understanding of the key principles of effective safeguarding practice, in addition to highlighting the necessary skills for professional responses and inter-agency working.

Reed, M. and Canning, N. (2012) (eds) *Implementing Quality Improvement and Change in the Early Years*. London: Sage. This book emphasises the importance of reflective practice and its impact on improving the quality of services for children and their families, with a range of themes pertinent to students developing understanding and practical competence.

Level 6

Hingley-Jones, H. and Allain, L. (2011) 'Safeguarding children: The complexities of contemporary practice and the importance of working with emotions', in C. Cocker and L. Allain (eds), *Advanced Social Work with Children and Families*. Exeter: Learning Matters. Although this chapter is written primarily for newly qualified social workers, the authors offer helpful insights into some of the challenges and dilemmas of child protection and multi-disciplinary work.

Wilkins, S. and Price, M. (2012) 'Safeguarding and promoting well-being', in N. Edmond and M. Price (2012) (eds), *Integrated Working with Children and Young People: Supporting Development from Birth to Nineteen*. London: Sage. This chapter addresses the wider implications for the role of practitioners in promoting the well-being of children and the assessment of risk and responses to concerns.

References

Arild Vis, S., Strandbu, A., Holtan, A. and Thomas, N. (2011) 'Participation and health – a research review of child participation in planning and decision-making', *Child and Family Social Work*, 16(3): 325–35.

Brandon, M., Sidebotham, P., Bailey, S., Belderson, P., Hawley, C., Ellis, C. and Megson, M. (2012) *New Learning from Serious Case Reviews: A Two Year Report for 2009 –2011*, Research Report DFE–RR226. London: Department for Education.

Broadhurst, K., White, S., Fish, S., Munro, E., Fletcher, K. and Lincoln, H. (2010) 'Ten pitfalls and how to avoid them: What research tells us'. Available at: http://www.nspcc.org.uk/inform/publications/downloads/tenpitfalls_wdf48122.pdf (accessed 2 September 2013).

Cleaver, H., Unell, I. and Aldgate, J. (2011) *Children's Needs – Parenting Capacity. Child Abuse: Parental Mental Illness, Learning Disability, Substance Misuse, and Domestic Violence*. London: The Stationery Office.

Cuthbert, C., Rayns, G. and Stanley, K. (2012) *All Babies Count: Prevention and Protection for Vulnerable Babies*. Available at: http://www.nspcc.org.uk/inform/all_babies_count_pdf_wdf 85569.pdf (accessed 2 September 2013).

Department for Children, Schools and Families (DCSF) (2010) *Working Together to Safeguard Children: A Guide to Inter-agency Working to Safeguard and Promote the Welfare of Children*. Nottingham: DCSF Publications.

Department for Education (2012) *Statutory Framework for the Early Years Foundation Stage*. Cheshire: DfE Publications.

Gardner, R. and Cleaver, H. (2009) 'Working effectively with parents', in H. Cleaver, P. Cawson, S. Gorin and S. Walker (eds), *Safeguarding Children: A Shared Responsibility*. Chichester: Wiley-Blackwell.

Ferguson, H. (2005) 'Working with violence, the emotions and psycho-social dynamics of child protection: Reflections on the Victoria Climbié case'. *Social Work Education*, 24(7): 781–95.

Field, F. (2010) *The Foundation Years: Preventing Poor Children Becoming Poor Adults*. London: HM Government.

Hingley-Jones, H. and Allain, L. (2011) 'Safeguarding children: The complexities of contemporary practice and the importance of working with emotions', in C. Cocker and L. Allain (eds), *Advanced Social Work with Children and Families*. Exeter: Learning Matters.

HM Government (2013) *Working Together to Safeguard Children: A Guide to Inter-agency Working to Safeguard and Promote the Welfare of Children*. [Online] Available from: http://www.media.education.gov.uk/asst.files/pdf/working%20togetehr.pdf (accessed 20 April 2013).

Laming, Lord (2003) *The Victoria Climbié Inquiry*. London: The Stationery Office.

Laming, Lord (2009) *The Protection of Children in England: A Progress Report*. London: The Stationery Office.

Lansdown, G. (2011) 'Children's welfare and children's rights', in L. O'Dell, and S. Leverett (eds), *Working with Children and Young People*. Milton Keynes: The Open University.

Lynch, M.A. (2009) 'Should I be worried?', in H. Cleaver, P. Cawson, S. Gorin and S.Walker (eds), *Safeguarding Children: A Shared Responsibility*. Chichester: Wiley-Blackwell.

Munro, E. (2008) *Effective Child Protection*. (2nd edition). London: Sage.

Ofsted (2011) *The Voice of the Child: Learning Lessons from Serious Case Reviews*. Available at: http://www.ofsted.gov.uk/resources/learning-lessons-serious-case-review (accessed 2 September 2013).

Powell, J. and Uppal, E.L. (2012) *Safeguarding Babies and Young Children: A Guide for Early Years Professionals*. Maidenhead: Open University Press.

Radford, J. (2010) *Serious Case Review. In Respect of the Death of a Child. Case Number 14*. Birmingham Safeguarding Children Board. Available at: http://www.lscbbirmingham.org.uk/downloads/Case+14.pdf (accessed 30 December 2012).

Richards, C.M. (2012) 'Quality matters because quality protects', in M. Reed and N. Canning (eds), *Quality Improvement in the Early Years*. London: Sage.

Spyrou, S. (2011) 'The limits of children's voices: From authenticity to critical, reflexive representation', *Childhood*, 18(2): 1–15.

UNCRC (1989) United Nations Convention on the Rights of the Child. UNICEF. Available at: ®http://www.unicef.org.uk/Document-pdfs/UNCRC_PRESS200910web.pdf (accessed 18 December 2012).

Wilkins, S. and Price, M. (2012) 'Safeguarding and promoting well-being', in N. Edmond and M. Price (eds), *Integrated Working with Children and Young People: Supporting Development from Birth to Nineteen*. London: Sage.

15

Management and Leadership

Judy Stevenson

This chapter will:

- Consider the differences between leadership and management and the place of both within early years practice
- Examine the historical/political context of leadership in early childhood care and education
- Explore the leadership vision
- Consider different leadership styles
- Look at how teamwork with colleagues is built and developed
- Explore how leadership behaviour affects the team
- Examine the challenges of making changes
- Consider the reasons for conflict and how it might be resolved
- Reflect on the specific requirements of Ofsted
- Examine the concept of 'supervision'.

When you go into any bookshop nowadays, there is generally a whole section on leadership, management and teamwork. There are also countless self-help manuals with quick fix suggestions to enable individuals to improve their performance in these areas. However, most of these relate to the field of business and industry, and whilst many of the principles apply to early childhood, it is often difficult to see how to put them into practice. It is also unfortunate that the titles of 'leader' and 'manager' have come to represent a somewhat false layer of hierarchy, where people holding these positions are thought to be more important than those actually being managed.

This chapter aims to look at the role of management and leadership within early childhood settings. It will consider how this has evolved in a political and historical context, looking at the importance of working with colleagues and how your behaviour and leadership style impacts on this. It will also consider two of the major challenges that face practitioners. The first is managing the many changes that need to be implemented with increasing frequency and the second is how you can resolve conflict professionally. It will conclude by looking at one of the unique situations we all face that needs specific thought: leadership and management when Ofsted arrive.

Management and leadership

There are many myths held about management, but the reality is that it is something we do all the time, from birth into old age. The youngest baby quickly learns to manage its need for attention and food through crying, smiles and cooing. Similarly, you only need to look at young children playing to see how they organise their available resources, their games, and frequently each other. As adults, we all manage ourselves and our complex technological lives through domestic activities, balancing work and home lives, planning holidays and the like. Gardner (1997) suggests the best managers are those who are able to draw on the intuitive approaches they developed in childhood.

Leadership is less easy to define, yet if any of us were asked to draw up a list of leaders, we could probably do it with ease, and it might include such people as Nelson Mandela, Winston Churchill, Mother Teresa or Mahatma Ghandi. But what is it about these people that give them the title of being a leader? Some might attribute this quality to intelligence, determination, charisma or vision, but through his research in the early 1990s, Daniel Goleman (1996) introduced the idea of emotional intelligence, and suggested that the most effective leaders have a high degree of emotional intelligence, which includes self-awareness, self-regulation, motivation, empathy and social skill.

Management and leadership are words that are used all the time within the early childhood field. Although all settings have someone who holds ultimate responsibility, often referred to as 'The Manager', the reality is that the majority of early childhood practitioners are involved with a range of children, carers, colleagues and other professionals and therefore use both management and leadership skills all the time. Although there is frequently an assumption that they refer to the same thing, they actually have different meanings and serve different, but equally important purposes. However, in care and education, they need to co-exist side by side, and it could be argued that management without leadership is ineffective, whilst leadership is equally ineffective without management.

Within a school, the hierarchy is more clearly defined with a Headteacher, Deputy Headteacher and frequently Co-ordinators for the various Key Stages, including the Foundation Stage. Whilst these layers have their own leadership and management responsibilities, these do not detract from those of the practitioners who also need to lead and manage their own routines and their work with children and families.

Reflection

Think about the differences between leadership and management highlighted above. Make a list of the tasks you do every day which have to be managed, from getting organised to leave for work or study, working during the day and through to your return home in the evening. Do you recognise yourself as a manager? Read through your list again. Are there any occasions when you used leadership skills instead?

Having established that we are all managers in every aspect of our lives, we need to think about what this actually means in terms of our work in our early years settings. If we accept that it is a process of organising and getting things done, this would include a range of tasks, such as planning, communicating, solving problems and maintaining resources, to name but a few. More senior managers might be involved in budgets, recruitment, personnel policies and legislation, and monitoring outcomes and results.

The leadership role is less clear to define in the early years. If we agree that it is leadership that inspires and motivates others towards a better future, an early years leader is the person who works with others to form visions, to plan next stages for developments, to initiate new projects and to react to crises in such a way that equilibrium is restored. Finally, the best leaders are also experts in delegation; they are aware of their own limitations and entrust others to carry out the daily tasks.

Smith and Langston (1999: 11) drawing on the work of Shea (1993) describe the leader as a person who 'inspires, thinks, motivates, initiates change, dictates, takes decisions, sets objectives, sets the pace, inspires loyalty' and is 'self-sufficient' while the manager 'controls, does, organises, accepts current practice, administers, follows through, co-ordinates' and is 'motivated by discipline'. This list clearly points towards leadership as taking others on a shared journey with the vision and the ability to motivate and empower them, while management is more about defining the task, working out how to achieve it, and designing and putting systems in place.

Reflection

Think about the different people who have had a senior role to you. What does it feel like when someone is managing you? Does it feel different if they are leading you?

The historical and political context of leadership in early childhood care and education

Leadership in early childhood care and education has gone through many changes in a relatively short period of time. Nowadays, we tend to take the variety and forms of pre-school provision for granted, with a range of private nurseries, state nurseries, pre-schools, schools, classes and Children's Centres across the country. However, this has not always been the case, and the evolution to our current situation has great implications for the way leadership and management of these settings has also developed.

If you look back to the origins of the nursery school movement in the nineteenth century, it was clearly linked to the Industrial Revolution. Mothers suddenly had the opportunity, and were frequently expected, to work long hours in factories, which meant there was often no one to look after the youngest children (Cunningham, 2006). The first nursery school in the United Kingdom was opened in 1816 by Robert Owen in New Lanark to care for children while their mothers worked in his cotton mills. When compulsory education for children over 5 was introduced in 1870 younger children also started to attend, and this unofficial system was ended in 1905 when the Board of Education recommended separate facilities for children under 5 (Cunningham, 2006). There was no requirement for any adults looking after our youngest children to have any formal training. There were no qualifications, ratios or minimum standards, but it is immediately obvious that those involved must have displayed many of the leadership and management skills we look for today. How else would they have created and sustained such innovative practice?

Reflection

What difference do you think training and qualifications are making to your practice? Are you a better practitioner because of them? What would it feel like to be starting your career with no training?

As time moved on, within the United Kingdom, early years care and education developed into two distinct strands. One of these was nursery education for 3- to 5-year-olds, and the other became known as early years care, or daycare. These two systems had vastly different functions, administrative structures and expectations of staff qualifications (Nutbrown, 2008). Nursery schools and classes, run by the local education authority, offered almost exclusively part-time education for 3- and 4-year-olds and were staffed by qualified teachers and by nursery nurses with a lower level of qualification. Daycare centres were run by the local authority social work departments, offered part-time or full-time care for children from birth to 5, and were staffed by nursery nurses and similarly qualified staff. Neither provided a universal service, and this public provision was supplemented by private provision, playgroups and childminding. A system developed whereby some settings were led and managed by those with teaching qualifications, others by nursery nursing qualifications, and some by those with no qualifications at all. Deep divisions were formed across all sectors which related to levels of pay, terms and conditions of work and to a system where a qualified nursery nurse could be the manager of a daycare centre, yet in education, could only be employed when a teacher held the management and leadership role.

From the 1970s onwards, a new form of provision began to emerge, driven by settings such as the Hillfields Centre which opened in 1971, and the Pen Green Centre which opened in 1983. These centres were set up as multi-functional centres for children and families, staffed by multi-disciplinary teams and combining care and education for children from birth to 5. With the election of the Labour Government in 1997 such centres increased through the Early Excellence Centres, Sure Start Programmes, Neighbourhood Nurseries and the legislation around Every Child Matters. These were all part of the Government's strategy to raise standards, increase opportunities for employment, reduce social exclusion and reduce child poverty. All offered a one-stop shop where families and children could have access to high quality integrated care and education services delivered by multi-agency partners with one centre or a network of centres. These forerunners led to the development of the Sure Start Children's Centres we now see across the country (Nutbrown, 2008). Alongside these developments came debates about the professionalisation of the workforce and new requirements for qualifications, collaborative working and, inevitably, the leadership and management of settings.

Reflection

What are the benefits for children and families of a combined education and care system? Can you think of an example where this type of provision has made a real difference for children and families?

The Nutbrown Review, *Foundations for Quality* (DfES, 2012b), has again considered early education and care qualifications both for young people who are new to the early education and childcare sector, and for those already employed there. It also considered how to promote progression through an early years career and into leadership roles.

Two new qualifications for leadership and management began to emerge: the National Professional Qualification in Integrated Centre Leadership (NPQICL), piloted by the Pen Green Centre and developed by the National College for School Leadership (NCSL, 2004), and the Early Years Professional Status (EYPS), developed by the Children's Workforce Development Council (CWDC, 2007). These are currently not linked, with NPQICL being the recommended qualification for Children's Centre leaders and EYPS being a curriculum leadership role linked to every setting including a graduate member of staff. Both are validated at a postgraduate level.

NPQICL is currently being revised, but has traditionally been linked to a set of National Standards, reflecting the challenges faced by Heads of Children's Centres. (DfES, 2011). A key feature is how the leader establishes a vision that is shared by all the different agencies involved in the Centre that will not only welcome children and families, but will also enable them to develop and thrive. The NPQICL is awarded to those who can demonstrate their competence against these standards, although the programme itself is highly experiential and encourages participants to *reflect* on their leadership work, *practice* their leadership and *discuss* leadership with other colleagues.

The Early Years Professional Status (EYPS) is a professional accreditation endorsed by the Government and currently awarded by the Teaching Agency (TA) to graduates working with young children aged 0–5 years. The aim of the programme is to develop and validate graduates who are leading practice from birth to the end of the Early Years Foundation Stage. EYPS is awarded to those who can demonstrate competence against a set of professional standards which cover essential aspects of high quality practice and leadership. As a result of 'More Great Childcare' (DfES, 2013), Early Years Professional Status is currently under review and the launch of Early Years Teacher Status is expected in 2013.

In highlighting these relatively new developments in leadership and management within early years education and care, the question must be whether meeting a set of standards is a reliable indication of high quality leadership and management. In practice, it is the skills and attributes of the individual, the views of others and the quality of provision for children and families which will answer this – qualifications and a professional status are an added bonus.

It is noticeable that despite the Government agenda to raise leadership qualifications, this has yet to permeate through to the Early Years Foundation Stage where the Statutory Framework (DfES, 2012a: 3.12) requires the manager to hold a full and relevant Level 3 qualification with at least two years' experience of either working in an early years setting or other suitable experience.

The leadership vision

As we have seen already in this chapter, establishing and maintaining a vision is one of the essential aspects of being a leader, so it is important to define exactly what this means and how it is established. Visions can be seen as something we see in our minds; they are our dreams and our glimpses of what the future might look like. However, they need to be developed into something more concrete than this. For our visions to become reality there has to be a clear picture of the future in terms of 'how we want things to be'.

Goleman et al. (2002: 209) suggest that 'the invisible threads of a compelling vision weave a tapestry that binds people together more powerfully than any strategic plan' and it is this binding of people together that is therefore so important. Any vision for our settings needs to be shared by everyone who is involved in the setting, regardless of their role or professional background, regardless of whether they are employed, a volunteer or a parent – the vision must be common to everyone for it to succeed. And it is the role of the leader to begin this process.

Smith and Langston (1999: 20) suggest that: 'Leaders should be visionary yet realistic; sensitive but demanding, innovative yet practical'. Sharing in a vision can raise aspirations and create excitement, it can encourage experimentation and risk taking, and increase the motivation to succeed. A shared vision can rarely be 'official', although many have tried to create this through Mission Statements. It is not solely the task of the leader to establish the vision – it is important that we all consider what inspires, motivates and excites us. It would be unrealistic to expect everyone to share our individual passions, but it is important to be able to explain our vision and what can be achieved through it.

Reflection

Does your setting have a Mission Statement? Who was involved in writing it? Does it reflect your vision for the setting?

Vision is not to be seen as a solution to problems, but rather a driving force for development and change. It involves constant attention to three fundamental questions: what does the future we are seeking to create look like?; why are we pursuing this particular vision?; and how do we behave to be consistent with the vision we are committed to?

However, for a vision to become shared, it is also important that a staff team consider their personal and shared values, that is, what they consider individually and collectively to be valuable and important about their work with children and families. Sharing and understanding each other's values is an important stepping stone to beginning to share a vision of the future.

Once those involved in a setting are clear about their shared values and visions, it is important to put the vision into action, which might well be deemed a managerial role. Visions only become reality if they are broken down into goals, tasks and action plans which may form the basis of a development plan. Again, the art of delegation is crucial here, but there is a much greater likelihood of this being successful if everyone has embraced, and is motivated by the vision.

The different types of leadership and management approach

There is a wealth of literature around leadership styles and characteristics and, again, much of it is hard to relate to our work with children and families. In this section, we will consider some of the theories around leadership styles and characteristics and whether any particular style is more suited to early years settings. This is particularly important in terms of gender, as it has to be acknowledged that we are working in a profession where the majority of staff are women. Also, the early years environment is socially complex: early years leaders work directly not only with staff, but with other agencies, families and children. Leadership is often considered from two perspectives: the tactics used when carrying out a task, and the concern paid to the relationships with staff, families and children. These two aspects need to be balanced, demanding equal energy and attention.

CASE STUDY

Marisha is the Head of a Children's Centre. She works with a large staff, many of whom have different cultural and professional backgrounds. The Centre has been asked to increase the number of places for 2-year-olds, but this creates a variety of dilemmas. The Centre has a space which could be converted into a toddler room, but this would mean moving the library and stock room, which some of the staff are against. It will require creating a new team, but the staff are settled and many want the new room to be run by a newly recruited team. Parents and health and social workers are keen for the room to open as quickly as possible as there is a need for more childcare in the locality.

Marisha needs to make decisions. She has tried involving everyone in her discussions and has listened to their points of view – but it is clear to her that she cannot accommodate everyone's wishes. She also needs to get on with the task of creating a room. In this instance, she refers the staff back to their shared vision for the Centre and decides to trust her instincts.

In looking at leadership approaches in the early years and which approach might be more successful than another, it can be helpful to think about your favourite cookery books. Many books contain the same recipe, but the ingredients will vary according to both the author and individual taste. Similarly with leadership, what works in one situation will be disastrous in another. For this reason, a leader needs a shelf of cookery books and to develop the personal knowledge of which ingredient will make the difference. For example, in periods of uncertainty, the leader might need to be very directive and give clear instructions, whilst at other times, a more democratic approach based on discussion and suggestion might be best. To develop this knowledge, a leader needs to be highly reflective and continually analyse what works and why.

One view of leadership identifies traits, such as intelligence, self-confidence, determination, integrity and sociability. Another considers heroic leadership where individuals are charismatic, inspirational and persuade others to their view, alongside its opposite – post-heroic leadership, where the leader is more consultative and facilitates discussion, taking on board suggestions and ideas. Transactional and transformational leadership focus on how leaders work with others. Transactional leaders think about how to achieve tasks quickly and efficiently, often using rewards and sanctions, while transformational leaders think more about the process and base their decisions on values, ethics and the long-term goal (Rodd, 2013).

Another popular view is to consider leadership styles. Goleman, Boyatzis and McKee (2002) identify six styles: visionary, coaching, affiliative, democratic, pacesetting and commanding. They point out that all these styles are useful at different times and in different situations, but that any one used continuously will be less effective.

Rodd (2005: 15) cites Bogue (1985) and suggests that the following five characteristics, known as 'The Five Cs' are relevant for early years leaders:

- Curiosity (an interest in learning)
- Candor [sic] (principles and action being open to public scrutiny and a willingness to speak the truth)
- Courtesy (treating others with respect and dignity)
- Courage (a willingness to risk and dare, and a willingness to make mistakes and learn from them)
- Compassion (creating trust, empathy, high expectations, hope and inspiration and providing opportunities for individual, group, personal and professional development).

However, others have expanded this list to include more personal characteristics and Rodd (2005: 27) includes softer descriptions such as patience, kindness and self-awareness alongside harder qualities such as being knowledgeable, rational, logical, professional, assertive, proactive and goal orientated.

Whilst it is helpful to understand this range of theories and to recognise the various styles and characteristics, they do not necessarily make the role of the leader any easier or clearer. Thinking again about cookery books and recipes, you cannot remove individual tastes and preferences, but, as already stated, the important thing is to try, to test and reflect on what works for you and why.

Building, developing and supporting a multidisciplinary team

Whilst we have been focusing on the individual leader or manager, this has little purpose if you ignore the teams that exist in every early years setting. Increasingly, we work with a range of individuals with different qualifications and different professional backgrounds, who are of different ages, cultural backgrounds and gender. These may include workers from education, care, health, social work or community development backgrounds. Whilst everyone might share a concern with the daily lives of children and their families, their approaches might be very different, depending on the individual and their professional heritage. In many Children's Centres there is the added difficulty of staff teams who work different hours with different terms and conditions. These may include people who are bought in through the commissioning of services and have their own line management and code of professional practice. Building and developing a sense of a team working towards a common, shared aim is a complex and often daunting role for a leader. In this situation, it is helpful for a leader to think in terms of distributed leadership, a term which is often used interchangeably with shared or democratic leadership, where individuals take responsibility for leading particular teams or areas of provision.

Rodd (2005: 146) describes teamwork as a process 'in which individual interests are subordinated in order to engage in joint, coordinated activity to achieve the common goals and purposes of a united group', that is to say, individuals put the needs of the team before their personal needs. If this is the aim, the question must be: how does the leader accomplish this feeling of team spirit? Establishing a collective vision will help them to share a common purpose and aim, but this does not resolve the issue of members of staff actually getting on with and relating to each other. It is important for people to feel happy in their work, and when team morale is high, everyone works better. For many years, the relationship between a nursery class teacher and a nursery nurse was described as being like an arranged marriage – the two individuals have to learn to get on with each other – and there is much anecdotal evidence that, as in a successful arranged marriage, in time, the team grows together, understanding each other's strengths, passions and challenges.

This is much the same in larger teams – it takes time. There is a trend for staff to have 'team building days' and to take part in 'team building exercises', where individuals engage in a range of fun and interesting activities to increase their sense of belonging.

However, there is no quick fix and team spirit cannot happen overnight. We have all experienced reservations when we join a new team or have to work with others for the first time. Three issues are of particular importance: inclusion – will I feel involved and accepted; control – how much influence will I have; and affection – will the other team members like me. A leader can help a team to recognise these insecurities and help people individually and collectively to work through them.

Handy (1990) drawing on the work of Tuckman (1965) suggests that all teams move through a number of stages of development. These are: forming, storming, norming and performing. At the forming stage, the team is a group of individuals coming together and beginning to form views on each other. In the storming stage, the individuals feel confident enough to start to challenge each other and storms ensue. Once a team has reached the norming stage, they begin to feel more united and new ways of working together become more established and normal. As a team reaches the ultimate stage of performing, everyone works together, supporting each other and creating their best performances.

Reflection

Think about any team you have been part of. Do you recognise these stages? Did you go through them in this order?

Whilst we might agree with the stages of team development, it is important for the leader to think about their role in it. Whilst it can be tempting to be a spectator, a leader can help the team move on to the next stage by assessing, supporting, discussing and reviewing progress with the team.

Leading a multidisciplinary team which includes a range of professional disciplines can have its own specific challenges. The days where a manager could be an expert in all areas are long gone, and, again, the idea of distributed leadership is important. If the expertise within the staff is harnessed into a leadership team, there is less likelihood of an area being neglected through lack of knowledge of what needs attention. However, as already highlighted, this is far harder where settings are working with partners who have their own leadership and management.

CASE STUDY

Jun is the SENCO in a private nursery and recently one of the children, Tom, has been allocated regular speech therapy. On the first day that the speech therapist visits, she enters Tom's room and asks Tom to go with her to the story room where they can work quietly.

Jun is very unhappy about this. The nursery has a policy of not withdrawing individual children from their rooms but when she says this to the therapist, the reply is that Tom needs a quiet environment so he can listen carefully and not be distracted. Jun feels she lacks the knowledge of this particular discipline to insist further.

For staff with different professional heritages to work together, regardless of their line management, it is essential that everyone is committed to collaborative working and shares a common belief that it will improve the lives of children and families. This needs to be followed by the opportunity for individuals to get to know each other. In the case study on p. 293, had the speech therapist and Jun talked together about how she would be working? Jun could have explained the nursery policy and avoided any confrontation. As with any team, it is the initial stages of establishing ways of working together that are so important.

For a whole staff team to continue to develop, everyone needs access to continuing professional development. This might be through attending training leading to a recognised qualification, but could include focused short courses, conferences or wider discussion groups. Individuals often gain new interests and passions through learning about a specific area of practice, and providing they are given the chance to share this with other members of the team, this can have an invigorating effect on all the staff. The Early Years Foundation Stage Statutory Framework (DfES, 2012a) suggests that an important element of supervision is the coaching and training element, which highlights further skills the leader will need to develop in themselves.

The challenges of making changes

An everyday occurrence in the life of early years practitioners is the need to make changes. We are continually adapting our practice to meet the needs of the children in our care and the changes in our rooms and our routines. However, all of us face bigger changes in our work lives, and it is the role of the leader to help us through these changes.

Reflection

Think about the last time you faced a major change at work. What did the leader in your team or your setting do to help you? Is there anything they could have done better?

Any change is unsettling and will cause a certain amount of anxiety. In recent times, we have had to adjust to new curriculum frameworks and new expectations for integrated working; for example, many practitioners are currently adapting to having 2-year-olds in their rooms. But all of these are about changes in organisation and generally come with some guidance, albeit not as thorough as we would wish. Far harder to manage are the long-term changes in attitudes, thoughts and beliefs – the changes in heart and mind.

It helps if you can understand that change is a process, with stages that people need to go through before they are able to embrace it and move forward. We are not strangers to this process as we frequently observe it when children are settling in, and we have great experience in supporting them through the transition. One model that gives us an insight is the Change Curve, based on a model developed by Kubler-Ross in 1969 to explain the grieving process, but now used as a tool to help people understand their reactions to change. This has three stages; the first is shock and denial, which is frequently caused by a lack of clear information, fear of the unknown and the fear of doing something wrong. Once the initial shock is passed, individuals experience a sense of denial – everything was fine the way it was, why should anything change? It is not unusual for people to convince themselves that the change is not actually going to happen, or if it does, they won't be involved. At this stage it is crucial for the leader to keep up a high level of communication, giving clear information and reassurance as much as possible. The second stage is one of anger and depression. At this stage people find it important to focus the blame on someone or something, allowing them to continue to believe that nothing will actually change. The depression is the lowest point of a downward curve, when the anger wears off and the realisation that change is inevitable sinks in. It is important for the leader to stay focused, and people will be reassured by the knowledge that others feel the same. It is important that the team is given the opportunity to talk about their feelings, which can create an emotional environment from which to move on to the final stage. This is acceptance and integration when the curve begins to rise and a more optimistic and enthusiastic mood begins to emerge. Individuals accept that change is inevitable, and begin to work with the changes rather than against them. People begin to be excited by new opportunities and in some cases are impatient for the change to be complete. At the peak of the curve is integration, where the focus is on the future and the changed situation has become the new reality. Normal topics of conversation resume, and everything gradually returns to the accepted routines. Obviously, people will go through these stages at different rates, but it is important that when any change is complete, the leader celebrates the successes with all, whilst keeping a close eye on the team to review and check the understanding of new ways of working.

The behaviour of the manager throughout the process of change is very important. Too much speed and attention to getting things done will frequently run side by side with a lack of attention to how the team is feeling and a lack of nurture and support. We need to take time to prepare people for change, to involve them at all stages with clear information and communication, and to help them to embrace, rather than fear, the new.

The reasons for conflict and how it might be resolved

In a working environment where people are together for long hours and have a high involvement with children and families who are frequently under stress, it is not surprising that conflict occurs. Some of this will quickly blow over, but, unfortunately, some conflicts go on for longer, and then the leader needs to intervene to help restore harmony. This sounds simple enough, but it is often one of the more challenging aspects of being a leader and manager. It is best dealt with promptly and thoroughly, as conflict which is neglected often festers and can divide the happiest of teams.

Conflict often arises when someone believes that an individual isn't doing their work properly, when someone complains constantly about their role or responsibilities, when someone is continually sulking or moaning, or through fundamental differences in how to resolve a situation with a child or family. It can be based on personal or professional issues – or both. Adults are not unlike children, and sometimes conflict can arise as staff seek attention. It should also be recognised that not all conflict is bad – it can be a powerful tool in instigating change.

Obviously, it is best to try and avoid conflict and this can be done by creating an environment where people feel valued, where they are respected and where the leader knows each individual who is working in the setting. This will give them the confidence to approach you if they are unhappy. Communication is also critical, clear information delivered to everyone at the same time with further time for questions and discussions can do much to allay gossip and feelings of favouritism. This needs to be face to face and not delivered electronically by email or text, as can be the trend when staff are working different shifts and work patterns. It is also important to be transparent, straightforward and articulate.

Reflection

Think about a time when you have been annoyed with someone you work with. How did you resolve the issues? How did you feel afterwards?

Managers and leaders need to maintain a high profile at work and be seen in all areas, ready to pitch in when needed. Being around the setting rather than hiding in the office under a pile of paperwork allows you not only to be seen by the staff, but more crucially to sense any change in the atmosphere in a room and to ask questions to resolve issues immediately. Leaders need to use their emotional intelligence to tune in to the staff and sense when something is not right.

However, not all conflict can be avoided, and sometimes it is so serious that the only solution is to look towards employment legislation; but up to this point there are many situations which can be resolved and are better dealt with by the manager.

It is important to reflect on the different styles you use in different situations. In the 1970s Thomas and Kilmann (Thomas, 1974) identified five main styles: competitive, where the leader takes a firm stand and uses their status to win, which can leave everyone feeling bruised and resentful; collaborative, where the leader tries to meet everyone's needs and embrace everyone's points of view, which can end up with no one feeling better; compromising, where the leader expects everyone to give up something; accommodating, where the leader indicates a willingness to meet the needs of others at the expense of their own needs; and avoiding, a style used when you are trying to completely avoid the conflict. Once you understand the different styles, you can use them to think about the most appropriate approach (or mixture of approaches) for the situation you are in. You can also think about your own instinctive approach, and learn how you can change this if necessary. Ideally you can adopt an approach that meets the situation, resolves the problem, respects staff interests and mends damaged working relationships.

The specific requirements of Ofsted

The Early Years Foundation Stage Statutory Framework (DfES, 2012a) has few requirements for leadership and management other than qualifications and supervision, but when Ofsted visit they will be making specific judgements about this aspect of the setting and how well all aspects of the EYFS are led and managed. Although there are different regulations for different forms of provision, many of the underlying factors that the Inspectors will look for are the same. The guidance for the inspection of Children's Centres is currently under consultation. One of the principle tasks of any leader or manager is to reassure staff about the process and to try to allay the anxiety the visit will cause. It is worth remembering that by the time of the visit there is little you can do to change anything the inspectors will see, the work needs to have been done beforehand, be on-going and be supported by thorough evidence.

Inspectors will principally report on 'the effectiveness of the leadership and management in understanding and implementing the requirements of the Early Years Foundation Stage' (Ofsted, 2012). This will include the curriculum aspects of the EYFS, safeguarding and welfare requirements, the nursery environment, self-evaluation and target setting, performance management and arrangement for professional development, and, finally, the relationships with parents and other external partners. Much of the evidence around these areas will come from meetings between the inspectors and the manager alongside discussions with staff and parents and written samples of policies and procedures.

As already stated, the work in preparing for an Inspection needs to be done long before the inspector walks through the door. Staff need to see the Inspection as a positive experience whereby they can highlight all the things the setting is doing well, and if the quality of the provision is high and staff are well prepared, there is no reason why the Inspection outcome should not be good.

Supervision

The need for leaders and managers to provide supervision for all staff who have contact with children is a new requirement of the Early Years Foundation Stage Statutory Framework (DfES, 2012a). Whilst there is a rich tradition of supervision in some professions, this will be new for many with an education background. Rodd (2013: 167) summarises the aims of supervision as enabling early childhood practitioners to 'be clear about their roles and responsibilities; plan and monitor progress towards meeting service objectives; receive support for their work effort and outcomes; and access planned opportunities for learning and professional development'. The Tickell Review (2011: 5.17) goes slightly further and recognises that 'supervision should be expressed in such a way that encourages reflective practice and moves away from the perception that it is merely a tick-box approach to check what practitioners are, or are not, doing'. One of the challenges for those working in close contact with families is that of managing close emotional relationships with children whilst maintaining some professional distance. A skilful leader will provide an environment that both supports and challenges the practitioner in this role.

Journal Task

Shin, M.S., Recchia, S.L., Lee, S.Y., Lee, Y.J. and Mullarkey, L. S. (2004) 'Understanding early childhood leadership: Emerging competencies in the context of relationships', *Journal of Early Childhood Research*, 2(3): 301–16.

This article looks at the leadership behaviour of six children and the leadership characteristics they showed in their relationships with other children and staff.

Levels 4 & 5

Think about the children you are working with. Observe the leadership behaviours you see. Are there differences between different age groups or between girls and boys? Why do you think this might be?

Level 6

This article highlights two behavioural and personal characteristics shared by the young leaders: dynamic and powerful personalities; and a high level of awareness. Are these characteristics shared by the managers and leaders you work with? How would you develop these characteristics in yourself? When the opportunity arises at work, try out a new style of leadership.

To download this task as well as other useful online resources please visit:
www.sagepub.co.uk/mukherji

Summary

In this chapter we have considered many of the aspects that are important to leaders and managers of early years settings. It is worth remembering that although you may not yet hold this position, we all work in teams and lead the care and education of children. It is important to think about the role you play as a team member, a room leader or in time as the manager, and to reflect on the style and philosophy you are developing in your relationships with others.

Further reading

Levels 4 & 5

Hay, S. (2007) *Essential Nursery Management: A Practitioner's Guide*. London: Routledge. A practical book with many case studies that considers all aspects of effective nursery management.

Robins, A. and Callan, S. (2009) *Managing Early Years Settings*. London: Sage. A key text with discussion points and case studies that looks at both the skills and techniques needed in leading and managing early years settings.

Rodd, J. (2013) *Leadership In Early Childhood* (4th edition). Maidenhead: Open University Press. An accessible text recently revised and updated to reflect the changes affecting leaders in early childhood.

Level 6

Jones, C. and Pound, L. (2008) *Leadership and Management in the Early Years: A Practical Guide*. Maidenhead: Open University Press. This is a practical guide that encourages practitioners to recognise themselves as leaders and managers whatever their current role in the profession.

Miller, L. and Cable, C. (2010) *Professionalization, Leadership and Management in the Early Years*. London: Sage. This text will help to develop your critical thinking about yourself as a leader and manager.

Aubrey, C. (2011) *Leading and Managing in the Early Years*. London: Sage. This text combines theory, research and practice in relation to the childcare sector. It provides a clear context for leadership and management in the early years.

References

Aubrey, C. (2011) *Leading and Managing in the Early Years*. London: Sage.

Bogue, E.G. (1985) *The Enemies of Leadership*. Bloomington, IN: Delta Kappa Education Foundation.

Cunningham, H. (2006) *The Invention of Childhood*. London: BBC Books.

DfES (2011) *National Standards for Leaders of SureStart Children's Centres*. London: TSO.

DfES (2012a) *Statutory Framework for the Early Years Foundation Stage*. London: TSO.

DfES (2012b) *Foundations for Quality*. London: TSO.
DfES (2013) *More Great Childcare*. London: TSO.
Gardner, H. (1997) 'Multiple intelligences as a partner in school improvement', *Educational Leadership*, 55(1): 20–21.
Goleman, D. (1996) *Emotional Intelligence*. London: Bloomsbury.
Goleman, D., Boyatzis, R. and McKee, A. (2002) *The New Leaders: Transforming the Art of Leadership into the Science of Results*. London: Time Warner.
Handy, C. (1990) *Inside Organisations*. London: BBC Books.
Hay, S. (2007) *Essential Nursery Management: A Practitioner's Guide*. London: Routledge.
Jones, C. and Pound, L. (2008) *Leadership and Management in the Early Years: A Practical Guide*. Maidenhead: Open University Press.
Kubler-Ross, E. (1969) *On Death and Dying*. Oxford: Routledge.
Miller, L. and Cable, C. (2010) *Professionalization, Leadership and Management in the Early Years*. London: Sage.
Nutbrown, C. (2008) *Early Childhood Education: History, Philosophy and Experience*. London: Sage.
Ofsted (2012) *Evaluation Schedule for Inspections of Registered Early Years Provision*. Available at: http://www.ofsted.gov.uk/resources/using-early-years-evaluation-schedule-guidance-for-inspectors-of-registered-early-years-settings-req (accessed 7 December 2012).
Robins, A. and Callan, S. (2009) *Managing Early Years Settings*. London: Sage.
Rodd, J. (2005) *Leadership in Early Childhood* (3rd edition). Maidenhead: Open University Press.
Rodd, J. (2013) *Leadership in Early Childhood* (4th edition). Maidenhead: Open University Press.
Shea, M. (1993) *Personal Impact, Presence, Para-Language and the Art of Good Communication*. Sinclair-Stevenson Ltd.
Smith, A. and Langston, A. (1999) *Managing Staff in Early Years Settings*. London: Routledge.
Shin, M.S., Recchia, S.L., Lee, S.Y., Lee, Y.J. and Mullarkey, L.S. (2004) 'Understanding early childhood leadership: Emerging competencies in the context of relationships', *Journal of Early Childhood Research*, 2(3): 301–16.
Thomas, K. W. (1974) *Thomas-Kilmann Conflict Mode Instrument*. New York: Tuxedo.
Tickell, C. (2011) *The Early Years: Foundations for Life, Health and Learning*. London: DfES.
Tuckman, B. W. (1965) 'Developmental sequence in small groups', *Psychological Bulletin*, 63: 384–399.

Part 5

IMPLEMENTING THE CURRICULUM

This section looks at the delivery of the English Early Years Foundation Stage Curriculum (EYFS) (DfE, 2012), although early childhood practitioners working in other countries will still find the information relevant. The practice that is outlined is based on approaches and principles that are common to many different curricula.

As we have seen in earlier chapters, dividing learning and development into discrete areas, such as physical development and language is a somewhat artificial divide as all aspects of learning and development are dependent on each other. However, for practical reasons, the EYFS divides the curriculum into seven areas of learning and development; three prime areas and four specific areas. In this part of the book we have provided a chapter on each of the prime areas: communication and language, physical development and personal, emotional and social development. In addition there is an extended chapter that looks at three of the four specific areas: mathematics, understanding the world, and expressive arts and design. The fourth specific area, literacy, is included in the chapter on communication and language.

In Chapter 16 Julia Manning-Morton describes ways in which children's personal, social and emotional development can be promoted within early childhood settings. Julia sees this aspect of learning and development as fundamental to all other areas of learning, and as one that requires practitioners to develop sophisticated professional skills which need to be nurtured by strong leadership and management. To promote this area of learning for children, practitioners are required to understand the links between emotional learning, early relationships and children's sense of self and understanding of others. Julia provides a sound theoretical base which practitioners can use to help them deliver this aspect of the curriculum.

In Chapter 17, Louise Dryden discusses communication, literacy and ICT. Literacy and ICT are specific areas of learning and development under the EYFS (DfE, 2012) but have been included within this chapter as there are strong links between them. Louise explains that communication, in all its guises, is the foundation of all learning; within this chapter she gives an outline of the development of communication skills and how this development can be supported in early childhood settings. Louise explains how language development is related to problem solving, creativity and symbolic representation, and explains how practitioners can support early mark making and literacy.

Physical development is discussed by Rita White in Chapter 18, where she points out that that the development of physical skills is inextricably linked to all other areas of development. Rita looks at common patterns of physical development and at some of the factors that can influence the acquisition of physical skills. The chapter gives a sound introduction to how physical development can be promoted within early childhood settings.

In Chapter 19 Ros Garrick looks at three of the specific areas of learning and development; mathematics, understanding the world and expressive arts and design. Ros introduces us to some of the various theories that underpin our understanding of how to promote these areas of learning and development in early childhood settings. Throughout the chapter Ros focuses on supporting children's dispositions for learning whilst using her experience to support practitioners in planning quality provision for children.

Finally, Chapter 20, written by Hilary Fabian, looks at transitions. In this chapter the various transitions made by children both between and within settings are discussed. The importance of working as a team with all involved, listening to children and giving them a sense of control is emphasised. Hilary explains how successful transitions are linked to children's socio-emotional well-being; children who are resilient and confident being able to cope well with transitions, whilst transitions that are handled badly can have a negative effect.

Reference

Department for Education (DfE) (2012) *Statutory Framework for the Early Years Foundation Stage: Setting the Standards for Learning, Development and Care for Children from Birth to Five*. London: DfE.

16

Young Children's Personal, Social and Emotional Development: Foundations of Being

Julia Manning-Morton

This chapter will:

- Introduce some key theories relating to the personal, social and emotional development of babies and young children
- Explain processes of emotional expression and regulation in babies and young children
- Discuss the links between emotional learning, early relationships and how babies and young children develop a sense of self and an understanding of others
- Identify some aspects of practice that support babies and young children's personal, social and emotional development.

When it comes to purposeful planning in early childhood settings, thinking about children's personal, social and emotional development tends to be the poor relation, forming much more of the unplanned or 'hidden' curriculum. This tendency may arise from the emergence over the last 20 years of a notion of professionalism in the early childhood field that emphasises the importance of focusing on intellectual learning and cognitive skills, which in turn reflects a wider Western/European cultural bias towards valuing the rational and objective (and the mind) over the emotional and subjective (and physical) aspects of our lives (Manning-Morton, 2006; Osgood, 2010).

Judy Dunn describes how this bias has also been present in developmental psychology:

> Until quite recently, cognitive and socio-emotional developments were studied as separate domains. The mapping of children's discovery of the mind, which has proved so exciting, did not include a focus on the role of social experience in influencing the development of understanding, and little attention was devoted to individual differences in mind reading and their possible links with social relations. (Dunn, 1999: 56)

And yet, throughout my experiences of teaching and discussing the development and learning processes and needs of young children, students and practitioners consistently cite children's personal, social and emotional learning as being the foundation of all other aspects of development and a central concern of their practice. Thankfully, this concern has begun to be reflected in aspects of policy in early childhood, such as the guidance for practitioners on 'Social and Emotional Aspects of Development' (DCSF, 2008), the requirement to implement a 'Key Person Approach' (Elfer et al., 2003) in the Early Years Foundation Stage curriculum framework (DCSF, 2008) and, latterly, the Tickell review of the EYFS (Tickell, 2011), leading to a revised EYFS (DfE, 2012), which identifies three prime areas of the curriculum, one of which is personal, social and emotional development. Yet still, within this one area, three major aspects of development are combined, which, considering the amount of theoretical discussions involved in each of them, still means that the complexity of how they each develop and are also interrelated, is often reduced in curriculum development to areas such as self-help skills and behaviour management.

For this reason, and because it is not possible to do justice to the whole range and depth of theoretical and practice discussions in this area in one chapter, here we will focus on some key aspects of emotional learning and its links with early relationships, the development of self-awareness and an emergent understanding of other people.

Feelings and emotions

Reflection

Consider the range of feelings you have experienced over the last 24 hours, how many and which ones can you recall?

From this you may recognise that we often only take account of our feelings when we 'get emotional', that is, show a particular strength of feeling, even though there are a huge range of feelings going on in our minds all the time. Antonio Damasio, a neuroscientist, encapsulates how difficult it can be to notice this when he says that feelings are 'the bedrock of our minds' (Damasio, 2003: 3) but that we don't notice them because our minds are taken up with a lot of visual, aural and other stimulation.

This section will describe how we see emotions developing in young children and what this may mean for early childhood practitioners in practice.

Nearly 150 years ago, arising from the close observations of his son and naturalistic studies of peoples from across the world, Charles Darwin suggested that humans have an innate and universal repertoire of facial expressions denoting the primary emotions of happiness, anger, disgust, sadness, surprise and fear (Darwin, 1872, cited in Harris, 1989). One hundred years later, further studies showed how these emotional expressions could reliably be identified in very young babies (Ganchrow et al., 1983).

It could be argued that these expressions in infants arise from their ability to imitate facial expressions from birth (as identified by Meltzoff and Moore, 1983), but it should be considered that were these expressions solely learned socially, there would be different patterns of facial expressions in different societies rather than universal patterns (Barnes, 1995). Consequently, Harris (1989) endorses Darwin's view of the universality of emotional facial expressions, emphasising that this has been supported by more recent cross-cultural studies too.

These discussions are, so far, constructed within the nature/nurture debate, but it is clear that even if these primary or basic emotions are innate and universal, they are then built upon through the child's socio-cultural experience. In this way humans develop a range of secondary emotions such as hope, anxiety, excitement, frustration and so on that are blends of the basic emotions. These blended emotions take on slightly different meanings and modes of expression through growing up in a particular culture.

This brings an interactionist view to bear on the development of emotion, which would see babies and young children coming to understand their feelings through a combination of biological and social interactions. A 'dynamic systems' view of development (Schaffer, 2006) would describe how the physical system of the chemicals in the brain, the nervous system and muscles not only communicate together within their own system but also interact with the social system, such as the child's recognition of faces and voices, crying and vocalising.

CASE STUDY

Caitlin is hungry, which gives rise to internal feelings of anxiety and discomfort. This then causes the release of hormones and chemicals in the brain and the body and Caitlin cries. The expressive movements of her crying face activate the many receptors in the skin of her face, which are sensitive to the resulting stretching and

(Continued)

(Continued)

pressure changes. So Caitlin has a physical sensation of 'this is me crying'. This external physical awareness is linked in her mind with her internal feelings of discomfort and anxiety. Then her father's familiar face appears and she hears the soft reassuring tone of his voice, feels his arms gently holding her and smells the familiar scent of his body and the milk. These actual experiences are linked together and also to the internal feeling of comfort and fullness she experiences on feeding and perhaps then what it feels like to smile.

This example indicates the importance of the development of emotions in humans for evolutionary survival (Caitlin's emotional expressions ensure that she is fed). Daniel Goleman sets out how different emotions prepare our bodies to respond in ways that have enabled us to overcome threats to our evolutionary survival; for example, anger causes blood to flow to the hands, making it easier to grasp a weapon, while fear sends blood to our large muscles, making it easier to flee (Goleman, 1996: 6–7).

So we can see how emotions are a bodily phenomenon and how our bodily processes are closely linked to our feelings. Next we look at how these emotions are linked with conscious behaviours and social experiences in the structures of the brain.

Emotional development and the brain

Reflection

Study some illustrations of the structure of the brain in Carter (1998), Eliot (1999) or LeDoux (1996), or search 'brain' on Google Images. You can also find some useful video clips of lectures by prominent neuroscientists such as Susan Greenfield that will provide you with useful background learning.

LeDoux (1996) and Goleman (1996) identify the limbic system at the centre of our brains as the area that is mainly responsible for processing our unconscious emotions. In particular, they identify the amygdala as being the part of the brain that is our 'emotional sentinel'. When the brain receives information that is threatening to our survival in some way, rather than being transmitted to the cortex for consideration, it travels directly to the amygdala where basic emotions such as fear and anger trigger the fight or flight response, sometimes causing us to behave in ways that perhaps we would not have done had we consciously thought about it. Goleman (1996) calls this 'emotional hi-jacking'.

But of course, as with all neurological processes, the processing of emotions does not only take place in one area of the brain (Greenfield, 2000), the limbic system is densely connected to the cortex, making our thoughts and feelings inextricably linked. It is through the connections in the cortex that children start to be able to know and understand their emotional responses. As more connections are made between neurons, as a result of the child's expanding experience of the world and other people, pre-existing feelings start to become conscious (Carter, 1998). Children's social experiences also stimulate neural connections to send chemicals to the amygdala that inhibit emotional reactions, supporting their slowly growing ability to regulate their emotions. So, it is negative feedback from the connections in the cortex that enables children to delay gratification and to exercise the kind of self-control that is necessary for successful social interactions (Eliot, 1999). However, it should be noted that the process of firming up these neural pathways, only starts at about 18 months and is not completed until late adolescence. This gives a neurological explanation of the high level and constant flux of emotionality of young children that early years practitioners will be familiar with, and also helps to explain young children's immature ability to control aspects of their behavioural expressions of emotion. Practitioners with this understanding will have appropriate expectations of children and be able to think about how best to support the gradual emergence of emotional regulation throughout infancy and early childhood. They may also be able to reflect on their own level of maturity of emotional regulation.

Implications for practice: Play and emotion

A crucial area of professional knowledge, then, is to understand how babies and young children come to experience their feelings and express their emotions, and then to be able to apply that knowledge in practice. This means that practitioners need to feel comfortable supporting a range of emotional expression in children and need to develop skills in containing and comforting children in distress through gentle holding, providing words for feelings, and calmly and gently offering explanations, empathy and reassurances.

Practitioners also need to plan how they support children's expressions of emotion through play opportunities that are open ended and child directed, in which children can use materials in a range of ways. Being actively involved in social play opportunities with children means practitioners can name and suggest a wide range of emotional states, thereby expanding children's emotional vocabulary. It is useful though to monitor how much this happens with girls rather than boys, as it has been noted that mothers talk about feelings more with their daughters than with their sons (Dunn, 1988), which, it is suggested, results in the apparently more mature ability of girls to regulate feelings by the age of 8 (Malatesta and Haviland, 1982, cited in Saarni, 1984).

By supporting children's social play, practitioners can empathise with troubling feelings, reinforce pro-social behaviour and model behaviours such as negotiation and compromise, all of which will support children's learning about regulating their emotions. Practitioners providing as much stability and consistency as possible and encouraging co-operation between children, are also important strategies.

Practitioners also need to understand how children use play to explore their inner troubles and concerns. From a psychoanalytic perspective play is an activity in which children's anxieties can be worked through (Manning-Morton, 2011). Cath Arnold uses some of these ideas to discuss how children's explorations of particular schemas such as containing, enveloping or connection, help them to understand emotional events and are used to 'comfort, to give form to, and to explore and begin to understand complex life events and changes' (Arnold, 2010: 11).

Reflection

Think back over the last time you were playing and interacting with a child. Note down your thoughts about the following:

- The feelings you were experiencing
- The feelings you think the child was experiencing
- Which expressions and behaviours led you to think that.

Were any of those feelings explicitly acknowledged or discussed? If so, in what way?

Close relationships

Trevarthen and Aitken (2001: 18) stress that emotions are inter-subjective, they say: 'Affect is fundamentally dialogic … it happens between people'. They also emphasise the importance of the rhythmic attunement of the caring adult's responses, as emotionally synchronised interactions have a positive role in the social growth of children through deepening bonds with others. Stern (1998) describes 'affect attunement' as the process whereby an adult sensitively reads a child's non-verbal signals and is then able to align their state of mind with the child to engage with them in the way they need. This high level of empathy required by very young children of their caring adults is also central to Bion's psychoanalytic concept of 'container-contained' (Bion, 1962). In this perspective the adult's mind acts as a container and 'holds' the child's difficult feelings such as distress and anxiety, which would otherwise threaten to overwhelm the child, leading to a fragmentation of their sense of self.

These concepts derive from the object relations school of psychoanalytic theory, which focuses on relations with other human beings as the basis of psychological life (Anderson, 1992, cited in Manning-Morton, 2011). But the most influential theoretical idea from this perspective is John Bowlby's theory of attachment (Bowlby, 1969). The sensitively responsive care identified in the concepts of attunement and container-contained also constitutes the kind of caregiver behaviour that Bowlby suggests enables children to form secure attachment relationships.

Key ideas in attachment theory

It is impossible to cover the breadth and depth of thinking about attachment theory in this chapter, but its implications for effective early childhood practice are crucial so it is important that practitioners familiarise themselves with these key ideas and then read further, as suggested at the end of this chapter.

Bowlby proposes that the framework for mother–infant attachment is the co-ordination of 'care seeking' and 'care giving' (1988: 121). Care seeking is seen in behaviour that results in a child being physically close to a preferred individual and is a key feature of an attachment relationship. How close to the attachment figure the child needs to be depends on factors such as age, temperament, developmental history, and whether the child feels tired, frightened or ill. The extent of the proximity seeking will also depend on particular circumstances, for example a recent separation will lead to greater proximity seeking. Care giving is complementary to this attachment behaviour and is focused on maintaining the equilibrium of the relationship through caring responses, thereby enabling a secure attachment. When a child is securely attached, they feel safe; they are distressed on separation but allow themselves to be comforted on being reunited with their carer (Holmes, 1993).

For Bowlby, the development of a secure attachment relationship with their primary caregiver is fundamental to a child's mental health and future ability to develop stable relationships, as it is through their experiences of caring interactions that they develop an 'internal working model' of what relationships are like and how to behave in them (Holmes, 1993). So babies and young children who have loving responses to their signals are developing mental concepts of relationships in which people can be trusted, and within that relationship the child can feel worthwhile. Neurologically, the cortisol levels in these children's brains rise in stressful situations but reduce quickly. They seem able to weather occasional difficult or distressing situations because they have an expectation that things will soon return to a more comfortable norm (Gerhardt, 2004). They are also learning that the world is a benevolent place worthy of being explored (Lieberman, 1993).

The urge to explore and play is as important a part of attachment as the need to be close. As carers support both these needs through providing a 'secure-base' (Bowlby, 1988), the child gradually develops an inner trust in the possibility of feeling safe while also being outgoing, competent and independent. Secure-base behaviours can be observed as children fluctuate between confidently crawling, walking and running away from the caring adult and then clinging, following or calling when alarmed or anxious. These behaviours are the essence of the second year of life but can be observed in children throughout their early years. Indeed, how the carer balances their task of protecting the child with the need to let them go, will also influence the child's mental model of how to balance states of intimacy and independence in later life.

The organisation of attachment systems in a child's mind can be observed in their protestations when separated from their attachment figures. For Bowlby (1988), behaviours such as crying, screaming, shouting, biting and kicking are normal responses to a threat to an attachment bond, as separation increases the level of risk to the human infant's survival. Feelings of loss are an integral part of attachment relationships and, for a young child, experiences of separation and loss are inherent in the process of entering an early childhood setting, where they have to be (often for the first time) without their parent/carer. The work of Bowlby and the films of the Robertsons (Robertson and Robertson, 1953) about the distress of young children in hospital separated from their parents have had a major impact on our understanding of separation. A child will go through phases in this process, which practitioners need to be able to recognise.

The first phase is one of protest and is characterised by active distress behaviours as described above, which can be disturbing for children, parents and practitioners. In situations where there is a prolonged or repeated period of distress, inexperienced or unaware practitioners may seek to defend themselves psychologically by discounting or minimising the child's feelings, interpreting them as 'attention seeking', while parents may try to separate from their child as quickly as possible, for example (Elfer, 1996; Manning-Morton, 2006).

In the second phase the child will begin to despair of being able to make their attachment figure return and fall into apathy, punctuated by crying, before finally giving up and sinking into despairing sleep. Practitioners, in their keenness for the child to be recovering from their distress, may assume the child is settled but then be surprised or even frustrated when the child breaks down crying again at the next transition time in the day or when their parent returns.

If, during this phase, a child isn't given consistent and caring support from their key person, the child may enter a phase of detachment. In this phase the child can be seen seeking contacts with any adult available, which may be interpreted by the practitioners as further evidence of the child being settled. However, close observation would reveal that these contacts are superficial, indiscriminate and transitory and do not constitute the kind of secure relationship necessary for them to become 'healthily independent' (DfES, 2002) in the setting. It is the gradual formation of a trusting relationship with a key person through a prolonged settling in period that enables young children to gradually separate from and comfortably be without their parents (Manning-Morton and Thorp, 2003, 2006).

Unfortunately, some babies and young children do not get the kind of loving support they need at times of separation and even experience mis-attuned or inconsistent responses to their needs at other times too. These children are likely to develop an 'attachment behavioural system' in which they are learning to expect little from close relationships and would be assessed in the 'strange situation' (Ainsworth et al., 1978) as being insecurely attached. If children are insecurely attached they may feel intense love and dependency but also fear rejection, they may then either cling anxiously to the attachment figure or avoid contact with them (Holmes, 1993). Children with these patterns are often identified later on as difficult in some way; they may seek attention and emotional support in socially unacceptable ways or have difficulty focusing calmly on their learning in school. Clarke and Clarke (2000) claim that the basis of their difficulties lies in their lack of emotional security or strong affectional ties to anyone.

However, some children who may have had early negative experiences still develop into 'competent, confident and caring adults', apparently against the odds (Mental Health Foundation, 1999: 9). There are protective factors that may combine to enable children to be resilient in this way and a protective factor in the wider community includes good quality childcare provision. So, although the most influential factor in children's future well-being is the establishment of a secure attachment in their family, children may still develop resilience through having someone else in their lives who respects them and in whom they can trust.

Reflection

The need for a secure attachment relationship and a secure base is rightly emphasised as being important for babies and toddlers in settings, but of course continues to be important throughout early childhood. Undertake an observation of a child over 3 and identify as many attachment and secure-base behaviours as you can. How does the key person approach in the setting support this child's personal, social and emotional well-being?

Implications for practice: The key person approach

In the light of the discussion above we can see the importance of adopting the key person approach in early childhood settings where the key person becomes one of a child's small group of significant attachment figures (Manning-Morton and Thorp, 2003).

This, now accepted, good practice was initially discussed in early years policy in the principles in the Birth to Three Matters Framework, which state 'A relationship with a key person at home and in the setting is essential to young children's well-being' (DfES, 2002: Introduction: 5) which paved the way for the 'key person approach' (Elfer et al., 2003) to be made a practice requirement in the Early Years Foundation Stage Framework (DCSF, 2008). The Tickell Review of the EYFS supported the retention of having a key person as a welfare requirement in the revised EYFS (DfE, 2012), stating, 'the nature of a child's relationship with a key person in early years settings is crucial' (Tickell, 2011: 94). The Key Times Framework takes this aspect as its central principle, stating: 'it is the quality of relationships between practitioners and children that is the cornerstone of good practice' (Manning-Morton and Thorp, 2006: xxi). The authors go on to identify that in order for babies and young children to develop a positive, integrated sense of self, they also need high levels of continuity and consistency in their experiences and relationships. This means ensuring that the key person approach is focused on the interactions and relationships between practitioner and child and practitioner and family rather than reduced to lists of children allocated to a practitioner where the focus is more on writing reports.

Understanding others' minds

Colwyn Trevarthen views the child as a social being from birth – an 'innate companion and co-operator', who is born ready to learn through sharing other people's thoughts and feelings (Trevarthan, 1995). Siegel (1999) points out that 'joint referencing', where the baby becomes able to look at an object pointed out by another person, is a form of shared communication. The ability to not only understand what another's attention is directed at but also to infer the emotional implication of another's expression is clearly in place by the end of the first year of life. This 'social referencing' can be observed each time a child watches the adult's reaction to a person or situation and thereby works out how to respond themselves. Children also explore how their own behaviours provoke emotional responses in others. So the child who previously observed and experienced their carer's disapproving tone and facial expression in relation to electrical sockets, for example, may go towards one and then look back with a cheeky grin, anticipating the adults 'uh oh, no thank you'. In this way such emotional transactions form the basis of early socialisation.

This ability to live together and communicate in groups is central to human evolution, and to be able to do so requires an ability to understand how one's own and other people's minds work. As children develop awareness of other people's feelings, thoughts, wishes and beliefs, they are said to be developing a theory of mind (Schaffer, 2006), so called because it is not possible to actually know what someone else's intentions are, so we create a theory in our own minds based on what we already know about our own intentions and on our previous experience of that person and similar circumstances. Siegel calls this capacity to perceive the mind of the self and others, 'mindsight' (1999: 149). In his concept of 'interpersonal neurobiology' he locates theory of mind or mindsight as initially sited in the right hemisphere of the brain and it develops further as more connections between the two hemispheres are established. He links this growing theory of mind to security of attachment, identifying that where parents/carers do not focus on the mental states of the child or where their own mental states are intrusive on the child's, the acquisition of theory of mind is impaired (Siegel, 1999). This has important implications not just for the individual child but also for the community in which he or she lives, as it is the foundation for developing empathy and concern for others and for making moral judgements. It has been suggested, for example, that children with insecure attachments have no clear model in their heads of what a significant adult would do in a particular situation, and because of this they are unable to make judgements about the 'best' course of action to take (Gopnik et al., 1999).

However, as identified earlier, children are remarkably resilient. Siegel (1999) asserts that, although a much more difficult process later in life, people can be helped to overcome disadvantages that might have arisen from difficult childhoods by purposefully utilising mindsight in daily interactions. However, some neuroscientists are of the view that if these capacities are not exercised early in life they can easily be lost (Eliot, 1999; Siegel, 1999), and so Siegel identifies the importance of habitually acknowledging the feelings that underlie children's behaviours so that they will gain insight into other people's mental states.

Judy Dunn's seminal work on sibling relationships identifies young children as learning empathy and social competence from their interactions with family members – brothers and sisters as well as parents (Dunn and Kendrick, 1982). She identified that young children can modify their responses to either exacerbate or ameliorate their sibling's distress according to whether they caused the distress in the first place and observed joking and teasing behaviours in children as young as 14 months old (Dunn, 1988). Although parents and practitioners will rightly lead children to understand that behaviours such as teasing, using forbidden words and lying are not socially acceptable, it is useful to remember that the ability to do so shows a sophisticated understanding of other people's minds and, lying to avoid getting into trouble for a recognised misdemeanour, for example, shows the emergence of more complex emotions such as shame and guilt. The emergence and developing understanding of such feelings, coupled with the ability to understand and empathise with others' states of mind, contributes to the child's ability to regulate their behaviours and also to critique the behaviour of others according to social moral standards.

Another extremely important effect of secure attachment patterns in children is social competence with peers. Research by Carollee Howes et al. (1994) found that young children who feel secure with their practitioner are not only more gregarious but also display complex play with friends. A key way in which children develop and hone their social skills is through imaginative and socio-dramatic play, and although they can practice social skills when participating in collaborative thinking with adults, play with peers offers unique possibilities as it requires more adaptation to the perspectives of less socially skilled play partners (Rogoff, 1990).

The importance of supporting children's social competence and friendships cannot then be overstated as they are related to so many other aspects of development, including cognitive understanding. Positive social interactions and relationships are now widely accepted as important in children's cognitive development, as the process of thinking and talking about emotions in social relationships includes the kind of reflective, problem-solving processes that are fundamental to cognitive understanding. Cognitive development used to be thought about mostly in terms of an individual actively exploring and acting on the environment in an autonomous fashion. Now, however, all cognitive advances are seen to depend on social interaction. For example, as children mix with others, they learn to see that there is more than one perspective on a situation and so their minds are opened to new possibilities. Encounters with people and ideas that are different to our own literally broaden the mind; this is particularly important in addressing prejudices. In addition, securely attached children show a greater ability in *metacognition*; the ability to reflect on and piece together ideas about one's own learning (Main, 1991).

Self-awareness and self-esteem

Similar to metacognition is meta-awareness – the ability to make awareness itself the object of our attention and take note of the contents of our internal consciousness, as if we are witnessing ourselves from outside. Before we reach this kind of sophisticated self-awareness though, babies and young children first have to establish an understanding of their own existence. For children, this inner, existential self develops through becoming aware of their own agency, the impact they have on objects and people, and through becoming aware of their uniqueness and the continuity of their identity (Barnes, 1995). In addition, children are developing an understanding of themselves as part of different social categories, being a sister, brown eyed, clever, and so on, thereby constructing a self-image. Children will also receive social 'scripts' (Berne, 1970) about how a child in a particular social category is ideally expected to be. This 'ideal self' combines with the child's inner 'self-image' to make up their overall 'self-concept' (Lawrence, 1988). So, central to the development of self-concept are the verbal and non-verbal reactions of others, which give young children messages about themselves, whether they are troublesome or well-behaved, clever or stupid. However, where there is a large discrepancy between self-image and the ideal-self a child may feel a lack of approval, feel unworthy and have low self-esteem (Lawrence, 1988: 5). Such feelings of unworthiness, shame, jealousy and embarrassment are self-conscious emotions that require self-awareness, but because they are provoked by the reactions of others, they are also sometimes called other-conscious emotions (Saarni, 1999).

This idea helps us to see the profound effect our behaviours as adults can have on a child's self-concept and self-esteem, which in turn have a major influence on children's social behaviours and dispositions to learning. Marion Dowling (2010) identifies some strategies, which she proposes may help or hinder the development of children's self-knowledge. She suggests that adult evaluations using empty praise or criticism hinders such development, while allowing silence and giving children plenty of time to respond encourages reflection. Dowling also suggests that putting children's ideas into words for them may help to develop their sense of self but emphasises that this will only work in a climate where children feel able to challenge what the adult has said.

The ability of children to challenge adults and adults to challenge children is of paramount importance in attitudes towards social differences of class, sexual orientation, ethnicity, gender and disability, and the prejudices and stereotyped assumptions that may arise from those attitudes. Siraj-Blatchford and Clarke remind us that 'A positive self-concept is necessary for healthy development and learning and includes feelings about gender, race, ability, culture and language. Positive self-esteem depends on whether children feel that others accept them and see them as competent and worthwhile' (2000: 18).

Practitioners should also keep in mind that ideas about what constitutes an adequate self are socially and culturally constructed. The emphasis on the primacy of being an autonomous, unique individual, as presented in developmental psychology, reflects a western cultural view, whereas other cultures emphasise much more the importance of the individual as part of the social whole and therefore encourage different types of social behaviours. For example, in China inhibition is perceived as reflecting social maturity, but in North America it is perceived to reflect immaturity (Cole, 1998). These cultural values are also reflected in the different emphases of curricula. For example, the principles of the EYFS (DfE, 2012) in the UK forefronts the 'Unique Child' whereas the New Zealand early childhood curriculum Te Whāriki (Ministry of Education, 1996) focuses more on the interdependence of child, family, practitioner, community and culture.

Reflection

Consider your own cultural family values and what you believe to be positive attitudes, dispositions and behaviours for children to develop. Are they congruent with those in the Early Years Foundation Stage curriculum framework?

What are the implications of this for your practice?

Journal Task

Manning-Morton, J. (2006) 'The personal is professional: Professionalism and the birth to threes practitioner', *Contemporary Issues in Early Childhood*, 7(1): 42–52.

Levels 4 & 5

Early childhood practitioners, especially those working with children from birth to three years old, have struggled to be accepted as 'professionals', as what they do is often seen as being just an extension of home-based caring.

1. Why has this struggle towards professional recognition sometimes led to an over-emphasis on 'education' and a lack of attention to physical and emotional care?
2. In what ways do respectful physical care and the provision of positive physical experiences promote children's personal and emotional development?
3. How might the 'key person' way of working with very young children place great emotional demands upon early childhood practitioners and how can practitioners be supported?

Level 6

1. How has the traditional view of the care of very young infants been influenced by the Cartesian mind/body dualist philosophy (Manning-Morton, 2006: 45), and how can the writings of Damasio and others help us move away from this dualistic philosophy? How does this relate to the professionalisation of the early childhood workforce?

To download this task as well as other useful online resources please visit:
www.sagepub.co.uk/mukherji

Summary

This chapter has discussed the links between emotional learning, early relationships and how babies and young children develop a sense of self and an understanding of others, and in so doing has emphasised that this is a fundamentally important area of knowledge and practice expertise for early childhood practitioners.

In order to effectively support babies and young children's personal, social and emotional learning, practitioners need to have a sound knowledge of a range of theoretical ideas about personal, social and emotional development. But equally they need a discerning sense of the cultural values inherent in curriculum frameworks and how these influence practice as well as the ability to challenge their own and others' prejudices and stereotypes. Above all they need to be able to form attuned, caring relationships with their key children. This requires a mature understanding of their own values, experiences and motivations and how these impact on their practice.

It is not sufficient that these kind of sophisticated professional skills are seen to occur 'naturally' in caring practitioners. In order to give these kinds of skills the promotion they deserve, practitioners need effective leadership support that includes regular opportunities to discuss the emotional impact of practice and to develop a shared team vision that puts children's personal, social and emotional development at the forefront of the curriculum.

Further reading

Levels 4 & 5

Department for Children, Schools and Families (DfE) (2008) *Social and Emotional Aspects of Development: Guidance for Practitioners Working in the Early Years Foundation Stage*. London: DCSF Publications. This guidance document offers useful information on PSED and opportunities for reflection for practitioners.

Dowling, M. (2010) *Young Children's Personal, Social and Emotional Development*. London: Paul Chapman Publishing. This book gives a very useful overview of children's personal, social and emotional development in the early years.

Elfer, P., Goldschmeid, E. and Selleck, D.Y. (2011) *Key Persons in the Early Years: Building Relationships for Quality Provision in Early Years Settings and Primary Schools*. London: Routledge. This is the definitive text on the key person approach in early childhood settings.

Gerhardt, S. (2004) *Why Love Matters: How Affection Shapes a Baby's Brain*. Hove/New York: Brunner-Routledge. This book presents complicated information on brain development and how it is shaped by experience in a very informed yet accessible way.

Level 6

Barnes, P. (ed.) (1995) *Personal, Social and Emotional Development of Children*. Oxford: Blackwell Publishing. This book presents the key pieces of research relating to young children's PSED and is an excellent resource for Level 6 and postgraduate students.

Dunn, J. (1988) *The Beginnings of Social Understanding*. Oxford: Blackwell. This is a seminal text which was key in shaping the re-thinking in developmental psychology about toddlers' social understanding.

Goleman, D. (1996) *Emotional Intelligence: Why It Can Matter More Than IQ*. London: Bloomsbury Publishing. This book not only presents information about neurological processes in an accessible way, it also provokes reflection on emotional regulation.

Manning-Morton, J. (2006) 'The personal is professional: Professionalism and the birth to threes practitioner', *Contemporary Issues in Early Childhood*, 7(1): 42–52. This article makes useful links between children's PSED and professionalism in the early years.

References

Ainsworth, M., Blehar, M., Waters, E. and Wall, S. (1978) *Patterns of Attachment: Assessed in the Strange Situation and at Home*. New Jersey: Erlbaum.

Anderson, R. (ed.) (1992) *Clinical Lectures on Klein and Bion*. London: Routledge.

Arnold, C. (2010) *Understanding Schemas and Emotion*. London: Sage.

Barnes, P. (ed.) (1995) *Personal, Social and Emotional Development of Children*. Oxford: Blackwell Publishing.

Berne, E. (1970) *Transactional Analysis in Psychotherapy*. New York: Ballantine Books.

Bion, W.R. (1962) *Learning from Experience*. London: Karnac Books.

Bowlby, J. (1969) *Attachment and Loss. Vol.1: Attachment*. London: Hogarth.

Bowlby, J. (1988) *A Secure Base: Clinical Applications of Attachment Theory*. London: Routledge.

Carter, R. (1998) *Mapping the Mind*. London: Seven Dials.

Clarke, A. and Clarke, A. (2000) *Early Experience and the Life Path*. London: Jessica Kingsley Open Books.

Cole, M. (1998) 'Culture in development', in M. Woodhead, D. Faulkner and K. Littleton (eds), *Cultural Worlds of Early Childhood*. London: Routledge.

Damasio, A.R. (2003) *Looking for Spinoza: Joy, Sorrow, and the Feeling Brain*. New York: Harcourt.

Darwin, C. (1872) *The Expression of the Emotions in Man and Animals*. London: Murray.

Department for Children, Schools and Families (DCSF) (2008) *Social and Emotional Aspects of Development: Guidance for Practitioners Working in the Early Years Foundation Stage*. London: DCSF Publications.

Department for Education (DfE) (2012) *Statutory Framework for the Early Years Foundation Stage: Setting the Standards for Learning, Development and Care for Children from Birth to Five*. London: DfE/HMSO. https://www.education.gov.uk/publications/standard/AllPublications/Page1/DFE-00023-2012 (accessed 28 April 2013).

Department for Education and Skills (DfES) (2002) *Birth to Three Matters: A Framework to Support Children in their Earliest Years*. London: DfES/HMSO.

Department for Education and Skills (DfES) (2008) *The Early Years Foundation Stage: Setting the Standards for Learning, Development and Care for Children from Birth to Five*. London: DfES/HMSO.

Dowling, M. (2010) *Young Children's Personal, Social and Emotional Development*. London: Paul Chapman Publishing.

Dunn, J. (1988) *The Beginnings of Social Understanding*. Oxford: Blackwell.

Dunn, J. and Kendrick, C. (1982) *Siblings: Love, Envy and Understanding*. Cambridge, MA: Harvard University Press.

Dunn, J. (1999) 'Mindreading and social relationships,' in M. Bennett (ed), *Developmental Psychology: Achievements and Prospects*. Pennsylvania, PA: Psychology Press. pp. 55–71.

Elfer, P. (1996) 'Building intimacy in relationships with young children in nurseries', *Early Years*, 16(2): 30–34.

Elfer, P., Goldschmeid, E. and Selleck, D. (2003) *Key Persons in Nursery: Building Relationships for Quality Provision*. London: David Fulton.

Eliot, L. (1999) *Early Intelligence: How the Brain and Mind Develop in the First Five Years of Life*. London: Penguin.

Ganchrow, J.R., Steiner, J.E. and Daher, M. (1983) 'Neonatal facial expressions in response to different qualities and intensities of gustatory stimuli', *Infant Behavior and Development*, 6(4): 473–84.

Gerhardt, S. (2004) *Why Love Matters: How Affection Shapes a Baby's Brain*. Hove/New York: Brunner-Routledge.

Goleman, D. (1996) *Emotional Intelligence: Why It Can Matter More Than IQ*. London: Bloomsbury Publishing.

Gopnik, A., Meltzoff, A. and Kuhl, P. (1999) *How Babies Think*. London: Weidenfield and Nicolson.

Greenfield, S. (2000) *The Private Life of the Brain*. London: Penguin Books.

Harris, P. (1989) *Children and Emotion: The Development of Psychological Understanding*. Oxford: Blackwell.

Holmes, J. (1993) *John Bowlby and Attachment Theory*. London: Routledge.

Howes, C., Matheson, C.C. and Hamilton, C.E. (1994) 'Maternal, teacher, and child care history correlates of children's relationships with peers', *Child Development*, 65(1): 264–73.

Lawrence, D. (1988) *Enhancing Self-Esteem in the Classroom*. London: Paul Chapman Publishing.

LeDoux, J. (1996) *The Emotional Brain: The Mysterious Underpinnings of Emotional Life*. New York: Touchstone.

Lieberman, A.F. (1993) *The Emotional Life of a Toddler*. New York: Free Press.

Main, M. (1991) 'Metacognitive knowledge, metacognitive monitoring, and singular (coherent) vs. multiple (incoherent) model of attachment: Findings and directions for future research', in C.M. Parkes, C. Murray and J. Stevenson-Hinde (eds), *Attachment Across the Life Cycle*. New York: Basic Books.

Malatesta, C.Z. and Haviland, J.M. (1982) 'Learning display rules: The socialization of emotion expression in infancy', *Child Development*, 53(4): 991–1003.

Manning-Morton, J. (2006) 'The personal is professional: Professionalism and the birth to threes practitioner', *Contemporary Issues in Early Childhood*, 7(1): 42–52.

Manning-Morton, J. (2011) 'Not just the tip of the iceberg: Psychoanalytic ideas and early years practice', in L. Miller and L. Pound (eds), *Theories and Approaches to Learning in the Early Years*. London: Sage.

Manning-Morton, J. and Thorp, M. (2003) *Key Times for Play: The First Three Years*. Maidenhead. Open University Press.

Manning-Morton, J. and Thorp, M. (2006) *Key Times: A Framework for Developing High Quality Provision for Children from Birth to Three Years*. Maidenhead: Open University Press.

Meltzoff, A.N. and Moore, M.K. (1983) 'Newborn infants imitate adult facial gestures', *Child Development*, 54(4): 702–9.

Mental Health Foundation (1999) *Bright Futures: Promoting Children and Young People's Mental Health*. London: The Mental Health Foundation.

Ministry of Education (1996) Te Whāriki. Wellington: Learning Media Limited.

Osgood, J. (2010) 'Reconstructing professionalism in ECEC: The case for the "critically reflective emotional professional"', *Early Years: An International Journal of Research and Development*, 30(2): 119–33.

Robertson, J. and Robertson, J. (1953) *Film: A Two Year Old Goes to Hospital*. Tavistock Child Development Research Unit, Concord Films Council, Ipswich.

Rogoff, B. (1990) *Apprenticeship in Thinking: Cognitive Development in Social Context*. New York: Oxford University Press.

Saarni, C. (1999) *The Development of Emotional Competence*. New York: Guilford Press.

Schaffer, H.R. (2006) *Key Concepts in Developmental Psychology*. London: Sage.

Siegel, D.J. (1999) *The Developing Mind*. New York: Guilford Press.

Siraj-Blatchford, I. and Clarke, P. (2000) *Supporting Identity, Diversity and Language in the Early Years*. Maidenhead: Open University Press.

Stern, D. (1998) *The Interpersonal World of the Infant*. New York: Basic Books.

Tickell, C. (2011) *The Early Years: Foundations for Life, Health and Learning*. London: Department for Education.

Trevarthen, C. (1995), 'The child's need to learn a culture', in M. Woodhead, D. Faulkner and K. Littleton (eds), (1998) *Cultural Worlds of Early Childhood*. Routledge: London.

Trevarthen, C. and Aitken, K.J. (2001) 'Infant inter subjectivity: Research, theory, and clinical applications', *Journal of Child Psychology and Psychiatry*, 42(1): 3–48.

17

Communication, Literacy and ICT

Louise Dryden

This chapter will:

- Explore early communication in all its forms, and examine our attitudes towards spoken and written communication in the early twenty-first century
- Describe the way in which babies and young children acquire spoken language(s)
- Explain how language facilitates other areas of development, in particular supporting and enriching social and cognitive behaviours
- Explore symbolic representation and how this can be nurtured
- Consider the ways in which children can be introduced to narrative, and a rich literary diet
- Explore how children begin to express their ideas through drawing and early mark making
- Consider the impact of ICT on our current literacy practices.

Human beings naturally have the capacity to learn how to communicate; research has shown that in utero babies become familiar with their mother's voice and the languages spoken in their community. This chapter will provide an overview of the way in which young children enter their social environment and begin to develop skills and strategies which enable them to communicate effectively. The crucial role that adults play in supporting and enhancing children's linguistic development will be explored, and consideration will be given to the implications of living and communicating in multicultural, multilingual communities.

Language development theory in first and subsequent languages

Children across the world learn to speak effortlessly, unless they have a severe condition which affects either their hearing or their cognitive development. Research shows that the foetus is aware of sounds in the womb and that it responds to music and the sound of its mother's voice (Kisilvesky et al., 2009). The baby comes into the world equipped to produce noises, including its first cry, which is eagerly anticipated in the delivery room. Early communication with carers involves eye contact and also imitation. The focal length of a newborn baby is short, but is sufficient to ensure eye contact with the mother while it suckles (Doherty and Hughes, 2009). Experiments on newborns show that in the first hours of life, babies imitate facial expressions such as tongue poking (Meltzoff and Moore, 1977) and respond to familiar sounds by kicking and rapid sucking behaviours. This suggests that babies are already participating in a form of social interaction.

Whilst adults and siblings do not overtly 'teach' babies to speak, the home environment is full of sounds, and soon the infant is able to distinguish human speech from other background noises (Dryden, 2005). This aural discrimination begins very early when babies respond more positively to a nursery rhyme sung by a familiar voice (such as their mother) than to the same words sung by an unfamiliar female voice (Hamer, 2012). In this way, babies across the globe begin to hear the language of their home environment, and start to recognise its unique sounds and intonations.

Motherese (Snow, 1972) is a term used for the simple communications that are instigated by a baby's carer (male or female). This type of speech is characterised by a rhythmic pattern, with exaggerated stress patterns, and delivered at a higher pitch than 'normal' adult speech. During these 'proto-conversations', the adult behaves as if the baby's contributions (cooing, giggles, etc. from three months) are valid, and conventional turn-taking takes place (Hamer, 2012).

The sequence of speech development is universal, and babbling, early experimentation with sound production, begins at around 8 months, and is multilingual in nature (Doherty and Hughes, 2009). Babies practice babbling without need of an audience; they exercise their vocal chords and start to gain control over the tiny movements of mouth, tongue, jaw and throat which enable the production of specific speech sounds (phonemes), and also experiment with the way air-flow influences sounds (such as /s/ and /h/). Gradually the infant's babbling begins to imitate the sounds they hear in their home environment (patterned speech), and they drop those sounds not associated with their mother tongue (Gopnik et al., 2001).

Infants are very attentive and they soon understand the association between a particular sound sequence and what we would classify as a word. They become aware of the consonants and vowels that together make up the syllables in words. This is quite an achievement, since mature speech is rapid and it takes a long time before young children are able to recognise single-word units (Clay, 1991). This is where simplified sentence structures (such as Motherese mentioned previously) facilitate the child's ability to isolate key words and phrases.

Gradually, young children begin to produce their first words. From around their first birthday most will be able to use several words, though they understand a great many more than they can produce (Browne, 2007). These first words that children collect in their lexicon (their word-bank) are usually associated with subjects of particular interest, such as favourite people, foods and toys (Riley, 2006). Whilst children are moving towards speech production, they use gestures and particularly a pointing finger to indicate what they desire (Bruner, 1986). Later, this pointing behaviour is accompanied by a 'what's that' (or their equivalent *wot's dat*) where the child instigates the gathering of new vocabulary. By 18 months most children will understand around 150 words (Doherty and Hughes, 2009) and be experimenting with their unique approximations of adult speech. At this stage they find it hard to discriminate between subtle phonemic differences, and some sounds are harder to produce than others. This early word production is followed by what has been described as a 'vocabulary explosion' (Cattell, 2007: 6), where the child is increasing their lexicon by numerous words each day.

Table 17.1 summarises the sequence in which children begin to move from the production of single words to grammatical sentences. We should keep in mind that individual children will reach these stages at different ages, with some children slower to produce words than others.

Table 17.1 Development of speech

Stage	Child is able to	Examples
1 word utterances (holophrases)	Name objects, give commands, ask a question	Teddy Grandma
Over-extension	Use one word for a number of words in the same classification	Teddy for all soft toys
2 word utterances	Show relationship between two objects or ideas, but can have multiple meanings so requires listener to interpret	Teddy Grandma
Telegraphic speech	Express ideas using only essential words (nouns and verbs)	Teddy go Grandma
Functional speech	Give instructions, pose questions	Take Teddy Grandma's house?
Over-generalisation of grammatical rules	Invent words using formal grammatical rules, such as over-use of ed for past tense	I taked Teddy to Grandma's house
Grammatically correct + temporal understanding	Use language to express experiences outside the immediate context	Yesterday I took my Teddy to my Grandma's house

Note: For greater detail, refer to a text such as Doherty and Hughes (2009: 323) which provides a chart of the 'Language Milestones'.

Theories of language development

The average 6-year-old child has a vocabulary of around 14,000 words (Cattell, 2007). Let us examine the major theories which attempt to explain how children achieve this remarkable feat.

Behaviourist learning theories focus on imitation and the fact that humans learn by being rewarded (Skinner, 1957). In relation to language development, this theory suggests children learn to speak by imitating fluent speakers. However, critics of this theory (such as Chomsky, see below) counter that this means a child would need to have heard every possible sentence combination before they could use it. In other words, a young child would be unable to produce a unique sentence of their own.

Cognitive theorists, Jean Piaget included, have suggested that language develops in tandem with the maturation of a child's thinking, during the pre-operational stage (Piaget, 1959). He suggests that as the child's ability to use symbolic representation during their play develops, so does their capacity to symbolise their thoughts through words.

Constructivist theory, proposes that language develops through application, and stresses the importance of learning in context. Halliday (1975) suggests that children learn to use a variety of linguistic functions to make themselves understood.

Nativist theories, such as those suggested by Noam Chomsky (1965), consider that the facility to communicate is innate, and that the ability to tune in to language comes before cognitive skills begin to develop. Chomsky suggested that there is a Language Acquisition Device (LAD) which enables the young child to produce unique utterances using their knowledge of grammatical rules (leading to over-generalisations, for example inventing verbs such as *goed* in place of *went*).

Social-interactionist theorists, including Vygotsky (1962) and Bruner (1986), believe that language develops during interaction with other more competent speakers, and that it is used to communicate with others before a child can use words for internal thought.

Differences in acquisition

There is no evidence to suggest that any particular group of children are more advantaged than others in terms of first acquiring their home languages. There is some neurological research (Karmiloff and Karmiloff-Smith, 2001) which suggests that girls' physiological development matures more quickly than boys', which means that they may start to speak earlier. However, in terms of social equality, several studies demonstrate that whilst different social groups may speak using a different register (using a wider or narrower vocabulary, or ignoring or maintaining conventional grammatical structures, Bernstein, 1971), this does not affect children's capacity to learn to communicate (Tizard and Hughes, 1984).

Almost every child by the age of 5 years old will have become proficient in English grammar without a single lesson! However, there is research which shows that a crucial aspect of becoming a really fluent communicator relies on the quality and frequency of the child's interactions with adults (Hamer, 2012). Children who are fortunate enough to be born into multilingual families will effortlessly acquire two or more languages simultaneously, and research shows that there are many other cognitive benefits associated with this facility to switch between different languages (Baker, 2001).

Children who are new to English

Reflection

Many young children in Britain experience English for the first time when they enter some form of organised childcare. Do some further research on the different theories of acquisition (discussed above) and then consider the extent to which they may contribute to our understanding of how children learn subsequent languages. If you are currently working with children who are new to English, reflect on the ways in which they appear to be acquiring and practising their English.

Many children in Britain today speak English as a second or subsequent language (recent statistics showed that 300 different languages are spoken in London schools, London councils 2013), and those from newly migrated families may acquire their first words of English in a childcare setting. These children are competent language users, having gained fluency in their home language. They have a lexicon, use a grammatical structure required by their home language(s) and are competent communicators (Siraj-Blatchford and Clarke, 2000), and can use this knowledge as a foundation for the acquisition of English. Unlike the group of indigenous children entering nursery with poorly developed linguistic skills (ICAN, 2007), these emergent bilinguals are competent communicators, with research indicating many benefits (Baker, 2001). It also appears that the more languages a person knows, the easier they find it to learn new ones.

Chomsky (1965) suggests that the facility to learn languages with ease begins to fade as we reach puberty. The optimum time for language acquisition appears to be in early childhood, and the best possible conditions for this learning to take place are naturally in context (Siraj-Blatchford and Clarke, 2000). Young children entering nursery need to be supported as they begin their journey towards becoming a fluent English speaker. At first the child needs to listen to key vocabulary, become familiar with the rhythm and accent of the new language, and hear repetitive phrases. This is known as the 'silent period' (Browne, 2007) where, like the infant developing their first language, the child who is new to English listens and begins to understand, without themselves producing speech. This period lasts different lengths of time for individual children, and there is some evidence that those with more extrovert personalities are willing to speak more quickly than their less confident peers (Krashen, 1981). The most effective conditions for learning a new language are when the child plays or works alongside fluent speakers (adults or peers).

Bilingual children should be encouraged to use their home language(s) in educational settings, whatever stage of fluency they have reached (Brock and Rankin, 2008). Children must sense that these languages are respected, and feel comfortable about switching between English and their home language. Playing alongside other bilingual children and adults will facilitate their learning, as they can confidently grapple with new concepts in the language in which they have a richer vocabulary (Barratt-Pugh and Rohl, 2000).

Individual children progress at their own pace, but generally it takes between two and four years for a child to become 'conversationally fluent' (Browne, 2007: 28), and a further three years for children to use the new language confidently for cognitive and academic purposes. It is important for educators to be aware of this, because sometimes emergent bilinguals' needs are neglected once they appear to be verbally proficient. The extent of grammatical and syntactic errors may only surface when the child begins to write down their ideas in Key Stage 1.

Language for communication

Over the past decade there have been several changes to the curriculum for children under 5 (DfE, 2012; DfES, 2007a; QCA, 2000). Each successive piece of legislation has put more emphasis on the development of communication skills, and shown greater recognition of the way these skills support children's all-round development. Certainly, the capacity to use language for thought, for social interaction and for problem solving should be understood as central to children's educational journey towards adulthood.

The first step on this journey is taken when the young child is engaged in conversations. Speaking and listening skills develop (as discussed above) during everyday interactions within the family unit. Parents are the child's first educators, and the richness of verbal exchanges in the home helps to establish patterns for children's later linguistic behaviours, allowing the child to develop at their own pace. Classic research by Tizard and Hughes (1984) demonstrated that young children are eager to engage in domestic conversations, and their research highlighted the importance of developing skills within a familiar context. The 4-year-old girls in this study increased their communications skills through engagement in meaningful exchanges about domestic planning, current events and family history. The girls were supported, for example, in developing a better grasp of verb tenses whilst discussing what had happened previously, or might happen in the future. The mothers were able to scaffold their daughters' linguistic development because they mostly understood what the child was alluding to. This support was in stark contrast to the conversations that these girls had with adults in their nursery classes, where there were fewer opportunities for them to engage in one-to-one conversations, and most talk was adult-led. In the home environment, it was often the girls who led the conversations on topics of genuine interest, based on real experiences, but in the educational settings, discussions were frequently contrived conversations on subjects of no immediate relevance to the child.

This study still has relevance to our understanding of the role of the educator in our childcare settings today. Current curriculum guidance (DfE, 2012) emphasises that adults should focus on children's individual interests, and be on hand to work alongside them, providing appropriate support as they engage in activities of the child's choosing. Staff in educational establishments are required to monitor the linguistic progress and cognitive achievements of the children in their care. Careful observations enable them to create an exciting environment which supports the children's linguistic development and self-expression, providing opportunities to share ideas and feelings and engaging in meaningful discussions (Brock and Rankin, 2008). The availability of a wide range of activities encourages reflection, problem solving and negotiation skills, and helps to extend children's vocabulary in context.

Reflection

The current EYFS Statutory Framework (2012) states that children need ' ... to develop their confidence and skills in expressing themselves; and to speak and listen in a range of situations' (DfE, 2012: 5). Consider the activities available to the children you are in contact with. Make a list and match them to the appropriate aspects of the Developmental Matters in EYFS (Early Education, 2012).

Language is a very powerful tool in society, and social justice requires us as educators to ensure that every child has the capacity to express themselves clearly. For the past 10 years, there have been serious concerns expressed regarding the number of children entering nurseries with poorly developed verbal communication skills (ICAN, 2007). Sammons et al. (2008) reported as part of the EPPE project that children who had struggled to communicate in the early stages were often at a disadvantage throughout their primary education, still underachieving in Year 6. This in turn affects their ability to perform effectively when they move into the secondary phase of their education. The 'Every Child a Talker' initiative was designed to enhance the life chances of these children, and its mission was to equip young children with the confidence and breadth of vocabulary to begin their school careers. The 'Third Instalment' (DCSF, 2009) provides practical information, using examples of the way different authorities have worked in partnership to support parents, childminders and childcare teams. Sadly the funding for this project was stopped in 2009, but the excellent materials are available online.

Where a child has a speech delay or a specific speech impediment (difficulty in physically producing sounds), but is developing normally in all other areas, a brief course of speech therapy usually proves extremely effective. Once the concern has been raised, it is important for the child's hearing to be tested first. Then the appropriate agencies should be contacted quickly, as many authorities have long waiting lists for this type of service. The referral can be instigated by a health visitor, a doctor or the childcare setting. However, certain physical and developmental conditions may severely hamper children's linguistic development. It is important that adults working with children with complex needs work in partnership with the child's family and liaise with other agencies and specialists involved with the child's well-being. Sign language, Makaton and other visual vocabulary systems can help children to communicate their immediate needs when spoken language is difficult.

Language and cognitive development

The major classical theorists on this topic are Vygotsky and Piaget. Vygotsky (1962) considered that language begins as a way to communicate effectively within a social context and that later, language becomes a tool for organising thoughts (Bruner, 1986). Vygotsky's theory suggested that the child begins by thinking and planning aloud, before they begin to use this language as 'inner speech'. Piaget, however, recognised that thought is possible pre-linguistically, that babies are capable of cognitive function before they have the means to verbalise their ideas (Wood, 1988). In Piaget's view, children in the 'pre-operational' period use spoken language to represent their ideas, but find it hard to express themselves clearly because they are still egocentric and not able to understand the listener's point of view.

Recent research has stressed the importance of sustained shared thinking (EPPE project), showing that children make better progress in settings where adults actively engage in activities with the children, modelling appropriate language and posing stimulating questions and discussion (Brock and Rankin, 2008). Gussin-Paley has written a number of delightful texts which illustrate how to encourage discussion amongst young children; she demonstrates their capacity to tackle difficult topics in a thoughtful and empathic manner (e.g. *Wally's Stories*, Gussin-Paley, 1981).

Social aspects

Humans use language to communicate; it enables us to socialise, maintain relationships and to share ideas and experiences. Halliday (1975) discusses seven models or 'functions' of early language use, and demonstrates how the young child uses language to express their feelings, communicate their wishes and interact with others. Young children need frequent opportunities to engage in conversations and negotiate with their peers. These aspects are emphasised in current documentation (Developmental Matters; Early Education, 2012) which relate to listening to others in small groups (30–50 months) and being attentive and responding appropriately while working with others (40–60 months).

Symbolic representation

There is an extensive literature on symbolic representation relating to all aspects of children's communicative development. In the last century, Piaget (1959) observed how very young children begin to use one object to represent another, for example using a brick to represent a car. Many early play behaviours centre on the simulation of real-life events, using props and small-world toys to relive experiences, and this form of symbolic representation precedes the child's ability to express their ideas and intentions verbally. A young child may cuddle a doll as if it were a baby, feeding it invisible food, and the movements of the 'brick/car' are accompanied by car noises that dramatise the action.

Speech is a highly significant development in children's symbolic representation, as it allows them to express themselves beyond the present context, predicting the future, and describing the past. These verbal skills facilitate their ability to express ideas, speculate and problem solve, which are fundamental to developing critical thinking (Doherty and Hughes, 2009).

Imaginative play and role play are also important features of children's early experiences. Through imitation of adult behaviours and during fantasy play, the child explores their feelings, tests boundaries and gains an understanding of their environment. Resources such as soft toys, puppets and small-world figures provide excellent opportunities for children to practise expressing their ideas and engage in story-telling (Browne, 2007). Home corners and other imaginative play scenarios set up in home and educational settings empower children to direct their own play sequences.

At first children talk aloud to themselves, providing a running commentary to go with their actions, a form of 'egocentric speech' (Vygotsky, cited in Riley, 2006), but gradually they begin to engage in cooperative play sequences with their peers. Children enjoy instigating imaginative plays which often run for several days, like an adult soap opera, with participants re-enacting the previous day's episode before moving the storyline on. Play scenarios are a useful tool for children who are learning a new language. Drury (2004) describes the way Samia, a child who is very new to English, practises her two languages as she plays 'schools' at home with her 2-year-old brother. She enacts aspects of her nursery routine using their home language with fluency, but interspersing the dialogue with newly acquired English phrases.

Role-play scenarios are often set up by adults in childcare settings, providing resources relating to a story the class has shared (Browne, 2007). These activities give children the opportunity to dramatise the action and narrate the story in their own way, encouraging them to practise retelling a story in sequence and employ newly acquired vocabulary. This type of activity is useful for children who find it hard to engage with books, or for those who are new to English.

CASE STUDY

Arun is 3 years old and has been attending a Children's Centre for six weeks. He is still at the very early stages of acquiring English, though he is fluent in Urdu. His key person understands the importance of using props when telling or reading stories to groups of young children. During the morning session, she reads a popular picture book to her group; in preparation for this shared reading, she selected several small-world toys which complement the narrative, and she encourages the children to pass these around as she retells the story. She put these artefacts aside, but during the afternoon, she finds Arun sitting alone in a quiet area. He has taken the resources and is narrating the story aloud in Urdu, using the resources to represent the action. She does not intrude, in case her presence halts his enjoyment, but she makes a note to create a further opportunity for Arun and another Urdu-speaking child to revisit the story later in the week.

- Select a suitable picture book, and consider ways in which you could extend Arun's enjoyment of the book, suggesting resources which would help him to explore the story-telling in two languages.

Representation using 2D symbols

Drawing and mark making are important aspects of symbolic representation. Children naturally begin to make marks with whatever materials are at hand; babies spontaneously use their fingers to make patterns in spilt food. Multi-modal forms of visual expression continue to develop during early childhood, and research shows that young children enjoy experimenting with different media (making marks on paper and producing 3D models) to creatively express meaning and illustrate their narratives (Anning and Ring, 2004). Children's drawings develop as they gain control over their fine-motor movements. Clay (1991) notes that children develop their drawing skills over time, often working on a theme (or schema) for several weeks, modifying and playing with a basic pattern.

This playful aspect of mark making continues as children move towards conventional writing using established alphabetic symbols (DCSF, 2008). Children claim ownership of their initial (*'that's my S'*) as if it stood for the whole name, and Kress (1997) describes how his daughter Emily experimented with her first initial E, drawing extra horizontal lines, rather than restricting herself to three; she played with the visual effect long after she was capable of writing her full name correctly, producing a unique signature.

Early literacy behaviours

We live in a print-rich society, surrounded by texts. A child wakes in the morning with print on their pyjamas, logos on their trainers and lettering on cereal packets at breakfast time (Dryden, 2004). They become curious about these symbols and begin to recognise product labels and logos, particularly those relating to favourite foods, supermarkets and fast food outlets (Browne, 2007). Indeed the Sheffield Early Literacy Development Profile (Nutbrown, 1997) uses photographs of familiar products to assess young children's early 'reading' behaviours.

A literate environment

Early literacy emerges out of a social context, when children observe the reading behaviours of those they live with (Meek, 1991). Children observe adults reading materials such as letters, greetings cards and newspapers (Riley, 2006), and begin to understand the purpose of engaging in print. Electronic screens now feature heavily in our reading activities, and children watch adults reading from mobile phones and computers (Goouch and Lambirth, 2011).

Many, but not all, children are fortunate to have books and stories as part of their shared home routine. Schemes such as 'Bookstart Baby Packs' (http://www.bookstart.org.uk/) encourage new parents to understand the importance of sharing books with their babies, to establish a positive attitude towards books, and make reading a pleasurable shared experience.

According to the EYFS Statutory Framework (DfE, 2012), children need to be introduced to pertinent texts that 'ignite their interest'. Historically, children's books were quite dull, with worthy storylines (often with a strong moral tone) and few illustrations. However in the latter half of last century, publishers began to commission attractively illustrated books with simple, child-friendly texts. This multi-million pound industry now produces colourful, exciting books designed to stimulate children's enthusiasm for reading, literature with a dual purpose – to both entertain and educate (Eccleshare, 2009).

Sharing texts

The first books children own are generally cloth or board books, often with simple illustrations, one object to a page. It takes time for a small child to associate the banana they eat, with a 2D printed illustration. However, these simple books engage babies' interest in print (Meek, 1991) and are an excellent way to expand their vocabulary. As their lexicon grows, young children enjoy listening to new words and attempting to pronounce them, adding them to their memory bank of useful words.

Nursery rhyme books are the next to capture young children's interest, engaging them with both rhyme and repetition, providing opportunities to recognise characters, and study the illustrations. Many children's rhymes and songs are now available on CDs, DVDs and on screens where the rhymes are accompanied by moving images (for example, www.bbc.co.uk/cbeebies/songs).

In their second year, children are ready to engage with the illustrations in storybooks and there are many titles incorporating features which the young reader can touch, move, or explore, such as flaps and peep-holes (Meek, 1991). As children experience more complex picture books, they begin to learn about how books 'work' (Meek, 1991) and understand the difference between spoken language and the language of books (Clay, 1991). They enjoy the rhythm of different textual formats, and enjoy repetition, in particular the refrains (such as 'who's been eating my porridge?') which enable them to participate in the story-telling process.

Early storybooks focus on familiar topics, often relating to home, family and pets, and some become particular favourites (Browne, 2007), which the child never grows tired of hearing. Illustrations in picture books are very important, with the printed text sometimes taking a secondary role. Meek (1991) discusses the picture book *Rosie's Walk* which has a simple, descriptive text, but the humorous sub-plot is told through the illustrations. Books like this teach children to abstract meaning from texts, encouraging the development of important higher order reading skills, which children need to develop in order to become successful readers. This simple storybook encourages the child to share in the storytelling by uncovering the sub-plot, scrutinising the illustrations and making predictions. Children know from other literature that foxes like to eat hens, so they are delighted to see how the fox is thwarted, and they eagerly scan the illustrations for clues to the next accident that will befall him. In this way, children learn about story structure, traditional literary themes and plots. Children continue to rely on illustrations to help construct meaning as they move towards becoming independent readers (Clay, 1991).

Children need to experience the pleasurable nature of reading if they are to become successful readers (Goouch and Lambirth, 2011), and there is evidence to suggest that a rich literary diet is an important indicator of future reading success (Browne, 2007). By their third year, children are becoming confident language users, enthusiastic about playing with language, and appreciative of the humour found in many children's stories and rhymes. They should be exposed to a wide range of genres, including fiction and non-fiction texts.

Learning to read

Traditionally, pupils have been taught to read through an eclectic mix of phonic knowledge, sight vocabulary (high-frequency words committed to memory, Riley, 2006) and reading for meaning using the higher-order reading skills discussed above. However, research carried out in Clackmannanshire (Johnston and Watson, 2005, cited in Goouch and Lambirth, 2011) changed educational policy by proposing that the ability to build and dissect words phonetically provides beginners with the best tools to tackle print. Whilst there has been a great deal of criticism within academic circles (Goouch and Lambirth, 2011), government policy currently requires that pupils are initially taught to read using a 'systematic synthetic phonics approach' (DfES, 2007b). Using this method, children are taught letter-sound correspondence, and begin to decode simple words, out of context, blending their component letters and sounds. The EYFS Developmental Matters (Early Education, 2012) emphasises the importance of children acquiring phonic knowledge as they enter the 40–60+ month range, enabling them to blend (decode) and dissect words (encode, needed for spelling) to promote independent reading and writing development. In the earlier stages children are encouraged to take part in activities which help them to listen attentively, noticing sounds in the environment and developing an awareness of rhyme and alliteration (DfES, 2007b).

One difficulty of phonic approaches to reading English is that pronunciation and spelling frequently do not correspond to the 26 letters of the alphabet. There are 44 phonemes (sounds) in English, and these are spelt using approximately 140 different grapheme (letter) combinations. In addition, many frequently used words do not conform to the spelling rules, so children still need to memorise a lengthy list of 'irregular' words (DfES, 2007b).

The 'Simple View of Reading' (DfES, 2007b) was the result of recommendations made by the Rose Review (DfES, 2006), and this reading strategy acknowledges that there are two dimensions (skill sets) required for children to become confident readers. They need to have the tools to decode words by blending the phonemes, but they also need to use comprehension skills to make sense of a text.

Reflection

Consider the following quote.

> *If reading success is so dependent on oral language skills, should we not be placing more emphasis on vocabulary and rich language environments in the home, pre-school and the primary grades, rather than assuming that word reading skills alone will suffice?*

Catherine Snow, 'The centrality of language: A longitudinal study of language and literacy development in low-income children', Institute of Education, University of London, 2010. (Thorne, Cited in National Literacy Trust. Website: http://www.literacytrust.org.uk/talk_to_your_baby)

- What are the counter-arguments?

Mark making and writing

As described earlier, children begin to make marks on paper and gradually gain control of drawing and writing tools; there is a long journey between what Clay (1991) terms 'formless scribble', and conventional handwriting. Children experiment with 'emergent writing' (Riley, 2006) which begins to imitate the alphabet in much the same way that children's early babbling mimics adult speech. This stage is an important step towards understanding the symbolic nature of the written word (Browne, 2007), and develops at the same time as children are becoming aware of print in other contexts. Once a child recognises the difference between drawing and writing, they have grasped the concept of written texts (Clay, 1991).

As children begin to explore this medium, they should be encouraged to 'write' for a purpose. Children enjoy using emergent writing in imaginative play scenarios, such as filling in an MOT form in a garage (Hall and Robinson, 2003). As children move towards more conventional writing, they often begin by copying their own name, or memorising the spelling of favourite words. Gradually the child's phonic knowledge becomes evident, where initial sounds may represent whole words and consonants are used to build words such as RUDF (Bissex, 1980), a written plea from Bissex's son when she failed to respond to him.

We should keep in mind that many children in our multi-cultural society become literate in two or more languages simultaneously. Kenner (2000) has considered the way in which parents can help monolingual educationalists to include different literacies in childcare settings. When we look at young children's drawings we should be aware that they often contain elements of their emergent writing in their home alphabets (Czerniewska, 1992).

Journal Task

Collins, F.M. and Svensson, C. (2008) 'If I had a magic wand I'd magic her out of the book: The rich literacy practices of competent early readers', in *Early Years: Journal of International Research & Development*, 28(1): 81–91.

(Continued)

(Continued)

Levels 4 & 5

The 10 children in this study exhibited a range of early literacy behaviours. As you read this article, reflect on the way in which the illustrations in the selected texts supported their comprehension, enabling the children to enjoy the narratives on several different levels. Also, notice the way the children spontaneously made connections with other stories with which they were familiar.

Select one of the texts used in the research and share the book with a group of children.

1. Compare the way these children respond to the text with the responses discussed in the article.
2. How can you focus on these important early reading strategies in your professional work, and how important is the parental contribution?

Level 6

The researchers in this article explored children's enthusiasm for books, but also scrutinised the children's emergent writing for evidence of grapho-phonic knowledge. Currently, the Government's early reading objectives focus on the teaching of systematic synthetic phonics (SSP). However, many practitioners consider that this can stifle children's enthusiasm for reading independently. Research further into the literature on both sides of the argument (e.g. The Clackmannanshire Report (Johnston and Watson, 2005) as well as the counter arguments of those who oppose the imposition of SSP, such as Henrietta Dombey, 2008) and consider your personal position on this crucial subject.

To download this task as well as other useful online resources please visit:
www.sagepub.co.uk/mukherji

Communication in the early twenty-first century

The rapid emergence of new technologies over the past twenty years brought with it fears of a possible decline in traditional communication skills. In fact it appears to have done the opposite. When the technologies behind email and mobile texts were developed, the inventors had no idea that they would become so popular with the general public; they were designed originally for information sharing and technical support between scientists, not to arrange to meet for coffee. The majority of adults (and teenagers) in Britain own a mobile phone, and are constantly communicating in spoken and written forms. Just when we thought writing was going out of fashion, it has become an important part of our social networking.

ICT has certainly become a very important part of all our lives and children are growing up in a technological world that was not dreamed of twenty years ago.

Many young children are computer literate long before they start formal education, and children as young as 2 years old can understand how to navigate around a touch-screen on an iPad. Today, young children have access to texts on screens which literally 'dance across the page' (Goouch and Lambirth, 2011). In the current EYFS (DfE, 2012) ICT comes under the specific area: 'Understanding the World'. ICT is mentioned briefly in the Reading section (p. 29), but not in the Writing section of Developmental Matters (Early Education, 2012). Perhaps it is time to have a debate on the advantages of helping young children to develop keyboard skills (Dryden, 2007).

Summary

This chapter has attempted to address an enormous topic, the acquisition of communication skills, which are at the foundation of all learning. We have explored how very young children begin by breaking the verbal code, and then move on to representing spoken language in its other forms. We have briefly considered the importance of linguistic development as a tool for self-expression, negotiation and problem solving. Above all, I hope that this chapter will have underlined the importance of creating vibrant linguistic experiences which excite children and engage them in communication in all its guises.

Further reading

Levels 4 & 5

Department for Children Schools and Families (DCSF) (2007) *Supporting Children Learning English as an Additional Language: Guidance for Practitioners in the Early Years Foundation Stage*. Nottingham. DCSF. Available from: http://webarchive.nationalarchives.gov.uk/20110208164652/http:/nationalstrategies.standards.dcsf.gov.uk/node/84861 (accessed 20 May 2012). A practical resource considering ways to support young bilingual and multilingual children in early years settings.

Hall, N. and Robinson, A. (2003) Exploring Writing and Play in the Early Years (2nd edition). London: David Fulton. A book which explores the importance of purpose in mark making and writing.

Karmiloff, K. and Karmiloff-Smith, A. (2001) *Pathways to Language: From Foetus to Adolescent*. London: Harvard University Press. A classic text considering linguistic development.

Marsh, J. and Hallet, E. (eds) (2008) *Desirable Literacies: Approaches to Language and Literacy in the Early Years* (2nd edition). London: Sage. An excellent edited text with chapters addressing various aspects of early literacy.

Meek, M. (1991) *On Being Literate*. London: Bodley Head. A classic text which conveys the joy of early encounters with books, with an emphasis on 'reading' (in its broadest sense) as a shared experience.

Level 6

Cattell, R. (2007) *Children's Language, Consensus and Controversy* (Revised edition). London: Continuum. A book providing a detailed account of current thinking on linguistic development.

Kenner, C. (2000) *Home Pages: Literacy Links for Bilingual Children*. Stoke on Trent: Trentham Books. This book considers the importance of providing a multilingual literacy environment and encourages parents to participate in early years settings.

Kress, G. (1997) *Before Writing: Rethinking the Paths of Literacy*. London: Routledge. A more challenging text, which encourages the reader to re-examine the notion of early literacy.

Minns, H. (1997) *Read it to Me Now! Learning at Home and at School* (2nd edition). Buckingham: Open University Press. This book looks at the early literacy experiences of five 4-year-old children from a variety of cultural backgrounds.

References

Anning, A. and Ring, K. (2004) *Making Sense of Children's Drawings*. Maidenhead: Open University Press.

Baker, C. (2001) *Foundations of Bilingual Education and Bilingualism* (3rd edition). Clevedon: Multilingual Matters.

Barratt-Pugh, C. and Rohl, M. (2000) *Literacy Learning in the Early Years*. Buckingham: Open University Press.

BBC: http://www.bbc.co.uk/cbeebies/

Bernstein, B. (1971) *Class Codes and Control (Volume 1)*. London: Routledge & Kegan Paul.

Bissex, G.I. (1980) *GNYS AT WRK: A Child Learns to Write and Read*. Cambridge, MA: Harvard University Press.

Book Start: http://www.bookstart.org.uk/

Brock, A. and Rankin, C. (2008) *Communication, Language and Literacy from Birth to Five*. London: Sage.

Browne, A. (2007) *Teaching and Learning Communication, Language and Literacy*. London: Paul Chapman.

Bruner, J. (1986) *Actual Minds, Possible Worlds*. London: Harvard University Press.

Cattell, R. (2007) *Children's Language, Consensus and Controversy* (Revised edition). London: Continuum.

Chomsky, N. (1965) *Aspects of the Theory of Syntax*. Cambridge, MA: MIT Press.

Clay, M.M. (1991) *Becoming Literate: The Construction of Inner Control*. Auckland, NZ: Heinemann.

Collins, F.M. and Svensson, C. (2008). If I had a magic ward I'd magic her out of the book: The rich literacy practices of competent early readers,' *Early Years: Journal of International Research & Development*, 28(1): 81–91.

Czerniewska, P. (1992) *Learning About Writing*. Oxford: Blackwell.

Department for Children, Schools and Families (DCSF) (2008) *Mark Making Matters*. Nottingham: DCSF Publications.

Department for Children, Schools and Families (DCSF) (2009) *Every Child A Talker: Guidance for Consultants and Early Language Lead Practitioners*. Nottingham: DCSF Publications.

Department for Education (DfE) (2012) *Statutory Framework for the Early Years Foundation Stage*. Nottingham: DfE Publications.

Department for Education and Skills (DfES) (2007a) *The Early Years Foundation Stage*. Nottingham: DfES Publications.
Department for Education and Skills (DfES) (2007b) *Letters and Sounds: Principles and Practice of High Quality Phonics*. Nottingham: DfES Publications.
Doherty, J. and Hughes, M. (2009) *Child Development: Theory and Practice 0–11*. Harlow, Essex: Pearson Education.
Drury, R. (2004) 'Samia and Sadaqat play school', in E. Gregory, S. Long and D. Volk (eds), *Many Pathways to Literacy*. London: Routledge Falmer.
Dryden, L. (2004) 'Showing signs', *Nursery World*, 22 April, pp. 22–3.
Dryden, L. (2005) 'Language and literacy', in L. Dryden, P. Mukherji, R. Forbes and L. Pound, *Essential Early Years*. London: Hodder.
Dryden, L. (2007) 'Emergent typing', *English Four to Eleven*, 31: 15–18.
Early Education (2012) *Developmental Matters in Early Years Foundation Stage*. London: Early Education/DfE.
Eccleshare, J. (2009) *1001 Children's Books You must Read Before You Grow Up*. London: Octopus Books.
Gopnik, A., Meltzoff, A. and Kuhl, P. (2001) *How Babies Think*. London: Phoenix.
Goouch, K. and Lambirth, A. (2011) *Teaching Early Reading and Phonics: Creative Approaches to Early Literacy*. London: Sage.
Gussin-Paley, V. (1981) *Wally's Stories: Conversations in the Kindergarten*. London: Harvard University Press.
Hall, N. and Robinson, A. (2003) *Exploring Writing and Play in the Early Years*. London: David Fulton.
Halliday, M.A.K. (1975) *Learning How to Mean: Explorations in the Development of Language*. London: Edward Arnold.
Hamer, C. (2012) 'Parent–child communication is important from birth', *Perspective*, December, pp. 15–20.
ICAN (2007) 'Language and social exclusion', ICAN Talk Series, Issue 4, ICAN. http://www.ican.org.uk/ (accessed 19 September 2012).
ICAN (2009) 'Speech, language and communication needs and the early years', ICAN Talk Series, Issue 7, ICAN. http://www.ican.org.uk/ (accessed 19 September 2012).
Johnston, R.S. and Watson, J.E. (2005) *Insight 17: A Seven Year Study of the Effects of Synthetic Phonics Teaching on Reading and Spelling Attainment*. IAC.
Karmiloff, K. and Karmiloff-Smith, A. (2001) *Pathways to Language: From Foetus to Adolescent*. London: Harvard University Press.
Kenner, C. (2000) *Home Pages: Literacy Links for Bilingual Children*. Stoke on Trent: Trentham Books.
Kisilvesky, B.S., Hains, S.M.J., Brown, C. A., Lee, C.T., Cowperthwaite, B., Stutzman, S.S., Swansburg, M.L., Lee, K., Xie, X., Huang, H., Ye, H.-H., Zhang, K. and Wang, Z. (2009) 'Fetal sensitivity to properties of maternal speech and language', *Infant Behaviour Development*, 32(1): 59–71.
Krashen, S.D. (1981) *Principles and Practice in Second Language Acquisition*. London: Prentice Hall International.
Kress, G. (1997) *Before Writing: Rethinking the Paths of Literacy*. London: Routledge.
London Councils http://www.londoncouncils.gov.uk/londonfacts/default.htm?category=2 (accessed 7 August 2013).
Meek, M. (1991) *On Being Literate*. London: Bodley Head.
Meltzoff, A.N. and Moore, M.K. (1977) 'Imitation of facial and manual gestures by human neonates', *Science*, 198(4312): 75–8.

National Literary Trust (2013) *Talk to you Baby*. London: National Literary Trust. Available at: http://www.literacytrust.org.uk/talk_to_your_baby (accessed 25 November 2013).
Nutbrown, C. (1997) *Recognising Early Literacy Development: Assessing Children's Achievements*. London: Paul Chapman.
Piaget, J. (1959) *The Language and Thought of the Child*. London: Routledge.
QCA (2000) *Curriculum Guidance for the Foundation Stage*. London: QCA.
Riley, J. (2006) *Language and Literacy 3–7*. London: Sage.
Rose Review (2006) *Independent Review of the Teaching of Early Reading*. Nottingham: DfES.
Sammons, P., Sylva, K., Melhuish, E., Siraj-Blatchford, I., Taggart, B., Hunt, S., Jelicic, H. (2008) *EPPE: Influences on Children's Cognitive and Social Development in Year 6*. London: DCSF.
Siraj-Blatchford, I. and Clarke, P. (2000) *Supporting Identity, Diversity and Language in the Early Years*. Buckingham: Open University Press.
Skinner, B.F. (1957) *Verbal Behaviour*. Englewood Cliffs, NJ: Prentice Hall.
Snow, C.E. (1972) 'Mothers' speech to children learning language', *Child Development*, 43(2): 549–65.
Tizard, B. and Hughes, M. (1984) *Young Children Learning, Talking and Thinking at Home and School*. London: Fontana.
Vygotsky, L. (1962) *Thought and Language*. Cambridge, MA: MIT Press.
Wood, D. (1988) *How Children Think and Learn*. Oxford: Basil Blackwell.

18

Physical Development and the Role of the Physical Environment

Rita White

The chapter will:

- Investigate the physical development of young children
- Describe some of the stages, sequences and milestones relating to physical development in young children
- Suggest a range of practical ideas regarding how to support babies and young children in the Early Years Foundation Stage (Early Education, 2012).

In order to assist young children's care and education adults working with young children need to consider how children develop holistically, which enables them to recognise and understand the interrelatedness of areas of development, and ensures they are better able to support children's individual needs. Physical development is essential for good posture and a healthy lifestyle, which if enjoyed throughout the early years should provide children with the confidence to continue to engage in sports through their later years in school and socially as an adult. It is essential for adults working with young children to have a sound understanding of the theory that underpins child development and this chapter aims to support adults to make links between the areas of learning, with a specific focus on physical development. It explores ways in which adults can enhance children's learning through the interrelatedness of areas of development and make use of available resources and outdoor areas in multicultural settings.

In the revised Early Years Foundation Stage Curriculum (DfE, 2012) and in the non-statutory 'Development Matters' (Early Education, 2012), the seven areas of learning and development have been divided into prime and specific areas and physical development has been given prominence as being one of the prime areas of learning for the youngest children. The three prime areas are Physical Development, Communication and Language and Personal Social and Emotional Development and the specific areas of learning relate to Literacy, Mathematics, Understanding the World and Expressive Art and Design (DfE, 2012; Early Education, 2012). In care and education settings, early years practitioners monitor children's progress through ongoing observations and assessments, compiling a summative report outlining each child's individual progress in the prime areas of learning when they are 24–30 months of age (Early Education, 2012). This summative report correlates to the two-year check carried out by health professionals with reference to the same areas of development. This is not coincidental as young children are naturally inclined to show rapid progress in these areas, transitioning from limited communication and movement to acquiring speech and developing mobility.

Developing a holistic view of the child

Babies start life dependent on adults to care and provide for their needs, which they are unable to do for themselves. Developing mobility not only aids the child physically, but cognitively too, as practising and refining skills helps them to consolidate learning which enhances their confidence, ability and self-efficacy (Greenland, 2006). May (2011) concurs that 'Physical development and its attendant refinement of motor skills is interrelated to children's emotional and cognitive development' (2011: 27). There are many theories related to child development showing differing opinions about how children develop, for example Arnold Gesell (1928) believed maturation and development were due to genetic factors affecting the rate, growth and development of young children. He carried out research on twins, providing one with more practice of motor skills than the other. His findings showed little difference in the rate at which both twins acquired motor skills, leading him to conclude that it was maturation rather than experience that had the greater impact on development (Keenan and Evans, 2009). Gesell's theory was in contrast to that of John Watson (1928) who believed the environment was more significant. Both theories, focusing on how culture and social experiences affect learning (Bertram and Pascal, 2006), have contributed to the ongoing debate regarding development and learning and the impact of nature versus nurture.

Patterns of growth from pre-natal development onwards

In order to understand the physical development of Nursery and Reception aged children, it is important to have a good understanding of the previous stages of development. Physical growth begins in the embryonic stage of pregnancy, ending around eight weeks when the foetal stage begins. During the foetal stage organs gradually form, starting around three weeks, and are developed between 10 and 12 weeks. The foetal stage of pregnancy lasts till birth at approximately 38–40 weeks. During the gestation period development follows a sequence of head to toe, known as *Cephalocaudal development*, and downwards and outwards, *Proximodistal development*, with organs forming before limbs (Johnson and Nahmad-Williams, 2009). As the foetus develops its bones and muscle tone, it begins to move its limbs, hands and feet, thereby demonstrating that movement begins in the womb. Following birth, babies develop at a rapid rate, and, as they do, their body changes significantly; you will know this if you have seen a newborn shortly after birth and met them again a few months later, the physical changes are quite pronounced.

When babies are first born it is usual for the midwife to check a number of involuntary primitive reflexes which can be identified when parts of the baby's body are stimulated. These innate reflexes are temporary patterns of movement which are precursors to the voluntary planned movements that develop at a later stage through experience (Doherty and Hughes, 2009). One such reflex, the grasping reflex, or palmar grasp, is an example of an involuntary reflex which can be identified as a baby clasps a finger placed in the palm of its hand. Often the grasp is so strong it is not easy for the baby to let go. This reflex disappears by about six months and is replaced by purposeful voluntary movements such as reaching and holding. These innate reflexes are thought to exist to aid survival, for example in young animals that are carried by the adults it is essential for the offspring to be able to hold on whilst the adult travels. In mammals and specifically young babies, the rooting and sucking reflexes allow them to search for the breast in order to drink milk. Other survival reflexes include the Moro reflex which disappears around two months and can be recognised by the baby extending its limbs in an outward thrust when startled (Macintyre, 2012). When handling young babies it is important to be aware of these reflexes and support them accordingly.

Stages of physical development and milestones

At birth babies' heads and brains are fairly developed, and as they grow they gradually gain control of their body; starting with the head, then the torso, followed by the limbs. A baby's head requires support, and holding them correctly with your hand or bent elbow underneath is essential. Around four months of age babies begin to roll from one side to another. This development can appear quite unexpectedly so it is important for their carers to be aware and take safety precautions to avoid babies rolling off changing mats or cushions. Initially babies have enough muscle control in their neck to raise their heads up slightly when placed on their stomach. As they gain more control they can push with bent forearms to raise their head and shoulders off the ground and once their muscle control and strength increases they are able to raise their head and chest off the floor using outstretched arms. All of this requires practice and speaking to babies will encourage them to raise their head to see your face; initially it may be easier if they are laid on a raised area slightly above the floor level until they gain greater control of their neck muscles.

By six months most babies begin to crawl, followed later with standing and walking, which can start as young as nine months, or as late as 17 months, although the average age is between 12 and 14 months (Keenan and Evans, 2009). You may be aware that some babies omit the crawling stage, or shuffle on their bottoms either forwards or in a sideways movement. With practice babies' legs become stronger and their balance more stable. As they become more mobile they will explore further and gradually begin to pull themselves to a standing position. When this milestone is achieved, and as they gain confidence, they will usually begin to take steps, cruising round furniture or objects; this development can be supported by placing stable items in close proximity to encourage the toddler to take steps unaided.

Movement and the brain

Movement is controlled by the brain which plays a significant role in development, controlling the spinal cord, nervous system, emotions and learning (Johnson and Nahmad-Williams, 2009). The body relies on the brain to direct movement such as fine, gross and locomotor skills, for example our fingertips are connected to tissues in the frontal cortex of the brain (Winkley, 2004). Research into brain development concludes that children learn best from hands-on experiences (Keenan and Evans, 2009). Each learning process involves neurons and synapses which transmit signals to each other in the brain through connections, and as babies develop and explore and learn, the neurons become stronger (Johnson and Nahmad-Williams, 2009). Babies have significantly more neurons in their brain than adults, which are gradually pruned when not used regularly, affirming the 'use it or lose it phenomenon' (Blackmore, 2007). The more the children practice and learn through exploratory play using their senses, the more likely they are to retain the learning (Riddall-Leech, 2009). These experiences will assist the neural connections in their brains to develop into neural pathways, which without repeated experience fade away, along with the learning. The Development Matters guidance, used by adults working in care and education settings, identifies 'Characteristics of Effective Learning' as including 'playing and exploring, active learning and creating and thinking critically' (Early Education, 2012: 4).

Although movement skills are closely linked, there are specific differences between them, and acquisition is acquired gradually through maturation and experience. Stages of development are sequential, with some physical skills being required before others in order to perform certain tasks (Macintyre, 2012). For example, a young child needs to develop gross arm motor movement and wrist control before being able to use a pencil effectively to achieve legible handwriting. As you observe babies and young children you will become aware that development cannot be hurried. Macintyre (2012) dissuades adults from rushing young children as 'babies have an inbuilt sequence of development that suits their stage of development. They will walk when they are ready, i.e. when they have the musculature and the co-ordination to do so' (2012: 59). The current Development Matters guidance is useful in that it provides guidance to support adults' understanding of the ages and stages of development and learning in children from birth to 5 (Early Education, 2012). Through observations you will see the range of motor movements in action, for example children using their limbs and muscles to create whole body movements when climbing, standing and sitting. The Development Matters guidance (Early Education, 2012) can be referred to as you take note of how abilities vary between babies and children of the same age.

Reflection

Imagine what it feels like for a young child to begin taking steps from one object to another and the emotions involved in moving from one piece of supporting furniture to another? Not only does the child have to reach and step they also have to retain their balance. If you have seen young children in the early stages of walking you will notice how often they fall back on their bottom or hesitate and sit down before trying again or crawling instead. Consider what resources you could provide for babies in a setting to encourage them in taking their first steps?

Developing early coordination

As babies and young children make sense of their world, they also develop perception. Perception is developed not only by experience but also well-being, previous learning, and motor development, all of which are inextricably linked. The development of distance perception, along with visual awareness, aids their acquisition of hand-to-eye coordination later on. From a few months, babies can track objects if they are moved slowly in front of them. If you have been in contact with newborns you may notice they sometimes appear cross-eyed, this is due to the lack of muscle control around the eye area which is underdeveloped in the womb because of an absence of light (Macintyre, 2012). Placing mobiles or other stimuli close to the baby or singing to them softly as you hold them will encourage them to focus on the movement of your lips and facial expressions.

Reflection

Babies are able to distinguish their mother's voice from other voices (see Chapter 17). You may have witnessed a very young baby turning in recognition towards a familiar voice and becoming attentive when sung lullabies. Singing softly to babies is an adult behaviour common to most cultures, as babies are soothed by the singing.

What kind of physical responses do you think you might elicit from singing to a young baby?

Babies often respond to singing by waving their arms, smiling and making noises such as squeals of delight, gurgling and babbling. Singing and talking to babies encourages turn taking, but leave suitable pauses between responses to give the baby time to respond. Babies achieve control over their bodily movements from their midline outwards; for example, whole arm movement is achieved before manipulation of the fingers (Meggitt, 2012). You will notice that babies appear to initially kick and move their limbs in unplanned movements. Once the baby develops control of its limbs, it will find that flaying its arms or legs sometimes results in contact with toys and objects of interest, hung or attached to the cot or pram. Initially babies have limited control, and their movements may result in them banging themselves, causing distress, therefore you should provide them with toys that are soft and suitable for mouthing, so that any jerking or sudden movement will not cause injury. At six months old most babies have learnt to calculate distance more efficiently, and after much encouragement and concentrated effort they can reach out and grab the desired object, which May suggests is in part due to a 'rise in expectations that drives the child to become ever more skilful' (May, 2011: 27).

You may have noticed how babies mouth objects before holding them at a distance, focusing on them, transferring them between hands before mouthing them again. Playing with objects, termed by Piaget as 'sensory motor play', begins 'as soon as infants can grasp and hold on to them; early investigative behaviours include mouthing/biting, rotating whilst looking, rubbing/stroking, hitting and dropping' (Whitebread, 2012: 68). With further fine motor development a 10-month-old baby will usually be able to pick up smaller objects between the thumb and forefinger, a skill which Woodfield (2004) explains is acquired in a three-part process; acquisition, development and consolidation. A baby or child first acquires a skill, for example reaching, and with practise the movement is developed more accurately before finally becoming internalised to a point where conscious effort is no longer required. Movement and cognitive development are interrelated, an idea acknowledged by developmental psychologists and early years theorists including Maria Montessori (Lillard, 2005). Adults support babies' development by moving objects slightly out of their reach which encourages them to move in different ways.

Health and exercise

As children's bodies grow and mature their ability to acquire skills and movement increases. As we have learnt, their progress will be determined by nature as well as their environment, and although developmental progress tends to be steady, it can also be very rapid, or plateau, and in some instances decline. Progress is dependent on other aspects of development such as social, emotional, linguistic and cognitive development, all of which can hinder or increase the likelihood of babies and children meeting milestones earlier or later than expected – for example, a sick or unhappy child may appear to regress.

Reflection

Consider how a young child's behaviour might be affected by illness, or a medical condition. How might certain types of physical incapacity hamper a child's physical development?

Physical activity stimulates the appetite (Keenan and Evans, 2009) and children need to replenish their energy with regular eating and drinking. These everyday tasks provide additional opportunities to improve fine motor skills in the mouth through chewing and tasting and developing hand-to-eye coordination as children feed themselves. Fine motor skills develop after gross motor skills and involve smaller physical movements and manipulation, such as movement of the tongue, eyes and fingers (Macintyre, 2012). As adults we have full control over our lips and tongue, but it is only when the muscles in the tongue and mouth are developed that young children can achieve specific planned movements, which include manipulating their lips to make audible and recognisable speech (Keenan and Evans, 2009).

Regular exercise also has an additional benefit of tiring children, which enables them to sleep better and produces a sense of well-being. Achievement and acquisition of new motor skills improves children's emotional and cognitive development; most children are thrilled and excited when they are able to achieve a skill that an older child or sibling can do. May (2011) explains that 'For a child to feel positive about learning something new there needs to be both a cognitive challenge – i.e. something that awakens the child's curiosity – and the desire to learn' (2011: 13). As you watch children moving you can observe a range of skills in action, such as gross and locomotors skills and spatial awareness. It is not uncommon to see children running, moving, turning, changing direction, speeding up and slowing down; occasionally stopping to pick up objects, which requires balance, coordination and stability, as well as manipulation of the wrist, hand and fingers. Macintyre (2012) suggests that it is important for parents and practitioners to observe and encourage the development of children's movement patterns: 'This is because movement, as well as being very important in its own right, helps children to become confident learners in all aspects of their development – social, emotional and intellectual' (2012: 50).

Children benefit from praise when they practice or achieve a physical skill, which Bandura suggested can lead to self-efficacy (cited in Keenan and Evans, 2009). Whilst it is good practice to praise effort, encouragement can be more effective, leading to intrinsic motivation. Theorists, including B.F. Skinner, acknowledge that children respond well to praise and behaviour reinforcement ('operant conditioning theory'), noting that when a child receives attention, the behaviour is likely to be repeated (cited in Johnson and Nahmad-Williams, 2009). Bandura recognised that learning was also reinforced through socialising with others; however he differed from Skinner in that he recognised that just by watching others, children's behaviour changed, and he termed this 'social learning theory' (cited in Keenan and Evans, 2009). Physical play involving other children lends itself to practising turn taking and improving communication and social skills. Children respond to each other's achievements by copying and refining their own skills in comparison to their peers. For example, playing in mixed aged groups can help a child develop confidence by achieving more than their peers, while another may be encouraged to attempt what they observe more capable children doing.

Professionals support babies and children in their care to develop their physical skills by being aware of what they can do, what is expected for their age and what the next steps in development might be; these are outlined in the Development Matters guidance (Early Education, 2012). Practitioners in care and educational settings are required to have a good understanding of each child, and this includes acquiring information regarding their previous experiences and developmental progress from their parents; a process which can start before the child enters the setting. (This partnership is explored further in Chapter 13.) Children are continuously observed on a daily basis, in order to facilitate their learning and development, through carefully planned interaction at appropriate times. A skilled practitioner will know when to support or demonstrate skills, by having a secure understanding of the 'normalised' milestones and stages in children's development, although children are unique and vary considerably, having 'their own innate timetables of development' (Macintyre, 2012: 50). Macintyre's view is widely accepted and in contrast to Piaget's work on the developmental stage theory. The development stage theory identified by Piaget, acted as a 'normalizing device' to calculate whether children were 'in line with developmental norms' (Fabian and Mould, 2009: 18). Through experience and with support from other specialist staff, adults learn to recognise when other issues may be delaying children's progress.

Encouraging physical development through play

Resources which develop early manipulative skills

Young children love exploring everyday objects and engaging in heuristic play, a name which originates from 'the Greek "eurisko" which means "I discover" or "I find"' (Riddall-Leech, 2009: 2). Adults can be creative and use everyday objects rather than manufactured toys which have limited imaginative value.

Treasure Baskets, pioneered by Elinor Goldschmied in the 1980s are used in many early years settings to enhance heuristic play which is unhurried, independent and open-ended, as babies and children choose how to use the objects, learning according to their own exploration (cited in Hughes, 2006). Treasure Baskets, which Hughes likens to 'food for the brain' (2006: 3), can be filled with everyday objects, for example small kitchen utensils and wooden objects together with natural materials such as leaves and feathers. The objects should be supplemented regularly, and for safety reasons, nothing should be small enough to fit into a child's mouth. As soon as a baby can sit unsupported they are ready to be left alone to explore the materials for themselves.

Around 2 years old, most children will be walking confidently and able to pick up toys from a standing position. Adults should provide suitable activities which support this development, such as baskets to encourage them to tidy away resources. Picking up toys from a standing position is familiar to most children of this age, either by grasping the objects in their hands or using the pincer grip.

Using other play resources such as bricks, Lego® or small-world resources can support manipulative skills and spatial awareness. Small children have a preference for floor play rather than sitting at tables, however, Howard (2010) found that older children had perceptions about what was and was not play in educational settings, noting that floor-based work was play, whereas table top activities were not. When organising table-top activities it is not always necessary to have chairs, as standing whilst playing encourages movement such as reaching and stretching, which can be completed more easily from an upright position than a sitting one.

CASE STUDY

At 3 years of age, Ahmed was new to the children's centre, but settled in well with his key person Michael. Michael recognised that Ahmed showed a particular interest in shiny materials and observed him selecting foil and metallic objects from a range of resources. Ahmed's interest moved to collecting other metallic

(Continued)

(Continued)

and shiny objects from around the setting and placing them in a doll's pram which he used to collect and transport his finds. In subsequent weeks, his play developed further, with him placing the metallic objects in rows, rearranging their order from time to time.

- Consider aspects of Ahmed's schematic play and how his 'transporting' and sorting behaviours were also developing his physical skills.
- What other experiences might provide Ahmed with opportunities to use his gross motor skills.

The 'Prime Area of Learning: Physical Development' also includes the aspect of health and self-care (DfE, 2012: 2). Eating and preparing food to share in the setting will provide opportunities to discuss healthy eating, likes and dislikes and choices (Albon and Mukhejri, 2008). Children like to explore food using their senses including their hands. For the younger children, adults can provide plates with suction or non slip surfaces, so they do not need to manage the movement of the plates as they grapple with the skills required to pick up food. Young babies will grasp food in their hands until they have developed finger control and are able to pick it up with their forefinger and thumb as outlined in The Development Matters guidance, which suggests that between eight and 20 months a child 'Grasps finger foods and brings them to mouth' (Early Education, 2012: 25). Once they notice children becoming more independent, adults can provide child-sized forks and blunt knives.

Moving on

The Development Matters guidance recommends a cycle of observation, assessment and planning as good practice for supporting young children's learning and development (Early Education, 2012: 3). Whilst observing young children at play, you will have noticed they begin by using whole arm movements when painting and mark making, before gradually learning to use their wrists to make more precise movements. For example, children can create marks using large movements, such by using domestic paint brushes or rollers to paint on large surfaces, using paint on rolls of paper, or buckets of water to create large images on the ground or walls. In addition, by engaging in shared play with smaller mark-making tools, practitioners can create pictures together with the child, supporting and encouraging their fine motor development. The children may recognise symbols being created and talk about them as they develop pictures with you; this will be an opportunity to make links to literacy and mathematics (Early Education, 2012).

Between the ages of 40 and 60 months age, children become more independent and relish opportunities to dress and undress themselves, despite the challenges of buttons and zips (Early Education, 2012: 27). The Development Matters guidance describes the 'Characteristics of Effective Learning' under the heading 'A Unique Child' and suggests professionals observe whether children show signs of concentration, being involved and persisting with tasks (Early Education, 2012: 6). Practitioners should consider ways to support children by providing a well-resourced role-play area which includes a range of clothing representing all cultures (Dowling, 2010). It is advisable to make sure the clothing has large buttons and fasteners that children can manage themselves, including shoes with Velcro and wellington boots which will give children opportunities to learn about pulling and pushing as they dress and undress. Fiddly clothing will frustrate and deter the children from playing and exploring independently.

Malleable materials are excellent for developing fine motor skills, but children's fingers can become tired easily, so providing a range of textures is important. There are many conventional materials such as sand and clay which are used in early years settings, but there are more exciting materials which children can experiment with which provide a variety of textures and require different handling skills. The practitioner can be inventive, providing shaving foam or wet spaghetti, for example. For more ideas refer to the 'Exploring and using media and materials' section of the Development Matters guidance (Early Education, 2012: 43).

When children are frustrated or angry, dough and clay is often used to allow them to vent their feelings, and is also used widely in play therapy sessions. 'Play-dough provides not only the obvious elements of expression of anger by rolling, folding and pounding but the not-so-obvious elements of recognition, modulation and control of anger and its two cousins, frustration and aggression' (White, 2006: 288). You may have noticed that the process of thumping, pulling, stretching and squeezing can alleviate frustration, and by the time children are finished they become engrossed in making something. As noted, dough and other malleable materials have wider benefits than just physical development; cognition is developed as children explore size, shape and transformation, changing a piece of dough from a small round ball to a flat pancake or rolling it into a long sausage.

Reflection

When using play dough or clay with children, providing them with a choice of cutters, shapes and tools helps them to make decisions and explore effects. However, limiting the number of tools also encourages turn taking and sharing.

(Continued)

(Continued)

Consider the benefits and challenges for children with reduced resources available during play and how adults can support their sharing and turn taking. Refer to the Development Matters guidance and note the age identified when a child 'Begins to accept the needs of others and can take turns and share resources' (Early Education, 2012: 13). How does this age-related expectation relate to children you have worked with, and why do you think some children find sharing more challenging?

Activities using water and sand are part of the continuous provision both inside and outside the classroom, offering multiple benefits in terms of promoting physical development and ludic play (Johnson and Nahmad-Williams, 2009). As adults play alongside children, as recommended by many approaches including Reggio Emilia and HighScope, they can engage in dialogue whilst the children play. Talking to children helps them to focus and verbalise their actions whilst introducing new vocabulary related to their physical movements. Modelling like this is necessary because children can find it hard to express themselves aloud (Dowling, 2010). Facilitating learning in this way not only promotes language, but also physical development whilst retaining children's 'autonomy' as they 'take ownership of their learning', directing it in self-initiated ways (Whitebread, 2012: 3).

Another important area of provision involves those opportunities provided for creative development including gluing and sticking with reclaimed materials. Children love to use tape and scissors, which may initially require assistance or modelling to show children how to hold the materials properly. You can help them develop scissor control by first holding the paper as they snip and attempt to cut lines on the page. Later, with more experience, they will be able to hold the paper and control the scissors to follow a wider zigzag line drawn for them, and in doing so develop hand-to-eye coordination. Some children will be ambidextrous when they are young, but you will become aware of children who show a strong preference to use their left hand (and foot). Left-handed scissors are usually recognisable by differentiated colouring; if a child is struggling to cut, adults can offer these to see if they find them more manageable.

Moving outside

As well as traditional outdoor equipment, home corners and other imaginative play resources should be made available outdoors, and not confined to indoor play provision.

Extending play into the outdoor area

Reflection

Having washed some dolls' clothing, for example, the children could be encouraged to make decisions about where best to hang them. Consider how you could support children in making these decisions without redirecting and leading their learning. For example, would they recognise that a safely positioned, brightly coloured washing line hung low would be helpful? If not, how could you encourage this decision?

Reflect on the physical movement required in lifting wet items from the water tray, squeezing them dry, shaking and arranging them on the line, and attaching pegs to hold them in place. Children will have different needs in terms of support as they carry out the task; it is always best to wait for them to request help rather than rushing in to help. Reflect on what you observe the children being able to do alone in relation to the Development Matters guidance, focusing on 'Physical Development: Moving and Handling' (Early Education, 2012: 23).

One of the benefits of outdoor play is that it can take place on a large scale, and also, noise is less restricted. Creating a low stage from large building blocks or milk-crates that are fastened together securely makes an ideal platform for children to engage in dancing and singing. Providing music from different cultures is beneficial, and where possible staff or parents from a variety of communities can contribute, for example modelling cultural dances and movements.

The outdoor area provides opportunities for imaginative play with greater freedom of movement, and children need no adult interference in engaging in long-running narratives which frequently extend over a series of days. By observing their play you can plan ways to extend their learning, providing them with equipment which enhances their 'stage'.

Developing gross and loco-motor skills and spatial awareness outdoors

In all early years settings professionals are required to ensure children have daily access to the outside (DfE, 2012). Making use of the outside space is possible in all weathers with a canopy or suitable all-weather clothing. Easy access from the inside areas of the setting, to the resourced outdoor space will provide children with the opportunity to move freely, and with sufficient staff ratios it should be possible for children to choose where they wish to play at all times.

Opportunities for children to be physically active are extremely important, as recommended in the Development Matters guidance (Early Education, 2012). A well planned outdoor area with plenty of provision and stimulation should enable children who do not have access to a garden or park to engage in physical play. The EYFS (DfE, 2012) includes a theme related to 'Enabling Environments', and guidance regarding access to outdoor provision is stipulated in the Statutory Framework for the Early Years Foundation Stage (DfE, 2012):

> Providers must provide access to an outdoor play area or, if that is not possible, ensure that outdoor activities are planned and taken on a daily basis (unless circumstances make this inappropriate, for example unsafe weather conditions). (DfE, 2012: p. 24, para. 3.56)

The outdoors provides a perfect space to explore movement, for example travelling in different directions by darting, twirling, spinning and stopping. Gallahue and Ozmun's stages of motor development (2005) include the 'Fundamental Movement Phase', in which locomotion, stability and manipulation skills are developed. Stability is required in order for children to come to a standstill after travelling at speed. As you observe children standing and bending you may notice the stability required, particularly with the younger children. Responding to movement is often practised by young children (Early Education, 2012: 24), which Whitebread (2012) suggests 'begins to emerge during the second year of life and typically occupies around 20% of children's behaviour by the age of 4–5 years' (2012: 68). When children are engaged in vigorous activities they need to develop spatial awareness, and providing objects for them to run around and travel under, over and between, can aid this development (Early Education, 2012).

Many well-resourced early years settings have chosen to buy fixed provision such as climbing frames, boats and other play material. Settings with less funding may be more creative and resourceful, using everyday objects for multiple purposes. For example, using an 'A' frame (support) and planks of wood designed to be held as slides, platforms or ladders, enables a range of obstacle courses to be created, thus promoting different levels of challenge. When this equipment is not being used for climbing and travelling along, it can provide the perfect support for fabric, so that children can use their imagination to create dens and tents, play which Vygotsky identified as symbolic representation (cited in Karpov, 2005). Creating tents encourages children to move into and out of spaces, and bending, carrying, stretching fabric, reaching, pulling and fixing are just a few of the movements that require coordination of different motor skills.

CASE STUDY

Maria first came to the Children's Centre just after her first birthday. Now aged 4 she is in her last term before transitioning to the local primary school. Being one of the oldest, she plays confidently and happy with the staff and children, showing a preference for outdoor play. Her physical skills have developed beyond expectations and her key worker notices how she uses all available resources in her imaginative play, particularly when creating dens and tents in the warmer weather. At times she becomes quite controlling over the space available, which causes disagreements amongst her younger peers.

- Consider how your planning reflects the needs of the different aged children in your setting? Does it provide a range of experiences in all weathers, taking into account how the space is shared?
- Are the children aware of which areas are designated for bikes and balls or for quieter stationary activities, through identified zoned or marked spaces?
- Do you provide adequate storage or trolleys and boxes of resources positioned in areas close to where they are required?
- Talk to your colleagues about ways in which the available space can be redesigned to enhance the learning experience for all children.

Safety factors

Johnson and Nahmad-Williams suggest key aspects of quality play inside and out are 'time … and space … to move freely' (2009: 273). Most settings will consider the safety aspect of outdoor play as part of their Health and Safety policy. Always read this policy when you spend time in settings to ensure you are compliant with the requirements. Practitioners should be mindful of children with restricted mobility; consider their needs and plan ways of enabling them to engage in all play. Children who use mobility aids or wheelchairs will need to feel confident that they are safe in a busy, bustling outdoor area. The Statutory Framework proposes inclusive use of the outdoor space where the 'facilities, equipment and access to the premises are suitable for children with disabilities' (DfE, 2012: 24).

Reflection

Reflect on the resources available as part of outdoor provision in a setting you are familiar with, and consider whether they encourage independent or group play. Balls, hoops, skipping ropes, two-person trolleys and tricycles are a few of the resources that require assistance from a friend and, in doing so, encourage manipulation skills of the hands and feet.

(Continued)

(Continued)

What other resources can be used to develop hand-to-eye coordination or gross motor skills, for example rolling, kicking, bouncing or passing balls between children?

If funding is limited be creative, a wet bean bag thrown at a numbered target drawn on the wall with chalk can be just as effective as a bought resource in developing accurate hand-to-eye coordination and gross motor skills. Adults can initiate play by drawing circles, squares and triangles on the ground with chalk and then naming the shapes and using positional language as children jump into and out of them, or hop around or beside them. This will enhance their mathematical vocabulary and understanding as well as the physical skills as referred to in 'Development Matters, Mathematics: Shape, space and measure' (Early Education, 2012: 3). If there are bilingual children the practitioners can learn the key words in the children's home languages to support engagement and identity.

Older children can be introduced to physical games that have rules and require participation and cooperation with others. Piaget recognised the benefits of games in aiding children's social and moral development (cited in DeVries, 2006) as does Whitebread (2012) who claims: 'In children from a very early age, a considerable proportion of time and energy playing any such game is devoted to establishing, agreeing, modifying and reminding one another about the rules' (2012: 82).

Journal Task

Dyment, J.E. and Coleman, B. (2013) 'Factors that limit and enable preschool-aged children's physical activity on child care centre playgrounds', *Journal of Early Childhood Research*, 25 January, doi: 10.1177/1476718X12456250.

Levels 4 & 5

The settings in this article explain that their main priority is to ensure children are safe whilst playing outside. Consider how this approach hinders children's development and confidence to take risks whilst reflecting on your own concerns regarding the safety of children in your setting.

Level 6

This research outlines how settings' Health and Safety policies also influence the likelihood of staff encouraging children to engage in more exploratory outdoor play. After reading the article, consider the recommendations from the Health and Safety Executive Statement, 'Children's play and leisure – promoting a balanced approach', September 2012 (available at: http://www.hse.gov.uk/entertainment/childrens-play-july-2012.pdf). Reflect on your setting's Outdoor Play and Health and Safety policies and consider ways in which these policies could be adapted to enhance the children's learning opportunities.

To download this task as well as other useful online resources please visit:
www.sagepub.co.uk/mukherji

Summary

This chapter has outlined ways in which children develop, prior to birth and afterwards. Reflecting on how you can support young children's physical development holistically in relation to theory will ensure you provide learning experiences that engage and enhance children's learning in all areas of the curriculum. Talking with friends and colleagues who have children, and comparing the ages their children met milestones, alongside reading the Development Matters guidance (Early Education, 2012) will give you a broader picture of when stages of physical development are most likely to occur. Remember that you do not need expensive resources to support physical development; practitioners are the most valuable resource in aiding children's learning, as long as they acquire a good understanding of children's needs through regular observations and assessments, and engage in child-initiated play.

Further reading

Levels 4 & 5

Albon, D. and Mukherji, P. (2008) *Food and Health in Early Childhood*. London: Sage. This book looks at the factors that affect the health of very young children, looking in more depth at the topics covered in this chapter.

Bilton, H. (2010) *Outdoor Play in the Early Years*. London: David Fulton Publishers. This book offers comprehensive advice for practitioners to analyse, review and improve their outdoor provision, including helping children to manage risk taking in their play, and will support your understanding of outdoor play.

Ouvry, M. (2003) *Exercising Muscles and Minds: Outdoor Play and the Early Years Curriculum*. London: National Children's Bureau. Another useful book which will support your understanding of planning for outdoor learning for 3–5-year-olds.

Level 6

Hodgeman, L. (2011) *Enabling Environments in the Early Years: Making Provision for High Quality and Challenging Learning Experiences in Early Years Settings*. London: MA Education Ltd. This book will help you to reflect on your provision, enabling you to consider ways you can support children safely in their self-initiated play, with a particular focus on outside areas.

Lindon, J. (2012) *Understanding Child Development: 0–8 Years (Linking Theory and Practice)* (3rd edition). Abingdon: Hodder Education. This book makes links between theory and practice, highlighting research and ideas to support secure learning and holistic care for young children.

Wilson, R. (2012) *Nature and Young Children: Encouraging Creative Play and Learning in Natural Environments* (2nd edition). Abingdon: Routledge. This book offers practical advice and guidance on how to maximise the use of outdoor space whilst promoting environmentally friendly learning opportunities. It will enhance your understanding of how to use outdoor space to develop creative play opportunities.

References

Albon, D. and Mukherji, P. (2008) *Food and Health in Early Childhood*. London: Sage.

Bertram, T. and Pascal, C. (2006) Introducing Child Development, in Bruce, T. (ed.), *Early Childhood: A Guide for Students*. London: Sage.

Blackmore, S.J. (10 August 2007) *Why it is never too late to grow. Times Educational Supplement*, Available at: www.tes.co.uk/article.aspx?storycode=2419075 (Accessed 4th May 2012).

Department for Education (DfE) (2012) *Statutory Framework for the Early Years Foundation Stage*. Nottingham: DfE Publications.

DeVries, R. (2006) 'Games with rules', in D.P. Fromberg and D. Bergen (eds), *Play from Birth to Twelve,* (2nd edition). Abingdon: Routledge.

Doherty, J. and Hughes, M. (2009) *Child Development: Theory and Practice 0–11*. Harlow, Essex: Pearson Education Ltd.

Dowling, M. (2010) *Young Children's Personal, Social and Emotional Development*. London: Sage.

Early Education (2012) *Development Matters in the Early Years Foundation Stage*. Available at: http://www.foundationyears.org.uk/wp-content/uploads/2012/03/Development-Matters-FINAL-PRINT-AMENDED.pdf

Fabian, H. and Mould, C. (2009) *Development and Learning for Very Young Children*. London: Sage.

Gallahue, D.L. and Ozmun, J. (2005) *Understanding Motor Development: Infants, Children, Adolescents and Adults* (6th edition). Boston: McGraw-Hill.

Greenland, P. (2006) 'Physical development', in T. Bruce (ed.), *Early Childhood*. London: Sage.

Howard, J. (2010) 'Making the most of play in the early years: The importance of children's perceptions', in P. Broadhead, J. Howard and E. Wood (eds), *Play and Learning in the Early Years*. London: Sage.

Hughes, A. (2006) *Developing Play for Under Threes*. London: David Fulton Publishers.

Johnson, J. and Nahmad-Williams, L. (2009) *Early Childhood Studies*. Harlow, Essex: Pearson Education Limited.

Karpov, Y.V. (2005) *The Neo-Vygotskian Approach to Child Development*. Cambridge: Cambridge University Press.

Keenan, T. and Evans, S. (2009) *An Introduction to Child Development*. London: Sage.

Lillard, A.S. (2005) *Montessori: The Science Behind the Genius*. New York: Oxford University Press.

Macintyre, C. (2012) *Understanding Babies and Young Children from Conception to Three*. London: Routledge.

May, P. (2011) *Child Development in Practice: Responsive Teaching and Learning from Birth to Five*. London: David Fulton Publishers.

Meggitt, C. (2012) *Child Development: An Illustrated Guide*. Harlow, Essex: Pearson Publications.

Riddall-Leech, S. (2009) *Heuristic Play: Play in the EYFS*. London: Practical Preschool Books.

Watson, J.B. (1928) *Psychological Care of Infant and Child*. New York: Norton.

White, P.R. (2006) *CLAYtherapy: The Clinical Application of Clay with Children*. New York: Guilford Press.

Whitebread, D. (2012) *Development Psychology and Early Childhood Education*. London: Sage.

Winkley, D. (2004) 'Grey matters: Current neurological research and its implications for educators', seminar: www.keele.ac.uk/depts/ed/kisnet/interviews/winkley.htm in C. Macintyre (2012) *Understanding Babies and Young Children from Conception to Three*. London: Routledge.

Woodfield, L. (2004) *Physical Development in the Early Years*. London: Continuum International Publishing Group.

19

Specific Areas of Development and Learning (Mathematics, Understanding of the World, Expressive Arts and Design)

Ros Garrick

This chapter will:

- Explain the rationale for the age-related distinction between prime and specific areas of development and learning, while acknowledging the holistic nature of early learning
- Present theories of learning that support an understanding of children's development in the specific areas and in related dispositions
- Enable reflection on case-study examples of children engaged in play and activities that support developing stores of knowledge and dispositions within the specific areas.

Prime and specific areas

The revised framework for the Early Years Foundation Stage (EYFS) (DfE, 2012) for children from birth to 5 years in England identifies, for the first time, a set of prime areas of learning and development, and a set of specific areas. It explains that the prime areas, identified as communication and language, physical development, and personal, social and emotional development, underpin young children's capacity to learn, and are essential if children are to thrive, make positive relationships and engage with learning. The EYFS requires early childhood practitioners working with the youngest children to focus strongly on these areas, increasing their focus on specific areas only as children gain confidence and skills in the prime areas. Specific areas, building on the prime areas, offer meaningful contexts for further learning and include skills children will need for successful participation in society. The specific areas of mathematics, understanding the world, and expressive arts and design are the focus of this chapter. A fourth specific area, literacy, is considered elsewhere in the book, alongside communication and ICT. It is important to note that, while Development Matters (Early Education, 2012), the guidance supporting the EYFS framework, highlights the distinction between prime and specific areas, it also explains that all areas of learning and development are interconnected.

While there are valid arguments for distinguishing prime and specific areas, you are encouraged to ask critical questions about this distinction throughout the chapter, drawing on your own experience and findings from research. For example, you may have family and/or professional experience of caring for babies, who are precocious communicators through early smiles and vocalisations (Whitebread, 2012). Additionally, you may know babies who are highly motivated to practise new physical skills, for example rolling over and learning to crawl (Keenan and Evans, 2009), and babies who build close relationships with carers and other family members from birth (Whitebread, 2012). These are all examples of early development and learning in the prime areas. This chapter, however, will explain how babies also show precocious abilities in the specific areas. For example, babies respond to music prenatally (Shore and Strasser, 2006) and are sensitive to differences in displays of small sets of objects from the first months of life (Sarama and Clements, 2008). Therefore, in examining how practitioners can support children's development and learning in the specific areas, this chapter will acknowledge the early appearing abilities and interests of babies and toddlers, as well as those of young children.

Holistic learning

While focusing on play and activities that support the specific areas of learning and development, you are also encouraged to keep in mind the holistic nature of young children's learning. As a first example, consider the case study below.

CASE STUDY

Amina, Dale and Simone are 4-year-olds, attending Butterflies Nursery. They had been very excited the previous afternoon because Simone's father, Ed, visited the

(Continued)

(Continued)

group with his racing bike, special clothes and equipment. The children listened intently to Ed and asked many questions. Simone, who knew lots about her father's favourite sport, even answered some questions on his behalf. She also asked her own questions about how the brakes worked when he was going fast downhill.

Today the children are enjoying painting pictures of bicycle wheels of different sizes, brought in by Emma, a practitioner. Before painting, they looked at the wheels together, talking with Emma about the shapes and patterns they could see. Children noted the wheels' circular rims and the straight spikes, radiating out from the central hubs. After talking, the children settled down to their paintings. Simone worked carefully, painting the rim, the hub and then the spokes. She enjoyed choosing her favourite colours. Looking at the nearly completed picture, Simone decided to add some 'spotty patterns for dad'.

Reflect on the play provision and different activities you provide for children during one session. Select an area of provision or activity that provides opportunities for development and learning in at least one prime area and aspects of two or more specific areas. The case study above shows the interrelated nature of mathematics with the expressive arts and design. Can you identify other commonly related areas of learning and development?

In the case study above, Simone's learning relates to several prime and specific areas of learning and development. Both activities build on and extend her communication and language skills (prime area) and, while painting, she is developing the physical skills of handling a brush and paint (prime area). At the same time, Simone is exploring and using paint as a medium, and she is being imaginative in representing the wheel. These are two aspects of expressive arts and design (specific area). Simone is also developing knowledge and understanding of shape, space and measures, for example developing mathematical language relating to shape, size and pattern (specific area). This exemplifies the interconnected nature of young children's learning (Early Education, 2012).

Mathematics

Issues for mathematics teaching and learning

Simone and her friends in the case study above enjoyed developing mathematics knowledge and skills in the context of creative activities and they were confident in using new mathematical language, for example the words 'centre' and 'pattern'. A team of European researchers is currently investigating creative approaches to mathematics and science teaching in early childhood settings, with the expectation that linking mathematics and creativity will support positive dispositions for mathematics learning (Creative Little Scientists, 2012). This is important because many adults have negative memories of school maths teaching and low self-esteem in this area. The Williams Review of mathematics teaching in early years settings and primary schools notes that 'the United Kingdom is still one of the few advanced nations where it is socially acceptable – fashionable even – to profess an inability to cope with the subject' (2008: 3). It raises particular concerns about the confidence and subject knowledge of early years practitioners to support young children's mathematical development.

Related to this relative lack of practitioner confidence in mathematics, the longitudinal study of English pre-schools, Effective Provision of Pre-school Education (EPPE) (Sylva, 2010), evaluates learning environments for mathematics as of lower quality generally than environments for other areas, such as literacy. Additionally, the Millennium Cohort Study (Hansen, 2010) identifies wide differences in outcomes for children's mathematical development at age 5, relating to aspects of disadvantage, such as low income. Therefore, if all young children are to achieve their potential and develop positive dispositions for learning in mathematics, this area of learning will require particular attention. Fortunately, effective teaching and learning in mathematics builds on approaches that are very familiar to early years practitioners, as explained below.

Theories of mathematical development and learning

To best support young children, it is important to understand the key characteristics of mathematical development and learning. Reviewing theoretical accounts of learning pathways, Sarama and Clements (2009) highlight three main frameworks:

- Empiricism
- (Neo)nativism
- Interactionalism.

These frameworks link to longstanding debates about the respective importance of nature and nurture in children's learning. Traditional empiricist accounts of learning start from a view of young children as 'blank slates' who learn by repeated experience or by direct transmission in formal teaching contexts. In contrast, nativist theories emphasise how children's inborn capabilities develop very early in life or are easy to learn. Nativists argue that such early appearing abilities are evident across cultures and underpin future learning. An example is the early sensitivity of babies to the numerosity of displays of very small sets of objects, identified in habituation experiments with babies of just a few weeks (Sarama and Clements, 2009). The third framework, interactionalism, validates both empiricist and nativist theories, recognising the interacting contributions of both nature and nurture to learning. Building on more recent research in mathematics and extending the theories above, Sarama and Clements (2009) propose a fourth theoretical framework, 'hierarchic interactionalism'. This links well to the identified 'characteristics of effective teaching and learning' (DfE, 2012: 6) in the EYFS framework. The section below summarises key elements of this theoretical account of children's mathematical learning and development.

Developmental progressions

Sarama and Clements's (2009) first claim is that there are developmental progressions in levels of mathematical thinking within particular cultures. A second claim is that progressions in mathematical thinking relate to specialised domains of mathematics, such as counting or shape. Both claims are reflected in Development Matters (Early Education, 2012). The authors also identify important interactions between domains, such as between children's levels of thinking about counting and measurement. For example, children need relevant counting skills and a conceptual knowledge of number to measure the length of the nursery garden by counting strides.

Incremental learning

Sarama and Clements's (2009) third claim is that new levels of understanding and skills in any domain build incrementally on existing concepts and processes. This makes it important to assess children's levels of thinking in number in order to plan for small steps in their learning, an approach reflected in the EYFS (DfE, 2012) focus on formative assessment. For example, children who are confident in reciting the number sequence to five and can recognise small sets of objects to three will enjoy learning to count small sets of objects to five. However, if practitioners disregard incremental learning, children are likely to become anxious in ways that take up memory space, interfering with mathematics learning (Gifford, 2008).

Sensory-concrete to generalisations and abstraction

Sarama and Clements's (2009) fourth claim is that children's progression is often from sensory-concrete understanding to more explicit, verbally-based generalisations or abstractions. For example, a toddler might point to their eyes or ears when asked to show two, evidencing a sensory-concrete understanding of two. Later the child will develop a more generalised and verbal understanding, for example, selecting a set of buttons with two holes from a button box and explaining what they have done. Development Matters (Early Education, 2012) charts progressions of this kind.

Concepts, skills and dispositions

Sarama and Clements (2009) make a fifth claim, which is that there is an interaction between the development of mathematical concepts and skills, for example the concept of number and the skills of counting. At the same time, successful learning depends on the development of positive dispositions. Development Matters (Early Education, 2012: 5) similarly highlights dispositions for learning under the heading 'active learning – motivation', one of three characteristics of effective learning.

Initial bootstrapping

The final claim outlined here is that initial bootstrapping is important. Bootstrapping refers to the pre-mathematical and general cognitive processes, present at birth or very soon after birth, guiding mathematical development across cultures. An example is babies' early sensitivity to small numbers, outlined above.

Sarama and Clements's (2009) theory of 'hierarchic interactionalism' has informed the development of learning trajectories within particular domains of mathematics. A learning trajectory involves a learning goal or important cluster of concepts and skills that contribute to future learning; a developmental progression or pathway of learning; and activities that match to increasing levels of thinking on the pathway. Development Matters (Early Education, 2012) sets out learning trajectories for two main aspects of mathematics. However, these are not as detailed or clearly sequenced as trajectories in US guidance materials (Sarama and Clements, 2009).

Numbers and counting

The EYFS framework (DfE, 2012) identifies two domains of mathematics for young children, firstly, number and secondly, space, shape and measures. The Early Learning Goal for mathematics sets the expectation that children will develop confidence with numbers up to 20 by the end of the EYFS. This includes counting forwards and backwards, ordering numbers, knowing one more and one less, and solving simple problems. While this is a challenging goal for some children, in particular summer born children who are just five at the end of the EYFS, other children will enjoy counting and recognising patterns in the number system to 100.

The case study below encourages you to consider how best to support the learning trajectory of a 4-year-old in the area of number.

CASE STUDY

Ricky is 4 years old and has just started nursery. His mother, Diana, was reluctant to take him initially because he is the youngest of her five children and she knew that she would miss him when he started school. Ricky has settled happily, making good friends, and he particularly enjoys active outdoor play, construction play, singing and stories. Generally, Ricky is making good progress across areas of development and learning. In mathematics, he can recognise and name small sets of one, two and three objects without counting, a competency known as subitising. However, he shows little interest in numbers beyond three or in counting. Diana disliked maths at school and is concerned that she lacks the skills to help her own children, although wanting to work with practitioners to help Ricky avoid problems like her own.

Reflect on how you advise parents who are keen to support their children's early development of number concepts and skills, including parents of children with special educational needs (SEN) or at risk of SEN. Consider Ricky's case and identify the next stage of his learning trajectory, taking account of his existing skills in subitising. What activities could Diana undertake with Ricky at home to support progression? In what ways could Diana strengthen Ricky's dispositions for learning about number, drawing on his interests? The journal task below may help you to develop your ideas further. Also, see the suggestions for further reading to identify potential activities.

Journal Task

Notari-Syverson, A. and Sadler, F.H. (2008) 'Math is for everyone: Strategies for supporting early mathematical competencies in young children', *Young Exceptional Children*, 11(3): 2–16.

This American article examines the content of a high quality mathematics curriculum for young children and effective teaching strategies for children with SEN. It is relevant to working with a wider range of children.

Levels 4 & 5

1. Identify similarities and differences between the five components of mathematics in the American curriculum and the components of mathematics in the English EYFS framework (birth to five years). Are the differences significant for children's learning and development in mathematics?

2. Look at the examples of intentional teaching strategies for teaching early mathematical concepts and identify a set of strategies to use during the everyday routines of your setting to teach early number concepts and skills. Work systematically to identify strategies from children's arrival time through to the end of the session or day. Ensure that planned approaches are enjoyable and build confidence.

Level 6

Review the key competencies relating to numbers and operations (Table 1 in the article). Children develop these competencies slowly over time before they achieve mastery in counting objects to 20. Identify a child at an early stage and a child at an advanced stage of counting and invite them to participate in counting during play and informal activities over several days. Assess both children in relation to Table 1 competencies. Evaluate this set of competencies in terms of its value in extending your knowledge and understanding of children's levels of thinking in the area of number.

To download this task as well as other useful online resources please visit: **www.sagepub.co.uk/mukherji**

Shape, space and measures

The second aspect of mathematics within the EYFS framework (DfE, 2012: 12) is shape, space and measures. Guidance highlights the importance of mathematical talk about everyday objects and shapes, and the need for practitioners to support children's developing concepts of 'size, weight, capacity, position, distance, time and money', as well as pattern. This aspect of mathematics interconnects in multiple ways with the prime areas of physical development and language development. For example, babies delight in early explorations of the physical properties, including shape, size and weight, of toys and everyday objects. They then learn how to stretch to reach objects, roll over, crawl and walk, exploring new spaces and aspects of space (Forbes, 2004). Caregivers often talk informally about the salient aspects of babies' and toddlers' experiences, using mathematical language such as *big*, *little*, *round*, *far*, *in* and *on*.

Schema

Chris Athey (2007), a researcher and educationalist, highlights the importance of enabling environments and adult talk for early mathematical development. Athey drew on the ideas of Piaget (1896–1980), a Swiss scientist who developed influential theories of child development, informed by close observation of his own three children as babies and toddlers. Piaget's theory highlights the concept of schema, beginning with early sensori-motor behaviours. He identifies tracking and gazing at objects as the first schemas to develop in the baby's early exploration of the physical world (Gray and MacBlain, 2012), followed by schema such as grasping, reaching and kicking. On one occasion, Piaget (1936, in Smith,

2010) observed his daughter, aged four months, explore kicking movements in her cot. Having excitedly discovered that she could strike a doll, held over the cot by her father, she did this repeatedly. This repetition of patterns of behaviours is characteristic of the early schemas that Athey (2007) went on to identify in children's play at nursery.

Athey (2007) led the Froebel Early Education Project with children up to 5 years. Its aim was to identify developments in children's thinking as well as appropriate curriculum content to enrich and extend thinking, particularly for disadvantaged children at risk of SEN. A further aim was to work in partnership with disadvantaged parents to support children's development. Athey (2007) identified a range of early appearing graphic and action schemas, important for children's developing ideas about shape, space and measures. Table 19.1 identifies key aspects of this strand of mathematics, matched to relevant schema. The table also provides examples of play and appropriate practitioner language.

Table 19.1 Schema supporting aspects of shape, space and measures

Aspects of shape, space and measures	Schema	Activity	Practitioner language
Size	Going round a boundary (action schema)	Eleni (2:10) and Na Wei (3:1) played a chasing game, running around large and small tyres on the grass.	"You're running around the big tyre."
Weight	Containing (action schema)	Tom (2:6) filled a shopping bag with home corner food and took it outside.	"That bag has lots of food in it. It looks heavy."
Capacity	Containing (action schema)	Jamal (1:11) was digging in the sandpit, filling his bucket with sand.	"Your red bucket is full. It holds lots of sand."
Position	Going over, under and on top of (action schema)	Fay (3:7), building a wide tower with unit blocks, stretched up tall to place the two final blocks on top.	"I can see you putting those last two blocks on top. Look they are next to each other."
Distance	Dynamic vertical (action schema)	Ahmed (3:4) climbed to the top of the climbing frame and dropped his toy parachute.	"Your parachute fell a long way, from high up, all the way to the ground."
Pattern	Horizontal and vertical lines (graphic schema)	Fabi (4:1) played with pegs and a pegboard, selecting red pegs and making parallel lines of pegs.	"Look, you are making red lines; one, two and almost three lines of pegs."

Athey (2007) advises that adults provide a running commentary on children's schematic behaviours to support progression from sensori-motor behaviour to the representation of ideas in language. Representation, means making one thing stand for another, and is an important development in young children's thinking. From about 2 years, children use an increasing range of ways to represent their experiences, for example through language, graphic representation (drawing) and role play.

Learning about space, shape and measures begins with early play and exploration, supported by the verbal commentary of adults or older peers. Children first build implicit mathematical knowledge and understanding, and this provides a foundation for the development of more explicit knowledge, for example, knowledge of shape names, the features of shapes and the relationships between shapes.

Reflection

Reflect on the areas of play provision in an early childhood setting that you know. Consider which areas offer children good opportunities to enact the following action schema.

- Going over, under and on top
- Containing
- Dynamic horizontal and vertical lines
- Going round a boundary

Focusing on these areas, identify additional resources to extend opportunities for children to enact particular schema. How could you help children to represent their sensori-motor experiences?

Heuristic play

It is particularly important to support and extend schema-based play for children under 4 as well as slightly older children with SEN. We sometimes offer the youngest children scaled down versions of typical provision for 3–5-year-olds. This can result in children appearing to play without purpose, for example flitting between activities and tipping out baskets of resources. Elinor Goldschmied, a pioneering educationalist, developed a distinctive approach to schema-based play for younger children, including disadvantaged children at risk of SEN. Her heuristic play sessions for small groups use a range of natural, household and reclaimed objects and different kinds of receptacles. When this is working well, children's play appears calm and purposeful, with children often sustaining attention for extended periods.

Goldschmied's developed heuristic play for children from about 12 to 20 months. Twelve months is the age when many children start walking and particularly enjoy their new ability to transport objects from place to place. The period ends as children's interest in representational play develops, for example, when a child picks up a brick and makes *brmm brmm* noises, pretending it is a car. Hughes (2010) argues that heuristic play is most appropriate for this age group because the question 'What can I do with it?' shapes children's early play with objects. She reminds us of the artificiality of categorising play in terms of particular areas of learning and development. In fact, while heuristic play supports mathematics, it is also significant for other kinds of learning, particularly knowledge of the world.

Heuristic play has some distinctive features, which contrast with other kinds of play provision in terms of the approach taken to space, time, resources and the adult role.

Table19.2 The distinctive features of heuristic play sessions

Dimensions	Distinctive features of heuristic play
Space	• Play takes place in a dedicated space or small room, separate from continuous play provision.
Time	• Play takes place during a defined period and is distinct from periods of free-flow play.
	• A small group of children stays together for the full play session.
Resources	• Children play with collections of special resources, which are not part of the everyday play provision (15+ sets).
	• Collections of open-ended household materials, reclaimed materials and natural objects are used (50 objects per collection approx.).
	• Varied receptacles are included e.g. baskets, boxes, mug trees, tubes, cans.
	• There are few, if any, traditional toys.
Adult role	• Adults observe children's play attentively but do not interact actively with children during the session.

These features, which are set out in Table 19.2, support 'children's natural development and creativity' (Hughes, 2010: xiv).

Reflection

What resources would you provide for heuristic play with a group of six children, aged 12 to 20 months, to support children's informal knowledge and understanding of mathematics? Identify resources and receptacles to promote the following mathematical concepts:

- one, few and many
- big and little
- heavy and light
- long and short
- capacity (e.g. how much a container holds)
- hollow and solid shapes
- solid shapes that roll
- similarities and differences
- pattern.

Block play

Gura (1992) explains the long history of block play in early childhood education and argues that it has special affordances for young children's mathematical learning and development. She explains how Froebel (1782–1852), the first educator to develop a theory of play and learning, introduced blocks and other manipulatives into his programme. Having studied the natural sciences, he recognised recurring geometric forms in the natural world, mathematics and architecture, and this informed his structured set of geometric blocks, the Gifts, developed for play in his first kindergarten. The more open-ended blocks, used today, were influenced by two American educators, Patty Smith Hill, who introduced a range of large, open-ended play materials in the 1870s, and Caroline Pratt, who developed unit blocks. The mathematical proportions of unit blocks, based on multiples of two, contribute to young children's mathematical learning and their continuing use today. Community Playthings (2012) now produces high quality blocks in four sizes: traditional unit blocks and hollow blocks for children from age 3; mini-hollow blocks for use by children from age 2; and mini-unit blocks for children from age 1.

Sarama and Clements (2009) identify unit blocks as significant for young children's spatial thinking, in particular for spatial visualisation and imagery, highlighting the importance of ensuring girls have equal opportunities for such play. During free play with blocks, children develop an implicit understanding of the properties of different 3D shapes and the interrelationships between shapes. They use this knowledge for problem solving, for example working out how to build a set of enclosures to house small-world farm animals. Gura (1992) explains how use of precise mathematical language enables young children to develop mathematical thinking about space and geometric shapes. Adults can support mathematical learning through talk that enables children to make such thinking about space and shape explicit.

Understanding the world

Understanding the world is a broad area of learning and development within the EYFS (DfE, 2012), with three aspects: people and communities, the world and technology. Although this is identified as a specific area, it is important to note that understanding the world begins with babies' and toddlers' early physical explorations of the world and their social interactions with family members and other carers.

People and communities

CASE STUDY

Ning was just 3 and had attended a childminding setting since a baby, along with her older brother Jiang, aged 8. Today she was bringing photographs of her third birthday party to show everyone. Dorothy was keen to see the photos and asked if

(Continued)

(Continued)

Ning would like to choose one for her profile and one to put up on the special 'All About Me' boards in the playroom. Each child had a board to display pictures, certificates and other important information relating to family lives, special interests and achievements. Jiang also had a new photo to bring, one from a recent gymnastics competition where he had won a medal. Ning helped Dorothy choose where to put the new photo and told Dorothy about the party food, including some special cakes which she said were 'very delicious'. Not having seen these cakes before, Dorothy said she would ask Ning's parents for the recipe so they could make some for the other children.

Dorothy works closely with parents and supports children to talk about their lives and those of family members, encouraging them to appreciate similarities and differences between families, communities and traditions. She uses wallboard displays as a focus for talk and celebrations, highlighting similarities and differences between cultures. What other strategies could Dorothy use to encourage children to share information about the different aspects of their lives in families and communities?

The starting point for young children learning about people and communities is learning about themselves, their families, their peers and the lives of those who work with them. This learning is important because researchers have identified that children begin to form positive and negative views about similarities and difference by the age of 3 or 4 years (Robinson and Diaz, 2006). MacNaughton and Williams (2009) offer a range of strategies to use with young children to address such issues, highlighting the areas of race and culture, gender and disability.

Practitioners can also support the development of children's understanding of the social world and promote positive attitudes to difference through play provision, pictures books, songs and rhymes reflecting diversity in positive ways. This is important for all children but particularly for children in mono-cultural communities. The EPPE study (Sylva et al., 2006) reports findings on how different kinds of settings reflect aspects of diversity in positive ways, for example through planning for individual needs, race and gender equality. Using the Diversity item 'Race Equality' from the ECERS-E scale, researchers gave high scores where settings drew children's attention to 'books, pictures or dolls that show black and ethnic minority people in non-stereotypical roles and familiar situations' (Sylva et al., 2006: 79). Unfortunately, average scores for Diversity across settings were below an adequate level and below the scores for other aspects of the learning environment. These findings point to planning for diversity as an important development area for many settings.

The world

The EYFS focus on 'the world' (DfE, 2012) extends the notion of 'understanding the world' from the primarily social focus on people discussed above to a focus on 'places, objects, materials and living things' (DfE, 2012: 9). Just as young children show early appearing dispositions to engage with other people, they also show dispositions to explore objects through sensori-motor play. Many early appearing schema involve object play and tool use.

Treasure baskets

The section on mathematics introduced Goldschmied's work on heuristic play for toddlers. Goldschmied also developed treasure baskets as a special approach to play for babies from about five months, just as they begin sitting up and reaching for objects (Hughes, 2010). Treasure basket play has gained in popularity amongst practitioners working with babies in early childhood settings. A baby or small group of babies sit close to a large basket filled with carefully selected objects. Babies select their own objects for play and become absorbed in exploring the properties of each object and sometimes two together. Adults sit close by and observe, protecting the babies from unwanted distractions. The careful selection of objects is essential for health and safety but also to ensure a range of objects in terms of sensory qualities, enabling children to feel, taste and smell objects as well as make sounds. Exploration and early play with objects represents a powerful way in which young babies find out about the physical world (Smith, 2010).

Natural world play

As babies become mobile, they will be keen to explore natural materials and objects in other ways, particularly through play in a garden or on regular visits to parks or woods. Children are motivated to explore the natural world and living things from an early age, and find animals particularly fascinating (Wilson, 2012). Therefore, well-planned outdoor provision, including garden and wild life areas, are essential to the development of early scientific understanding and skills. Watts (2011) and Garrick (2006) provide practical ideas for developing outdoor areas to extend young children's opportunities to explore and gain understanding of this aspect of the world.

CASE STUDY

Summerfield Nursery is an inner-city unit for children from 2 to 4 years. Many children come from disadvantaged families and live in flats with no or limited opportunities for outdoor play. The school is relatively new and the outdoor area is

(Continued)

(Continued)

large, comprising grassy and tarmac areas which are not landscaped. Summerfield practitioners are keen to develop garden and woodland areas and hope to provide children with opportunities to observe and talk about similarities, differences and change in relation to plants, animals and the weather on a daily basis, across the changing seasons. A group of parents is keen to help and Josie, a practitioner, is a volunteer with a conservation organisation that often works with early childhood settings. The team have been applying for grants to develop the garden and have £2,000 to start developments.

Summerfield nursery practitioners aim to give the children the following opportunities within the first year of development of the nursery garden:

- To observe and talk about similarities and differences in small animals, living in different habitats
- To observe and talk about similarities, differences and change in relation to plants
- To observe similarities, differences and change in relation to a range of natural materials
- To observe similarities, differences and change in relation to the weather and season.

Identify a monthly timetable of actions to develop the garden so that the nursery practitioners meet their aims within the first year. What resources would you introduce to support children to make observations and talk about them?

Observation is a key scientific skill that develops from children's first sensory explorations of the physical world. As well as supporting observation, practitioners should plan to support children to represent and communicate their findings about the natural world, for example orally, with pictures or sculpture and by taking photographs (Garrick, 2006). Picture books and ICT resources are also valuable tools that practitioners can use to extend early observation skills and understanding of the natural world (Howes and Davies, 2010).

Technology

Technology has an ever-growing role in contemporary society and the technologies that children will use as adults are likely to be very different to those used today. Therefore, from the early twentieth century onwards, technology, closely linked with design and science, has become an important focus within the school curriculum (Saracho and Spodek, 2008). Young children begin to build knowledge and understanding of technology from an early age, for example from their experience with action toys, everyday domestic equipment and specific ICT equipment. Families often give babies and toddlers toys and books with flaps and other parts that move and/or make sounds. Additionally, children experience at least some of the following domestic appliances: toasters, torches, ovens, microwaves, hair dryers, cameras and washing machines. They are also likely to encounter computers, laptops, smart phones and/or iPads. As they go out into the local community young children will also experience technology in the form of traffic lights, a bank 'hole in the wall' and large machines on building sites or at road works. Technology is found everywhere in the world of young children and often generates intense interest.

Some children will be supported by interested adults who talk with them and explain what is happening as equipment is used. For example, a parent with time may help a 3-year-old to select the setting for washing clothes. However, parents may be in a rush or may feel that play with toys is a more 'educational' way for children to spend their time. There is also a danger that early childhood practitioners focus exclusively on learning through play and neglect to involve children in everyday experiences that include technology, for example taking digital photographs for children's profiles. Therefore, a starting point for enhancing children's understanding of technology is to identify opportunities of this kind in the setting and plan to utilise them.

Reflection

Review the ways that adults with different roles in your setting use technology during their working day. Which activities currently include children? Which activities have potential for children's participation? Plan a programme of activities that enable all children to have opportunities to engage with technology within the setting.

Expressive arts and design

Music and dance

CASE STUDY

Nyah, Isabelle and Jon, all aged 5, had just come in from an umbrella walk around the Foundation Unit playground and they were excited by the heavy rain, pounding on the windows. Trying to decide what to do next, the children noticed

(Continued)

(Continued)

new instruments on the music table. 'I know', said Jon, 'we can make a rain song. Like the rain on our umbrellas'. 'And on the windows', said Nyah. The children eagerly chose instruments. 'This is good for rain', said Nyah, picking up the red maracas. Isabelle took the stripy claterpiller, while Jon took the wooden guiro. They played their instruments vigorously until Isabelle told them to stop. 'You're giving me a headache. You've got to make it light rain like Mrs Khan showed us in music. Start it quiet and very slow'. The children followed Isabelle's lead, alternating soft and loud sounds, sometimes at a steady beat and sometimes very fast. They also took it in turns to do a fast rain dance to music, using hands and feet to represent the rain.

The expressive arts and design area within the EYFS framework (DfE, 2012) has two aspects: the first is 'exploring and using media and materials', and the second is 'being imaginative'. Music and sound-makers are important examples of the media and materials that interest young children who regularly incorporate musical elements into their play, for example spontaneously singing, dancing and exploring sounds (Niland, 2009). In the case study, the children enjoyed exploring the qualities of the sounds made by their instruments, for example, exploring the differences between soft and loud sounds, and between slow and fast tempos. They were also imaginative in terms of choosing instruments to sound like rain and moving expressively to represent the rain.

While babies do not have this ability to represent ideas imaginatively through creative media, there is evidence of very early sensitivity to the expressive arts. For example, Keenan and Evans (2009) cite evidence of newborn babies' sensitivity to music, seen in changed patterns of sucking, and they note babies' abilities to discriminate musical sounds by two months of age. In addition, babies and toddlers enjoy music from early on, seen in the prevalence of lullabies across cultures, sung to help babies relax and sleep. Babies also enjoy nursery rhymes and action rhymes, which are important musically but also for early language development (Forbes, 2004). Anning and Edwards (2006) describe a successful musical project, including children of under 2, in an inner-city pre-school. Practitioners worked with families in a multi-ethnic community, learning about the rich musical traditions of families and producing a multilingual nursery songbook. While recognising the value of musical culture in its own right, the practitioners were also keen to realise the mathematical potential of musical play for young children, for example, acting out number songs and rhymes, and clapping to musical patterns.

Journal Task

Niland, A. (2009) 'The power of musical play: The value of play-based, child-centered curriculum in early childhood music education', *General Music Today*, 21 April. doi: 10.1177/1048371309335625.

The American article looks at child-centred musical play as a medium to support young children in exploring the world, while developing musical skills and concepts.

Levels 4 & 5

1. Most theorists and educators work from a definition of play that sees it as freely chosen, sustained by intrinsic motivation and enjoyable; they emphasise the process of playing rather than particular outcomes. Identify the range of forms of musical play that researchers have identified.
2. On-going assessment, known as formative assessment, is a requirement of the EYFS framework (DfE, 2012), undertaken, for example, through observation and listening. Explain how practitioners can use observation and listening to support their plans for children's musical learning and development.

Level 6

There is often a tension between a focus on skills and creativity in arts education. An adult-led curriculum tends to start from planning for skills development, while an emergent and play-based curriculum focuses on creativity. Compare books and journals for practitioners focused on the visual arts and those focused on musical education. Is there a difference in approach? Drawing on this chapter and Chapter 7 on play, explain the limitations of a skills-based approach to early music education.

To download this task as well as other useful online resources please visit:
www.sagepub.co.uk/mukherji

Role play

CASE STUDY

Noah and Karid, aged 4, had enjoyed a story about Noah's Ark told by their nursery teacher. Noah was excited to hear a story about someone with his own name. 'I have to be Noah' he said, 'so you'll have to be my wife'. Karid agreed, saying, 'OK, if I can choose which animals to take on the ark. We can choose children to pretend to be animals'. The two boys rushed outside to find the large hollow blocks, with tyres and crates nearby, and set to work to build their ark. Carla, their key worker, was outdoors

(Continued)

(Continued)

and encouraged them to fetch the picture book to look at details of the ark to help in their construction. When it was nearly finished, they decided they needed beds for the animals as well as food to eat on the ark. They rushed off to the woodland area with a bucket and began collecting twigs, grasses and leaves for food.

Review the opportunities for role play in your setting. What spaces and resources do you provide to support young children in developing their own ideas for role play?

Many children enjoy role play, identified as an aspect of 'being imaginative' within the 'expressive arts and design' area (Early Education, 2012). Garrick et al. (2010), reporting a study of 3–5-year-olds' experiences of the EYFS, explain that role play, labelled as 'pretend' by children, was the kind of play that children wanted to talk about most. Developmental psychologists have also been keen to investigate pretend play. Whitebread (2012), for example, identifies pretence/socio-dramatic play as one of five main types of play, the others being, physical play, play with objects, symbolic play, and games with rules. He explains how pretence/socio-dramatic play begins in the second year of life, usually as solitary play, as young children begin to make one object stand for another, for example pretending a block is a biscuit to eat. Most children soon begin to enjoy opportunities for dressing up and taking on different roles, for example animal, family, work and superhero roles. By 4 or 5 years of age, many children enjoy socio-dramatic play with peers and their play develops a narrative structure. Noah and Karid, in the case study above, were experienced in this kind of play and, like many children, often combined imaginative play with objects and role play. Flexible resources, for example the hollow blocks and natural materials used by the two boys, are particularly important for children's sustained engagement in play matched to their wide-ranging interests (Broadhead and Burt, 2012).

Smith (2010) summarises a range of recent evidence on the functions of pretence/socio-dramatic play for young children's learning and development. He explains that it supports children's increasingly complex narrative skills, their cognitive and language development, early literacy skills, and theory of mind development. Whitebread's (2012) review adds further evidence of the value of pretend in supporting young children's social and emotional learning, including emotional self-regulation. This is clearly a case where areas of learning and development are interrelated, with role-play supporting learning in a range of areas.

Visual arts

The infant-toddler centres and pre-schools of Reggio Emilia, a city in northern Italy, emphasise high quality services for children and families, and there is a strong tradition of education in the expressive arts and design. Children from birth to 6 years have rich opportunities to explore what is described as 'the hundred languages of childhood', with each language representing a particular media for exploration and meaning making. Early childhood centres have a professional artist, who supports the expressive arts, working alongside practitioners. Brunton and Thornton (2010) explain how, alongside music and movement play, the centres emphasise children's exploration of visual media and the representation of experience through drawing, painting and a range of 3D media, including clay. The visually striking quality of early years settings also enhances visual education, with careful attention given to the features of visibility, flexibility, light and shadow, reflection and multisensory spaces. Images of the Diana Pre-school and the Loris Malaguzzi Infants School in Reggio Emilia exemplify these features (Imagine Inspirational School Design, 2010). The visual aspect of the expressive arts is considered next, beginning with a consideration of babies' very early appearing visual abilities.

Visual perception in babies

As well as noting early sensitivity to musical sounds, Keenan and Evans (2009) highlight babies' early sensitivity to colour and pattern. The extent to which perceptual abilities are learnt or innate is not entirely clear. However, some researchers argue that babies discriminate colours across the spectrum by two months and that, by four months, they perceive colours in the same way as adults. Keenan and Evans (2009) cite additional evidence that newborn babies like looking at patterned stimuli rather than plain ones, and explain that, as babies grow older, they enjoy increasingly complex visual patterns, including patterns with high contrasts. Very young babies respond best to large-scale patterns, for example large, black and white checkerboard patterns, but soon begin to distinguish smaller-scale patterned displays. Some settings have responded to research by devising black and white areas and rooms full of high contrast patterns. Young babies may enjoy such high contrast displays but they are also highly responsive to human faces and moving objects. Therefore, providing varied visual experiences of people, places and objects indoors and outdoors seems important to stimulate babies visually. This can include high contrast, patterned displays, moving objects such as mobiles, and mirrored surfaces.

Mark making and drawing

As babies' and toddlers' fine and gross motor skills develop, young children often show an early interest in making marks with a range of materials. Forbes (2004) argues that early creative and movement experiences are interlinked, for example as children explore the sensory nature of messy play with materials such as gloop. She also suggests that practitioners working with babies and toddlers prioritise creative play with sensory and natural materials such as wet leaves and puddles, rather than providing scaled down versions of art activities for older children.

Athey (2007) documents children's mark making development from about 2 years as they begin to explore a range of action schema with, for example, pens, pencils and paints. She documents how the children gradually developed their use of lines to represent important experiences in their lives, including people, animals, vehicles and places. Practitioners supported children to develop this 'language of lines' by offering an enrichment programme of visits to places of interest. This was particularly important because the project worked with children from disadvantaged families where the opportunities for such experiences were limited.

Journal Task

Anning, A. (2003) 'Pathways to the graphicacy club: The crossroad of home and pre-school', *Journal of Early Childhood Literacy*, 3(1): 5–35.

This UK article takes a socio-cultural perspective on seven young children's experiences as they make the transition from enjoying personal and social drawing at home to narrower versions of literacies at pre-school and school, where visual literacy is undervalued.

Levels 4 & 5

1. Outline the different forms of representation that young children combine with their drawings before formal schooling. Identify some examples of multi-modal communication from your own observations of young children.
2. What does Anning mean by 'functional graphical behaviours'? What examples of this do young children experience in their homes before starting pre-school and school?

Level 6

What is meant by taking a socio-cultural perspective on children's graphic representations and how does this differ from a developmental perspective? What are the implications of a socio-cultural approach for the ways in which practitioners work with young children to support their meaning-making and communication through the visual arts?

To download this task as well as other useful online resources please visit:
www.sagepub.co.uk/mukherji

This section has considered young children's exploration of a range of media and forms of representations within the expressive arts and design. These motivating experiences lay the foundations for being imaginative, as children begin to represent their experiences in particular media, often in multi-modal ways. Finally, it is important to remember that the outdoors can provide a particularly stimulating context for the expressive arts and design. For example, outdoor spaces allow for exploration of expressive media on a much larger scale than indoors. White (2008) provides detailed guidance on a wide range of media to explore outdoors, including chalk drawing on paving stones, weaving on a wire mesh fence, dancing with ribbon sticks and exploring sounds on kitchen utensils strung between posts.

Summary

This chapter has explained the EYFS rationale for the age-related distinction between prime areas and specific areas of development and learning, while also highlighting the holistic nature of early learning. It has presented theories of learning that support understanding of children's development in the specific areas of mathematics, understanding of the world, and the expressive arts and design. Throughout, it has focused on the importance of supporting children's positive dispositions for learning. Finally, the chapter has introduced case study examples of children engaged in play and activities that can support developing understanding, skills and dispositions within the specific areas.

Further reading

Levels 4 & 5

Brunton, L. and Thornton, P. (2007) *Bringing the Reggio Approach to Your Early Years Practice*. Abingdon, Oxon: Routledge. Introducing the educational work of infant-toddler centres and pre-schools in Reggio Emilia, the authors bring an important perspective to thinking about provision for the expressive arts and design in UK settings.

Hughes, A. (2010) *Developing Play for the Under 3s: The Treasure Basket and Heuristic Play* (2nd edition). London: Routledge. This interesting and practical book provides a clear rationale for the use of treasure baskets and heuristic play with children from birth to 3.

Meade, A. and Cubey, P. (2008) *Thinking Children: Learning about Schemas*. Maidenhead, Berkshire: McGraw-Hill/The Open University. This book is a very useful introduction to the schemas of young children. It provides interesting case study examples of how practitioners can support schema learning.

White, J. (2008) *Playing and Learning Outdoors: Making Provision for High-quality Experiences in the Outdoor Environment*. London and New York: Routledge.

Level 6

Clements, D. and Sarama, J. (2009) *Learning and Teaching Early Math: The Learning Trajectories Approach*. London and New York: Routledge. This book usefully identifies learning trajectories for each area of early mathematics. Each trajectory is informed by research and includes a mathematical goal, steps in a developmental pathway, and motivating activities to support children's development.

References

Anning, A. and Edwards, A. (2006) *Promoting Children's Learning from Birth to Five: Developing the New Early Years Professional* (2nd edition). Maidenhead, Berkshire: McGraw-Hill/The Open University.

Athey, C. (2007) *Extending Thought in Young Children* (2nd edition). London: Paul Chapman.

Broadhead, P. and Burt, A. (2012) *Understanding Young Children's Learning Through Play*. Abingdon, Oxon: Routledge.

Brunton, L. and Thornton, P. (2007) *Bringing the Reggio Approach to Your Early Years Practice*. Abingdon, Oxon: Routledge.

Clements, D. and Sarama, J. (2009) *Learning and Teaching Early Math: The Learning Trajectories Approach*. New York and London: Routledge.

Community Playthings (2012) Blockplay [online] http://www.communityplaythings.co.uk/products/block-play (accessed 13 October 2012).

Creative Little Scientists (2012) [online] http://www.creative-little-scientists.eu/node/57 (accessed 6 October 2012).

Department for Education (DfE) (2012) *Statutory Framework for the Early Years Foundation Stage: Setting the Standards for Learning, Development and Care for Children from Birth to Five*. London: DfE. https://www.education.gov.uk/publications/standard/AllPublications/Page1/DFE-00023-2012 (accessed 3 June 2012).

Early Education (2012) *Development Matters in the Early Years Foundation Stage (EYFS)*. http://earlyeducation.org.uk/sites/default/files/Development%20Matters%20FINAL%20PRINT%20AMENDED.pdf (accessed 3 June 2012).

Forbes, R. (2004) *Beginning to Play*. Maidenhead, Berkshire: McGraw-Hill/The Open University.

Garrick, R. (2006) *Minibests and More: Young Children Investigating the Natural World*. London: Early Education.

Garrick, R., Bath, C., Dunn, K., Maconochie, H., Willis, B. and Wolstenholme, C. (2010) *Children's Experiences of the Early Years Foundation Stage. DFE-RR071*. Department for Education. https://www.education.gov.uk/publications/eOrderingDownload/DFE-RR071.pdf (accessed 22 April 2012).

Gifford, S. (2008) 'How do you teach nursery children mathematics? In search of a mathematics pedagogy for the early years', in I. Thompson (ed.), *Teaching and Learning Early Number.* Maidenhead, Berkshire: McGraw-Hill/The Open University.

Gray, C. and MacBlain, S. (2012) *Learning Theories in Childhood*. London: Sage.

Gura, P. (1992) (ed) *Exploring Learning. Young Children and Blockplay*. London: Paul Chapman.

Hansen, K. (2010) 'Teacher assessments in the first year of school', in K. Hansen, H. Joshi and S. Dex (eds), *Children of the 21st Century: The First Five Years*. Bristol: The Policy Press.

Howes, A. and Davies, D. (2010) 'Science and play', in J. Moyles (ed.), *The Excellence of Play*. Maidenhead, Berkshire: McGraw-Hill/The Open University.

Hughes, A. (2010) *Developing Play for The Under 3s: The Treasure Basket and Heuristic Play* (2nd edition). London: Routledge.

Imagine Inspirational School Design (2010) [online] Sponsored by Balfour Beatty Education and Partnerships for Schools. http://www.imagineschooldesign.org/ (accessed 22 April 2013).

Keenan, T. and Evans, S. (2009) *An Introduction to Child Development* (2nd edition). London: Sage.

MacNaughton, G. and Williams, G. (2009) *Teaching Young Children: Choices in Theory and Practice* (2nd edition). Maidenhead, Berkshire: McGraw-Hill/The Open University.

Meade, A. and Cubey, P. (2008) *Thinking Children: Learning about Schemas*. Maidenhead, Berkshire: McGraw-Hill/The Open University.

Niland, A. (2009) 'The power of musical play: the value of play-based, child-centred curriculum in early childhood music education,' *General Music Today*, 21 April. doi: 10.1177/1048371309335625.

Robinson, K. and Diaz, C. (2006) *Diversity and Difference in Early Childhood Education: Issues for Theory and Practice*. Maidenhead, Berkshire: Open University Press.

Saracho, O. and Spodek, B. (2008) 'Scientific and technological literacy research: Principles and practices', in O. Saracho and B. Spodek (eds), *Contemporary Perspectives on Science and Technology in Early Childhood Education*. Charlotte, NC: Information Age Publishing.

Sarama, J. and Clements, D. (2008) 'Mathematics in early childhood', in O. Saracho and B. Spodek (eds), *Contemporary Perspectives on Mathematics in Early Childhood Education*. Charlotte, NC: Information Age Publishing Inc.

Sarama, J. and Clements, D. (2009) *Early Childhood Mathematics Education Research Group: Learning Trajectories for Young Children*. New York and London: Routledge.

Shore, R. and Strasser, J. (2006) 'Music for their minds', *Young Children*, 61(62): 62–7.

Smith, P.K. (2010) *Children and Play*. Chichester: Wiley Blackwell.

Sylva, K., Siraj-Blatchford, I., Taggart, B., Sammons, P., Melhuish, E., Elliot, K. and Totsika, V. (2006) 'Capturing quality in early childhood through environmental rating scales', *Early Childhood Research Quarterly*, 21(1): 76–92.

Sylva, K. (2010) 'Quality in early childhood settings,' in K. Sylva, E. Melhuish, P. Sammons, I. Siraj-Blatchford and B. Taggart (eds) *Early Childhood Matters: Evidence from the Effective Pre-school and Primary Education Project*. Abingdon: Routledge.

Thornton, L. and Brunton, P. (2010) *Bringing the Reggio Approach to Your Early Years Practice* (2nd edition). London: Routledge.

Watts, A. (2011) *Every Nursery Needs a Garden: A step-by-step Guide to Creating and Using a Garden with Young Children*. London: Routledge.

White, J. (2008) *Playing and Learning Outdoors. Making Provision for High-Quality Experiences in the Outdoor Environment*. Abingdon: Routledge.

Whitebread, D. (2012) *Developmental Psychology and Early Childhood Education*. London: Sage.

Williams, P. (2008) *Independent Review of Mathematics Teaching in Early Years Settings and Primary Schools*. Nottingham: DCSF Publications. https://www.education.gov.uk/publications/eOrderingDownload/Williams%20Mathematics.pdf (accessed 22 April 2013).

Wilson, R. (2012) *Nature and Young Children: Encouraging Creative Play and Learning in Natural Environments*. Abingdon, Oxon: Routledge.

20

Transitions

Hilary Fabian

This chapter will:

- Outline the types of transition that children make
- Highlight some differences and challenges in the move from EYFS to NC and the impact of these on children's well-being
- Present practical ideas for supporting successful educational transitions
- Explore ways of personalising transition for children with specific circumstances.

There is widespread agreement that transitions have two main strands: *settling-in* to the new setting in terms of socio-emotional well-being; and *continuity* in terms of learning (Fabian and Dunlop, 2005). The process of change that children experience in making the move from one setting or educational phase to another is seen as an ecological transition (Bronfenbrenner, 1979) whereby the move is influenced by relationships and the environment. It often involves moving from a place or situation of 'feeling suitable' (Broström, 2002) to one of uncertainty, and a time during which children commute between two different cultural settings (Lam and Pollard, 2006). Some of the challenges of transitions can cause anxiety and tension between wanting to enter the transition stage and staying in the safety of the known environment. For example, myths about school; coping with physical, social and pedagogical differences; expectations of family; and the accepted ways to interact and behave, can all cause disquiet. The effect of transitions should not be underestimated as they involve intense demands which can bring about a significant difference in the way children participate in the family and community. However, to recognise and understand the impact that transitions make, they must be seen in the context of a child's life (DfES, 2003).

How well children adjust and cope with the new context – fitting into, or having difficulties, with the environment; comprehending the teaching methods; following the rules; and gaining a sense of belonging – can be seen as indicators of how well they have settled. In addition, children's ability to make friends and cooperate is related to their future academic and social success (Yeo and Clarke, 2006). Children's experience of transitions not only makes a difference in the early months of a new situation, but may also have a much longer-term impact because the extent to which they feel successful is likely to influence subsequent experiences. A successful transition has a positive impact on children's later success as it can affect the way in which they view themselves, their sense of well-being and their ability to learn, resulting in them feeling competent and able to handle new experiences with confidence. Conversely, high levels of behaviour problems, conflict and dependency in the first year of schooling can predict poor behavioural and academic outcomes up to six years later (Margetts, 2009). Many children develop coping strategies whereby they either change their interpretation of the situation to ease their emotional responses and/or change their behaviour in an attempt to fit into the new environment. Those who settle quickly are not only more likely to succeed than children who have difficulty adjusting, they will also respond better to future transitions (Margetts, 2009; Yeboah, 2002) and gain 'transitions capital' (Dunlop, 2007: 164).

Types of transition

Transitions are not just about moving from one educational setting to another as children grow older, there is also a trend towards children attending out-of-school-hours care settings, which often have their own significant social and cultural systems (Johansson, 2007). These two types of transitions can be described as *vertical transitions*, where movement is through education systems or programmes, and *horizontal transitions*, where there is movement across various settings within a short timeframe, such as a day. You can look at these in terms of the support that is required for each transition:

- When is support needed?
  - Home to early childhood settings
  - Children's Centres to nursery to school-based settings
  - Foundation Stage (FS) 1 to FS2 to Key Stage 1 (KS1)
  - Transitions within the daily routine, including to out-of-school activities.
- What needs support?
  - Curriculum continuity and learning modes
  - Socio-emotional well-being.

- Where do you need to support?
  - Either side of the physical and cultural border
  - In the boundary zones
- Who needs to support?
  - Parents
  - Organisations to which the child belongs
  - Domain members
  - Border keepers

Journal Task

Campbell Clark, S. (2000) 'Work/family border theory: A new theory of work/family balance', *Human Relations*, 53(6): 747–70.

While this article is focused on work and the workplace rather than school, there are similar issues that can be identified, such as emotional 'spillover' between settings; the need for a supportive family; the often differing cultural influences which shape expectations and behaviour; and notions of making a daily 'border crossing' between two domains. The resulting border-zone has areas that are described as having the possibility to be dangerous.

1. Who are the key border-keepers in each transition where you work?
2. Explore the 'dangers' that the border-keepers need to be aware of and their role in supporting children across the 'boundaries'.

Extension to Level 6

Border theory has been addressed further by Peters (2010) in relation to the way that interconnectedness between settings comes about through shared responsibility and strong links at educational borders and cultural intersections.
Consider ways in which you are responsible for providing links between various settings. How might these be improved?

To download this task as well as other useful online resources please visit:
www.sagepub.co.uk/mukherji

Different pedagogical positions prevalent in current early years and primary education

Transition to the next phase of education can present challenges that can prove to be a major obstacle in many children's learning careers. Not only do they face different surroundings and staffing ratios, but also differences in the length of the day, teaching styles and curriculum, which can result in a cultural shock. These differences include:

Curriculum organisation

- In England, children between the ages of 3 and 4 learn in a childcare setting, such as a nursery, through a play-based pedagogy – Foundation Stage 1 – which is integrated and flexible. Foundation Stage 2 takes place in the Reception Class of a school between the ages 4 and 5. When children make the transition to Year 1 they begin a more formal curriculum and experience the National Curriculum for KS1 which is divided into subject areas with prescribed programmes of study.
- In England most 3-year-old children attend early childhood settings run by private, voluntary or public providers and staffed by early childhood practitioners who usually have Early Years qualifications. Reception and Year 1 classes are located in schools and are staffed by teachers, usually with support from a teaching assistant. Children make the physical transition to the school-based reception class but continue with the FS curriculum. The transition to more formal learning does not coincide with the transition to school, resulting in both opportunities and challenges: It can make the transition to school easier because the curriculum requirements are the same, even though children are often moving to a new setting; but there is a danger that the subsequent move to Year 1 may not be deemed important because it takes place a year after children have physically started school (White and Sharp, 2007).

Curriculum philosophy

- In early childhood settings children have few time restraints and activities are organised to children's own sense of time. Children have space to play independently and take the initiative to direct the flow of their ideas. Learning is through play with an emphasis on activities that are relevant and motivating for each child. This means that children have opportunities to make choices about their activities directed by materials, choose with whom they play and take responsibility by initiating their own learning. In contrast, primary school learning is more structured and children are expected to conform to more formal rules and routines. In school, timetables are important tools for organising the day, there are more verbal instructions, there is a focus on literacy and numeracy and a more formal teaching style. In many primary schools children have to learn within a teacher-directed pedagogy that differs from the more implicit learning methods at home or in early years settings. This difference in ways of working between the autonomous, play-based pedagogy of the early childhood setting and the more formal, teaching-directed learning expectations of the primary school may cause anxiety for some children. Furthermore, a pre-set curriculum means that there are often constraints on the amount of time available for teaching and learning, making it difficult for teachers to plan for individual interests.
- In early childhood settings children are generally organised in small groups and are assigned a key person (DfE, 2012: para. 3.26) with whom they develop a strong attachment (Bowlby, 1988); they then move to a KS1 class with one teacher (and usually an assistant) per 30 pupils. With fewer adults it is likely that there are

increased waiting times and less supervision. In addition, there is a wider mix of age groups, more buildings and larger playgrounds. Consequently, you can see that functioning in an early childhood setting as a 'child' is different from becoming a 'pupil' in school – in early childhood settings there is an emphasis on care and social development; in school the emphasis is on teaching and learning.

Assessment

- During the FS formative assessments are made and progress checks shared with parents when the child is aged between 2 and 3; before starting Year 1 an EYFS Profile is completed outlining their readiness for KS1 (DfE, 2012: 10–12). In KS1 some assessments become summative. At this time children may be assessed in a more comparative manner which can affect the way in which they are viewed by others and, as a result, their self-esteem.

Mechanisms for smoothing the transition

The issue, then, is how you support the transition to school in order that all children make a successful start. First we need to know how to recognise success. Ladd (2003: 3) suggests that:

> A child can be seen as successful in school when she or he: (a) develops positive attitudes and feelings about school and learning, (b) establishes supportive social ties with teachers and classmates, (c) feels comfortable and relatively happy in the classroom rather than anxious, lonely or upset, (d) is interested and motivated to learn and take part in classroom activities (participation, engagement), and (e) achieves and progresses academically each school year.

Learning about one another: Developing communication systems

Parents want sufficient information and opportunities to understand the school environment, its curriculum and where they fit into the organisation. Teachers value having shared meetings before school begins and want to know about each child's learning and previous experiences from parents and early childhood practitioners (Broström, 2002). Therefore, it is not just children who are involved in transitions; parents, early childhood practitioners and teachers are also involved with this change (Dockett and Perry, 2004). If the transition is to be successful for all children then it needs to be a process of co-construction through participation between the early childhood settings, school and family communicating and working together (Griebel and Niesel, 2002). This places the family as equal partners in the transition process. If this is the case, then you need to consider communication systems which are going to provide opportunities for building meaningful and responsive relationships which will not only support the transition to school, but also form the basis for on-going interactions. This might be through face-to-face discussions, technology or home visits before the child begins school.

Journal Task

Greenfield, S. (2012) 'Nursery home visits: Rhetoric and realities', *Journal of Early Childhood Research*, 10(1): 100–12.

Levels 4 & 5

This article outlines the historical reasons for home visits and, through a substantial case study, explores the tensions between parents and practitioners concerning home visits. One of the key issues is about training to work with parents. The Statutory Framework for the Early Years Foundation Stage (DfE, 2012) seeks to provide partnership working between practitioners and with parents and/or carers.

Consider the training that you think you might need for working with parents both in terms of home visits and in dealing with transition issues.

Level 6

Kagan (2003) discusses children's readiness for school – for example, skills and abilities – and Graue (1999) outlines a school's readiness for children – for example, adapting contextual factors such as the curriculum and staffing to create an appropriate learning environment.

1. What aspects do you think need to be considered in order to form a match between child and school?
2. How might this differ between families/communities? For example, those living in isolated rural districts or low socio-economic areas.

To download this task as well as other useful online resources please visit:
www.sagepub.co.uk/mukherji

Parents usually connect with the school and have a sense of being valued as part of the school community. However, this can be difficult if they have no real understanding of school and tensions can arise if the expectations of school and parents differ (Dockett and Perry, 2005). In addition, schools need to recognise the particular perspectives of parents. For example, Crozier and Davies (2007: 311) outline the way in which white middle-class parents have a keen understanding of the need to 'compete for scarce resources and develop competitive strategies to maximise their children's opportunities', whereas the majority of Bangladeshi and Pakistani parents in their study believed that schools would simply provide the best they could for each child. Therefore, you not only need to consider how you are going to communicate, but also what you want to know and what parents need to know, in order to make sense of the information together.

How parents feel about the transition their child makes will be influenced by the nature of their relationship with the school and staff responsiveness to any issues which arise. Well-informed parents are less likely to be stressed about their child's transition and more able to assist their child in overcoming any confusion in adapting to the new environment (Bredekamp, 1987). Through sharing information and being provided with guidance and advice, each child will have a personal experience of the transition that is likely to be successful.

In England and Wales children do not have to attend school until the beginning of the term following their fifth birthday, but most schools have a policy of accepting children at the beginning of the term during which they become 5 and adopt a single-, two- or three-point entry system (Rogers and Rose, 2007). On their first day children might start with the rest of the school, have a staggered start before or after other children have begun, or start over a number of days. Although seasonal age has some effect on performance (autumn-born children tend to do better than summer-born children), it is the quality and type of provision experienced that makes the difference to achievement.

Reflection

The first day can be stressful when parents need to leave. How can children and their parents be helped through the separation on the first day?

Parents may have concerns about the way in which their child is settling into school during the first few days. How can you provide feedback about the way their child is responding to being in school and handling new routines?

Assessment

Just as it is important for parents and educators to communicate well, so is the need for staff to liaise between settings and pass on useful information and records. In the final term of the year in which the child reaches 5, and no later than 30 June in that term, the EYFS Profile must be completed for each child, with development being assessed against the early learning goals (DfE, 2012: para. 2.6). In addition, The Profile report should inform a dialogue between Reception and Year 1 teachers about each child's stage of development and learning needs, which in turn assists the planning of activities in Year 1 (DfE, 2012: 11, para. 2.8). However, do be aware that there are different views of the same child and an image of a child in the early years setting might not translate into the same image in school. For example, if a child is seen as sociable in the early years setting, in a school environment this might be seen as being talkative rather than concentrating on recorded work, and therefore, problematic.

Developing cultural understanding through cross-border visits

Schools sometimes have a transition policy which encourages children and their parents to make visits in the term before starting. These can be a combination of: single visits; a series of half-day visits; talks to parents either in an afternoon or evening; parents staying with their child; parents leaving their child with the teacher; and experience of lunch time and the playground. In tandem with visits, staff from school often visit the local early childhood settings to observe and meet the children. These meetings can be used for gathering information about individual children or groups and to share practice. This can help teachers to become familiar with the children as individuals, assess their levels of attainment as learners, and gauge any behavioural or developmental difficulties.

Rogoff's (1990) 'guided participation view' sees children as apprenticing to become competent members of their environment. Visits can offer opportunities to become familiar with the new setting during this in-between time. Indeed, the border-zone has become a state in itself – a transitional period which has acquired a certain autonomy, a stage which needs to be gone through before balance and routine are once again restored (van Gennep, 1960). It provides an orientation for understanding the intricacies of school, preliminary to the event itself and the potential for a connection between settings. The issue for schools, however, is to identify the prime purpose of the pre-entry visits and activities. Is it for children to meet their teacher and develop friendships? Is it for staff to assess children's skills? Is it to provide a taste of the way in which learning takes place? Familiarity with the classroom, its materials and people, may facilitate adjustment but curriculum continuity and developing similar learning approaches between settings could also assist transition and help to avoid 'dips' in learning (Dunlop, 2007: 164).

CASE STUDY

In a joint project about fairy stories the FS2 children and KS1 children worked on the theme of Jack and the Beanstalk. Part of the project involved making a beanstalk that wove its way from the FS room to the KS1 classroom, enabling children to learn the physical layout of the building. Children then painted pictures of their favourite

(Continued)

(Continued)

stories and acted them for the KS1 class. These included traditional stories such as 'The Three Little Pigs' and modern classics such as 'The Hungry Caterpillar'. When the FS children started KS1, the teacher displayed their paintings in the classroom at the beginning of term (Fabian and Dunlop, 2005). This joint working meant that the setting was familiar to the children; they were able to recognise certain books; they had a sense of belonging; and they gained self-confidence.

Plan a joint project across the next 'border' which will encourage children to move confidently from one setting to another. How can curriculum progression be included?

Visits can also take place between settings by the children themselves through buddying or pairing, which can support the integration of children into the school community. One school began by inviting older pupils in the school to complete application forms and be interviewed for the role of buddy. They then visited the early childhood setting regularly to play and talk with children. Later in the year, groups of buddies were matched with groups of early childhood children and escorted them on visits to school. The buddies were then able to support the new intake at playtime when they started school (Fabian and Dunlop, 2007a).

Expectations

With the start of school comes expectations of, and for, children. Formal expectations – those from parents and teachers – include the development of meta-cognitive skills, taking responsibility, behaving appropriately and self-regulation. The home exerts the strongest influence on children's learning. However, parents' intuitive expectations and preconceptions based on their own experiences in a different context might mean that they do not fully understand the processes of formal education, including the language and thought needed for abstract thinking. Informal expectations – pupils' hopes for their learning, relationships amongst peers, and the way they view themselves – are shaped by the child's home context, parental support, attitudes, the media, out-of-school activities and the school philosophy. Children's beliefs about school build expectations, but they may be confronted by a different model and have to reassess their goals.

Social well-being

A key factor influencing transitions is friendships. Those children who start school with a friend in the same class have an advantage as they feel more secure (Hamre and Pianta, 2001), settle more easily, and have less problematic behaviour and better social skills than those who start school without a friend (Fabian and Dunlop, 2007b). Other studies (Faulkner and Miell, 1993; Ladd, 1990; Margetts, 2002), have also found that having friends creates a supportive learning environment, resulting in the establishment of positive school perceptions and enhanced school performance. They suggest that friendships and social competence influences children's ability in a range of learning activities, particularly those which involve collaboration and cooperation. This is because being an active participant in conversations and being able to communicate effectively with peers is central to the many classroom activities which are based on discussion. This strong link between children's social behaviour and academic achievement implies that supporting children's social adjustment is necessary for their learning.

Reflection

Maintaining friends in the transition can be enhanced by providing information about which children are 'going to the same school, providing resources to support the establishment of friendships in the context of play, allowing mixed-aged friendships (which provided modelling and protection) and the direct teaching of social skills' (Peters, 2003: 52).

Given that one of the overarching principles of the Statutory Framework for the Early Years Foundation Stage is developing positive relationships (DfE, 2012: 3), identify the social skills necessary to make a successful transition, including those related to cooperation, personal responsibility, independence and peer relationships. What can you do to help children develop these skills and build social capital?

Emotional well-being

During the transition to school, children are expected to 'develop the skills and attitudes to learn well whatever the conditions' (Claxton, 2002: 15), that is, to develop resilience. To help children adjust to change by developing coping skills, they often go through stages, or rites of passage (van Gennep, 1960). For example, in the early stages transitioners may be given glimpses of their forthcoming move by parents talking about 'big school' or practitioners in early childhood settings discussing visits to school. This provides children with the opportunity to express their views, discuss their feelings, talk about their expectations, and be informed about school. You can use a child-sized school-uniformed puppet to answer children's questions, show them photographs of the classroom, teach them songs about starting school and put forward problems that 'he' has encountered at school to discuss (Ofsted, 2012). The next stage is represented by children making visits to school in the border-zone and through preparations such as buying their school clothes. This stage can be eased by encouraging established friendships, and using stories and illustrations about difficult aspects of the day, such as lunchtime or playtime, to empower children by asking them what they might do in similar circumstances and work out solutions for themselves (Cefai, 2008; Fabian, 2002). In addition, Key Stage 1 children can create eBooks about school for the new children, and children's confidence can be built through the use of transitional objects (Campbell Clark, 2000) such as a photograph or toy. The final stage is when children begin school and their pupil identity gradually evolves as they acquire the new culture and adopt particular dispositions to cope with the challenges presented in the classroom.

A sense of belonging

The way in which children adjust to the meeting of cultures partly depends on past experiences, social competence, problem-solving skills, self-reliance and determination (Fabian, 2002). In the border-zone children often have to cope with two institutional cultures: the early childhood setting and the school. The school culture – its values, traditions and beliefs – is not always obvious to children, but can be a powerful force in creating expectations and shaping behaviour. A sense of belonging to the school community is an important contributor to the way in which children and families adjust to school and gain a sense of emotional well-being. Children do not necessarily fit in passively, following the rules and behaviour expectations of the setting, but acquire and understand the culture through 'living it'. Through observing and copying others, and by drawing on their experiences, children construct their own realities and meanings, interpreting and shaping the culture to suit themselves. In this way, the school's culture, language and patterns of behaviour are gradually absorbed without conscious thought through 'learning by osmosis' (Claxton, 1998: 20). However, children's adaptation to the environment is influenced by their confidence and their ability to detect what is going on within the classroom. They can be given the opportunity to enter the culture with an awareness of how to participate, and bring their own culture to the setting, through stories and social processes in which knowledge is co-constructed within the group – referred to as 'situated learning' by Lave and Wenger (1991). Thus they gain an understanding of the rules; a knowledge of symbols such as the sounding of a bell; the name of their class groups; and understand the language of the new environment and the way in which physical spaces are used. As a result, they are likely to have increased motivation and move quickly towards full participation in the socio-cultural practices of the classroom community. The way children cope and adapt to the classroom is critical to their careers as pupils, so teachers need to be sensitive and responsive to each child's background, skills and abilities.

Teacher behaviours

Teachers act as role models for children by demonstrating the knowledge, skills, values and attitudes required for successful performance. In addition, their behaviour can support the settling-in process by acting 'as if' children were making sense of the classroom and the way in which learning takes place (Edwards and Knight, 1994: 15). There is clearly a connection between teachers' actions and children's perceptions: where a teacher's actions facilitate and promote a positive image, this supports the child's peer relationships and a positive cycle of learning. However, if a teacher does not value the child's approach to learning this can bring about a negative cycle of deteriorating relationships and a loss of motivation and enthusiasm for school (Pollard with Filer, 1999).

Children learn and develop well in environments where the experiences offered support individual needs and there is a strong partnership between practitioners, parents and carers. Making the environment a friendly, secure and welcoming place is one aspect of Development Matters in the Early Years Foundation Stage (Early Education, 2012), in which enabling environments value people and learning, and offer:

- Stimulating resources, relevant to all the children's cultures and communities
- Rich learning opportunities through play and playful teaching
- Support for children to take risks and explore (Early Education, 2012: 2).

However, it is social practices in the broader environment of school, family, friends and the local community which enable learning to take place. Supporting continuity of experiences for children requires policies and procedures that foster liaison between settings, the transfer of relevant information to promote curriculum continuity, and the close involvement of all those involved in constructing the transition process together. Rites of passage will help children to gradually absorb the culture of the school, gain their pupil identity and feel 'at home' in the new situation.

Reflection

Lam and Pollard (2006: 137) identify three elements for assessing how well children have adapted to the new setting: patterns of formal outcomes (curriculum attainment) and informal outcomes (self-confidence, motivation, autonomy and a sense of belonging); patterns of strategic actions; and an evolving sense of pupil identity. What signs would you look for to identify those children who are having a difficult transition?

Consideration of specific needs relating to particular children

For many educators, working with children and parents from diverse backgrounds has become a common feature of their professional practice. Some work with vulnerable groups, such as children who grow up thinking that conflict, misbehaviour and abuse on the part of a parent is normal behaviour; others work with children who have severe, profound or multiple health and learning needs or disabilities. Whatever the individual needs and background of the children, there must be a supportive programme of activities in place as well as strategies for exchanging information with parents and/or carers, health and social services which ensure that problems are identified at an early stage and a package of support is provided, tailored to the needs of the family.

Reflection

There are many picture books for children about starting school that explore socio-emotional issues and learning.

Look at some of these books and consider the types of messages that children and parents are receiving about school from the pictures and text. What do they say about children with specific needs?

Pupil mobility – those children who change school as a result of parental occupation or lifestyle, or specific events such as family break-up, as well as refugee families (Stead et al., 1999), travellers (Jordan, 2000), or children of Armed Forces personnel (Ballinger, 2001; The HoC Select Committee on Defence, 2006) – can pose a problem because the move disrupts their education. In addition, these children can have difficulties making new friends or suffer emotional upset. However, the reason that a pupil moves school, rather than the change of school itself, is probably the most important factor in relation to attainment (Strand, 2002).

Children moving from abroad might have experienced a school with a different curriculum or pedagogy, others might arrive in a traumatised state with no understanding of English. Barriers to involvement may also come in the form of a lack of cultural awareness which results in parents not being able to prepare their children for school. The organisation of time and space can also cause cross-cultural misunderstandings. For example, the way the classroom is physically organised and the amount of time that children work with the teacher might be different from that experienced in the previous setting. Parents from most cultures are usually concerned that their children 'fit in' to school and feel a responsibility to make sure that their children know how to behave in relation to eating and in talking to teachers (Hamilton, 2011). They are also concerned that teachers should not judge children who are having difficulties moving between languages as incompetent. So, when assessing children on arrival, be sure of the difference between children's skills in English and any possible learning difficulties. For children whose home language is not English, you must provide opportunities for them to develop and use their home language in play and learning (DfE, 2012: para. 1.8). Also be aware that tensions can arise for parents who do not speak English if they are unable to access information about the school in their home language.

As well as supporting newly-arrived children, you can also provide for the needs of children transferring out of school and for those who are 'left behind' as a result of their friends having moved. For children who change schools there are three steps in the transfer process, comprising a disengagement phase, an interim stage and a reintegration phase (Ballinger, 2001). The disengagement phase is characterised by children spending more time and energy preparing to leave rather than living in their current culture. However, once relocated, it can take up to 12 months before children have fully engaged with the new culture.

Pupil mobility does not necessarily have a negative effect on children. Pollock and van Reken (2001) point out that many pupils also gain valuable learning experiences and benefits because they develop resilience, adaptability and flexibility, become confident with change, value relationships and gain a wide network of friends, develop a sense of realism and the importance of 'now', and become adept at 'closure' skills.

Journal Task

Laoire, C.N., Carlene-Mendez, F., Tyrrell, N. and White, A. (2010) 'Introduction: Childhood and migration – mobilities, homes and belongings', *Childhood*, 17(2): 155–62.

This article is the introduction to a series of papers about migration. It questions the fixed and stable nature of childhood by exploring the fluid and dynamic way in which migrant children make connections. It explains that identities are developed through relationships and suggests that identities are multiple and intersecting. Furthermore, these children have different ways of belonging as they have culturally blended lives.

Levels 4 & 5

Read the article and consider the ways in which children develop their identity and notions of belonging. How did you build your sense of self when you moved to your current setting?

Level 6

Pollock and van Reken (2001) have argued that roles and identities of Third Culture Kids – those children who are raised in a highly mobile and genuinely cross-cultural world – become confused as a result of new relationships encountered in transitions. How can you help children from diverse backgrounds relate to the school ethos, and develop who they are in relation to the surrounding culture?

To download this task as well as other useful online resources please visit:
www.sagepub.co.uk/mukherji

Links to other transitions

The issues discussed in this chapter focus on children starting school, but similar principles apply to any transition process, such as babies and very young children beginning at an early years setting or children transferring from KS1 to KS2. While goals, demands and expectations might change, the aspects of clear communication and exchange of information, familiarisation with the environment and personnel, the development of socio-emotional well-being, and continuity of learning, remain as key features throughout any transition.

Summary

Children experience both vertical and horizontal transitions. Most children respond well to moving between settings, thereby gaining 'transitions capital' (Dunlop, 2007). Co-constructing the transition programme with all those involved both clarifies procedures and provides 'ownership' of the process. Curriculum continuity requires policies that support liaison between settings and enable a smooth and successful transfer. This can be harmonised through border-zone activities. Empowering children by developing resilience and confidence, contributes to children's sense of being in control of the transition and promotes their feelings of belonging. In addition, friendships ease the anxiety of new situations and provide socio-emotional well-being which enables learning to take place. For children with specific needs, information and programmes are best if personalised.

Further reading

Levels 4 & 5

International Journal of Transitions in Childhood, https://extranet.edfac.unimelb.edu.au/LED/tec/journal_index.shtml. This is an online, international journal which publishes academic research articles and practitioner papers that explore thinking about the variety of transitions experienced by children. It provides a forum for publications that describe and extend approaches to the theory and practice of childhood transitions.

Lam, M.S. and Pollard, A. (2006) 'A conceptual framework for understanding children as agents in the transition from home to kindergarten', *Early Years*, 26(2): 123–41. This journal article begins with a review of the concept of transitions and presents a conceptual framework to understand children as agents in the transition from home to early years settings. Major elements of the conceptual framework come from socio-cultural theory and highlight the interconnectedness of context, stages of transition and acculturation.

This discussion is illustrated and extended further in:

Lam, M.S. (2009) 'Crossing the cultural boundary from home to kindergarten in Hong Kong: A case study of a child's strategic actions', *European Early Childhood Research Journal*, 17(1): 125–45.

Fabian, H. (2002) *Children Starting School*. London: David Fulton Publishers. This book draws on research, theory and practice to present ways in which practitioners, working in partnership with parents, can provide children with a successful start to school. This book, along with

Brooker, L. (2008) *Supporting Transitions in the Early Years.* Maidenhead, Berkshire: Open University Press/McGraw-Hill Education. This book focuses on socio-emotional well-being during transitions. Through case studies these books identify some of the key qualities required to foster and achieve effective transitions.

Level 6

Dunlop, A.W. and Fabian, H. (eds) (2007) *Informing Transitions: Research, Policy and Practice.* Maidenhead, Berkshire: Open University Press/McGraw-Hill. This book explores early transitions from a variety of international perspectives, including, amongst other issues, parental involvement, children's views and the construction of identity.

Jindal-Snape, D. (ed.) (2010) *Educational Transitions: Moving Stories from Around the World.* Abingdon, Oxon: Routledge. This provides an in-depth journey from the earliest transitions, through primary and secondary school, to employment.

References

Ballinger, A. (2001) 'Mobility: Information for teachers and other staff who work with Service Children.' paper presented at The Shropshire Service Schools' Conference: 'Pupil Mobility: What Does It Mean?/What Can We Do?', 9 July, Albrighton, Shropshire.

Bowlby, J. (1988) *A Secure Base: Parent–Child Attachment and Healthy Human Development.* Tavistock Professional Book. London: Routledge.

Bredekamp, S. (ed.) (1987) *Developmentally Appropriate Practice in Early Childhood Programs Serving Children from Birth Through Age 8.* Washington DC: National Association for the Education of Young Children.

Bronfenbrenner, U. (1979) *The Ecology of Human Development: Experiments by Nature and Design.* Cambridge, MA: Harvard University Press.

Broström, S. (2002) 'Communication and continuity in the transition from kindergarten to school', in H. Fabian and A-W. Dunlop (eds), *Transitions in the Early Years: Debating Continuity and Progression for Children in Early Education.* London: RoutledgeFalmer.

Campbell Clark, S. (2000) 'Work/family border theory: A new theory of work/family balance', *Human Relations,* 53(6): 747–70.

Cefai, C. (2008) *Promoting Resilience in the Classroom: A Guide to Developing Pupils' Emotional and Cognitive Skills.* London: Jessica Kingsley Publishers.

Claxton, G. (1998) *Hare Brain, Tortoise Mind.* London: Fourth Estate Limited.

Claxton, G. (2002) *Building Learning Power.* Bristol: TLO Limited.

Crozier, G. and Davies, J. (2007) 'Hard to reach parents or hard to reach schools? A discussion of home–school relations, with particular reference to Bangladeshi and Pakistani parents', *British Educational Research Journal,* 33(3): 295–313.

Department for Education and Science (2003) *Every Child Matters.* Norwich: The Stationery Office.

Department for Education (DfE) (2012) *Statutory Framework for the Early Years Foundation Stage 2012.* Norwich: The Stationery Office.

Dockett, S. and Perry, B. (2004) 'Starting school: Perspectives of Australian children, parents and educators', *Journal of Early Childhood Research,* 2(2): 171–89.

Dockett, S. and Perry, B. (2005) 'Starting school in Australia is "a bit safer, a lot easier and more relaxing": Issues for families and children from culturally and linguistically diverse backgrounds', *Early Years*, 25(3): 271–81.

Dunlop, A.W. (2007) 'Bridging research, policy and practice', in A.W. Dunlop and H. Fabian (eds), *Informing Transitions: Research, Policy and Practice*. Maidenhead, Berkshire: Open University Press/McGraw-Hill.

Early Education (2012) *Development Matters in the Early Years Foundation Stage (EYFS)*. London: Early Education.

Edwards, A. and Knight, P. (1994) *Effective Early Years Education*. Buckingham: Open University Press.

Fabian, H. (2002) 'Empowering children for transitions', in H. Fabian and A.W. Dunlop (eds), *Transitions in the Early Years*. London: RoutledgeFalmer.

Fabian, H. and Dunlop, A.W. (2005) 'The importance of play in the transition to school', in J.R. Moyles (ed.), *The Excellence of Play* (2nd edition). Maidenhead, Berkshire: Open University Press/McGraw-Hill.

Fabian, H. and Dunlop, A.W.A. (2007a) 'The first days at school', in J.R. Moyles (ed.), *Beginning Teaching, Beginning Learning* (2nd edition). Open University Press/McGraw-Hill.

Fabian, H. and Dunlop, A.W.A. (2007b) *Outcomes of Good Practice in Transition Processes for Children Entering Primary School. Working Paper 42*. The Hague, The Netherlands: Bernard van Leer Foundation.

Faulkner, D. and Miell, D. (1993) 'Settling into school: The importance of early friendships for the development of children's social understanding and communicative competence', *International Journal of Early Years Education*, 1(1): 23–45.

Graue, M.E. (1999) 'Diverse perspectives on kindergarten contexts and practices', R.C. Pianta and M.J. Cox (eds), *The Transition to Kindergarten*. Baltimore, MD: Paul H. Brooks. pp. 109–42.

Greenfield, S. (2012) 'Nursery home visits: Rhetoric and realities', *Journal of Early Childhood Research*, 10(1): 100–12.

Griebel, W. and Niesel, R. (2002) 'Co-constructing transition into kindergarten and school by children, parents, and teachers', in H. Fabian and A.W. Dunlop (eds), *Transitions in the Early Years: Debating Continuity and Progression for Children in Early Education*. London: RoutledgeFalmer.

Hamilton, P. (2011) 'The Inclusion of Eastern European children into primary schools in North Wales: A case study', PhD thesis, University of Wales (unpublished).

Hamre, B.K. and Pianta, R.C. (2001) 'Early teacher–child relationships and the trajectory of children's school outcomes through eighth grade', *Child Development*, 72(2): 625–38.

Johansson, I. (2007) 'Horizontal transitions: What can it mean for children in the early school years?', in A.W. Dunlop and H. Fabian (eds), *Informing Transitions: Research, Policy and Practice*. Maidenhead, Berkshire: Open University Press/McGraw-Hill.

Jordan, E. (2000) *Traveller Pupils and Scottish Schools: Spotlight 76*. Edinburgh: The Scottish Council for Research in Education.

Kagan, S.L. (2003) 'Children's readiness for school: Issues in assessment', *International Journal of Early Childhood*, 35(1–2): 114–20.

Ladd, G.W. (1990) 'Having friends, keeping friends, making friends, and being liked by peers in the classroom: Predictors of children's early school adjustment?', *Child Development*, 61(4): 1081–1100.

Ladd, G.W. (2003) 'School transitions/school readiness: An outcome of early childhood development', in R.E. Tremblay, R.G. Barr and R. DeV. Peters (eds), *Encyclopaedia on Early Childhood Development* (pp. 1–10). Montreal, Quebec: Centre of Excellence for Early Childhood

Development. Available at: http://www.child-encyclopedia.com/documents/LaddANGxp.pdf (accessed 12 April 2012).

Lam, M.S. and Pollard, A. (2006) 'A conceptual framework for understanding children as agents in the transition from home to kindergarten', *Early Years*, 26(2): 123–41.

Laoire, C.N., Carlene-Mendez, F., Tyrrell, N. and White, A. (2010) 'Introduction: Childhood and migration – mobilities, homes and belongings,' *Childhood*, 17(2): 155–62.

Lave, J. and Wenger, E. (1991) *Situated Learning: Legitimate Peripheral Participation*. Cambridge: Cambridge University Press.

Margetts, K. (2002) 'Transition to school – complexity and diversity', *European Early Childhood Education Research Journal*, 10(2): 103–14.

Margetts, K. (2009) 'Early transition and adjustment and children's adjustment after six years of schooling', *European Early Childhood Education Research Journal*, 17(3): 309–24.

Office for Standards in Education (Ofsted) (2012) *Early Years Foundation Stage to School Transition Project: Carousel Children's Centre*. URN 20386. Reference: 120043.

Peters, S. (2003) '"I didn't expect that I would get tons of friends . . . more each day": children's experiences of friendship during the transition to school', *Early Years*, 23(1): 45–53.

Peters, S. (2010) 'Shifting the lens: Re-framing the view of learners and learning during the transition from early childhood education to school in New Zealand', in D. Jindal-Snape (ed.), *Educational Transitions: Moving Stories from Around the World*. Oxon: Routledge.

Pollard, A. with Filer, A. (1999) *The Social World of Pupil Career: Strategic Biographies through Primary School*. London: Cassell.

Pollock, D.C. and van Reken, R.E. (2001) *Third Culture Kids: The Experience of Growing Up Among Worlds*. Maine: Intercultural Press.

Rogoff, B. (1990) *Apprenticeship in Thinking: Cognitive Development in Social Context*. Oxford: Oxford University Press.

Rogers, S. and Rose, J. (2007) 'Ready for reception? The advantages and disadvantages of single-point entry to school', *Early Years*, 27(1): 47–63.

Stead, J., Closs, A. and Arshad, R. (1999) *Refugee Pupils in Scottish Schools. Spotlight 74*. Edinburgh: The Scottish Council for Research in Education.

Strand, S. (2002) 'Pupil mobility, attainment and progress during Key Stage 1: A study in cautious interpretation', *British Educational Research Journal*, 28(1): 63–78.

The House of Commons Select Committee on Defence (2006) *Educating Service Children: Select Committee Report: HC 1504*, 6 September 2006. Norwich: The Stationery Office.

Yeboah, D.A. (2002) 'Enhancing transition from early childhood phase to primary education: Evidence from the research literature', *Early Years*, 22(1): 51–68.

Yeo, L.S. and Clarke, C. (2006) 'Adjustment to the first year in school – a Singapore perspective', *European Early Childhood Education Research Journal*, 14(2): 55–68.

van Gennep, A. (1960) *Rites of Passage*. Translated by M.B. Vizedom and G.L. Caffee. London: Routledge and Kegan Paul.

White, G. and Sharp, C. (2007) 'It is different … because you are getting older and growing up': How children make sense of the transition to Year 1', *European Early Childhood Education Research Journal*, 15(1): 87–102.

Glossary

Aesthetics Concerned with the beautiful appearance of the environment.

Affect The observable behaviour that represents the expression of emotion.

A-Frames Metal frames used in settings which can be adapted with wooden ladders and planks to create a variety of climbing and travelling challenges for children.

Alliteration A literary feature in which a series of words begin with the same phoneme (angry alligators ask awkward questions).

Amygdala A set of neurons located deep in the brain shown to play a key role in the processing of emotions.

Anthropometric A comparative study of human body measurements, proportions and properties.

Anthroposophy A philosophy founded by Rudolf Steiner which aims to develop faculties of perceptive imagination, inspiration and intuition through cultivating a form of thinking which is independent of sensory experience, in order to support inner and spiritual development.

Attachment behaviour Forming a close emotional bond with a parent or carer. Feelings of anxiety and distress are caused by the absence of the attachment figure.

Attunement The ability of an adult to 'tune in' and respond sensitively to a child's moods, expressions and behaviours and to adjust their actions and responses accordingly.

Aural discrimination The ability to hear/differentiate between different sounds.

Behaviourism An approach to psychology which focuses only on observable elements of behaviour.

Bodily-kinaesthetic intelligence The ability or capacity to use hands and body skilfully.

Border/boundary area A neutral zone between established systems.

Cephalocaudal development Development starts from the head in a downwards direction.

Change Wilhelm (1967) makes a distinction between three kinds of change: non-change, cyclic change and sequent change. Non-change is the background against which change is made possible – a fixed point to which change can be referred. Cyclic change is recurrent, or the rotation of phenomena with each succeeding the other until the starting point is reached again. Sequent change is the progressive, non-recurrent change of phenomena produced by cause and effect.

Child Protection Plan Plan, based on the assessment of risk to the child and information shared at the child protection conference, specifying roles and responsibilities of those involved in the care of the child.

Co-construct Adults or peers and children working together to build their learning.

Cognition Mental processes involved in thinking, knowing, remembering, problem solving and evaluating. Using language, perceiving, imagining and planning all depend upon cognitive processes.

Common Assessment Framework (CAF) Framework offering an opportunity for early identification of the child's additional needs, enabling the sharing of information as part of multi-agency working practices.

Communication Ability to express ideas, thoughts and feelings to others through gesture, facial expression, signs, symbols or spoken language.

Concrete operational The stage between 7 and 11 years of age in which Piaget suggested that children could use logical thought, but only in relation to concrete or tangible objects.

Constructivist theory A theory of learning, and an approach to education, which emphasises the way in which meaning is created by individuals in the light of experience and interaction with others.

Cortex The outermost sheet of neural tissue of the brain where most of the conscious information processing in the brain takes place.

Cortisol A hormone produced by the adrenal glands in response to stress.

Deficit model In education, this term is used to indicate instances where children's under-achievement is explained in terms of something being 'wrong' with them or their families (such as poor parenting), rather than attributing under-achievement to failures in the education system and in society.

Designated Safeguarding Officer Member of staff in an agency who is the main point of contact for other staff to discuss concerns about a child's safety and welfare.

Developmental A scientific approach to studying changes that occur over the course of the human life span.

Dialogic As in a conversation; communication between two people.

Discrimination Treating one group of people less favourably than others because of perceived differences such as their religion, ethnicity, sexuality or lifestyle.

DLO Desirable Learning Outcomes, a set of goals used to assess children's progress and development.

Domain of development An area or aspect of development such as physical development and cognitive development. Because of the holistic nature of children's development there are a number of different ways of dividing development into domains.

Dynamic systems The view that development happens through the mutual interaction of all aspects: the biological, psychological, social and cultural.

ELG Early Learning Goals: a set of goals/outcomes used to assess children's progress and development.

Emotional regulation The process of learning how emotions make you feel inside and how to cope with feelings, leading to developing healthy ways of showing these emotions to others.

Empiricism A theory of knowledge asserting that experience and, in particular sensory experience, is the primary source of knowledge.

Enactive Knowledge or learning acquired through 'doing'.

Epistemology A branch of philosophy which examines the nature of knowledge.

EPPE Project 1997–2004 Effective Provision of Pre-School Education Project. This was a longitudinal study conducted by Kathy Sylva and others. The findings suggest that children achieve best in high-quality pre-school education delivered by well-qualified staff.

Extrinsic rewards A reward that comes from outside, such as money, sweets, praise.

Formative assessment Assessment designed to help the practitioner (and parent) understand the stage of development/learning of a child in order to plan appropriate activities and experiences to further the child's learning and development.

Fully functioning person In Rogerian therapy such a person demonstrates openness, spontaneity, compassion and self-direction.

Gene Genes are bundles of DNA (genetic material) on specific sites on chromosomes which are responsible for physical and other inherited characteristics.

Gestaltists Psychologists holding a holistic view of the mind – rather than its being the sum of its parts.

Grammatical structures Conventions of word order, which differ between languages.

Heuristic play A play session designed to enable young children to find out about objects and what can be done with them.

Hidden curriculum The aspects of a child's experience in a setting, which, although unplanned, still have a big impact on their learning, such as the layout of the environment, the physical care routines or the attitudes of the practitioners.

Higher order reading skills A set of cognitive skills which enables the reader to use pictorial and contextual clues, grammatical structures, and comprehension, to predict unknown vocabulary and facilitate fluent reading.

Humanistic psychology An approach that views every individual as unique and as possessing an inherent capacity for making rational choices, achieving positive growth and ultimately, achieving maximum potential.

Iconic mode of representation The second of Bruner's stages of development, where mental pictures begin to emerge through the use of a variety of means of representation.

Ideal self An idealised version of self, created out of the demands of society and role models: what you wish you were really like.

Innate Inborn, natural.

Interactionalism A perspective in psychology that recognises the continuous and multidirectional interaction of the person and their situation.

Interactionism The idea that meaning or learning is created between the individual and society or the theory that the mind and the body act on each other.

Interpersonal An adjective describing the relationships and communication between the child and other people.

Interpersonal intelligence One of Gardner's multiple intelligences relating to relationships with others.

Inter-subjectivity Mutual engagement and participation between two people, which influences their respective experience.

Intrapersonal intelligence One of Gardner's multiple intelligences relating to understanding of self.

Intrinsic rewards An outcome that gives an individual personal satisfaction such as that derived from a job well done.

Introspection The process of 'looking inward' and examining one's self and one's own actions in order to gain insight.

Learning Theory Behaviourist understanding of learning which assumes that all learning is shaped by responses that are rewarded or punished.

Learning trajectory A developmental pathway leading towards a learning goal, and including activities matched to increasing levels of thinking.

Legislation A law/legal procedure which informs practice and must be adhered to.

Lexicon Word bank, stored vocabulary.

Limbic system The innermost part of the brain, which is the home of emotions, responses to emotion and motivation.

Local Safeguarding Children Boards Required by the Children Act 2004 to ensure the cooperation of relevant agencies to promote and safeguard the welfare of all children in a local area.

Majority world That part of the world formally referred to as being 'underdeveloped' or the 'third world'. The word 'majority' is used in recognition that most of the world's population live in these areas.

Makaton Communication system using signs, symbols and speech: see http://www.makaton.org/aboutMakaton

Maturational theory Theory generally associated with Gesell that assumes that children mature at rates according to their biological clock.

Minority world That part of the world formally referred to as 'developed'; generally understood to include the industrialised nations of western Europe, Australasia, the USA and Canada.

Multi-modal Combining two or more systems of communication or meaning making.

Nativism A perspective in psychology that emphasises how inborn capabilities develop very early in life or are easy to learn.

Neuron A brain cell, usually consisting of a cell body, axon and dendrites, that transmits nerve impulses and is the basic functional unit of the nervous system.

Phonemes Individual speech sounds made up of one or more graphemes (letters).

Policy A statement of intent in order to practice within the law.

Prejudice Negative attitudes about a group based, not on factual information about that group, but on stereotypes; for example, believing that all Gypsies or Travellers are thieves. Prejudice can lead to discrimination. In this example it may lead to local people refusing to let Travellers settle in the area.

Pre-operational Piaget's second stage of development, from the ages of 4 to 7, during which the child begins to go beyond recognising and is able to use words and images to refer to objects.

Proximodistal development Development which starts from the centre and proceeds in an outwards direction.

Psychoanalytic theory The theory of personality developed by Freud that focuses on repression and unconscious forces.

Psychometrics The field of study concerned with the theory and technique of psychological measurement, which includes the measurement of knowledge, abilities, attitudes, personality and intelligence.

Qualitative approach An approach to research that uses methodology designed to provide an in-depth understanding about how individuals think and behave, using methods such as observation and unstructured interviews.

Quantitative approach An approach to research that uses scientific methodology involving the collection of numerical data from a large sample.

Racism A particular form of prejudice which involves the belief that 'races' have distinctive characteristics which render some groups superior to others. Racism can give rise to discrimination and abusive behaviour. In its extreme form it has led to apartheid and genocide.

Receptors A nerve ending that is sensitive to stimuli and can convert them into nerve impulses.

Reconstituted family Sometimes known as a blended family, the reconstituted family is one where the adults have children from previous relationships, so that the children may be related to only one parent. Within a reconstituted family there may also be children born from the new partnership who are related to both parents.

Representation Making one thing stand for another, e.g. using a word to represent an object.

Resilience Normal development under difficult circumstances or the human capacity to face, and overcome, life's adversities and challenges.

Rhyme A literary feature in which words end with the same sound pattern.

Schema An organised and repeated pattern of thought or behaviour.

Self-actualisation Most often linked to Maslow's hierarchy of needs, this describes the final level of psychological development that can be achieved when all basic and mental needs are fulfilled and the 'actualisation' of the individual's full personal potential takes place.

Sensori-motor The stage identified by Piaget as the period between birth and age 2 during which an infant's knowledge of the world is limited to his or her sensory perceptions and motor activities.

Serious Case Review Review set up when a child dies, and where abuse or neglect is suspected as being a factor in their death.

Setting This refers to a variety of childcare facilities such as childminding, daycare, nursery school, nursery class within a school, pre-school or school.

Social capital Informal social relationships and cooperation based on trust and reciprocity which collectively bring benefits to individuals and groups.

Social constructivism Process by which groups construct knowledge for one another, collaboratively creating shared meanings.

Socio-cultural A perspective in psychology that emphasises how higher order functions develop out of social interaction within cultural contexts.

Strange Situation An experimental procedure developed by Mary Ainsworth and colleagues (1970) to observe different forms of attachment between mothers and infants.

Sub-intelligences Each of Gardner's intelligences consists of a variety of sub-intelligences which mean that the intelligence may be demonstrated in many different ways.

Subitising Recognising and naming small sets of one, two and three objects without counting.

Sustainability Used to describe the idea that the resources we use to support and meet the needs of this generation should not compromise the ability of future generations to meet their needs.

Syllables Rhythmic divisions in words, each syllable contains one vowel sound (pear = 1 syllable; melons = 2; banana = 3).

Symbolic The third of Bruner's three stages of representation in which thinking moves to the abstract, using a variety of means of symbolising thoughts, feelings and ideas.

Theoretical model A generalised explanation about a phenomenon, which helps us understand the factors that influence this phenomenon and aids prediction about what may happen in certain circumstances.

Transitioners Those who are in the process of transition.

Ways of knowing The variety of modes available to find new knowledge. They include intuition, bodily ways of knowing, problem solving, practical experience, and scientific inquiry.

Yoked view of development Theories in which stages reached in different areas of development are assumed to be the same. Piaget's theory of stage development suggests, for example, that a child reaching a particular stage mentally may also be at that stage physically or morally.

Zone of Proximal Development (ZPD) The gap between what a child can achieve independently and what can be achieved under adult guidance or in collaboration with more experienced peers.

Index